{Unexpected}

Stories of a Down syndrome diagnosis

As told by families around the world

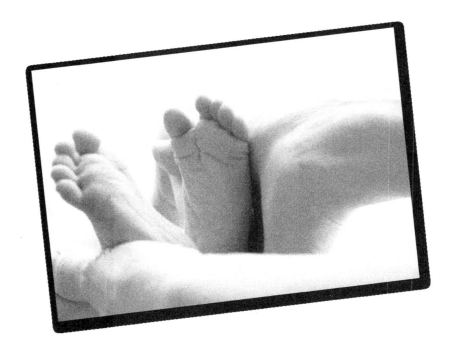

Compiled by Jennifer Jacob and Joelle Kelly

www.missiont21.com

This book is not intended as a substitute for the medical advice of physicians. The reader should regularly consult a physician in matters relating to his/her health and particularly with respect to any symptoms that may require diagnosis or medical attention. These stories are written by parents of children with Down syndrome. This book is not written as a medical reference, it is written as a reflection of memories from the diagnosis time from parents' perspectives.

Because families from around the world contributed to this work, spelling, phrases and language were kept in the context of the geographic location.

ISBN 978-1-312-07711-9

Visit our website @ http://www.missiont21.com/

Made available through support and funding by Down Syndrome Diagnosis Network (DSDN)
http://www.dsdiagnosisnetwork.org/

{Unexpected}

{Appreciation}

This book really is a true work of heart. So many mothers and fathers poured their hearts into these stories so that other families might feel a bit less alone in this journey. None of us expected to be on this adventure, but as you read, you realize how life-changing it has been for many families. Our greatest hope is that you see bits of yourself and your story here and that you will feel the tremendous sense of community, family and support that is the world of Down syndrome.

We are so grateful to all the moms and dads that were honest, vulnerable and sincere in what their diagnosis story was. As you authored your story, your genuine selves were shown. It was fantastic therapy session for many of us and uncovered much learning and understanding.

Many thanks to the many moms who shared their talents in editing, marketing, artistry, publishing and creativity to help this novice team pull together a great work; sharing your talents has made all the difference in this project. From all over the world we came together for a common focus and what a result!

Most of us never imagined that our lives stories would become intertwined together. To all the women around the world that we now count as friends and family, THANK YOU. What a difference this will make in the lives of families for years to come.

~ Jen and Joelle

{Welcome to the family}

Odds are that if you are choosing this book, you or a loved one has entered into the world of Trisomy 21 (T21), also known as Down syndrome, probably with little warning or preparation.

It is also highly likely that you may be scared, confused, anxious, or even terrified. Often those feelings are al so accompanied by deep love and concern for your new or unborn baby. It is quite a paradox and can really send you into a tailspin. You love your child so much, yet all your background knowledge (which for many of us was very limited) and inner voice may scream out, "This is the worst news possible!"

Breathe.
Stop Googling.
Breathe again.

We have been there. And we want to tell you this: it really gets better. *Really.*
Not long ago we were in your shoes and feeling exactly the same things.
Through our stories, you will see bits of yourself. You will see pieces of your family. You will see your new baby and, potentially, his or her future.

You will see that life does not come crashing down and that your child will fold into your family like any other baby. Well, maybe not like any other baby. You may notice the intense stare as your baby seems to look into your heart and soul.

Our purpose in writing this book is to add to the resources for new and expecting parents with a T21 diagnosis. We want to share our experiences and stories and provide a realistic view of what it means to welcome a baby into your family with Down syndrome. Our hope is that, through our words and photographs, you are able to glimpse into the future and more easily accept your baby and all that may come and see that it truly is a blessing, like any other child.

{Expecting the Unexpected}

Receiving a Prenatal Diagnosis

Words that a parent is never prepared to hear from a medical professional: We have reason to believe that your child may have Down syndrome.

Receiving a prenatal diagnosis for Trisomy 21 (Down syndrome) can leave you feeling a range of emotions. Confused. Scared. Isolated. Terrified. Angry. Anxious. Love. Many feelings are similar to those faced in the grieving process. The dream of the baby imagined is now replaced by a new child surrounded by so much uncertainty and, perhaps, fear. All of these feelings are valid and normal.

Prenatal testing has come to the forefront in the headlines recently, although parents may not understand the depth of the ramifications involved. Perhaps you did the prenatal testing without a second thought based on the doctor's recommendation.

Perhaps you went for the ultrasound scan just to could catch a glimpse of your baby, never imagining there would be anything wrong. Perhaps you requested the testing based on your pregnancy history. Regardless of the exact path of diagnosis, life changed in a moment with one extra chromosome.

For many mothers, there is a lot of time spent processing the diagnosis, analyzing it inside out. Some mothers report feeling that they get to a point in the pregnancy where nothing more can be processed until meeting the baby at birth. At this point, there is generally a feeling of acceptance. There is excitement, as you realize that your baby is going to be very loved and will require just the same amount of care as any other baby. This renewed sense of hope at what was initially perceived as doom and gloom is worth holding on to. Once that baby is placed in your arms, all those undesirable feelings will disappear and be replaced ten-fold with love.

Every mother's journey along the prenatal path is different, yet the similarities are undeniable. It is our hope that as you read these stories you will find your own feelings validated and know that you are not alone

{Our Stories}

{Our Stories}

{Natalie}

My first pregnancy and the first few months of my son's life were tumultuous. We had an early miscarriage scare, and then there was a thickened nuchal fold (which turned out to only signify a minor heart defect that resolved on its own), long-lasting morning sickness, cord issues, a two-day induction, a NICU stay, and weight gain and milk supply issues. It was an exhausting and stressful year. So when I found out that I was pregnant again in October 2011, I was determined to have a happy, healthy pregnancy, pop the baby out with no intervention, and exclusively breastfeed my baby who would get fat and happy. After everything I had been through, I deserved it, I said.

But at my nuchal translucency scan, about 12 weeks into my pregnancy, I knew something was wrong immediately. The nuchal fold was large again, larger than it had

been with my son. The doctor came in and gave us the rundown. We already knew it all: chromosomal issues, heart problems, high rate of fatality. They told us that they could do a CVS (chorionic villi sampling) right away, and we accepted. My husband could not come in with me because our son had come to

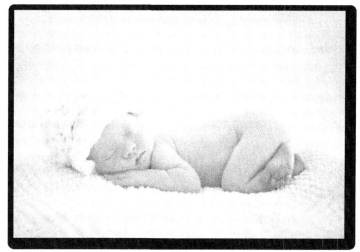

the hospital with us, so the genetic counselor held my hand during the test. I went home and wept, because I knew no matter what the outcome, I had been branded. My pregnancy was "high-risk", a title I so desperately had convinced myself I would escape this time.

For the next 10 days, I told myself that everything would be fine. The genetic counselor had said that she believed our baby would probably have the same kind of heart defect our son had... no big deal. But I think that despite what I told myself, I knew the news wasn't going to be what I wanted. When I considered the worst case scenarios, Down syndrome was always scarier in my head than the fatal trisomies. Maybe because I'm a terrible person, maybe God just has a sense of humor, but I had always had issues knowing how to talk with people who had intellectual disabilities. I could never look them in the eye, always felt uncomfortable around them. Having a child like that, I thought, would be the end of my world.

The genetic counselor called a week before Christmas, around 11:00 in the morning. "It's a good thing we did the test, because your baby has Trisomy 21, Down syndrome," she said. I held it together long enough to ask if it was a boy or a girl. She didn't want to tell me, but I told her I wanted to know. A girl. A girl, like I had wanted, just with an extra chromosome.

I fell down. I screamed and cried and begged God for it to be a mistake or to take it away. My son almost cried when he saw my distress, but then in classic toddler style decided to take advantage of the situation by obtaining the forbidden remote control. When I finally looked up from the floor he was one click away from ordering "Cowboys and Aliens" on Pay Per View. First I called my husband, and without even telling him the news, begged him to come home right away. Then I called my parents, who managed to hold me together for the next 30 minutes while I waited for my husband, each in their own ways. My dad shared my sorrow and prayed. My mom expressed her joy at a new baby girl. The two totally different responses were both exactly what I needed right then.

I spent the next few weeks over the holidays in a deep darkness. Every once in a while I would see a glimmer of light. Emails from friends that said, "Congratulations on your baby girl!" and "We can't wait to meet her!", along with uplifting blogs or online videos, like the one that talked about the statistics showing how overwhelmingly happy people with Down syndrome and their families are, helped me start thinking about how what I thought was an end to my life could actually be the start of a new, better one. But mostly there was sadness and crying and wishing that it would all go away. There were days when I would stand at the top of our steps with a laundry basket in my arms wondering if I could make myself fall and somehow end the pregnancy without hurting myself too badly.

God's grace was enough to keep me from falling, literally or otherwise. Before the diagnosis we had told the genetic counselor there was nothing that would make us consider termination. But then a few hours after she had delivered the news and we called her back for more information, she asked what we were thinking about keeping our baby. I kept putting her off, trying to think of another question to ask. Honestly, I wanted to end it. I did not think I wanted this baby anymore, and the only thing that kept me from telling her that was fear of committing a deep sin. Eventually I managed to get out the words that we would not terminate. I wanted to call her back, I prayed for a miscarriage, I even got a little hopeful when I would have Braxton Hicks contractions that they would result in pre-term labor. These words are true, but they cause heart to ache now. Over time I adopted a "not my will but thine" attitude. I could believe that God had given us this baby for a reason: a test or trial or maybe a punishment even. It was something we would accept and overcome. I could not believe that this baby herself was a gift.

Finally on Valentine's Day we had our first moment of joy since the diagnosis. We went back to Johns Hopkins for a scan of Baby Girl's heart. After an incredibly long ultrasound in a very hot room followed by a lecture from the doctor on the many heart conditions that babies with Down syndrome could have, she said, "But your baby doesn't have any of these". She was healthy! At that point I was probably more relieved for myself, thankful to escape living in a hospital for a few weeks after surgery and scores of cardiologist appointments. But I marked the occasion by buying her a dress; or rather, letting my mom buy her a dress. And we finally named her: Natalie.

It's funny how a tiny pink dress and a name changed so much for me. All of a sudden, I was excited. I was ready to decorate a nursery and buy some more clothes and figure out logistics. I decided to devote my time to these endeavors and "gave up Down Syndrome" -- that is, the obsessive research I had been doing on it -- for Lent. After Easter, we were getting close, and I went on planning, preparing, but still taking Benedryl almost every night to avoid the fears and worries that would otherwise come in the early morning hours. Breastfeeding was something that was incredibly important to me, so I found an online lecture on how to succeed in breastfeeding a baby with low muscle tone. I started a binder and jotted down the phone number for Infants and Toddlers in our county so I could call them as soon as we were home from the hospital and settled. And I went to the doctor, a lot. My doctor wanted me to have two non-stress tests a week. Natalie was pretty lazy, so these tests were often long and, despite their name, pretty stressful. I would sit there for over an hour while the nurse prodded my belly and encouraged me to drink juice and eat crackers. Natalie would usually wake up and start kicking like crazy right as the maternal fetal medicine staff started talking about sending me to Labor and Delivery.

On June 15, 2012 we headed into the hospital for an external version. Natalie was breech, though it was a bit unclear exactly what part was where. We only knew she definitely wasn't ready for launch, and I had held off my doctors to 39 weeks so that she could grow. I desperately wanted to avoid a C-section but after 45 minutes of my OB trying to push on my belly to make her turn, I conceded. A nurse in the operating room exclaimed, "Let's have a birthday party!" The C-section was... unpleasant, mostly thanks to an incorrectly placed spinal. My feet were very numb, but my midsection, not so much. Eventually the OB pulled out Natalie who still had her legs crossed and her back arched like they had found her inside me. "Take a picture dad!" the OB exclaimed. "I'm not feeling so good", my husband said. And then he blacked out and fell to the floor. "Someone get his camera," was my only comment. The nurses did what I asked and took some pictures, and then after my husband came to and then passed out again, they wheeled him out of the OR and set him up with some cookies and a drink while I got sewed back together under partial anesthesia.

My husband's failure to stay upright did result in something positive besides giving me a permanent way to shame him. After Natalie was checked out by the NICU doctors and deemed 'OK' she was rolled into the recovery room with him, and he got to spend a few moments alone with her before I could join them. He was smitten. I hadn't really talked to my husband very much about how he felt in the previous six months. I was so wrapped up in my own grief that I couldn't bring myself to ask how he was dealing with it. But then I saw him holding our sweet little girl, and I knew we would make it.

Later that day, the hospital lactation consultant came in with what seemed like 50 ways to feed our baby. She had several types of bottles, a supplemental nursing system, nursing shields, and more. She told us that babies with Down syndrome could often learn to breastfeed, but sometimes it took a while for them to catch on. I had prayed and prayed that nursing would work out for us. I had gone through weeks of pumping, supplementing, and taking all sorts of disgusting herbs to be successful in exclusively breastfeeding my first baby. I knew with two kids at home I would not have the time to do much, but I desperately wanted to nurse. God answered that prayer. Natalie latched on and nursed perfectly. My milk came in before I left the hospital, and she was back at birth weight within a few days. She is definitely fat and happy like I had hoped. This answer to my small prayer was a huge blessing for me. Nursing my baby has given me time to sit, reflect, relax, and love her. And love her I have.

When I was pregnant, I never spent any time thinking about what type of person I had growing inside of me. Most of my time was occupied with thinking about her health, her future, and how I might be inconvenienced. Natalie started to show us her personality early. By two months I had dubbed her "Princess Indignation". She tolerates most things, but when we cross the line to what she will not tolerate she immediately transitions from

pleasant smiles to bloodcurdling screams. She is fiesty, determined, cuddly, and sensitive. Best of all, she adores her brother. Brother (or, "bruddah") was her first recognizable word. She is always happy to see him and will cry when he is upset, but she also will not hesitate to shriek at the top of her lungs when he takes a toy from her, or grab his hair and pull hard when he is too close for her liking. Just like every sibling relationship at these ages, it is full of love and loyalty mixed with a little bit of resentment and wariness. It is so normal, and I love it.

Life with Natalie all around is normal, actually. We have been very lucky that Natalie has been healthy. She spent a few days in the hospital when she was around seven weeks old for a urinary tract infection, but we have had no major concerns. Life has been completely chaotic and fun, just as we expected it would be with two children. At 14 months, she does have some developmental delays, mostly in the realm of gross motor skills. In other facets of her life, she is developing right on par with other children her age. We spend a little extra time with Natalie trying to help her reach milestones, and she gets physical and occupational therapy each twice a month. To me, it's just another way I spend time and play with her.

Natalie is perfect. She brings us so much happiness and amazement every day. There are still many days I'm sad that she has Down syndrome. I wonder what it would be like to have a typical toddler at this stage, a running baby instead of a rolling one. I worry about her health, affording everything she will need, and what will happen to her when we are too old to take care of her. But the sadness, fear, and insecurity I've faced since the diagnosis, I am coming to realize, are all mine. They are my issues, not hers. The unknown baby/child/adult with Down syndrome in my head, I think, will continue to haunt me through my life. But the Natalie playing on my floor, eating in my kitchen, and sleeping on my chest has and will only be a source of joy and light. She is a beautiful gift from God.

~Anna, Natalie's mom; age 31; Maryland, United States

{Nicholas}

Minutes after we received the news that our third baby had a confirmed diagnosis of Down syndrome, 18 weeks into our pregnancy, there was a thunderous downpour of rain. It was quite appropriate, really, dramatically drawing a distinct line between before and after the moment where our lives changed forever.

Early into the pregnancy, we were rather surprised by the discovery we were expecting our littlest love, and it took four pregnancy tests to convince me that our third child was in progress. Coming from a family of seven children, I knew in my heart my family wasn't quite complete after having our two boys, but I'm not sure I'd really come around to the

thought of being pregnant again quite yet. But we were happy, albeit slightly terrified, about having three children under four years old. We shared our good news with close family and friends, and planned to keep any public announcements until after our 12 week scan. But that's when things got a bit rocky.

On September 12, my husband Ben and I went along to our 12 week nuchal translucency scan where we saw our tiny baby, looking very healthy and 'structurally good' according to the sonographer. We gave a sigh of relief. We then met with the consulting doctor who put all the numbers in the boxes and waited for the computer to process our 'risk result' for Trisomy 21. The answer was 1:14. I remember the doctor talking about what the next steps could be in terms of further testing, but I felt like I was having an out of body experience.

We stopped at a park on our way home. I cried, and we began Difficult Conversation Number One of what would be many. While I don't consider myself particularly religious,

I felt as though I heard God say, "Just trust me." While comforted by that, I didn't get the sense that He meant "Trust me, I'm going to make this easy"... more like "Trust me. This might be a cracker of a journey, but I'm here with you." I think in hindsight I had a sixth sense that this pregnancy was different.

The next few weeks were difficult, to say the least, and I fluctuated between feeling completely lost, and hoping that it would turn out I was just being a drama queen. Ben and I talked about our fears, thoughts, possible action plans, and then had times where we just couldn't talk about the baby anymore. I would love to say that we were immediately unified in our decision to keep this baby, but we come from different families with different beliefs, and we didn't know if we were up to the task of raising a child with a disability. Most of all, we were afraid. We both considered all options. The turning point for me came when we were sitting on the couch one night, and I was researching on the iPad. I began reading posts on a forum where women were discussing their regrets after having a 'termination for medical reasons', which was difficult enough. I then read about the physical process of terminating a pregnancy, and it broke me. I cried so hard I could barely breathe. I had felt this baby kicking inside my belly since 12 weeks into the pregnancy, and he was already so much a part of me. While challenged and terrified by a potential positive diagnosis, we came to the decision that we would have this baby regardless of his chromosome count. We made decisions based on the assumption the diagnosis would be positive, but we still clung desperately to that 7% chance everything would be okay.

The next question we needed to address was whether we could 'wait it out' for a diagnosis at birth, and the answer was that not knowing was killing us. After much research and discussion, we booked an amniocentesis, which couldn't be performed until after 16 weeks into the pregnancy, and settled in for the next wait.

The amnio was the easy bit. I wasn't exactly looking forward to the process of having a needle inserted in my belly, and was almost ready to pack up and go home when the sonographer couldn't see any of the usual 'markers' for T21 on our very healthy baby. But I stayed. I felt confident in the hands of the doctor we'd chosen, and the procedure went really well, with little, if any, pain. We were due to receive the results by phone call, from either our obstetrician or the doctor who performed the procedure, within 48 hours.

On day one post-procedure, I settled in at home, enjoying the peace and quiet of being temporarily child free, and put the thoughts of getting an early phone call out of my mind. On Day Two, my stomach churned from the second I woke up. Mid-morning, my mobile rang, and my OB's phone number came up on screen. "This is it," I said to Ben. Deep breath. It was the receptionist from our OB's office, completely unaware of our current situation and innocently calling to rearrange our next appointment. False alarm. By lunchtime, I am sure I could have been diagnosed clinically insane. At 3pm, I told Ben we needed to call them, but we were only able to leave messages. More waiting.

By the time we got the call at 4pm, I was beside myself. I couldn't answer the phone and didn't want to hear the news on speaker phone. In my heart, I knew what the answer would be. I watched Ben's face as he listened to our obstetrician on the other end of the line. He just nodded, "It's positive. Baby has Down's." We cried and hugged each other. The rain came down so heavily we could barely hear ourselves think. Then Ben went to pick up our eldest son from daycare. I sent a text to the loved ones who were waiting in the wings for news. The world kept turning, and life had to go on.

We each went through the various stages of grief over the next few months, but never at the same time, it felt. While we had made the decision to keep our baby after the nuchal test result, a confirmed diagnosis made it all so real that it was difficult not to re-question our beliefs. Initially after the amniocentesis, I was really careful about any heavy lifting and potential risks to the baby as a result of the amnio – but then we received the T21 diagnosis, and I wondered whether it would be easier if this baby did just pass away, if all these difficult decisions were taken out of our hands. We chose to see counsellors both together and separately as we talked through all our options. There was much anger and sadness, and oh so much silence between us as we each stumbled our own way through the darkness. I participated in online forums and read lots of information. Ben spoke to a few close friends and decided to do his information gathering once he could meet our baby in person. We just had to lean in and love each other through the pain and trust that it would all be okay.

Over time, we started sharing the news of our baby's diagnosis with friends and extended family, and usually via email. It was really important for me to be able to share our news in a positive way (and without me being a visible, blubbering mess), to let everyone know we were okay, that we were excited about meeting our beautiful baby, and that we wanted them to be, too. I wanted other people to be able to process the news and grieve in their own way without being worried about how they may react, and I am grateful for the many beautiful, heartfelt and honest responses we received. While no one else could walk in our shoes, we knew we were well supported in this journey, that our baby already had a strong network waiting to love him. A few weeks after the diagnosis, we went to a detailed ultrasound to check on our baby's health. After feeling as though we had been greeted with bad news at every recent turn, we waited expectantly for more challenges – but were thankful to discover that Baby Love seemed to be growing and developing beautifully, with no apparent health concerns. I was comforted by how active he was in utero – always such a busy baby. As the pregnancy progressed, we continued to have regular ultrasounds and breathed a little easier each time, hearing that our baby appeared healthy and well. The specialist we consulted at each appointment often commented that, without the amnio results, we never would have known about the T21 diagnosis until birth. With each prenatal scan and appointment, we tried to avoid finding out our baby's gender and let him reveal at least one surprise at birth.

Some days I felt invincible, facing our new future with strength and peace. Other days, the roller coaster of emotions dipped and turned with such ferocity, I just couldn't put on another brave face, and it was easier to stay inside and hide from the world. Some days, trying to put on the façade that I had it all together was just plain exhausting. I expected the emotional recovery to improve day by day, but in all honesty, there were good days and bad days. However, having an almost-two and almost-four year old afforded me little time for self-pity.

My two big boys were very excited about meeting their new baby brother or sister, and especially our eldest son who was now old enough to understand the concept of a new family member. As the weeks went by, I began to feel a glimmer of excitement at welcoming our new baby too. There were so many unknowns, but we were ready to hold that squishy new baby in our arms, to get to know him, and just face any challenges as they presented. I was also quite looking forward to being able to bend over again. A few days before reaching 40 weeks gestation, I went along to a scheduled appointment with my obstetrician one Monday afternoon, and had a strong inkling that we would soon be meeting our baby. I went home, tucked our boys into bed, tidied up loose ends, added the last bits and pieces to my hospital bag, and went to bed, but was woken by a very strong contraction at about 11.40pm. Within two hours and 55 minutes, after a smooth and speedy delivery, we met our very beautiful and perfectly healthy third son, who we named Nicholas.

As Nicholas was delivered onto my chest, I did a quick glance at his almond-shaped eyes, silently confirming the T21 diagnosis, and then soaked in every inch of my new little 3.8 kilogram bundle. He had his first breastfeed within 15 minutes of being born, continued to be a champion feeder, and was back to his birth weight by the time we went home four days later. I can honestly say that our grief and sadness became part of history the moment we laid eyes on our youngest baby boy, and he continues to bring joy into each day that we are blessed to spend with him. As difficult as it was, I would go through those months of heartache again in a flash in order to have him in our lives.

Nicholas has white blonde hair, with a big curl that stands up on the top of his head like something out of Dr. Seuss, and big, sparkly blue eyes. He

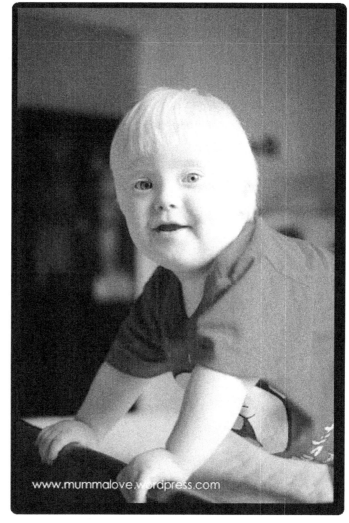

www.mummalove.wordpress.com

is loved – by us, our wide network of friends, his grandparents, his 16 cousins, his uncles and aunties, and most especially, by his two big brothers. He may take a little longer to do the things that kids of his age are doing, but it's not a competition. Nicholas is writing his own story. Every day that I get to snuggle his little body, see his big beaming smile, see how loved he is, I am thankful for the journey that guided us to this place. Ironically, we received Nicholas' Trisomy 21 diagnosis in October, which is Down

Syndrome Awareness Month, and he arrived into the world on March 20, the day before World Down Syndrome Day. I think he was always meant to be part of our love story.

Nicholas is 17 months old. He has been really healthy from birth, and is a fun, happy, engaged, playful little boy with white blonde hair and amazing blue eyes. He has just started moving from his tummy up to sitting position, loves to roll pretty much everywhere, and he can pull himself up to stand. His favourite words are dad and hello, and he loves music, especially doing the actions to his favourite songs. He is happy to eat anything, but loves fruit, and was breastfed up until very recently. Nicholas is adored by his extended family and wide circle of friends, but most especially by his mum, dad and two big brothers. We can't imagine our life without this gorgeous boy in it.

~Annie, Nicholas' mom; 33; Brisbane, Australia

Blogging @ http://www.mummalove.wordpress.com

{Josee}

We had two beautiful healthy children when I felt the need to extend our family just one last time. This yearning for a third child began at the ripe old age of thirty two, and went on for about a year. In that time I had many lengthy discussions with my closest girlfriends and my husband about what to do. I had a real sense of now or never, and when I visited my local family doctor, he too gave me the now or never lecture, which I thought surely must be a sign I needed to make a decision sooner than later.

I decided to go off the pill, and that same month I fell pregnant. My husband wasn't happy; I think he wanted a few more months to practice! I had a great first few weeks, and felt fantastic, but I just couldn't shake the feeling that something wasn't right. Ever since those little lines early on my pregnancy test announced very boldly that I was pregnant, I had an inkling that something was up.

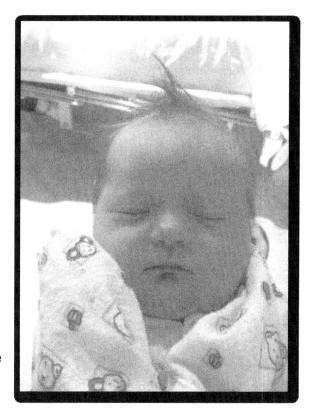

Our 12 week ultrasound was booked for the Wednesday afternoon, with the plan being that we could announce it to friends and work on the Friday before breaking up for the school holidays. I met my husband at the radiology clinic, and sent my kids off with a friend to go and have some afternoon tea whilst they waited. They were very excited to hear how the baby was.

As the technician began, she showed us an ultrasound image of what a foetus with an enlarged nuchal fold looks like. I nodded, as we had both been through this scan before, but at the same time also thought to myself, "That's interesting, no one has actually explained that to us before." I took note of the image of what an enlarged fold looked like.

As our baby came onto the screen, I breathed a sigh of relief. It was there, I could see it moving, there was a heartbeat. Phew! All the worry that I had that something had been wrong was unfounded. When she showed us the full length image I briefly glanced to where the nuchal fold was and thought to myself momentarily, "That kind of looks like what she showed us in the picture beforehand." But then I thought that it was probably hard to tell anyway, and pushed the thought aside. The technician began her measurements and my husband and I marvelled at this new life.

My husband left after about thirty minutes as he had to go back to work, believing all was ok. The technician finished up her measurements, she had become quieter and edgier the longer she went on. She turned the equipment off and looked at me to explain that before I had the ultrasound my chance of having a baby with Trisomy 21 was 1:350, based on my age. She then went on and said but your chances after having the nuchal fold, coupled with your bloods puts your chance at 1:2. I could barely breathe, and I could hear blood pumping through my ears.

"You're kidding," I said. I felt like someone had just dropped a bomb. She explained that she had seen babies with a higher fold that had gone on to have typical chromosomes. But it was in vain, I just knew. The rest of what she said was a blur as I was numb, and felt physically ill.

She went out of the room to see if there was a Doctor that could come and speak to us. In that time I messaged a few friends and said the scan wasn't looking good. I also messaged my friend who had my children, and told her to prepare for some bad news.

As she came back in I could barely hold back tears. I felt like I had been delivered a death sentence. I could barely speak, barely think, and I just wanted to turn back time to when I wasn't pregnant.

I rang my husband in tears, saying, "They think the baby might have Down syndrome, I'm sorry, I'm so sorry." I repeated my apologies over and over. He made his way back to the clinic and told me to stop apologising. My friend who was minding my children brought them back to me, and through tears, I broke the news that their sibling may have

Down syndrome. In the midst of the chaos I had forgotten that my children went to school with a child who has Down syndrome. My eldest child looked at me and said, "But Mummy, why are you crying? We love him, why are you so sad?" Her reaction really made me stop in my tracks as I tried to explain why I was upset. From that moment I tried to be brave and put on a front for my children, but on the inside I was breaking.

We organised a second opinion scan to be conducted the next week, hoping that the first scan was wrong. In those six days from the first scan to the second scan I was like a zombie, functioning on auto pilot. The only reason I managed to hold it together was for the sake of my children and the fact that I was on holidays from work.

At the next ultrasound we were confronted with even further bad news. The nuchal fold, which was already enlarged, had doubled in size, with the fluid now going up and over the back of the baby's head. There was also fluid noted in the baby's chest cavity and all under the skin. We were given the grave news that our baby had hydrops and was in heart failure. We were advised to go ahead with a CVS in two days time, so that we knew what was going on, but were solemnly told that the baby would most likely pass away within 24-48 hours of the CVS. We sadly made the appointment for the CVS and two days later, with heavy hearts, we headed into the hospital for what was a cold and clinical procedure. I could barely look at that tiny little body fighting for its life on the screen. Watching the biopsy needle come onto the ultrasound screen within centimetres of our baby was an image that I couldn't handle.

Once the biopsy was complete I rested for ten minutes. The Doctor then turned the ultrasound machine back on to check our baby. As the screen flickered on we could see our little fighter, kicking and moving about, oblivious to the world outside. We took what we thought was one last look at our baby on the ultrasound after the CVS and went home to wait for a miscarriage, but began praying for a miracle.

This grave diagnosis certainly put our initial fears in perspective. We initially thought there was nothing worse than a diagnosis of Down syndrome, but to be told that your child would not survive was definitely the worst news. We decided that we would enjoy every day that we had left with our child, and began to purposely find joy in each day. A deep sense of peace washed over my body as I knew that, no matter what, this child was loved and wanted.

We were called into the hospital four days after the CVS for the FISH results. We had already decided to love this child no matter what, and when the Doctor gave us the diagnosis that our baby had Trisomy 21, we just smiled and said thank you. We asked the gender, and were told it was a little girl. We were overjoyed! The doctor began to explain all the downfalls of our diagnosis and the multitudes of illnesses and challenges our baby would face in her lifetime. It fell on deaf ears. We had read so much in the short time from the scan to diagnosis that nothing we heard was new nor valued. This was our child, and to have their lifetime mapped out in doom and gloom was not something any parent would want to hear. The doctor then went on to discuss termination and that one could quickly be arranged. We said no, and then listened to him discuss what we could do if we changed our minds. We thanked him for his time and left.

Out in the hospital corridors, we went to our children, where we had left them in a little sunny nook overlooking the city. They jumped us as we approached them, and we gave them a cuddle as we told them they were having a sister. We all smiled and did a big family hug just as the doctor who gave us the diagnosis walked past. The look on his face was almost amusing... I think he thought we hadn't understood the bad news of the diagnosis!

My husband and I named our little girl that day with the name we had both liked early on in the pregnancy: Josee, which means "God will add". We thought it was fitting, as God had chosen to add to our family. My husband had a giggle as he said her name had a whole new meaning now, because God had also added an extra chromosome!

We went home that day, and tried to get on with life as we awaited our next scan. Each day we were grateful that our baby was alive, and I began to feel her move inside of me. We talked a lot to our children about finding joy in the every day, ordinary things in life. Already this little girl was changing our lives, perspectives and attitudes.

It was a long wait until our next scan, and when the day arrived we set off to hospital with apprehension, anxious to see if she was still alive and whether the fluid had increased. As the screen came on we saw our beautiful girl kicking around. My goodness, she had grown! Immediately my husband and I began scanning her body for signs of fluid, which show up as black spaces on the scan. A miracle had occurred! Our little girl's fluid had not only diminished, but disappeared, and she was growing beautifully! We were amazed, overjoyed and ever so thankful.

The rest of my pregnancy was reasonably uneventful. I was monitored well with a few extra scans here and there. Josee continued to grow, and all of her heart and gastrointestinal testing appeared fine. Having such a poor prognosis early on made me very anxious and fearful throughout the remainder of my pregnancy. I found it difficult to accept that she was ours to keep, and unfortunately, many doctors liked to remind me of the gloomy fact that 30% of babies with Trisomy 21 miscarry or are stillborn.

We prepared for our baby to come early, as so much of what we read talked about premature birth. For weeks on end we waited and waited. In the end I was induced after being ten days overdue. This baby was in no hurry.

As the contractions began, I suddenly became extremely irrational and overly anxious. It was as if the culmination of all the worry and fear in my pregnancy came to a head. I was so fearful of meeting Josee, but at the same time, I was desperate for her to be in this world. I was made to stay on the bed whilst I was constantly monitored, and I found this to be a complete contrast to my other children's active water births. The whole time my husband kept reassuring me that her heart rate was ok, and that she was doing fine. The labour was intense and quick, and she arrived naturally within a couple of hours. As soon as she was born my husband reassured me she was ok. I couldn't believe it! She was here and she was ok, what a Godsend!

My first cuddle with Josee Hope was the most magical moment of my life. I was so utterly amazed that she had made it into the world, and she was just beautiful and big! She nuzzled at my breast without feeding as the paediatrician wanted to check her digestive tract before she fed. We were given a short amount of time together where we just cuddled her and had skin-to-skin contact. I was, and still am, so thankful that the hospital staff allowed this.

Josee Hope spent two days in special care for observation and to monitor breast feeding. She came home five days after birth, and was initially slow to gain weight due to her low tone. She required top up feeds of pumped breast milk via a bottle after breast feeds for the first few months. Josee Hope continues to grow beautifully and has no medical issues. Today she is a gorgeous, social, and lovable baby with a smile that melts your heart. She is a true miracle and a blessing to our lives.

Josee Hope has just tuned 7 months, and is the light of our little family. She is extremely social and demands to be smiled at and talked to -- don't walk past her without acknowledging her! Her big brother and sister are in love; they are her biggest advocates and protectors, they relish in every moment with her. Josee Hope began rolling early on but at the moment spends most of the time on her tummy wanting to move forward, flapping those little arms and legs determinedly! She prop sits, and loves to stand up in our laps whilst we sing and talk to her. What I imagined my life would be like a year ago with our prenatal diagnosis, and what our life is actually like, are polar opposites. Her health is great, she breast feeds and eats food beautifully, and has such a little personality. She has enriched our lives, and we are so grateful for all the little things in life. No prenatal diagnosis can predict this kind of happiness!

~Joelle, Josee's mum; 33, Queensland, Australia

{Benjamen}

Chris and I were blessed with a wonderful surprise in January of 2012. We found out that we were expecting Blessing Number Three! Logan, our second blessing, came after years of infertility and was considered a miracle baby, so you can only imagine our surprise. Brittany, my first blessing, started her second year of college in the fall, so we had literally just started with diapers and bottles all over again. It was somewhat overwhelming to find out about my pregnancy with Benjamen, but we got over it, and got on to being excited!

On April 16th, Chris and I decided to have an amnio done because our penta screen came back positive for Down syndrome. Our doctor assured us that the test often had false positives, and did not really recommend an amnio unless we just had to know for sure. I knew with all my heart that it would not make one difference to me either way, but felt a pull to know. In fact, I felt a special little surge of love just at the thought of it being confirmed -- my favorite Uncle Tommy had Down syndrome, and was adored by our entire family until he passed in his 60s. But by nature, I'm a list maker, a planner, and a researcher. I needed to know, because if it were really true, I had a lot of work to do to get Benji's little world ready to greet him.

On April 27th, we found out that the amnio also came back positive. I ended up being told over the phone by my doctor while I was at work. Sitting at the nurses station in front of God and everybody, he said, "I'm sorry Stef, but the amnio came back positive. Your baby has Down's." It was true. All the thinking about it before was so abstract. Now it was real. I went completely numb. I remember being in the middle of something and just putting the phone down and walking away. Without a word, I walked down the hall, down the stairs, out the door, and into the parking lot. I honestly think I held my breath that entire time. And then I cried and cried -- not because I was having a child with Down syndrome. But I had researched, as I always do, and there was more than just the joy of the personality that I remember of my Uncle Tom in the little bundle that I would be bringing home. There were so many potential health complications. I had not planned this! The vast amounts of information available at your fingertips had done me in. I was suddenly scared for him. And what did I know about having a child with special needs? I had doubts about myself; would I be a good enough mother for him? I went through literally every range of emotion in what felt like a second: happy, sad, joyful, fearful. But mostly, I was fiercely protective, from the second the doctor confirmed the diagnosis. I was hesitant to tell people because I didn't want to see a look of pity, or get an "I'm so sorry". I didn't trust myself at first to react kindly to what I knew were well intended comments. I looked back painfully, and realized that I myself had made them to others before, with no clue how badly they had likely stung. I wanted people to be joyful, to see

the beauty of Ben, regardless of the number of chromosome he had. Ben's now godmother was one of the first people that I told. I blurted it out and watched, waiting for her reaction. Her eyes lit up, and she hugged me and told me "Congratulations! He will be just perfect!" And I cried again to have had such a loving reaction, the opposite of what I feared. And slowly but surely I started opening up to others. And most were wonderful reactions. Others were well intended. I perfected the response, giving them a smile and replying, "No need to be sorry, he is perfect, and we are so excited for him to get here!"

It was time to let go of my fears and start working on figuring out what I could start doing to make sure we had every option available for a safe pregnancy and healthy delivery. A dear friend of mine sent me an email after hearing about the positive penta screen with the story "Welcome to Holland".

It's a beautiful analogy to learning your child has any disability. I'm very thankful to have read that before we had our official diagnosis; it helped me summarize my feelings, and also realize that we were not alone.

Benjamen is now 12 months old and thriving after open heart surgery at 3 months for complete AVSD and PDA repair. He sits up beautifully, pulls to stand, and jabbers all day long. He has no problems telling us what he does and does not want to do! He is the light of our life. He is an inspiration and a blessing every single day. I cannot imagine our lives without him - he completes us!

~Stefanie, Benjamen's mom; 38; Florida, United States

{Cade}

In July 2012, we found out to our utter shock that we were expecting baby number three. Why was I so shocked? First, because I'm the ultimate planner. Nothing happens without me planning every last detail. Second, it took three years to conceive our older son. We had medical interventions, lots of tests, months of temping and taking ovulation tests. I honestly never thought that we'd get pregnant without these interventions. But despite all of that, here we were.

It took me a long time to get used to being pregnant again. It didn't help that I was sick for 18 weeks. Just as I was feeling better, I had some routine blood tests. A few days later my doctor called. "Your tests show a high risk for Down syndrome. We want to do an ultrasound and some more testing," they told me. Normal risk for any pregnancy is 1:700. Normal risk for a 36 year old woman is about 1:300. My risk after this blood test was 1:28.

No problem, I thought, those tests are never accurate anyway. We scheduled a Level II ultrasound with a specialist, and were excited to find out the gender of our little bundle.

But not so fast. During the ultrasound, they found two markers for Down syndrome. Our risk was now a life-altering 1:3.

We held it together in the doctor's office. Afterwards, we went for a quiet dinner before picking up our kids. Neither of us ate much, and I fought tears for most of the dinner. Down syndrome? Really? That night I lay awake long into the wee hours, pleading with God to make our baby be okay. Just make him healthy, I begged.

We went back to the specialist for a blood test called MaterniT21. At the time of our test, MaterniT21 was fairly new, but it was accurate enough to be a great alternative to amniocentesis. After the blood draw, the wait began.

We had Thanksgiving, where we bravely went ahead with my plans to do a gender reveal pumpkin pie. I cried as I made the cheesecake with a hidden blue layer, and was

solemn as I later cut it in front of my husband's entire family. A few days after that, as we waited impatiently, everyone in our family came down with the stomach flu. It was miserable, but it took my mind off of the wait. Finally, two weeks after the blood draw, the genetics counselor called.

"The test is positive for Trisomy 21. Your baby has Down syndrome."

I would like to say I took the news stoically. I did not. I cried and cried. My husband was home at the time, but missed hearing the phone call. He came out to where I had been working in the garage and asked a question about something work-related. But one look at me stopped him mid-sentence. He got down on his knees and hugged me tight. We stayed that way for several minutes. Eventually, he said something about it being okay, that we'd be okay. The baby was perfect the way he was. We'd love him just as we love our other two.

The next days are a little blurry in my mind. We met again with the genetics counselor, who politely offered to tell us about our options for termination or adoption. We met with our regular OB, and with our new specialist OB. We scheduled an echocardiogram to look at our baby's heart, and stumbled through those first two weeks after the diagnosis. I read a lot on Down syndrome, I joined the local support group, and we secretly Googled pictures of babies with Down syndrome when we thought no one else was looking. And gradually, it was okay. We told our families, we started telling our friends, and the more we talked about Down syndrome, the more okay it was.

After those first few weeks, I gradually began to enjoy my pregnancy, and take joy in the new life forming inside me. We looked forward to our son's birth with the same happy anticipation that we awaited the births of our first two children. The day before Easter in 2013, our son was born. Yes, he has Down syndrome. But, just as I'd asked from God, he was also born perfect and healthy.

Cade is nearly five months old and doing great! So far, he's a very typical baby who loves to laugh, snuggle with his older sister and brother, and look at himself in the mirror. He has no health issues whatsoever. Everyone he meets falls in love with him, and he charms them all with gummy smiles.

~ Heather, Cade's mom; 36; Oregon, United States
Blogging @ www.321mama.com

{Wyatt}

My son was only six months old when my husband and I found out I was pregnant again. We were shocked, but happy. Having our children so close together certainly hadn't been part of our plan, but we would soon find out that very little about this pregnancy would go according to plan.

Right away, we knew that the timing wasn't great. Matt, an active duty Marine, was scheduled to deploy soon. He was already going through his pre-deployment work-ups, which meant that he was away for training and preparations for weeks at a time. And he would not be home for the birth of this child. We were disappointed, but being a military family, we had always known this might happen one day and just prepared to deal with it. Meanwhile, I made my prenatal appointments.

As with my first son, I agreed to a first trimester screening test called the nuchal translucency screening. I had never thought much about it beyond knowing that it meant I would get an ultrasound that I wouldn't otherwise get, and who wouldn't want to see their baby if they could? The test consists of an ultrasound and a blood test, and those two combined give you a risk factor for Down syndrome.

In the week before the ultrasound, I couldn't shake this feeling of dread I had. I kept thinking that something would be wrong. I just knew it, deep down. So when the ultrasound screen came up and the heart was beating and everything looked good to me, I was immensely relieved. But that relief was short-lived. I soon found out that the screening came back positive -- I had a high risk factor for carrying a baby with Down syndrome, with odds of 1:6. For a 26-year-old woman, this was especially unusual.   I felt numb and confused, and agreed to a referral for a maternal-fetal medicine specialist, where they would do a higher-level ultrasound to try and find some soft markers.

This would be the last appointment my husband came to.   For the most part, everything looked fine aside from a buildup of fluid behind the baby's neck.   The doctor gently told us that this could be indicative of a heart defect, which could potentially lead to stillbirth. He cautioned us not to get too worried though, as it could go away and mean nothing at all.   He also told us that now was the time to decide whether or not we wanted to get an amniocentesis done and find out for sure if the baby had Down syndrome.   We agreed to get the amnio done, and I cried the entire way home.

Within a week, Matt deployed to Afghanistan, with lingering questions and fears left in the air.   And I would have to get this test done, which I was somewhat scared to do, alone.

During the test, another wife from my husband's unit came with me to hold my hand. We noticed during the test how very active this baby was: kicking, moving, working out those little arms and legs.   We gushed over the adorable little nose and thought how very perfect he looked.   It turned out I didn't need to stress much about the amnio; it ended up being much less painful than I thought, and it was over in less than a minute. Now, all we had to do was wait.   The doctor told me I would have the results in a few days.

Three days later, on a Friday around 6:00 in the evening, my phone rang.   It was my doctor's assistant, asking if I could hold for the doctor.   I knew right then it was bad news.   I knew the test came back positive.   Sure enough, he got on the phone and informed me that the results had come back as a male, positive for Trisomy 21, or Down syndrome.   I tried to remain calm on the phone while he asked if I had any other questions.   I said no, made my next appointment, and hung up as soon as I could. And then I immediately burst into tears.

The first person I called was my mother, who I had kept up-to-date on what was going on with my pregnancy.   We talked for about 45 minutes, and I unloaded all of my fears and heartache onto her.   Would he be accepted?   Would he have friends, go to school, get married?   What kind of life would he have?   Would he live with us forever? Could he work?   I felt scared, trapped, and resigned to a life of misery and fear.   My mother remained calm on the phone, but she told me much later that once we hung up, she cried.   She had wanted to remain strong for me, and it wasn't the diagnosis she was crying over -- it was my anguish.

Luckily, my husband was able to call that night from Afghanistan, and I told him that our son had Down syndrome.   His response?   "OK."   To him, it was a non-issue.   I wished I had more of his strength and acceptance.   I spent the next three days crying pretty much non-stop.   And I didn't even know why.   I just knew that this was devastating to me, and the fact that it was just made me feel even worse.   Abortion had never been, and would never be, an option for us, but all the same -- I couldn't help but wonder what kind of mother felt this way about her child?   Was I some kind of shallow, prejudiced person who hated people who were different?   What was the big deal?   It was just an extra chromosome.   But that extra chromosome sent my world into a tailspin.   Every time I thought about the baby, I cried again.

Over the next few weeks, I was on an emotional roller coaster.   I had brief moments of acceptance, and then plunged back into despair again.   Matt and I had discussed naming our son Wyatt, after a good friend.   I liked that name because I had read somewhere that it meant "little warrior".   Now it felt stupid, because how could a baby with Down syndrome be a warrior?   He would be weak and helpless, someone who I would need to take care of forever.   He wasn't my little warrior anymore.

Then, as I slowly started researching Down syndrome, I found an interesting fact. Babies who have a chromosomal abnormality are overwhelmingly likely to end up as a miscarriage or stillbirth.   This happens about 80% of the time.   Evidently, many times when a woman has a miscarriage and the remains are tested, it is found that the baby had Down syndrome or a similar chromosomal defect, like Trisomy 18.   And suddenly, I was looking at my baby in a whole new light.

No longer did I see him as someone who was helpless and fragile, someone who I would have to nurture forever.   This baby was a fighter, a survivor.   This was a baby who had already beaten the odds, just by surviving this long.   I realized that this was my little warrior, and together, we would fight and forge a new path together. There may be rough patches, but we could take them on -- together.

Now that we had an official diagnosis of Down syndrome, it meant that I would have twice as many doctors appointments to go to. I would have to continue seeing my regular obstetrician, who would monitor me, as well as continue to see the maternal-fetal medicine specialist, who would monitor Wyatt. This meant driving for an hour at least once a month, and as I got further into the pregnancy, once every other week. I actually didn't mind that much. Seeing the high-risk doctor meant that I got an ultrasound at every single appointment, and I knew that Wyatt was being well taken care of.

One thing that was incredibly frustrating to me was the stigma surrounding prenatal testing. I constantly was asked by people if I found out while I was still pregnant because I had considered termination. The answer is a resounding no, but it came up all the time. I found it very unfortunate, because it gives women the idea that prenatal testing is done solely so that they can abort the pregnancy. This attitude doesn't let anyone know how valuable it is, medically speaking, to know in advance. It also gave me time to process the diagnosis and accept it. It took a little while, but eventually, I could be happy about the pregnancy, and look forward to his birth. I couldn't even imagine what it would be like to get a surprise diagnosis, and feel all of the things I felt -- which I continue to feel a measure of guilt over -- while I was holding my son.

Medically, I was astounded at how much I was able to learn about Down syndrome from my specialist. From what I have heard since, many high-risk doctors are not very knowledgeable about Down syndrome, or up-to-date on what kind of lives people with Down syndrome are able to lead. I was thrilled to know that not only did my doctor know a lot about the medical aspects of Down syndrome, he was also free of the outdated stereotypes and negativity that I myself had even fallen into. He was able to explain why we would have multiple fetal echocardiograms, to check his heart, as well as what risks there were with other organs. He knew that the placenta, being formed from the baby's DNA, also contained the extra chromosome, and therefore was at a higher risk of failing early. As we got later into the pregnancy, this meant constant monitoring. I had two non-stress tests a week, as well as a weekly ultrasound. This was solely to make sure that the placenta was still functioning as it should be. It got a little bit old, to be honest, but I was still grateful. If there was even the slightest hint that the placenta was failing, they were ready.

Thankfully, Wyatt appeared to have no health problems whatsoever. His heart appeared to be fine in all of the fetal echocardiograms, and all of his other organs were growing and developing normally. All the same, knowing in advance once again proved to be beneficial. My doctors had a plan for my delivery, and then a back-up plan, and then another back-up plan on top of that. If Wyatt decided to surprise us after birth with any surprise health issues, they were prepared. I appreciated that, because it allowed me to go into the delivery with no anxiety. I had a great medical team standing by, who was ready for whatever might happen.

Because I had an emergency c-section with my first baby, I had a second c-section with Wyatt. The surgery went well, and out Wyatt came. He was big and pink and crying loudly. He was healthy, and we were all excited and relieved. My husband was able to Skype into the operating room from Afghanistan. Everyone also knew that I already knew about the diagnosis, so no one was tiptoeing around our room. No one offered their sympathy or acted sad. All of the staff treated the birth as the joyous event that it was. It was wonderful. Wyatt had some physical features of Down syndrome, but that didn't matter to me or anyone else, because he was still so stinking adorable.

After the birth, we still had to do follow-up echocardiograms. Wyatt turned out to have three minor heart defects: two tiny holes, and a PDA, which is when the ductus arteriosis in the heart doesn't close after birth like it is supposed to. None of these ended up being bad enough to prevent us from going home after a few days. We followed up with a cardiologist for the next few months, and slowly, we saw all of his heart defects resolve themselves completely on their own. Since then, Wyatt has been the picture of health. I had braced myself for a million complications and health problems, but he has had none.

The hardest thing about raising Wyatt has been the developmental delays. Day-to-day, I don't usually notice them. He's just a baby. He cries, he eats, he poops. He also gives me huge, excited grins when I get him up in the morning, and he loves being cuddled and bouncing on my lap. Down syndrome doesn't really affect our regular life much. But every now and then, I can't help but notice how far behind other babies he is, and it is disheartening. Babies with Down syndrome typically take about twice as long to reach milestones, which describes Wyatt to a T. So I know that this is completely normal and nothing to be worried about. But it can still be frustrating, knowing that at 15 months old, he still can't crawl, can't pull himself to standing, and can only sit on his own if he's propped there first. I have to just try to remind myself that he will get there in time, and in five years, it won't matter when he started sitting or crawling or walking. The important thing is that he will get there.

I don't know what our future holds, but I no longer have the anxiety about it that I did in the beginning. Life with Down syndrome may have its challenges, but overall, it really isn't that bad. I have two adorable sons who love me, their father, and each other. An extra chromosome doesn't change any of that. Life is still good.

Wyatt is 15 months old today. We have been very lucky to have no health issues to worry about. He likes to cuddle, loves hearing his mommy sing, and can also be pretty stubborn when he wants to be. He's able to sit on his own if placed into position, and can rock back and forth on his hands and knees. He can eat Stage 3 baby food. He is a much-loved member of our family and makes our lives better every day!

~ Cassy, Wyatt's mom; 27; North Carolina, United States
Facebook contact: https://www.facebook.com/cassy.chesser

{Quinn}

I knew I was pregnant the moment I conceived. Call it a woman's intuition or a case of mother-knows-best, but I knew. As the weeks went on and I could finally take a pregnancy test and receive reliable results, my husband Brian and I stared at the giant plus sign and I said, "I told you so." As things progressed, I also knew I was having another boy. Friends and family members would wink and say, "Oooh, what if it's a girl this time?" And I would smile and nod and join in the what-ifs, but I always knew deep down that our oldest, Atticus, would be getting a little brother. And when our doctor confirmed this at 16 weeks, I just shrugged at my own intuitive nature.

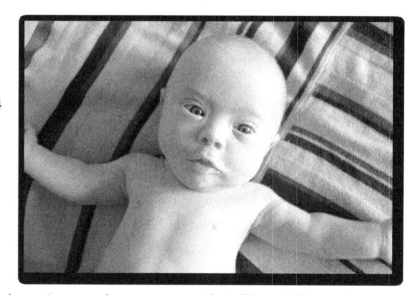

So when I got the news at 24 weeks about our son, I was shocked that I didn't already know.

It all started at our 20-week ultrasound. It's supposed to be a fun glimpse at the life growing inside, a check of basic anatomy, and a reassurance that all is well. For most moms it is. Our doctor found that our little guy had slightly dilated kidneys, but she wasn't worried about it too much. Even so, she sent us off for a level II ultrasound the following week, just to make sure that it wasn't anything serious.

I did a little research into what dilated kidneys could mean, and learned that it could be anything from a temporary fluid build-up that corrects itself before birth, to a marker for Down syndrome. As I was lying on the table with the unbearably cold ultrasound jelly smeared over my abdomen, it became clear to me that the ultrasound tech was looking for other signs of Down syndrome. She measured the heart, the level of fluid behind the neck, the length of the arms and legs, and the shape of the pinky finger. It turned out that in addition to the dilated kidneys, the baby also had an echogenic intracardiac focus. This is a calcification on the heart muscle that usually, like the kidneys, clears up on its own and isn't a cause for alarm. But it's also another marker for Down syndrome, and coupled with the kidneys, was therefore a cause for concern.

A genetic counselor came to talk with me and recommended that I have a new test called MaterniT21 that can definitively say whether or not the baby had a chromosomal anomaly. She stressed that there was still less than a 1% chance that anything would be wrong, and the test was merely a tool to give me peace of mind. The results would take a few weeks and she'd call me when they came in.

Enter the longest weeks of my life. I must have googled every variation of the words "soft markers for Down syndrome" a thousand times. Sometimes the results made me feel better, but more often than not they sent me into a tailspin of worry. It was a dark time. And then I got the call that would forever change my life.

Our second child would be born with Down syndrome.

The news was mind-shatteringly, heart-wrenchingly painful. I managed to cycle through a wide series of emotions in the matter of minutes. I grieved for the "normal" child I expected. I cursed whatever higher power would place this on our shoulders. I stared dumbfounded at the wall thinking that if I remained still long enough, the room would stop spinning.

We were suddenly faced with a multitude of choices. According to recent statistics, 90% of prenatal Trisomy 21 diagnoses end in termination of the pregnancy. I can't judge women who take this path when faced with such severe news, even when they are as far along as I am. The emotional, financial, and physical implications of raising a child with Down syndrome were mind-boggling to me at the time. But for us, at 24 weeks along, this wasn't a choice we could make. Our baby was no longer a clump of cells. I'd been feeling him roll and tumble in my stomach for weeks. We gave him a name. We gave him an identity. Termination was not an option for us.

Apparently, there are waiting lists for infants with Down syndrome, so the option of placing him up for adoption seemed a legitimate choice. Despite all that I had said about this child at this point in my pregnancy, he was still an abstract idea. He wasn't anyone I had met yet, and our bond had not developed. I only had attachments to what this child could become, and now my expectations had changed. Nevertheless, we decided we couldn't let someone else raise our child. And despite my surprise at this new challenge when my intuition into every other aspect of my pregnancy seemed so strong, I did know for certain that I would love him no matter what when he arrived.

Because of the diagnosis, my pregnancy was closely monitored. I went in for weekly ultrasounds, and each visit seemed to reveal possible worst-case scenarios. His kidneys remained dilated and now, in addition to the calcification on his heart, more calcification was showing up on his liver and stomach. The doctors told us it could be a manifestation of the Down syndrome itself, or a sign of something more serious, like a life-threatening infection. But the scariest finding by far was when we went in for the fetal echocardiogram to check for heart problems, and the doctor found a pleural effusion, which was fluid in the chest cavity near the heart and lungs. If it grew, it would likely kill him. But with each subsequent appointment, we saw that it remained small enough to be asymptomatic, and we crossed our fingers that it would stay that way. The doctors told us our best hope for his well-being was for me to deliver as close to full-term as possible. Since my first was two weeks early, our medical team put me on modified bed rest to prevent pre-term labor. I could go to work and handle basic tasks at home, but was advised to put my feet up as often as possible. As a teacher with a rambunctious two-year-old at home, this was easier said than done.

But one night just shy of 35 weeks, I woke up at around 2:00 in the morning with a pretty intense, but short-lived contraction. I knew that this tends to happen toward the end of pregnancy, so I ignored it and fell back asleep, but it continued for most of the morning. At around 5:00, I decided to start timing the duration and frequency of the contractions. They hurt, but there was absolutely no pattern to them at all. Most labor and delivery rooms have a strict policy that laboring women are not admitted until their contractions are four to five minutes apart and at least 60 seconds long. I was nowhere near there, so I decided to head into work. I needed to help my students prepare for their final exams, and after laboring with my first for 19 hours before any real progress was made, I felt like I had time even if this was the real thing. But I nevertheless put in a call to my doctor and she confirmed what I was suspecting: it was likely prodromal, or false labor. Still, she wanted me to come in and be monitored to make sure that the baby and I weren't in any distress. I figured I'd be slapped with an order for true bedrest and a prescription to assist with the pain. I called in for a substitute, hopped in the car, and drove to the hospital to see my doctor, texting my husband along the way to let him know what was going on.

When I made it to the doctor's office, the contractions became pretty frequent and painful. My OB/GYN wasn't in the office that day, but another doctor in the practice came in to check on me. The look she gave me was one I'll never forget: it was a mixture of shock, urgency, and a how-the-hell-did-you-not-realize-you-were-in-labor? I was almost fully dilated, and the baby was coming. Soon. They ordered a wheelchair to send me downstairs to labor and delivery, and told me to call my husband and order him to hurry or he would miss it. When we got downstairs, the

delivery room was already packed with a whole team, including the delivery doctor. Within the hour my husband arrived, I pushed a few times, and Quinton Robert Emil Mennes was born at just 35 weeks, over a month early

Weighing in at a healthy 6lbs, 13oz and over 18 inches long, we spent most of the day in shock. How did this happen so quickly? How was he so healthy for being born so early, especially after such a terrifying pregnancy? How the hell did I manage to teach three classes that morning, drive myself to the hospital, and deliver a baby before lunch? We asked and attempted to answer these questions for hours, telling and retelling the story to anyone who would listen. Had I decided to stay and teach my fourth period, like I really wanted to, I probably would have delivered this baby in an ambulance or along the side of the road. It turns out our little dude was in a hurry to meet us. He spent a week in the NICU for jaundice and some minor breathing issues, but was released to us the day before Christmas Eve.

Now, 8 months later, he is doing remarkably well. We've been blessed that he is healthy and happy and have numerous resources available to help us navigate the unknown waters of special needs parenting. We know we'll face some challenges ahead, but we've fallen so deeply in love with this sweet boy that we're willing to take on the world to give him what he needs.

Parenting is the hardest job I will ever have. This would be true even if my son did not have Down syndrome. But he does. And we love him not in spite of it or even because of it. We love him because he is our son, our Quinn, and he just happens to have Down syndrome. It does not define him, it only enhances him. And it makes me so appreciative of everything I have in this life, especially my children.

~Megan, Quinn's mom; 30; Houston, United States

Blogging @ "Define Crazy": www.meganmennes.blogspot.com

{Owen}

This being baby number four and not having major issues, I didn't reschedule my 20 week anatomy scan when I found out my husband couldn't join me that morning. I had already waited two extra weeks to schedule once the kids were in school, and we were seasoned parents. I skipped off to my appointment, anxious to see the little one moving and grooving around.

The tech was wonderful as she measured and checked all the pieces and parts of the

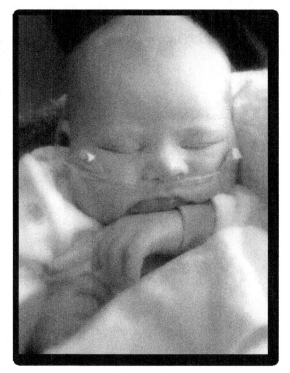

baby. She talked to me as she worked and printed out many photos for me to bring home. I was on cloud nine knowing that all the parts were there, and breathed a huge sigh of relief.

I waited to meet the doctor, and continue to plan for the rest of the pregnancy. I waited much longer than I believed I would, and my stomach dropped a bit when I met the xzcv ttdoctor's eyes as he walked in. He asked me a few questions, and then asked me to join him sitting down. I won't soon forget his words. "These are difficult ultrasounds to go over and share," he said. At that moment I felt like I was watching myself from afar or on television. I felt like I was listening in on the conversation as a third party. The doctor continued to show me the images from the ultrasound and assured me that all the baby's functions looked good and is healthy. Then he stopped when he got to the baby's face and profile pics. He talked about the baby missing a nasal bone, and how this was a marker for Down syndrome. He assured me the tech was quite qualified and usually saw things clearly. I remembered back to the scan as she struggled to get a good profile picture, and had to make me move around a bit. I never noticed anything off, but it was odd that she looked for a long time. He went on to show how everything else looked just fine; there were no other markers.

As he finished, his other comment still remains in my heart. "You will need to talk with your husband and decide what to do." I listened as he talked about a referral to a perinatalogist for a level two ultrasound and possible amniocentesis for a diagnosis. I left the office and cried on the way out to the car. I was so worried about all of the medical and social ramifications of what I had just heard. I had planned to go to the store and pick up a cute gender-specific outfit to share the news with daddy. Now I just wanted him to hold me. I drove, crying, the 30 minutes to his office, praying he wasn't on a job site and called him to come out to my car.

I felt such a heavy heart as I shared with Brian that our baby may or may not be "perfect." My emotions overwhelmed me, and my husband comforted me. He reminded me that our baby would be our baby no matter what. If I wanted more information, schedule an appointment. He was a rock of strength and his faith was unfaltering.

I decided at that moment leaving his office, that we indeed would be just fine. This baby was meant for our family in whatever form it took, and we would welcome it just as we had the other babies. A little retail therapy was called for, and after buying a few cute outfits, I was ready to face what was headed our way. Don't get me wrong, I had a billion questions and doubts, but I also felt a sense of calm that we would all be ok.

I called that afternoon and scheduled an appointment with the specialist. It would be two weeks of waiting and Googling and reading and researching. The nasal bone was a new marker to look for in scans, and it was often hard to detect. I was sure that this was the case and that our follow-up would show a nasal bone, and I could go back to worrying about my cervix as usual. Although I was anxious to go, I was more looking forward to some answers and moving forward from there.

We walked in ready for anything. The tech doing the ultrasound was very detailed, and talked us through much of what she was doing and seeing. Parts and pieces were all still measuring on track, so we were pleased about that. She took a very long time looking at the heart. I kept giving Brian the "oh no!" look, and we waited while she went to got get the doctor. We did get to see baby in 3D, too, which is always incredible to me!

When the doctor came in, they spent some time together looking at the heart and discussing quietly what they did or did not see.   The tech was unsure whether there was tissue between two of the heart chambers, but the doctor believed that he did see tissue, so he said that was nothing to worry about. Phew!   We knew from our research that heart defects can also be more common in babies that have Down syndrome.

The doctor then showed us the areas of concern.   They still did not see a nasal bone, which was the strongest marker.   In addition, they saw a bit of fluid around the heart and a dilated kidney.   The last two markers, he said, would not be of any concern typically -- in an ultrasound he wouldn't even mention them -- however, they are both soft markers for Down syndrome.   Together, the puzzle was coming together. He let us know that these are just screenings.   An amnio would give us a definitive answer, but we were unwilling to take that risk and lose the baby.

Our other option was a blood test.   They were newer on the scene, but would tell us with 99% accuracy whether there were issues with the top four chromosal abnormalities. The test we were offered was called Verifi.   It was non-invasive, just a blood draw for me.   We would know results in eight days.   We decided to go ahead with this test, so that I could have peace of mind for the remainder of the pregnancy.

Eight days. Eight days can be a flash or an eternity.   For me, it was a mix of both, somehow.

I truly believe I already knew the answer we would be getting.   There were several signs sent our way that week that may have seemed coincidental; however, I believe it was all there to confirm my thoughts so that we could continue on this journey.

The hardest part of this time was how to deal with it.   I am a talker.   My husband, thankfully, understands this and was fabulous, especially during this wait.   We didn't really want to share what was going on with anyone, but did tell a few people.   I didn't want people to worry.   I didn't want to have them drawn into this craziness until we knew for sure.   I didn't want looks of pity or sympathy, depending on the outcome. This was our baby, either way, and we never considered otherwise. I spent many sleepless nights that week.   I found support online. I searched and searched about absent nasal bones.   The more I looked, the more confident I felt that our little one would have "designer" genes, as one mom put it.

The call came exactly eight days after drawing blood.   The genetic counselor asked whether I wanted to talk about the results in person or on the phone.   I had a sense of calm as I verified my information so we could talk over the phone.   I knew what I was about to hear, and prolonging the inevitable was not going to change anything.   She explained that the test results were indeed positive for Trisomy 21. That would indicate our baby has Down syndrome with 99% probability.   She explained about the test, and what this would mean for our pregnancy and life.   She offered a meeting to go over things, so we set a time for the following week.

As I got off the phone, I let out a long, slow breath. I dialed Brian at work, and the tears began... although this time, they were from the relief and contentment of knowing, rather than from fear or worry.   I am sure Brian loved having this conversation on the phone, but I could not hold the information in. I had to let it out and let it be real.

Next, we called our moms to let them know, as they had been patiently waiting with us. Their love and responses were so crucial in the process of acceptance.   They were with us.   This was their family too, and they were more ready to meet the new little arrival.

I found it interesting that two days later, just before my 24th week, my OB called to see how I was doing with everything. I found it interesting that he called me; that was not his bedside manner in my experience. In retrospect, I know that he called because in Iowa, medical terminations can be done until the 24th week of pregnancy. He called to check in; but he really called to see if I wanted to abort my son.

After receiving the official diagnosis, I decided to switch hospitals for delivery, which also meant finding a new OB. In our area, there are two health systems, and my kids and I were not in the same one. We had a bad experience with one of the pediatric specialists in my system, hence the change for the kids, and I didn't want our new baby to be seen by that doctor either, if needed. So, with an already labeled high-risk pregnancy due to advanced maternal age and history of preterm labor, I was off to find a new doctor. It didn't take much time to find a perfect fit, and I was seen at the new office within the week. We created a plan and scheduled appointments with the maternal fetal medicine (MFM) office to evaluate our son further.

The rest of my pregnancy was quite uneventful. I went to appointments each week. The MFM completed an echocardiogram and determined his heart was structurally sound, although he had a thickened heart wall and pericardial effusion: fluid around the heart. I alternated seeing the MFM and my new OB. As the time got closer, I had appointments twice a week for a BioPhysical Profile (BPP) and a non-stress test (NST). Both were fairly quick, and baby boy was doing great.

Otherwise, it was Iowa in the winter. A week before we had him, we lost power for a full 24 hours. I was grateful to get through that storm without having to worry about digging out or, worse yet, delivering at home. But as the days grew closer, I became a bit more nervous about having him here. I was currently protecting him and sheltering him from whatever would be. Once he was born, that would become more difficult. I worked past my worries and was ready to meet him soon.

Christmas passed, and we went for a check up to the MFM. During the ultrasound and BPP that day, it was determined that the fluid around his heart was increasing. The MFM sat to meet with us, and consulted with our OB on the phone. They concluded that it was best to deliver the little squirt, and we agreed. We could head over the hospital after lunch, or wait until the next morning. Always the planner, I asked for the next day. I like the birthday of December 28th, and I really longed to have one more night with my kids at home as a family of five. We left with an induction scheduled for the morning and I savored the evening with my family.

The next day I had three worries: baby's heart, what/who he would look like and what we would name him. Within hours all my fears were put at ease.

I have been blessed with quick labors with my children. Number three was interesting. My water broke at midnight, we arrived at the hospital at 1:00 am, and delivered him at 2:00 am. That experience was very empowering, because I delivered without any medication. So this time around, my goal was to try to go without again. My water was broken a bit after 10:00 am, and within a few hours it was a go. Grateful for not needing Pitocin, I waited out other pain meds. By noon, I was progressing, and needed something to take the edge off. I was given a dose of Fentanyl, and told subsequent doses would be less effective. Thankfully, it helped enough to ease me through, and one dose later, I was ready to meet the little guy. My OB made it just in time to catch him as he arrived into the world at 1:04. Nothing in the world is like welcoming a new child. He cried, and I was able to relax a bit as we saw him, and watched the NICU team check him over.

Everyone said how great he looked, and I was able to nurse him a bit before they took him to the nursery while we switched rooms. Owen Henry was born at 38 weeks, 5 days. We welcomed our precious son on December 28, 2012. He was seven pounds, seven ounces and 19 ¼ inches long. And he was perfect.

After a while, the doctor came in to explain that his oxygen levels were not great, and that they were going to transfer him to the NICU. I was so disappointed, but I knew that we should go with it. I was a wreck worrying about his heart, but a short time later, the cardiologist performed an echocardiogram and found no concerns at all. What an answered prayer! That night, though, it was determined that his hemoglobin numbers were off. They believed he had extra hemoglobin in his blood, which was thickening it, so it was harder for him to get it moving around his body, especially his extremities. So they did a procedure to exchange out some blood for saline to dilute his blood, essentially. It worked, and he was resting comfortably that evening and stable. He was also on billi lights for a bit to help stay ahead of jaundice issues, and also received a low flow of oxygen. Pulmonary hypertension was the diagnosis, and the doctors were convinced it was just something that would take time to resolve as his body worked to stabilize.

In the NICU, there were ups and downs, but he progressed nicely and fed wonderfully. I had a huge worry about eating, but he nursed well and took bottles well. After going through a 30 day NICU stay with our oldest 7 years earlier, we decided to pump breastmilk and bottle feed to work on getting home. He did great and after 5 days, the team decided he could go home the next day. It was wonderful to take him home and have our family of six under the same roof.

The next weeks were filled with appointments and checkups to monitor the little guy: a pulmonologist, an audiologist, an ENT, and a pediatrician. Dealing with the oxygen and monitor was frustrating at home, with lots of tubing and waking to the pulse ox monitor several time a night. After visiting with the pulmonologist two weeks later, the oxygen was discontinued. Owen continued to sleep relatively well, although he did breathe quite loudly and wake himself several times a night. But over time, this lessened. We had scheduled a sleep study to look into the possibility of sleep apnea, but a bit before, he developed an ear infection and during the antibiotic treatment, his sleeping quieted and his breathing calmed.

Hearing concerns remained throughout his first months, as he did not pass any of the screens at the hospital or afterwards. His ear canals were tiny, and that was believed to be part of the problem, along with fluid in the inner ear. Owen's first ABR showed mild to moderate hearing loss, and after a few appointments with the ENT and audiologist, we prepared for hearing aids. We visited the ENT one day before our hearing aid were to be picked up and we had progress; he could see his ear drums! This was great news, until he shared that he did not see any evidence of

fluid. This led the ENT to believe that Owen's loss was most likely permanent hearing loss. It wasn't the news we were hoping for, but we were grateful that there were supports in place to help.

At the audiologist the following day, she wanted to run the screens one more time while we prepared to learn about the world of hearing aids. She ran all three screens and he passed every single one. We were in awe and so happy to know that this would not be another hurdle in the Owen's journey.

With the hearing and oxygen issues resolved, Owen became one boring baby. Our appointments decreased dramatically. His lower tone was evident, but he was still keeping on track developmentally. Physically, he consistently measured near the 50th percentile on the typical charts. Boring has never been so wonderful and appreciated!

Today, Owen is 14 months old. He has been very healthy and we are working towards milestones like standing and walking. He crawls like crazy and loves to torment his older siblings by climbing on them and pulling their hair. He loves to eat mashed potatoes and carrots. Our three older children love him to pieces and love to make him smile! It has been over a year since our diagnosis, and although it has been a roller coaster at times, we are so grateful he is here and well!

~ Jenny, Owen's mom; 35; Iowa, United States

{Jude}

Everything with Jude seemed okay at first. I opted for early testing which involved an ultrasound. Piper, my third child, came with me and we laughed at Skippy's, Piper's nickname for the fetus', antics. She was rolling around, standing on her head, and just being super active. I felt her rolling around very early on, and was reassured by her energy.

Then we got the call. My results from the first trimester blood test had come back with a 1:5 odds of the baby having Down syndrome. I was devastated. I sobbed and cried. I got really angry at God, at the universe, at the world. I felt like I was being punished for

wanting too much. I mean, come on. I already four children, and this is what happened when I pushed for five. I knew this was not a diagnostic test, but I was convinced that it was, and lived my life with that conviction. I had this feeling for months now. I had even debated with a friend, because I had said I would not terminate for Down syndrome. As much as I am not woo woo, I felt that I had known about Jude for a long time.

For two days, I cried. I researched tons of information and tried to bolster myself with some hope. Her nuchal neck count was two mm, which was normal. The doctor had not mentioned anything about her nasal bone, and I scanned her ultrasound pictures, hoping I could find the bone. But deep down I was convinced she had Down syndrome. My husband and I decided to go ahead and get an amniocentesis done. I felt that I had to know, that I couldn't bear to live in this half space of not knowing.

A week before the amnio, I stopped feeling Jude move. Because I was also at risk for Trisomy 18, I believed she had this much more severe chromosomal disorder, and that she was dead. I had suffered a miscarriage months before conceiving Jude, and I was scared it was happening again. At this point, there was a small shift in my feelings. Down syndrome was by far better than having a dead baby.

My mom came down Sunday, and on Monday accompanied me to my appointment. I wrapped my white rosary around my wrist, and brought a Mary card with The Memorare on the back. During the hour I waited, I prayed that prayer about ten times. Mary was a mother, and she had lost her son. I felt very close to her as I sat there waiting for them to jam a giant needle into my womb. I wavered, even then, over whether or not I should have even the test.

When we were finally called back, I was near panic with fear. And then there was the baby, moving around, heart beating perfectly, and I started to sob. The baby was alive. Suddenly, Trisomy 21 didn't seem like the worst option possible. What mattered in those few seconds was that the baby was kicking, swallowing, pumping blood through her tiny heart. The tech was very thorough, but acted impatient with me, and kept saying "This is all really hard to see at 16 weeks. We usually do these tests at 20 weeks," and then, "If you choose to do the amniocentesis... " It was clear that she had no idea why I was there. I finally said "Um... we are here for the amniocentesis." And then my mom said something about not aborting for Down syndrome, and the woman again began acting very annoyed, and said, "Well, you have two soft makers. She has no nasal bone and her bladder looks bright, but we'll have to ask the doctor what he thinks." And then she left. I cried and texted my husband the news. I told him the baby was a girl first, because I knew he was hoping for another girl. I softened up for the blow... not just high risk, but two soft markers. He wrote back, "So?" The doctor came in, and performed a careful but really long amniocentesis. He refused to speculate on the soft markers, but the lack of a nasal bone confirmed what I had accepted three weeks ago. I knew deep down that this baby, now Jude -- I had made a promise to St. Jude that if she was alive I'd name her Jude -- had Down syndrome.

We got the call two days later. Jude had Down syndrome. Initially, I just felt relief from knowing. I cried a lot at how kind my friends were. And when I started to reach out to the Down syndrome community, I was drawn right in and welcomed, which made me cry.

But really, I was also crying because Jude was not perfect. I was crying because I was not going to have a "typical" baby. I was crying because I was terrified of the future. I was crying because I was worried about how her care would effect the rest of my family. But then, I didn't dare express those feelings. My husband and my mom were so positive and supportive. My husband already loved Jude with the fierce passion that he shows for all our children. I loved her, but that love was overshadowed by grief and fear.

For the rest of my pregnancy, I'd swing between despair and hope. It helped that Jude was showing no health problems and that my pregnancy was going well. Usually at night when I was alone, I'd cry a lot about her future. I worried that she would never read, go to college, have an independent life. I wasn't sure how she was going to fit into our homeschooled, eccentric family. On other days, I felt that there was no better place for her. But what carried me is that I loved her no matter what.

Jude was born quickly in the midst of a rain storm in mid-December. I didn't even have time to get into a hospital gown before I started to push. Even with the furious rush of her coming, she was born into a quiet and calm space. The young midwife who caught her was still in awe of this miracle as were we despite this being the fifth time. And then they put Jude on my chest and she, the first of all my children to do so, lifted her tiny face towards mine. Our eyes meet, and there was a lot resting in that look she gave me. We knew Jude had Down syndrome. And I thought I was prepared. When I looked at her all I could see was the Down syndrome, and it was a shock. It was a crack in my expectations of how I would react. Of course it was not the shock, a woman feels with a post natal diagnosis but I wasn't expecting it to be a shock at all. I didn't feel like I didn't love her, or that she wasn't mine....I just felt this distance. I am aware that this could be from the shock of such a quick birth (I thought we had at least a few hours to go) but I'm honest enough to admit that some of it was the shock of seeing those features, and sadly my inability to see Jude. But as the night wore down, and my husband finally handed her over to me (he was in love right from the start), I was able to just be with her. I first noticed that when she was sleeping she pursed her lips into a little kiss just like my three year old daughter used to as a newborn. When she was getting ready to squawk, her face got all red and crinkly like my third child's face. The shape of her lips were similar to my second child and her tiny size reminded me of my sweet first born. And as the night turned into the day after, the light did come in, and suddenly Jude wasn't the face of Down syndrome. She was Jude. The baby who completed our family. She was what we needed and were waiting for even though we did not know it.

Jude does have Down syndrome but that is not her only qualifying characteristic to being human. She, like the other children, will surprise us with her own expectations of herself and her world. Her light, shining through my cracked bottles, will join with the light that we already have let into our family. She will have different, sometimes harder, challenges of course. We are not naive. But we are hopeful, and we all feel pretty lucky that this sweet baby has graced us with her life. I hope that we're worthy of such grace.

~Ginger, Jude's mom; 40; Georgia, United States

Blogging @ www.greenteaginger.blogspot.com

{Ada}

Taking the first trimester screening test was just a checkbox for us. We hardly gave it a second thought, because it came back with very low risk with my first, and we thought it would with our second also. They measured the nuchal translucency (NT), and it was small just like my son's. She took the largest measurement, which was 1.5mm. A week later, I got a phone call on a Friday afternoon from the OB nurse. You never want to get a phone call -- it seems they always have bad news. She said the risk of our baby having Trisomy 21 was 1:92. I tried to tell myself that a 1% chance of having a baby with Down syndrome was still very unlikely. Somehow, I still just had a feeling. My husband thought the risk was so low that we didn't even need to research or talk about it, but I still started researching on my own.

It seemed like forever -- it was actually a week and a half -- before we could get in to see the genetic counselor. By the time we met with the genetics counselor, I was 13 weeks pregnant, and I had researched all the new blood tests. The genetic counselor explained to us that my PAPP-A was low (0.2 MOM), and that was the reason our risk was elevated. She offered me the MaterniT21 blood test, and we had the blood draw done right away. However, two weeks later, she called to tell me that the blood tests came back inconclusive. We could either redraw, or I could proceed with the amniocentesis. Waiting had been agony, and I didn't want to go through two more weeks just to be told the results were inconclusive again. We scheduled the amnio. We had to wait almost two more weeks, and it was beginning to look like we would have to wait through our second weekend without the amnio results. Then, my OB called just before 4:00 pm on Friday, six weeks after the first phone call. They always like to call on Friday, it seems. My husband was on the way home, so I was alone with my 15 month old son. She congratulated me on having a baby girl. Just what we wanted - one of each! However, she proceeded to tell me that my daughter had Trisomy 21. At that point, I could feel myself breaking down. She gave me the cell phone number of the genetic counselor, and said I could call her right away if I wanted. Right after I got off the phone with the OB, my husband called, and there was no way I could keep the tears and fear out of my voice. I broke down the second I answered, and told him everything while he drove home.

That weekend, we spent most of our time reading about Down syndrome. We mostly read stories about adults. We were concerned that our daughter would suffer, that our family would suffer. Would my son get everything he needed if we were in and out of hospitals for our daughter? By the time we met with the genetic counselor, we were leaning heavily towards termination. I even wrote a letter to my unborn daughter apologizing for not being able to raise her and care for her. I placed the letter in a box with the only thing I had bought, hoping for a baby girl. It was a bib that said "My big brother is pooh-rific!" We discussed all of the options with the genetic counselor. She scheduled for us to have a fetal echocardiogram right away. The fetal echocardiogram didn't show any heart defects and the ultrasound technician couldn't find anything else either. We were told that if we hadn't had an amnio already, then they wouldn't have thought she had Trisomy 21. We tried to go ahead and schedule our termination, thinking we would schedule it for a couple weeks away, and think about it until then. But she said that she wouldn't schedule the termination until we were certain, and we had a few weeks to think about it since we were only 17 weeks along. I also spoke with our OB, and told her we were considering termination because we were worried how this would affect our son. She told me she had a nine year old niece with Down syndrome, and her two siblings hardly even know that there is anything different about her. I was amazed that everyone was encouraging us to continue our pregnancy when 90% of women decide to terminate.

We still weren't sure what to do, but I started reading blogs about younger children with Down syndrome, and I saw less doom and gloom, and many more happy stories. Yes, there were still struggles, but no one was spending 50% of their time in hospitals, and no one was suffering. This was a very different picture than the one I had originally painted in my head. When we got home, I continued to do some major soul searching. What was the purpose of life anyway? Some people say people with intellectual disabilities are a drain on society, but is the ability to work independently and earn enough money to care for yourself the only thing that matters? In my opinion, the ability to make people smile and change lives is far more important. Our daughter's health, from what we could tell at this point, didn't seem like she would be physically suffering. Even if she did have some health issues, it doesn't mean her life is any less valuable. We can't guarantee anything in life. In the end, I knew there would be one decision that I, personally, couldn't live with, and we decided to accept that our life wouldn't be what we expected. However, it would be what we wanted, and maybe even more. We would have our happy little family with one boy and one truly special girl.

The rest of my pregnancy went by without any issues. I had extra sonograms and no issues were ever noticed. I was expecting it to be a long haul because I went past my due date with my first. There were definitely times when I was scared for the future, but I was mostly just excited to finally meet her. One day, I found a box hidden under a desk and unpacked it. I found that special bib and the note I wrote her. It was very emotional reading how upset I was when seriously considering the possibility of giving up my daughter and how much things had changed since then. She had changed me so much and she wasn't even born yet. I remember and smile every time she wears that bib now.

Three weeks before my due date, I started having contractions. They were off and on for two days, but they were still inconsistent. Finally, they were painful enough to make the 45 minute drive to the hospital, but I was still expecting to be sent home. When we got there, I was six centimeters dilated already. My first labor went from one centimeter to pushing in a few hours, so I was prepared for a quick labor. However, my nerves got the best of me, and my labor stalled. I had an unmedicated birth with my son, and I had hoped to have another unmedicated birth. I think the fear of the future, both near and far, was causing me to slow down labor. My contractions were still very inconsistent. After several hours, I ended up getting the epidural, which really sped my labor up. It was only about an hour later that my baby girl was born. All nerves were out the window, and I was in love. She was so precious, and I couldn't figure out why I was ever nervous. She got great APGAR scores and was very alert.

However, she couldn't figure nursing out. We tried and tried to get her to latch, but something wasn't working. Multiple lactation nurses were trying to help, assuring me that I was doing a great job. I had a lot of practice with my son, after all. She was taken to the nursery to be under a warmer for a bit because she was having trouble maintaining her body temperature. She only spent an hour in the warmer before being sent back, but over half a day had gone by, and she still hadn't nursed. Finally, her pediatrician came to see her and with one glance in her mouth, he told us that she had a cleft palate. We were definitely surprised, but I don't think the shock was anything compared to her prenatal diagnosis. We handled it very well. She spent a couple weeks in the NICU because she was very small, had jaundice, and needed to get the strength to learn to feed from her special bottle. At first, I continued to try nursing her with lots of encouragement from the lactaction consultants and NICU nurses. Not once did anyone tell me that it was probably impossible, like trying to drink from a straw with a hole in it. For the first few days, I spent most of my time trying to get her to nurse and then giving her expressed breast milk through a tube in her nose (NG tube). I finally researched and realized that if I wanted to get her home, I would have to give her a bottle. Two of my biggest concerns for her, hospitalization and not being able to nurse, came true. It's amazing how those things didn't even matter that much to me anymore. All that mattered was that I could take this precious little girl home to meet her big brother!

Ada is 7.5 months. She has only been hospitalized once for RSV, which was more because she was only 3 weeks old and about 6lb when she got it. She is eating great and just started prop sitting. Her big brother loves her and she is a huge momma's girl. She will have surgery around 18 months to repair her palate. No other surgeries are expected. She is amazing!

~ Jaime, Ada's mom; 28; Arizona, United States

{Jacob}

It all began at the twelve week ultrasound and blood test. This was my fifth pregnancy, after having three miscarriages and our daughter, who was three. We had the twelve week nuchal translucency test, and it came back with a 1:52 chance of our baby having Down syndrome. We were offered invasive testing to confirm or deny Down syndrome, but after having three lost pregnancies, we decided against it because the risk was too high of miscarrying again. To say we were frightened is an understatement, but being strong Christians we decided to pray and put it all into God's hands.

Things went along merrily until the 19 week ultrasound. We had arrived to have the scheduled scan, and the ultrasound technician was taking a long time to do everything. She stopped after about 40 minutes and said that she needed to go check something with the doctor. I knew right in that moment that something was wrong. You get that sinking feeling in your gut, and you just know that "I'll just get the doctor" comment means that something is up.

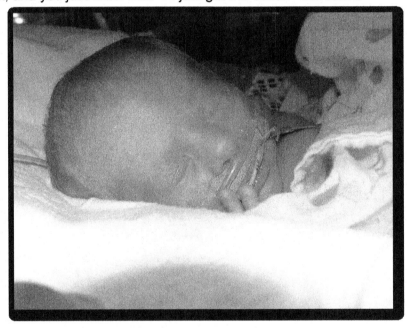

The doctor came, and we were ushered into another room and shown the extensive array of ultrasound pictures. The most troubling thing was our baby's heart. They could neither confirm nor deny whether our baby had a life threatening heart condition, and that we needed to be referred to a specialist as soon as possible. Also, the baby's limbs were measuring shorter than what was expected at that gestational age. They were pretty sure that with both of these indicators, our baby had Down syndrome. They again offered us the amniocentesis, and after some time on our own talking and praying, we decided to go ahead with it. It was pretty horrible, but still, our greatest fear was that we were going to lose this baby. We were also worried about the issue of Down syndrome, but at this point in time we were more afraid about the baby's heart, and if the baby would survive the invasive test. We left feeling very deflated and unsure of our baby's future.

The day we found out the truth about our baby's diagnosss was the hardest yet, and I will never forget it. The doctor called three days after the amniocentesis. It was a Friday, I had been waiting all day, and finally the call came at 2:00 pm. It had been the longest and hardest three days of crying, and praying that our baby would not have Down syndrome, and just be healthy. I will never forget his words on the phone. "I'm sorry love, it is Down syndrome," he said, "And, oh, it is a boy." I hung up the phone and rang my husband, and the grief and sadness we both felt was overwhelming. I have never cried so much for the baby I thought I was going to have, and never felt so helpless in all my life. To be honest, I cried for days, and struggled with all the 'what if' questions about his future. All I felt was a tremendous sense of grief, anger and fear. In saying this, though, there was never a time when we felt that termination was an option. We knew with a certainty that this baby was our son, and that we were having him no matter what. But it was still a confusing and emotionally challenging time.

After some days of feeling sorry for myself, I decided to get some help and support, and to educate myself about Down syndrome. I had spent the last several years as a high school teacher, and the last four of those working in the educational support unit. I had experienced teaching children with Down syndrome, but now this had become personal for me. I was now becoming the parent, the shoe was on the other foot, and I would be lying if I said I wasn't scared. So, I took my mum, and we went and visited the Down syndrome society. It was the best thing I could have done. I was able to talk to a mother who had been in my shoes, and ask her all about my fears for our son's future. I also spoke to a friend and colleague at work who had an 18 year old daughter with Down syndrome, and she was honest and supportive and full of encouragement. I think it really helped me to dispel a lot of the fears I felt, and for the first time, to actually feel hope for the future.

What then followed was a pretty difficult and worrying pregnancy. Our baby boy was not growing well, and at the 28 week ultrasound, he was only measuring a tiny 500 grams. One relief, though, was that we were able to see an amazing doctor for our baby's heart, and it was confirmed that he had holes in his heart -- but it was not life-threatening. This was an immense relief.

We made it to 32 weeks gestation, and after three days in the hospital, we were asked to make another tough decision: to have an emergency C-section as our son's umbilical cord was not working properly, and he was not growing. He was born weighing 1009 grams, and went straight to the NICU, were he spent the following nine weeks and one day. The moment he was born, and hearing his tiny little screech, changed everything for me. I just felt fierce love and protection for him, and all the sadness and grief just melted away. I really felt that it was time to get over myself, to stop feeling sorry for myself, because he needed me now more than ever, and that I had to be strong for him and to fight for him. I truly believe that was the defining moment for me of accepting his

diagnosis, and seeing him as just my son... nothing more and nothing less. I got to hold him the next day, and that was it. I was head over heels in love with my little man.

Since then, it hasn't been easy. There have been many health issues, and lots and lots of doctors visits, but he makes me and my heart smile everyday day, and I am always amazed at how he makes everyone in the waiting room at all these appointments smile too. I truly believe that God has a purpose for him, as he does for every child. He is truly blessed by God and he is incredibly brave, which is fitting because that is what his name, Jacob Coen, stands for.

Jacob is 20 months, 18 months corrected. He still is our little man, only weighing 8.3 kg after being born premature at 32 weeks. He has sleep apnea, and is on thyroxin for an under-active thyroid. He recently got his glasses for short sightedness, and he is doing lots of verbalising with his hearing aids on. He is crawling, but we call it the caterpillar crawl, because he crawls on his tummy. He is a beautiful, happy, and content little boy. His development is taking a while, but the joy and happiness he brings to our lives far outweighs any delays or health issues. Those we can continue to battle and fight while we enjoy having this beautiful person in our lives. His mum, dad, and big sister are so thankful for him and all the joy he brings to our lives.

~Sarah, Jacob's mum; 32; Sydney, Australia

{Edward}

In the fall of 2011, everything was starting to come together. I was 27, my husband was 31, and after two and half years of marriage, we were ready to start our family. After being diagnosed with a blighted ovum in the spring of that year we began to try again, and this time, it took a few cycles before those pink lines showed up again. When the "morning" sickness hit me, I was pretty sure that this time, things were going right. As much as I hated feeling constantly ill, I took it as a sign that there really was a life there this time around. This time, at our eight week ultrasound, we were both rewarded with

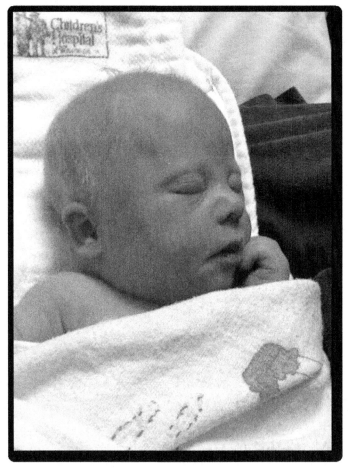

the sight and sounds of our little one's heartbeat. Sure, the image looked more like a Squidbilly character than a baby, but that heartbeat was more than enough for us. Despite confirmation of a real pregnancy, I was nervous and we waited until the end of the first trimester before announcing our pregnancy to the world.

The appointment for my anatomy scan was at 19 weeks, and although there were no concerns from my OB/GYN leading up to the scan, you better believe that I was still nervous, and had been checking for a heartbeat several days a week with my own home doppler. Although I am not the youngest of my siblings, I was the last to venture into the world of parenthood. My parents were already grandparents to six grandsons, with a seventh on the way, and no granddaughters... so you can imagine how much speculation there was regarding the gender of our child. I knew in my heart it would be a boy, and told people that the gender didn't matter as long as the baby was healthy -- but secretly kept wishing we would be blessed with a little girl.

The moment of our ultrasound arrived, and sure enough, we discovered we were having a boy. I remember feeling mildly disappointed, even though I already had a gut feeling about it. I internally repeated my mantra of "as long as he's healthy". The disappointment was fleeting, as I began to notice that the ultrasound tech was spending a lot of time focusing on the heart. While taking the other measurements she had been fairly chatty but now, as she increasingly pressed and pushed, trying to get new angles, she had fallen mostly silent. After 20 minutes or so of focusing on his heart, she told us she was going to go get the doctor so that he could try and get some different views. When she left the room my husband and I joked a little about some of the "cute" things we had seen while she was doing the measurements, like his relatively large head. I told him that it made me nervous that she spent so much time looking at the heart, and he admitted that it worried him too, but that it was probably nothing. It felt like forever before the doctor came in and introduced himself. He briefly checked the measurements the tech had done and then began to focus in on the heart. Time dragged and dragged, and then he finally announced, "There is a pathway in the heart that should not be there."

Now time didn't drag, it stopped. My husband and I squeezed each other's hands. We asked what that meant, and were told that our baby had a heart defect. He went on to say that the increased size of the nuchal fold and the shortened long bones of the arms and legs were indicative of a

chromosomal issue, most likely Down syndrome. He told us that we would need to get a fetal echocardiogram done to determine the exact heart defect, and that we could get an amniocentesis done to determine if there were any chromosomal abnormalities. We had declined prenatal screening at the 13-week mark, but being logical people and being faced with this unexpected turn of events, we both agreed that we needed to know. They did the amnio right then and there, and we were told that it would be a few days before the initial results were back, and even longer still before the full results would be available. On the car ride home, I cried, and we discussed what this would mean for our family.

It took three days for our FISH results to come back, which confirmed the presence of Trisomy 21 in every cell. Those three days were the roughest ones of our lives. I knew that I could not terminate this baby, and looked to the internet for information about Down Syndrome and what to expect. My husband wasn't sure that it was fair to our son to bring him into this world, where other people can sometimes work so amazingly hard to make sure that those who are different are denied the opportunity to thrive. In my darkest hour, I must admit that I sometimes felt the same way. After getting the FISH results, there was no point in waiting for the full results to make our decision. I told my husband that I understood if he needed to leave the relationship, but that I would be having this baby. I will never forget his reaction: he told me that there were an awful lot of things in this life that he could live without, but I was not one of them. He told me that we were in this together, and that our baby would be wonderful and that he would always love our son no matter how many challenges we had to face together as a family. Once those words were spoken, the worry and anxiety over the future were still there, but the tension and strain on our relationship was gone and we began planning for the next step.

~Jennifer, Edward's mom; 28; Wisconsin, United States

{Jesse}

At 16 weeks, I was referred for an amniocentesis after receiving a 1:10 chance of Down syndrome after undergoing the standard blood and ultrasound tests. I had the amnio without much thought. To be honest, while my lovely GP had been sounding cautious, in the back of my mind I was thinking, "He doesn't realize, this is a miracle baby." I had been told a few years earlier that I would have to go down the IVF path if I wanted kids. Then bang, after a lovely relaxing holiday to New Zealand, I found out I was pregnant.

Our world was turned upside down, in a nice way. After being in a stepfamily situation with all its challenges, my husband and I were enjoying a wonderful equally shared experience. It was an exciting time after what we had been through.

On Friday, May 29th, 2011 -- a day I'll never forget -- the obstetrician called and said, "I have the test results and they are positive for Down syndrome. I'm sorry," he said quietly, like he was delivering a death message; and I felt every bit like I was receiving one. I felt shock and disbelief, like when someone dies unexpectedly. Time stood still, and I felt numb as I hung up the phone. Ever the optimist, I would have hung onto a 1% chance, but this was an irreversible, no-hope diagnosis. I felt stuck.

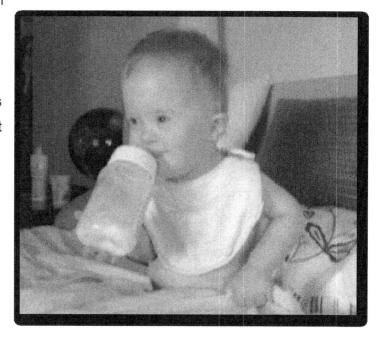

I sat on my bed and cried. When my husband got home, he just looked at me and didn't have to ask. He knew. We both cried together. I felt again that our lives were being turned upside down in a bad way. This pregnancy felt like a slap in the face. Why did I even fall pregnant if this was to be the scenario?

For anyone in my shoes right now, if I could be with you, I would say, go through what you have to and know it's normal, but trust me; it will change unbelievably. The single thing I regret the most is not having someone further down the road tell it was going to be alright... so much more than alright.

The first night was a sleepless night; and then I woke up Sunday morning, and a wonderful thing started to happen. Hope had started to slowly seep back into my heart. A Bible scripture was in my mind, and then I went to church, where this same scripture was preached. Somehow, I felt like I was in God's loving arms, and although I felt terrible, we would get through this the same way as other challenges we had faced.

When we caught up with the obstetrician a few days later, he was the first to utter the words that we would hear over and over: you have options. I looked at the photos of beautiful newborn babies lining his walls as we sat there. Not ONE of them had Down syndrome. Had every other parent taken the option, I wondered?

I will never judge anyone for aborting under the kind of pressure and negativity that surrounds Down syndrome in the medical field. You are so vulnerable during pregnancy, especially after receiving a bombshell. And if you haven't seen a living, breathing, cooing, smiling baby with Down syndrome and their adoring family, you forget about the child. None of the health professionals spoke positively about Down syndrome. Sure, Down syndrome is a condition, but what is overlooked is the person, the beautiful baby. It was like we were dealing with a cancer, and expected to have it cut out. At times, it was a little intimidating, and I kept having to say to a room full of specialists, "Before you go on, we have decided to keep the baby." They kept making sure we knew we had options, even up to later stages of pregnancy.

One of the hardest things for us was who to tell about the diagnosis and when. My husband is a fiercely private person, and while I'd told a handful of people, he hadn't even told his family late into the pregnancy. Breaking the news was usually a tearjerker, and we would fight to compose ourselves during these conversations. What I found helpful was to ask someone else to tell people, just so I wouldn't choke on the words. Once the news was out, I could talk pretty freely about things and let people know it was bittersweet, but we were still excited.

One of the most lovely and unexpected things about this whole experience was the way relationships became closer and stronger, and wonderful new relationships opened up.

The support was amazing, and one of the most helpful things was that they acted like it was not a big deal. We were spoilt with clothes and presents, and treated like something wonderful was happening, and not like the sky was falling.

It was also a powerful thing in our stepfamily situation, bringing love and bonding. Also, I look back on this time as one of the most intimate and special times in my marriage, building something amazing between us that still remains.

We knew we were having a boy, and soon after the Down syndrome diagnosis, we also found out he had a massive hole in his heart (AVSD). Our genetic counselor was very wise in organizing some visits for us to tour the Intensive Care Unit, seeing babies after heart surgery. That was tough. These days, which were so helpful later on, and also

when we had ultrasounds on the baby and his heart, were the bad days, but it would pass. Those were the days we held onto each other.

Finding out you are carrying a child who has complications of any kind is something you would never choose for your life. However, grief will be replaced with multiplied blessings. You will never be the same – in a good way. When you hold your baby in your arms, you will look at them and wonder what all the fuss was about. That's what happened to us.

Jesse is now 22 months old. It's hard not to use cliches, but the feelings of my prenatal diagnosis seem a lifetime away. He is an absolute joy in our lives, and not a disappointment in any way -- quite the opposite. He is very cute and confident and sure of himself. He is king of the kids at childcare, and the bigger kids love him. He is clever and has a real sense of humour. Tonight he fell over in the town library and cut his eye. He cried for about a minute, then jumped out of my arms and carried on playing and giggling. I thank God I have a house full of love where there would have been a void if we had decided to have a termination. I have met a wonderful new community of Down syndrome families, and we also love our mainstream mums group and friends as well. I sneak in at night and give him big kisses as he tries to sleep through the disruption... I can't help myself! Tonight, his eyes lit up and he smiled as I gave him a bottle on my knee before bed, and told him how he is terrific and the cutest kid in town... but to not tell the other kids and upset them.

~Jodie, Jesse's mum; 41; Australia

{Sibbie}

I had suspicions from very early into my pregnancy that my baby was extra special in a way that way that both exhilarated and scared me. I've had life experiences before that have led me to grow in ways that I may not have asked for, but have ultimately made my life very rich, and helped me to develop an appreciation for life beyond what I would

have without the bumps. I had a premonition that it was time for another of these experiences. And I wasn't afraid of the challenge. Still, I did not find out for sure until well into my third trimester that I was correct: my baby did in fact have that extra chromosome that I had wondered and worried about.

I had my nuchal translucency scan done in the hospital, and was already being treated by a neonatologist in addition to a regular obstetrician due to a previous uterine surgery, a c-section and my proud title of "Advanced Maternal Age." Being a very detail oriented person, I went into my nuchal translucency scan knowing that magic number. Three. If the fluid on the back of the neck was higher than three, there may be a problem.

As I lay on the table, I had one eye on my daughter's adorable profile, and one eye on the lower right hand corner of the screen, where numbers flashed and flashed as the tech did her work. The baby was very wiggly, and she had to measure many, many times. I saw 2.6, 2.9, 2.7, 2.9, 3.1, and then 2.7. When the neonatologist came in to review the pictures, he said all looked good. Since only one measurement out of the many, many taken was over 3, I'd passed that test. Bloodwork came next.

I got a call from my doctor a few days later. The combination of my nuchal translucency scan, my age and my bloodwork resulted in a 1:140 chance that my baby had Down syndrome. My doctor explained to me that this qualified as "high risk," but that my age had a lot to do with it, and although there were no promises, he wasn't overly concerned. In doing the math, I agreed, the chances were slim. But, in my gut, I knew.

I got my anatomy scan at 17 weeks. Everything checked out – two beautiful arms with 10 beautiful fingers. Again, the baby was extremely active, allowing for extra viewing time as the tech attempted to get all the pictures. When I visited my doctor to go over the results, he casually mentioned that there was a bit of "echogenic bowel", which basically means there are white spots present. According to him, it wasn't too concerning, and would most likely disappear on its own by the next ultrasound. It was also a soft marker for Down syndrome.

The bowel issue had not disappeared at the next ultrasound. I began to believe my gut more. This baby was special.

At the beginning of my third trimester, I decided to get a second opinion regarding an unrelated issue I was having with my doctor. I went to Dr. Hill with Ben and Raya one day after school to chat about birth options. We fell in love immediately, and promptly "broke up" with my original obstetrician. Although there was nothing wrong with him, it was one of the best decisions I've ever made. Dr. Hill took my concerns seriously. She wanted to investigate more, and ordered another anatomy scan at her office. A week later, we learned that the echogenic bowel was still present. She called me at work the next day and offered the Harmony test. I knew all about it, but had assumed since it hadn't been offered to me, that it wasn't available in my area. Wrong. It just hadn't been offered to me.

I went to her office for a blood draw that day. I needed to confirm my suspicion. I needed to know before my daughter's birth so that I could look at her for the first time and rejoice rather that pick apart her features, and wonder if she'd cause a silence in the room. The two week wait for results was tough. I was emotional. I had a lot of "What if's?" running through my mind. My phone became an appendage. And then it finally rang. I was in school teaching a kindergarten reading group. I took that call.

"The results of your test came back. They are over 99% positive that your baby has Down syndrome." The rest of the conversation was a blur. I hung up, grabbed my essential belongings and ran to my car. I didn't make it out of the parking lot before bursting into tears. Although I wasn't surprised, I was still shocked. I drove and cried for about five minutes before I felt the most beautiful little nudge from the innermost of my body. Kicks. Rolls. My baby, unaware that anything had happened, reminding me that she was still who she was. And I loved her more at that moment than I ever had before.

That was a Monday. The days to follow were a blur. I stayed up all night, searching the web for all things Down syndrome. I called off work Tuesday, thinking I needed a day to absorb. I called an acquaintance, who quickly became a true friend in every sense of the word, who also has a baby with Down syndrome, and asked her tons of very factual questions. I talked to my family and my soul sister, who was also pregnant at the time. I continued searching, reading, and asking questions on Baby Center's Down Syndrome Prenatal Diagnosis board. My husband jumped into action and started doing concrete tasks surrounding the diagnosis. I called off Wednesday, still in shock and unable to face the real world. I thought a lot about how others would react to this news. I hated that I knew this was news, and I needed to gain some type of control over how the information would be presented. Although I was scared and uncertain of so much, I did know that nothing at all had changed in the level of excitement I had to welcome this little girl into our family, and that in some strange way, we were extra blessed to have been granted her. I wanted to express my positivity before I sensed any whispers or pity glances as people began to hear through the grapevine. I also wanted to avoid the situation where people told me that they knew someone who had had a positive diagnosis and the baby ended up being "fine".

Thursday, I decided to send an email to those who I know love us, describing what we had learned and how we were feeling. I allowed them to share the news, and simply asked for people to welcome our daughter with the same love and light that we knew they would have done anyway. Eventually, after receiving the enourmous outpouring of love, I realized that I underestimated the people in my life. On Friday, I returned to work and to the comfort of the wild, but loving, students I worked with, the supportive staff, and the three flights of stairs I walked up and down over, and over, and over throughout the day as I serviced my small reading groups.

The rest of my pregnancy was a bit stressful. I was going into my doctor's office twice a week for non-stress tests and biophysical profiles of the baby. This was primarily due to the issue that caused me to change doctors, unrelated my baby's Down syndrome. My amniotic fluid level was high, and I was also diagnosed with gestational diabetes. Between the four daily finger pricks and the stress of the extra fluid putting me at risk for preterm labor, I was pretty miserable. During a biophysical profile, it was also found that the placenta was showing signs of deteriorating early, which is a big concern with Down syndrome pregnancies. The stress got to me, and my doctor and I decided it was best for me to stop working and focus on relaxing to hopefully keep this baby in for a while more. It ended up being the smartest move I could have made.

During the next four weeks, before my darling baby arrived, I got things sorted, I went to lunches with my dad and with friends, I put my feet up, went to movies, and ate more nuts and cinnamon than I thought was humanly possible. My sugars leveled. Things with the placenta looked good. And best of all... my sweet girl stayed safely in my womb until 38 ½ weeks.

It was a snowy March day. I was very excited because my best friend had given birth that morning to a girl. That afternoon, during my bi-weekly non-stress test, I watched as the little line that usually lay flat on the monitor make mountains. Contractions! Real, consistent contractions! I was sent to labor and delivery, where I found out within the hour that my baby would be joining us that evening. At 7:07, with her proud mommy and daddy smiling from ear to ear, Sibbie joined us with a cry so strong, it sent me to the moon! We had a NICU team in the operating room with us, but after a quick check, they left saying that our daughter was doing beautifully.

She has truly been the love of her big sister's life, and is our newest pride and joy. Sibbie is four months old and already, I wouldn't change one single thing about her. She lights up a room with her her sparkly, deep blue eyes. She is the blessing I didn't know I needed, and I am beyond thankful for her presence in our lives!

~ Joy, Sibbie's mom; West Virginia, United States

{Emery}

We went in for what we thought would be quick 20-week anatomy scan at my obstetrician's office. We found out the sex of the baby four weeks earlier by paying for a 3D ultrasound. The day we saw little Emery sleeping on the screen, it was our third time seeing her, and I was thrilled when the ultrasound tech said she indeed was a girl. We made small talk with the ultrasound tech, and she said the doctor would read all the images and call us tomorrow, which is routine for their office. When she came in the room and asked how I was feeling, the next thing that came out of her mouth was, "Are you going to do the blood test for Down syndrome?" I was caught way off guard, and a little nervous, but I also wondered if it was something she maybe asked all her patients around this time in their pregnancy. We said no, just as we had declined all of the other prenatal screening tests so far. The next day, I was at work when I received a call from my doctor telling me there was some fluid on the baby's

kidneys, which she wanted to monitor. After a scary Google search, we found that there could be a variety of reasons for dilated kidneys, most likely not life-threatening. When we went back in a week later for another ultrasound, again she mentioned the fluid on her kidneys had not changed, so we were referred to maternal-fetal medicine.

At maternal-fetal medicine, the ultrasound tech made no small talk. She took a lot of measurements, of her kidneys, heart, brain, and bones. There was silence in the room. When she left, my husband went over to read her screen, and most of the baby's measurements were small. He read that she had also marked down "no nasal bone". I saw the panic on his face. Then came the out of body experience that would continue for the next 16 weeks. The doctor came in and introduced himself. Then he told us, "Your baby has what we call soft markers for Down syndrome." We were in shock -- we wee only there for a little fluid on her kidneys, and I was only 29. He explained the absent nasal bone, echogenic intracardiac focus on her heart, overall measurements where she was measuring small, and the fluid on her kidneys were all the reasons he had his suspicions. He recommended that we undergo an amniocentesis, and we agreed. During the amnio, I felt completely numb. They said we would have the results hopefully within two days. We went home, cried, called some friends and family, Googled, and prayed that we were one of those people who has a scare like this and everything comes back ok. Overall, I wished we could push fast forward to hopefully put our minds at ease. I was clinging onto hope that this was all a false alarm that our baby indeed did not have any abnormalities.

Two days later, it was the Friday before Memorial Day. I went to work like I was scheduled. Around 3:30 pm, I received a call from the doctors office. When I answered, I told her I was still at work, and I would call her when I got to the car. I called Jeremy to tell him I finally heard from the doctor's office. I called her back, and she immediately said, "I'm sorry. Your baby does indeed have Down syndrome." She said we needed to set up an appointment in their office with the genetic specialist to go over our options. "What options?", I asked. "Options to continue on with the pregnancy or not," she replied. I really had no clue abortions were even allowed this late in pregnancy. Well, apparently we were one week from the cut off, which was 24 weeks, and this is why they had pushed for an amnio.

I called my husband on my way home. Before I got home, he had called both his parents and my mom. Bless him for making that call -- I was not in the mood to console anyone, and I am not the type of person who likes to be consoled. Great combination, right? The second phone call I made was to our son's pediatrician's office. Looking back, I was in freak-out mode, knowing that these current doctors would disappear in the next couple of months, and we would be reliant on the medical advice of our kids' doctors. I think I just needed to know that we would have medical support after she was born.

The rest of my pregnancy was filled with mostly positive interactions. There were lots of doctors appointments to monitor her growth and my placenta. As we prepared for her birth we feared the unknown. We were simply afraid of the future and of Emery's health after birth.

Emery entered this world fast with a fairly easy and uncomplicated delivery. I tried to prepare myself for the moment we would first see her. Experiencing meeting her for the first time was very calming. I knew we would be okay. I experienced the same feelings of joy and overwhelming love just as we experienced with our son. Today Emery brings us the same joy and overwhelming love. She is a thriving, fun, loving little girl. We are truly blessed.

~Julia, Emery's mom; 29; Georgia, United States

{Davis}

It was a Monday morning in November, slightly warm but otherwise monotonous. I awoke as my husband left for work, gave him a kiss goodbye, and began to get ready for work myself. As I brushed my hair, applied my makeup, and listened to the morning radio, I looked at my round belly in the mirror; I was nearing the end of my second trimester with my first child. I imagined what my baby looked like; maybe he already had hair, maybe he was long and lean like my husband, maybe he had my eyes... and maybe his little heart was beating strongly inside me, regardless that it wasn't properly formed.

The ultrasound performed two weeks prior confirmed the diagnosis of Atrialventricular Canal Defect. This meant that where my baby's heart should have two tiny valves, there was only one; he would require surgery as an infant. The doctor recommended an amniocentesis to check for chromosomal abnormalities that may have caused the heart defect. I had refused blood tests earlier in the pregnancy which screen for these types of abnormalities, but after learning about the heart issue, and having only minutes to make a decision about the amniocentesis, we decided that we would prefer to know before his birth about any other potential concerns.

That day was extremely challenging. I was not mentally prepared to have a needle stuck in my belly, much less hear that my precious son would need heart surgery. I left the office in tears and spent the next few days searching for answers: How did this happen? Did I somehow cause this? What are the chances of a chromosomal abnormality such as Down syndrome? (With this particular heart defect, the chance was 1 in 10.) And then I waited... and waited... and waited... for the call that would change my life.

So on this ordinary Monday, I ate my breakfast standing in the kitchen like I always did, staring at the clock, chewing quickly so that I was not late. Halfway through the meal, the phone rang - who could that be at 8:05 on a Monday morning? "Hello?" I said eagerly. The woman introduced herself, and then said those words I will never forget: "I'm afraid it's not the news you were hoping for; your baby has Down syndrome." And right then and there, in a matter of seconds, my whole world had changed.

Initially, I was shocked. I had not prepared myself for the diagnosis; but I was relieved to have an answer as to why my baby's heart had not formed properly. Fortunately, my work and educational experiences had familiarized me with special needs, including Down syndrome. I was not afraid of the diagnosis; I was afraid of my husband's reaction. I stayed home from work with the company of my sister, and waited until my husband arrived home to tell him the news. He took it better than I expected. We got online and did some research, shed some tears, and then named our special child Davis Matthew.

Two days later, after sharing the news with family and close friends, I shared this statement as my Facebook status: "The last two nights as I laid in bed, it was as if I could actually feel the love and prayers you are all sending our way. Maybe this is why I am able to take the news so positively. Learning that my baby will have special needs actually makes me MORE excited to be his Mommy; I feel like I know him better and feel more bonded with him... I know it won't be an easy road, but what road of parenthood is? I continue to celebrate my pregnancy and am SO excited to meet this little bundle of joy and watch him experience the wonders of life. So please, don't feel sorry for us - I don't. Share in the joy we feel as any new parent. And keep sending us peace and love!"

I realize that my reaction to my son having Down syndrome was quite positive in comparison to how other parents may have reacted. A more devastating reaction to this news is completely typical and acceptable. I was fortunate to have contemplated years earlier what it might be like to parent a special needs child, and I had decided that I would be completely okay with the scenario. After I had time to process the diagnosis, I just felt that this was my calling, this was how it was supposed to be, and this was how God wanted it to be; and I accepted it.

During the next few weeks, I visited doctors regularly for fetal echocardiograms, non-stress tests, and lots of ultrasounds. No medical expert or anyone else ever suggested that I should terminate the pregnancy, for which I will always be grateful. Despite no other issues besides a Down syndrome diagnosis and AV Canal defect, an induction was scheduled at 39 ½ weeks.

My labor was LONG. After about 40 hours, I finally pushed him out. I had a few seconds to hold his beautiful, wet, naked body to mine before he was whisked away by the NICU team. About two hours after his birth, my husband and I were able to visit him in the NICU. We were in love, but also crushed seeing our newborn son hooked to so many machines. We went back to our room, where we held each other and cried.

Davis spent ten days in the NICU. His primary issues were actually the result of a pneumothorax, which is a little air pocket in the lung, that sometimes happens with vaginal deliveries and, according to the doctors, had nothing to do with his heart defect. The pneumothorax combined with the way that his heart worked led to low oxygen levels. I cannot even tell you how many times I heard that oxygen monitor beep during our NICU stay! But the NICU was not a scary place. My only complaint is that the NICU is not very conducive to establishing a healthy nursing pattern because of feeding schedules, time limits to feed, and the need to measure how much is consumed. Therefore, nursing was quite a challenge, and his low muscle tone and heart defect made it even more difficult; so I pumped.

I resided in the hospital during Davis' NICU stay and walked the halls every three hours to feed and snuggle him. After our visits, I went to my room to pump, walked the milk back to the NICU, and spent the rest of my time sleeping, eating, etc. It was a very lonely, frustrating time for me. But I got through it, and was finally able to bring my adorable, sweet baby boy home.   However, this was nowhere near the end of our medical journey.

Davis' pediatrician and cardiologist kept a close eye on him over the next six months. We began medication when he was a few weeks old in order to combat the effects that the heart defect had on his body, so that he could wait for surgery until six months of age. Davis was actually quite a healthy eater, and gained weight appropriately. When he was six and half months old, he had his heart surgery at Vanderbilt Children's Hospital.

The AV Canal repair, in very basic terms, involves making one valve into two.   It is a very intricate surgery which has the possibility of resulting in all sorts of complications. The first forty-eight hours after surgery were extremely rough, and involved lots of scary moments. But believe it or not, we were only in the hospital for eight days. Somehow, I made it through those days. I blogged very openly about it, but even now, I have a hard time thinking about this time in my life, and looking at his pictures and what I wrote is heartbreaking. All I can say is, you just do what you have to do. You educate yourself, keep an open mind, think positively, and count your blessings.

Caring for Davis after surgery without the help of doctors and nurses was also very trying. I had zero medical experience, so the administration of medications, including an injection, was terrifying for me. Each day got easier, and each day Davis got a little closer to being himself again. After a few weeks, you could not even tell that he had

been through such a trauma. His physical and emotional bruises had diminished, and his happy, carefree, sweet spirit was back!

Davis's heart repair was not a complete, perfect success; but it is good enough for now, and he is no longer on any medications. He will continue to see a cardiologist, and may have heart problems as an adult. But for now, he is absolutely thriving. He remains low on the typical growth chart, but above average on the DS growth chart. He receives early intervention services, physical therapy once a week, and occupational/feeding therapy twice a

month. Davis is a social bug, and enjoys music class, play gym class, church nursery, play dates, DS support group outings, and a typical preschool program which he attends twice a week. He also enjoys books, Elmo DVDs, the outdoors, and anything involving a ball. He is learning sign language and already knows and initiates several signs.

Davis is an absolute jewel. I know I am his mommy and quite biased, but others feel the exact same way about him. He lights up a room and steals the show. There are countless people who have been positively impacted by his existence, and it makes me happy and proud to say that he has touched lots of lives already within his short life. Our journey has led us to meet some absolutely wonderful people along the way, and our lives are better because of that as well.

I hope that by sharing my experience, I can reach others who would otherwise not have known our story, and show that despite some of the scary stuff that Down Syndrome can bring, it is all worth it, and the joys far outweigh the pains. No matter who you are or what challenges life has brought your way, your ultimate path may be different than the one you had planned, and that is okay. Having a child with Down Syndrome is an incredible journey for which I will always be thankful. If I could revisit myself on that Monday morning knowing what I know now, and give myself some words of advice, they would be to let go of expectations, have faith that everything will be okay, and trust in the beauty of every day.

~Kari, Davis' mom; 32; Tennessee, United States

Blogging @ happyheartofdavis.blogspot.com

{Jonathan}

On March 21st, 2012, I got the call I had been dreading.   I knew it was him -- the doctor who would give me the news that would change my life forever.   He had told us, quite unsympathetically, that we would only hear from him if he had bad news.   So when the phone rang, and his number popped up, I knew.

Later that evening, as my husband and I sat prayerfully and tearfully considering our future with a child with Down syndrome, a sense of peace and calm settled over me.   I started to count my blessings, and realized I had them in abundance.   I had a beautiful family, strong faith, and caring, supportive friends.   I could feel my baby boy moving and stretching and kicking in my ever growing belly.   He was strong.   I could feel it.   I knew he was a fighter.

I began my research and information gathering in earnest.   I learned everything I could about Down syndrome.   I learned to cull out the often negative, outdated and archaic stereotypes.   I learned to choose doctors who supported our decision to cherish

our unborn child, and give him a chance at a good life, and to dismiss those who didn't. I learned to lean on the support of so many other mamas who had made this journey before me. I found comfort in the kindness of complete strangers, through websites and blogs and on-line support groups.   I networked with families in our area who had children of varying ages and abilities with Down syndrome.   I looked at these beautiful kids through new eyes; through the eyes of a mother.   I learned how frustrating it can be to have such little control over what's happening in your own womb, and yet how preparation for what is to come can be so therapeutic, and can make you feel as if you are reclaiming some control.   I learned who my truest friends were, and how to deal with those whose response to our situation was unintentionally hurtful.   I learned the meaning of true, unconditional love, and the fierce protectiveness one can feel towards her unborn child.   I learned to hear the ugliness in words commonly misused – like the "R" word.   It took on a totally different meaning for me, and I learned that it's not enough to say you don't like unkindness, bullying or exclusion of someone different, but that you have to take action to affect change in people's perception, because now it is personal.

When Jonathan arrived on July 22nd, 2012, I was unconscious.   He had to be taken by emergency C-section with me under general anesthesia because we had lost his heartbeat.   I remember my last thought as the anesthesia was taking hold: "Please save my baby."   When I opened my eyes, through my fog, I asked where he was.   Had he made it?   "He's beautiful," my husband said, "he's perfect."   And in fact he was.

When I finally held him 24 hours later, my heart melted.   His almond-shaped eyes, perfectly pink rosebud lips, button nose and wispy mohawk were so beautiful.   His tiny 4 lb body fit perfectly into my arms. He was no longer a diagnosis.   He was my baby, and his Down syndrome seemed such a small, insignificant part of him.   He was welcomed into our family by his proud parents, a brother and a sister who adore him beyond measure, and a host of other family and friends who have never left our

side.   He has grown strong, is smiley and giggly, loves Goodnight Moon, and to be tickled under his ribs.   He's a big fan of sweet potatoes, and has a fondness for Elmo. He hates to be alone, and thrives on the abundance of snuggles he gets every day.   He loves to sit up, and is working on perfecting his roll-over skills.   We don't know exactly what the future holds for Jonathan, but whatever the case, he'll never have to walk alone.   We will be his staunchest advocates, his fiercest protectors, his loudest cheerleaders, and his biggest fans.

I've heard it said that there are moments which mark your life, moments when you realize nothing will ever be the same, when time is divided into two parts – before, and after.   March 21st, 2012, which ironically was World Down Syndrome Day, was our before and after moment.   As we approached March 21st, 2013, I reflected on how our life has been after, and I have to say, it's been pretty darn wonderful.

~ Lara , Jonathan's mama; 43; Georgia, United States

{Audrey}

Our journey began at the 20 week anatomy scan ultrasound. Being my first pregnancy, I didn't know what would seem odd. The tech didn't mention anything to me, but when I went up to my see my obstetrician afterwards, she mentioned that she wanted a more detailed picture of the our little girl's heart. She made everything sound so casual that I didn't see it as a red flag, especially when everything else was normal on the ultrasound.

A week later, I was seen by a perinatologist for a fetal echocardiogram. After being there for a good while, the nurse left the room to get the doctor, and I knew something was wrong. The doctor told me about a white spot on the baby's heart and how it was a soft marker for Trisomy 21. She proceeded to tell me about a new non-invasive test called Harmony, and without even thinking for a second, I told her that I wanted to have it done. When I left the clinic, I called my husband, my sister, and my best friend. My husband assured me everything would be "normal", and quickly began searching the internet for information on other people's experiences. I only went on BabyCenter and asked on my birth club, which didn't really help. At the time, I didn't know that the Down syndrome Pregnancy board existed.

After a couple of weeks, I still hadn't received any results, and I began to think no news meant everything was fine. The clinic finally called to say I needed to go back so they could draw more blood and do the test over, because the results were inconclusive. I was angry and my blood was boiling. How could they put me through this again? I even considered not going back at all! Another two weeks went by, and then I finally heard from the doctor. She told me my pregnancy was high risk for Down syndrome, and that I needed to go in and be counseled. I had to go to work that day, right after receiving the news. The entire day I was lost, devastated, and even started doubting this new test. My best friend told me I should seek a second opinion, but somehow I knew it would be a waste of time. There was nothing to do.

In the first moments of telling my husband, he was very reassuring, supportive, and confident that our little girl would be fine no matter what. He and my sister were so accepting and ready to love this baby, and they really kept me together. When we saw the geneticist, I felt like it wasn't very helpful. I just kept telling her I didn't understand why. I told her I thought it was based on my age or family history -- at the time, I was 26, so I thought my age was not a factor. She began to take information about our families to make a family tree. It was so useless, I thought. I cried so much during the entire

appointment, and so much on the way home that my husband had to drive. The young geneticist gave my husband a folder full of literature. He read everything when we got home. He said, "Our daughter will be fine, it's just going to take her a little extra time to do and learn things." I admire him to this day for being so calm and understanding.

I shared the news with my best friend and my boss. That was it. My husband and I decided not to worry our parents yet, and tell them after she was born. I cried every day. Anytime I saw a kid, I would have negative thoughts of our baby not being able to do something because of the diagnosis. How silly of me!

On Tuesday, October 2, 2012, I began having contractions in the morning, and I stayed home because I knew it was time. I had a peaceful pre-labor at home, just walking around, taking baths, and preparing my hospital bag that I had left until the last minute. Around 8:30 pm, I had to go labor and delivery because I knew I was close. I was admitted at 5cm dilated, and I informed all the nurses and the attending doctors of my diagnosis. The night went so fast. I kept telling the nurses no medication, but they kept pushing for an epidural. The pain was brutal, but I made it through like I had planned. By 3:10 am, they said I was ready to push. Everything was very smooth and fast, and it all felt like a dream when I heard her cry. When I finally heald her in my arms, she looked up at me and greeted me by sticking her tongue out! I knew it when I looked into her eyes, the diagnosis was right, and it didn't matter. She was a dream, a little being so perfect, I would've never imagined her.

After the family and friends met her, my husband and I still stayed quiet, and decided to tell them later. We just didn't want to make a big deal about it yet. Plus, the attending pediatrician said she was runnig a chromosome karyotype just to make sure, saying, "It's hard to tell in newborns." It didn't really sink in with me because I was so in love with this amazing little person that I carried and finally met. I was in love no matter what.

I think it finally hit me when the pediatrician called me with the results of the karyotype. Then it all became real, and my brain began to process what my heart already knew. As it all became real, I had to begin my quest for information. I wasted four and a half months, and I really regretted not preparing more, and just accepting it. Thankfully, my parents were very accepting and supportive. They gave me so much confidence that Audrey was really going to do great. We were blessed with a healthy baby that thrived from day one.

Today Audrey is 11 months old, and we are grateful for a year full of good health. Her personality is blooming, and she shows no sign of being stopped by an extra chromosome. She's crawling, wanting to get into everything, loves to dance, is very sociable, and has the best laugh. We have worked hard to get her where she is, but we still have loads of fun. She's my life, and I try not to worry or think too much about the future. I just focus on each day, and enjoy every second.

~Magaly, Audrey's mom; 26; Texas, United States

{Alex}

"There are multiple complications with your baby." With those words, the world stopped spinning. I floated outside of my body, and I entered a new reality that was no longer filled with joy and anticipation, but instead was dark and scary and unknown.

I was 30 weeks pregnant. I had wanted to have a baby for what seemed like forever. I knew I was destined to be a mom, and finally, after a few years of getting everything in our lives in order, two pink lines showed up confirming we were going to have a baby. I was elated, and began to visualize what this new little baby would be like. Would the baby have his daddy's curly hair? Would he have my big brown eyes? What would his

profession be? I planned the perfect nursery theme, picked out names, and started reading all the books about pregnancy.

My pregnancy continued for weeks with no issue. I couldn't wait for that first ultrasound, and the chance to see our little peanut growing inside. My belly began to swell. I

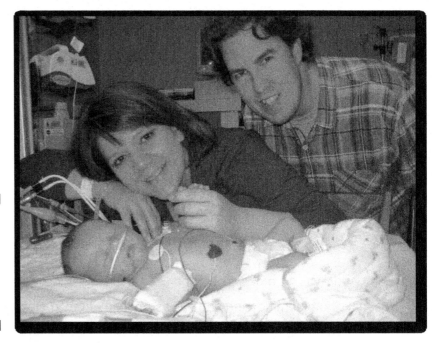

felt a few enchanting kicks. We gathered in the ultrasound room with anticipation. And there he was, floating around in his little cocoon, waving and kicking at us. He kept his hands up by his face as if he was already playing peek-a-boo with us. The technician invited us back in 8 weeks for a 3D ultrasound because she said that we deserved a good 3D image of our little guy. I felt so lucky to be able to come back and catch another glimpse of our little guy.

Eight weeks later, we were back in that same room, watching our baby swim and play. As we waited to meet our doctor, we stared at our black and white pictures trying to ascertain who he was going to look like. Our doctor finally called us in to his office, where he informed us he wanted us to go see a specialist in town who could do a Level II ultrasound. He remained calm, and explained that there were some minor liver calcifications that he wanted to get a closer look at. The doctor could sense our anxiety, and downplayed the severity of any potential issues, even when my husband asked for the worst case scenario. After some quick research, we convinced ourselves it was just a little bump in the road. This must be usual for first time pregnancies, we thought. We left for our appointment with this new doctor in separate cars and ready for work, because we were convinced this was just a precaution, and that within a few hours we would be on our way back to our lives and routines.

Within the hour all the hopes and dreams we fed on the last few months were shattered, and instead the reality was bleak and depressing. The doctor began to go over each complication one by one. She started with the duodenum, and pointed out how it made a double bubble, indicating a blockage. She ended with the heart that was only half formed, and not pumping blood properly. She began to speculate on syndromes, and was unable to positively diagnose Down syndrome or Edwards Syndrome. She explained the differences between the two, and we knew Down syndrome was the better option. She proceeded to say that no matter the results, there was no guarantee this baby would survive the next 10 weeks in utero, let alone the trauma of delivery, and it was highly likely we could be facing a still birth. She told me that while it was too late for an abortion in our state, she could provide me the name of the closest state that did allow late term abortions. She explained comfort care, and encouraged an amniocentesis so that we could be well informed as we weighed our options. The amnio, of course, came with a laundry list of risks -- the most threatening for me at my stage in pregnancy was preterm labor. After a quiet moment alone, my husband and I wiped our tears, embraced one another, and I entered the room where the procedure would be done.

Contractions started shortly after the procedure, and I was monitored, given a medicine to help stop them, and a few hours later, I entered the waiting room ready to go home. There sat my brother, stepdad and mom. In the mix of all the emotions, we had made a few phone calls, and those we loved were there waiting to pick up the pieces of our broken hearts. I embraced my mom, and whispered with all my strength, "Get me out of here." I looked around that room, at all the smiling expecting moms, and I knew I was no longer part of that world. I needed to be as far away from it as possible. Those moms wouldn't make eye contact with me either. They could tell we had just been given devastating news, and it was if I could read their thoughts and prayers to not let it be them. I couldn't stop asking myself "Why me? Why us?"

My mom drove me home. We didn't talk. We sat with the heaviness of the day. We arrived home, and I laid in our dimly lit living room, covered with a fuzzy blanket, and was comforted by the sounds of her cooking in the kitchen and my husband sitting by my side.

Two days later we received a call from our doctor that confirmed the news that our son would indeed have Down syndrome. In fact, he had translocation Down syndrome, and chances were either my husband or myself had passed on this gene on as a carrier. We clung to hope that translocation meant higher functioning. For a moment, we were relieved that we had avoided the more devastating diagnosis of Edward's syndrome. But of course, the questions of his health and complications remained. My husband and I both had seen that half heart, and heard the bleak prognosis of survival. We returned to work, we decorated for the holidays, we tried to entertain friends. We made phone calls to our family and closest friends. But mostly we clung to one another in our own ways, taking turns being the strong one when the other one needed us to be.

I dealt with guilt and blame. I had pushed for this baby, and painted a lovely quaint picture of a family for my husband, who was not as certain that a baby was what he wanted. I knew he would make a wonderful father, and dreamt about teaching him or her to play ball, Christmas mornings, trick-or-treating, sandcastle building, and little kid giggles. He loved me, and agreed that a baby should join our family. Still, I apologized to him for ruining our lives. Knowing that our son had translocation Down syndrome, I knew I was the carrier, and that I was to blame for this whole mess. I couldn't believe my doctor when she told me that neither I nor my husband were carriers, and that this was just a random act. But the question of why remained. I had done everything right -- went to college, had a growing career, fell in love, got married, and now was my time for a family. I deserved a "normal" baby just like everyone else. I cried myself to sleep on many nights, for the reality that the weight of parenthood now came with a whole new set of rules and responsibilities.

We started having numerous doctor appointments. We picked a hospital that was two hours from our house, but Johns Hopkins was known as one of the best hospitals in the country, and was the place for our son to be born. We met with surgeons who explained how they would repair the duodenal atresia on the first day of life. We toured the NICU, and had time to ask doctors and nurses there what to expect. I went to the doctor twice a week, and sat with a monitor hooked to my belly so doctors could monitor his heart rate, movement, amniotic fluid level, and monitor my progress. We had weekly ultrasounds where every nook and cranny of my baby was checked and rechecked. We had a fetal echocardiogram to check the progress of his heart. We sat in a dark room, where a silent technician took pictures of our baby's heart. I couldn't even watch the screen. I laid there quietly wiping my tears, trying to figure out how this had come to be my new reality. One of the best pediatric cardiologists in the country entered the room a bit later, hopped on a stool, and ignited a turning point for our journey when she said the sweetest words I had heard: "I'm looking at a fairly normal heart." She explained that it was possible that there might be some small holes, but nothing that gave her too much worry for the time being, and that she would see us again once our little one was born. A huge weight left our shoulders that day. Maybe, just maybe, this little one was going to live. Maybe, just maybe, everything was going to be ok. We didn't know how his heart had gone from being half formed to nearly perfect in just four short weeks, but we accepted the news with joy.

I started researching. I read blogs and memoirs written by moms of children with Down syndrome. I looked at pictures of babies with Down syndrome. I joined online support groups with other moms around the world facing my same reality.

Slowly a new vision formed in my mind. Gradually, our world seemed less dark and depressing. I would lie on the couch each night and feel my baby boy kicking and stretching. We started to laugh together again. My husband and I started talking about the things our son would be able to do. We talked about how much fun Christmas morning would be, and trick-or-treating, and sandcastle building. I started asking myself, "Why not me? Why not us?" I knew we would love this little boy. I knew we would teach him and support him no matter what. We wondered again would he have his daddy's curly hair or my brown eyes. We wondered what profession he would have. I planned the perfect nursery, and we researched the meaning of names until we settled on the perfect name. We couldn't wait to meet our son, Alex Daniel.

At exactly 38 weeks, I woke up with a new and intriguing pain in my abdomen. It didn't feel like anyone had ever described labor pains to me before, so I went about the day as normal. Throughout the day, I would stop as the pain would persist and then subside. We wrote the times down of the pains, but there was no pattern to them. Friends and family called to check on me throughout the day, each insisting we head to the hospital. We talked about it, but questioned the two hour drive. What if I wasn't really in labor and we drove two hours for nothing? Finally, after much deliberation, we decided it was better safe than sorry. We grabbed our already packed bags and headed for the hospital. We ran through a drive thru to get something to eat, and both of our phones started ringing off the hook. Within about one hour of the drive, it became clear that I was indeed in labor. The pains became more intense, and I was no longer able to talk through them. I glanced at my husband and he started to pick up the speed. We devised a plan for arrival at the hospital, and figured it was best to take me to labor and delivery, and then deal with the car.

We pulled into the curved driveway of the hospital, and when I stood up, my pants were soaked. I assured my husband I could walk myself the few steps to the elevator and that he should park the car and meet me upstairs. I waddled up to the desk, and with great excitement and a touch of fear informed the lady at the front desk of labor and delivery that I thought I might be in labor. They helped me to a room, and within a few minutes, my husband joined me. Nurses were in our room cleaning up the large puddle I had involuntarily made on the floor, and informing me that I was eight centimeters dilated.

We were quickly wheeled to a birthing room, and greeted by doctor after doctor and nurse after nurse. The NICU staff came and introduced themselves. I signed the waiver to receive an epidural. Contractions continued quickly and intensely. I didn't have the mindset to stop and count the people in our room, but at one point, there must have been 15 people total. Eventually, it was just me and my husband alone in the room with our fears and excitement. It was at this point, with no epidural, that I felt my son begging to enter this world. "He's coming, he's coming!" was all I could say. Soon, the doctors and nurses returned and told me it was time to push. I didn't think I could do it without the epidural, but the encouragement of my birthing team convinced me otherwise, and I realized that there was no going back. It was time to push. It was time to meet my son. There were pushes and screams and deep breaths and declarations of "I can't do this!!". They told me there was progress, and that he was crowning. Above all the commotion, the doctor forced me to focus, and explained that I had to get him out on the next push because his heart rate was dropping. She said if I didn't get him out, they would have to use a vacuum assist.

My mind flashed to the image of that half formed heart. My heart filled with fear. I remembered the words of our doctor telling us it was very likely our child wouldn't survive delivery, that he might be born blue and not breathing or not have a beating heart. I couldn't let this happen. I couldn't have come this far, fallen so madly in love with this unborn child, to lose him now. I instructed the doctor to use the vacuum now. I yelled at her to do whatever she had to do to get him out. And with that next contraction, he was out. I breathed with relief for my own body, but I couldn't hear Alex. The nurse next to me asked if I could hear him, and when I told her I couldn't, she yelled above all the noise for everyone in that room to be quiet so that mama could hear her baby. The sweetest cry I had ever heard came from across the room and filled my ears. I laid back against the pillow, filled with thanks for the first hurdle accomplished.

My husband crossed the room to sneak a peek. He told me he wasn't blue, that he was doing great, and I prepared to deliver the placenta. The placenta cord snapped, causing a look of confusion on the fellow, and the placenta remaining inside. That's when the resident explained that I would have to go to surgery. I begged to hold my son before I went.

They wrapped the most beautiful boy up in hospital blankets, and placed him in my arms. We posed for the first family picture. I looked into my little boy's eyes, and the love I felt is indescribable. I wish I had studied his face more. I wish I had whispered my promises to be the best mom ever to him. I wish I had cherished the weight of his little body in my arms. I didn't know it would be another nine agonizing days before I held him again.

I awoke from surgery to find my mom and brother sitting with my husband. They had all been to visit with Alex, and spoke of how beautiful he was. My mom told me how he grabbed her finger and stole her heart. I couldn't wait to go to his bedside.

The next morning launched me into a world I could never have dreamed of. I thought I was prepared. I had toured the NICU, I had met with doctors, I had asked questions. I knew what to expect. But nothing can fully prepare you for the despair you feel when your newborn baby lies in the NICU, hooked to wires and cords that beep and send chills down your spine.

We thought we would be preparing for surgery to fix the atresia. All the research we had done explained that once the atresia was repaired, it was a matter of learning to eat, and then we would be on our way home. We soon learned of a new challenge our little warrior would have to face. He didn't have enough platelets, and we didn't know why. Tests were ordered. I was about to be discharged from the hospital, and plans for where we would stay began. We found a hotel with a reasonable price, and my husband and I joined my mom in a double hotel room. The night I left my son behind in the hospital is a night I will never forget. I begged to go back. I had to see him one more time. We overpaid a taxi fee just so I could hold his hand one more time. No mom should have to leave her newborn baby, it's unnatural. Soon though, this became my new normal.

Soon I was waking at 5:00am to pump and catch the first hotel shuttle to the hospital. Bags would be packed for a full day of the hospital. I sat by his bedside as long as I could. I held his hand all day long, only letting go to go pump every 3 hours or eat lunch. If I couldn't be there, then someone else who loved him was ready for duty so that he wouldn't have to be alone. I cried each night as I had to catch the shuttle back to the hotel. I would grab a bite to eat and a few hours of sleep. I would pump some more. This was the one thing I could do for my son. He may not have been eating my milk yet, but I could provide him with a stock of nourishment when he was ready. I had a sense of accomplishment as I filled those little 2.5 oz bottles by the hundreds. Our day revolved around rounds. We forged relationships with nurses, and attempted to give a halfhearted smile to the other moms and dads we saw coming and going. We saw babies come to the NICU, we saw moms and dads take their babies home from the NICU. We waited for test results about platelets. We waited for surgery. My arms ached to hold my son. Family and friends came to visit when they could. Surgery was postponed longer and longer.

One day, a new set of doctors showed up by our bedside. They smiled and seemed nice enough, until they told us their specialty: oncology. "ONCOLOGY?!", I thought. "Why are they here? Make them go away! I don't want to be talking to an oncologist!" Our son was merely a few days old, how could his little body have cancer already? They explained the reason for low platelets. On this day, a few new words entered my vocabulary: Transient Myloplerative Disorder, or TMD for short. On this day, I learned that there is always another wild card to be played. As scary as it seemed, TMD was not the death sentence I thought it was. It was rare, but it should go away on its own. Unfortunately, it would place my son at an even greater risk of developing leukemia within the first four years of his life. When the doctors left our bedside, I clung to my husband in full despair, unsure of how much more I could take. He was once again my rock, reassuring me we would get through this.

On day 11, they prepped our warrior for surgery, and on day 12 we walked behind his bed all the way to the surgery door. The hours ticked by, and we waited for news that the surgery was over. Time  seemed to stand still, but eventually, we got word that he did great and was recovering. We ran to his bedside. Within days, he started to heal. He started eating. He started getting stronger. We waited eagerly for that first poop. With help from nurses and lactation consultants, and to the surprise of some doctors and fellows, our boy learned to nurse. It was such a tender feeling to have him nestled against my skin as he drank the nourishment intended for him. I finally felt like a mother.

On day 22, they told us we were going home. We were filled with joy. We couldn't wait to take him home, to see his room that we had prepared for him, to introduce him to his dog. We were also filled with fear. How could we be ready to take this tiny fragile special baby home? What would I do without the nurses there to help me? We strapped his tiny body into the oversized car seat and drove the two hour drive to our new life as a family of three.

We settled into as much of routine as new parents can. We entertained family and friends who had been eagerly waiting to welcome us home. We napped when Alex napped. I got up several times a night to nurse a hungry boy. Then we had to make a first monthly required visit to the oncology team. TMD came with the requirement of monthly blood draws by the team, so we could stay ahead of any threats to his body. We placed our tiny boy in his oversized car seat, and made the two hour trek back to the hospital. They stuck his tiny arm with a needle, and he screamed while they drew blood. Doctors entered the room and start talking to us about bilirubins, and how Alex's were way too high. They questioned the effectiveness of his liver. The doctor explained a sepsis liver to us, and once again, questions of survival became the topic of choice. We were readmitted for more tests. Our warrior had more battles to face.

We worked with more specialists, and tried to remain calm as once again, our little boy was threatened and challenged. Doctors ordered more tests, and severe threats such as biliary atresias were ruled out. We were placed on a heavy dosage of oral medicine and monitored weekly. One day, our liver specialists released us from the liver clinic with a healthy liver. We returned home and fell more and more in love with our son.

We found pleasure in watching Alex conquer the littlest challenge. The day he first smiled, giggled and rolled over gave us the greatest joy. Each day, I would look forward to spending some alone time with my son. I would sit and rock him for hours. I studied his features. I fell in love with his almond shaped eyes and his palmar crease. I would kiss the flat spot above his nose, confess my love, and give thanks for this beautiful child. The months continue to go by, and the baby that we thought would be so imperfect, that we feared would be such a burden, has proven time and time again to fill our lives with nothing but joy and happiness.

Today, Alex is a happy and thriving two year old boy. He is getting stronger each day. He uses over 50 signs, and some words to communicate his wants and needs. He loves to play ball, dance to music, and read books. Nothing makes him giggle more as bubbles and balloons. Our lives are so much better for having him in it. I still rock him to sleep nightly, and often end up wiping away tears because I am so filled with love for this person. The number of his chromosomes truly are not important, but the love he brings to this world is unexplainable and irreplaceable.

~ Megan; Alex's mom; 34; West Virginia, USA

{Sophia}

The sonographer ran the transducer over my belly. I was 16 weeks pregnant with baby number three, something I had not planned for, but it was a lovely surprise and I was looking forward to being a mum again.

"I'm sorry Mresa, we can't seem to find the bottom valves of the baby's heart. Can you come back tomorrow so we can try again?" asked the sonographer. I just shrugged and said "Sure, I'll make an appointment now."

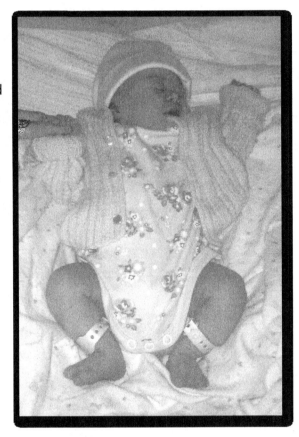

I went back the next day and again, the sonographer could not find the bottom valves of bub's heart.   I thought this was weird, but no one said anything.   I asked if everything was ok, and they assured me everything was fine. I was recommended to a specialist who deals with this kind of thing.   Still totally oblivious to anything, I made the appointment to see Dr. Dickinson in a month's time.

A month later, I was lying on Dr Dickinson's table, and she was doing an ultrasound on my baby. By this stage, I knew I was having a little girl, and I was so excited. I already had her named: Sophia Louise. I was in my own little world when I heard words that I had not prepared for: hole in heart... open heart surgery... Down Syndrome.

I looked at Dr Dickinson, and said to her "What are you talking about? My baby is fine, the lady at the hospital said so!" Poor Dr Dickinson was mortified. She said, "Melissa, don't you know that your baby has a hole in the heart?" I was shell-shocked. I was so sure she had the wrong person, and told her that it couldn't be right. She then pointed out the hole, and said, "Your little girl is going to need to have open heart surgery at some stage." I could not believe it, but then I remembered 2 other words, and said to Dr Dickinson, "I think you mentioned something about Down Syndrome." She looked at me.

"Yes, I think it is very possible. With all the factors I have -- your age, the shortness of your baby's limbs, the heart issues -- I would say you have a high chance of having a bub with Down syndrome."

I felt like I had just been slapped in the face.   How could she say that? Things like that don't happen to me! She suggested we do an amniocentesis, as when my baby was born the doctors would need to know everything about her. So I booked in to have an amnio done in a few weeks time. By the time I had it done, I was 25 weeks gestation.

Dr Dickinson rang me herself. It was a Tuesday afternoon.   I answered, and could tell by the tone of her voice what she was going to say. And she did. She gave me some phone numbers, and I made an appointment to see her in a couple of weeks for another scan.

I hung up the phone.   For as long as I could remember, every time I saw a child with special needs I would think to myself, "Thank God that's not me, I don't think I could do it." Was this punishment for not wanting a child with special   needs?   This was not fair.

I decided to go shopping. I have no idea why, but I just felt like I needed to get out of the house.   I went to Belmont Forum, and there were babies everywhere.   I hated the women who had these perfect babies. Mine would be different.   How was she going to fit into a society that doesn't like different people?   Would I have the capabilities to raise her like I did with my other two children?

I researched all I could on her heart issues, AVSD, and Down Syndrome, but by the end of it, it was so much information overload, that I had to take a step back. I found that it was the best way to be. I kept it quiet to start with, and I only told immediate family and very close friends.   Sophia's father had decided there and then that he wanted nothing to do with us, so he left me pregnant at 7 months, and at the time of writing this, we have not seen or heard from him.   He was not happy about the pregnancy, and I think perhaps, her Down syndrome and heart issues were the final straw for him, although he has never said so.

I went to Kind Edward Memorial Hospital on June 23, 2011 for my 36 week check up. The doctor was about to say goodbye, but he asked if I had any questions or queries and I told him that hse wasn't moving as much as she used to. Alarm bells started to ring, and he ordered a scan there and then. Half an hour later, he came back out and said "Well, your little girl is doing fine, but you on the other hand... " My placenta was dying off, the blood flow wasn't the best, the cord wasn't in very good conditio,n and there was no way I was going to last another three weeks. The baby was going to have

to come out now.   I was horrified! I told them that I can't have my baby now, I have plans for the next three weeks! But the doctor looked at me and said "Well, best you change your plans, you're having a baby today!"

I had to get a taxi home, throw some clothes in the case, text the kids to let them know whats going, ring my mum and calmly tell her to get to Perth, update Facebook (as you do), and get back to the hospital!

My little Sophia Louise was born later that night, at 11:05 pm.   She was perfect in every way.   I looked at Sophia and realized there and then that I was worrying about nothing... she was going to be fine. I loved her more than I could ever put into words. Her Down syndrome?   Pfft. Her heart issue took over from day one, so her Down syndrome has always come last. Most of the time, it's not even an issue.

Sophia is now two, and I look at her and can't believe how ignorant I was.   I had no idea about anything of Down syndrome.   I am ashamed to say that I didn't want a child with special needs, but having Sophia has opened my eyes to a whole new world that I probably never would have experienced, and I thank her every day for that. I love her so much, and would not change her for the world.

~Mel, Sophia's mum; 38; Western Australia

{Eli H.}

I was excited for this ultrasound. It was the only reason we opted to take part in a screening test. I wanted to see our baby on the "big" screen in the fancy office with the high tech equipment. I had no concerns that the baby I was carrying was anything but healthy. The maternal fetal medicine radiologist who was performing the ultrasound informed us of what he was doing each step of the way. He pointed out every ridiculously cute feature on our tiny baby. He took measurements while talking to us about everyday things like the weather. When he was finished he discussed the results with us. One measurement in particular stood out as a little high but not outside the normal range. It was the nuchal translucency thickness, the fluid beneath the skin behind our baby's neck. This is a marker for Down syndrome. He wasn't worried so we weren't either. We walked out of that appointment with 1 in 350 odds of our baby having a chromosomal abnormality, based on my age and the nuchal translucency measurement. I went to the lab for blood work without a second worry.

A week later we received a call from a genetic counselor. She left a message wanting to discuss the results of my screening test. I called my husband at work hysterically crying. Something was wrong. They said they would only call if there was a problem. I didn't want to call her back alone so we called her together. Her words were the most terrifying I have ever heard - "The results from your sequential screen show that you have a 1 in 3 chance of your baby having Down syndrome". I have no idea what she said next. We set an appointment to meet with her the next day. I hung up the phone and cried uncontrollably until my husband got home (he left work as soon as we found out). He remained optimistic. I did not. I was devastated. The following day we listened to our options of what to do next. We decided to take the new, non-invasive blood test (MaterniT21). Then we waited.

"May 8, 2012 at 1:15pm our world changed forever. We got the call from the genetic counselor that we had been dreading. The baby I have been carrying for 15 weeks, is not healthy**. He/she has Down syndrome. What?! How can this be? I've done everything right. I don't drink, smoke, take medicine, eat foods I'm not supposed to. Why me? Why us? Cause I'm old? But I'm not old! I'm only 36. What will this do to our family? I've gotten mad, sad, anxious, confused. Will I be able to love this baby? What does their future hold? Bullying, dependence, frustration? What does our older child's future hold? Constant defending? Other people's intolerance? Jealousy? What does our future hold??? I can't even go there right now. Everyone assures us that they'll love the baby regardless and that they'll always be there to support us. Will they? Will we? Can we? I have felt thoughts that I never thought I could feel about my unborn baby. Those thoughts make me angry, sad, and feel very un-mommy like. I've prayed for forgiveness of those feelings. Can I handle this? Can my husband? Will our marriage survive? Is it worth risking? Right now, I don't know the answer to those questions. I pray for clarity, for love, and for acceptance. I pray for peace. I pray that everything will just be alright." **Down syndrome does not make a child "unhealthy". (This was written before I knew better.)

I wrote that journal entry a few days after we found out that our baby does have Down syndrome. It makes me sad to read it now. I felt so out of control. So desperately trying to understand what was happening. I'd go to sleep and wake up not remembering if it was a dream or real. I would pray it was a dream then remember it was not. We cried a lot. We stopped praying. We felt betrayed by God. We worried and worried and worried. We grieved for the child we thought we were having and didn't know if we could ever come to terms with the child we were given.

After three long, insufferably challenging weeks my eyes were finally opened when my OB doctor (of all people!) quoted the Bible during an appointment. Jeremiah 1:5

Before I formed you in the womb I knew you, before you were born I set you apart.

All of a sudden, it all made sense to me. We were chosen by God to be this child's parents. He knows we are capable of loving this child unconditionally. He picked us for him and him for us. I walked out of that appointment knowing everything would be ok. There was a feeling of calmness and acceptance that was such a new, welcomed feeling for me. My husband still wasn't there. He was still depressed. I feared he may never get to a point of acceptance like me. But, a few days later, we named our son. He was no longer just a scary diagnosis. He was our baby. He was created out of love. He was who we had prayed for. He completed our family.

We spent the following weekend on the coast. If there's a perfect place to reflect and gain insight, it's the beach. There, we were surrounded by peace. We were filled with love. That weekend, amongst the crashing waves and the sunlit sand, we both accepted the child we were given. Not only accepted, but embraced.

Six months into the pregnancy, we learned our baby boy had a heart defect. At first we were told it was most likely a rare and complicated defect. We felt defeated. Once again, we found ourselves angry and depressed. Again we asked - Why our baby? Why us? We were sent to the cardiologist for an echocardiogram. She found it not to be the major defect that was originally suspected but instead a hole in his heart called a VSD. This is the most common heart defect amongst children. Oddly, we felt very relieved.

Our son was born via a scheduled repeat c-section at 39 weeks. The night before his birth, I wrote him the following letter: "My precious baby. Carrying you in my womb has been a journey that has strengthened my faith, enhanced my compassion, and changed my outlook on life. Let me start by apologizing to you. I am sorry that I ever questioned my capacity for love. I am sorry that I was afraid. Please know though, I never questioned my love for you. I was not afraid of you. You are our son. You were wanted. You were created out of pure love. You are a miracle, as is every baby. I have never taken that for granted. I promise to always protect you. I promise to be your biggest cheerleader and a foundation of support. I promise to always be proud of you. I promise to help you reach your fullest potential. I promise to always love you unconditionally. I am already proud to be your mama. I am already proud of you. Thank you for changing my perspective on living. Thank you for teaching me that through the rain and the clouds there will always be a rainbow. Life is beautiful. I know you'll be beautiful too. You are the true meaning of living. I can't wait to meet you tomorrow and hold you in my arms and tell you what I've learned from this long journey we've been on together - everything is going to be ok! With all my love, Your mommy"

I fully expected everything to go smoothly. I never envisioned that he wouldn't be placed in my arms. The surgery itself was uneventful. But, after he was delivered, he had trouble keeping his oxygen levels up. They held him up to me briefly then rushed him to the warming table. He wasn't crying. They gave him oxygen and then told me they needed to get him into the NICU. I asked my husband not to leave his side. They brought him over to me for a quick second. I told him I loved him and he was rushed out of the room. Just like that. All the anticipation turned into worry and fear. What was wrong with him? Would he be ok? So many feelings came rushing over me. I was terrified. What was happening? Was I being punished for my previous doubts and fears? I begged God not to take my baby. It turned out, he had a pneumothorax, or a hole in his lungs. The hardest part for me was being away from him while I recovered from the c-section. I had to wait 4 very long hours before laying eyes on him again. My husband stood by our baby's side the entire time, giving him comfort when he could. Eventually, I was able to be wheeled into his small room in the NICU where I was able to hold him and talk to him and pray for him. I was finally able to tell him, "Everything will be ok". At that point I wasn't sure if I believed those words. But, he showed us how strong he was. We already knew he was a fighter but I was hoping he wouldn't have to go to battle so soon. After seven very long, trying, tiring days in the NICU, our son was discharged. We were finally able to bring our baby home. We were ready and excited to start our lives as a new family of four.

I won't lie; the first couple of months were a struggle. Eli's heart was working too hard too often. He couldn't keep up the stamina needed to eat. He had trouble gaining weight. It was decided that he would need to undergo open heart surgery sooner, rather than later. Three days before he turned 3 months old, we handed our baby boy to the surgical team. The minutes leading up to that were the most excruciating moments I've experienced in all my life. While he was in surgery, I actually felt an unfamiliar calmness come over me. I trusted God to watch over him and I trusted our son's amazing cardiac surgery team to care for him as if he were their own. Thankfully, his surgery went smoothly and, incredibly, we were back home in five days with what seemed like a brand new baby. He now ate with a purpose. He gained weight and thrived. He smiled often. Each time he did, our hearts filled with pride.

We have encountered other health issues since heart surgery. Our son was hospitalized for seven days with bronchiolitis at 5 months old and then diagnosed with Infantile Spasms, a catastrophic seizure disorder with a higher incidence in children with Down syndrome, one week later. There may be nothing worse in the world than seeing your child slip away. Our once happy baby stopped smiling. He stopped playing. He stopped babbling. He stopped doing what babies do. After six weeks of intensive treatment (which involved me injecting his leg with a high dose steroid daily), he had a clear EEG and was officially declared seizure free. One month later, we found ourselves at yet another specialist's office. This time, we were reviewing a CT scan of our son's skull in the craniofacial department. Turns out, he has a very rare skull deformation called Lambdoid Craniosynostosis. One of the sutures on his skull fused in the womb. The only way to correct this is skull surgery, which he will undergo when he is 11 months old. This is NOT more common amongst kids with Down syndrome. In fact, I have yet to be connected with any other parent whose child has both. The chance of a child having this type of Craniosynostosis (Lambdoid) is 1 in 400,000. We haven't done the exact math, but combining the odds of a child having Down syndrome, a heart defect, Infantile Spasms, and Craniosynostosis makes our son truly one in a million. But we already knew that.

Rocky Balboa once said, "Let me tell you something you already know. The world ain't all sunshine and rainbows. It's a very mean and nasty place, and I don't care how tough you are, it will beat you to your knees and keep you there permanently if you let it. You, me, or nobody is gonna hit as hard as life. But it ain't about how hard you hit. It's about how hard you can get hit and keep moving forward; how much you can take and keep moving forward." Those words feel very true to us at times. This past year, our life has felt a lot like the tango - two steps forward, one step back. But, we always keep on moving. And you know what? I wouldn't change this journey for anything. I regret absolutely nothing. Where I once felt so scared, I now feel empowered. Where I was once angry, I am now enlightened. Where I was once filled with questions, I now patiently let the answers unfold themselves to me. Each day our son amazes us - with his strength, determination, and courage.

Very recently we reached the one year anniversary of the day we got "the call". One year ago we thought it was the worst day of our lives - the ending of our life as we knew it. Truth be told, it was just the beginning. The beginning of actually living life. A second chance to appreciate the world and all that is in it. My eyes were opened the day we found out our baby had Down syndrome. My heart was opened when our little boy was born.

We went back to the beach. The same beach that we went to last year that helped to cleanse our souls and pointed us in the direction towards acceptance. This trip, I spent a lot of time reflecting. I thought about the scared woman who cried so many tears after receiving that phone call. The husband who physically and emotionally checked out for a week. The friends and family members who offered their condolences. The baby that was growing inside me, completely  unaware that we were all so devastated. It seems like a lifetime ago. Yet I remember it like it was yesterday. If I only knew then what I know now, I wouldn't have wasted so much time grieving. I should have been celebrating. Rejoicing in the blessing that was being bestowed upon us. If I only knew...We are good enough parents to "handle" this. We can do more than we ever expected (and do it well!). If I only knew...I would be fortunate enough to meet a whole group of new friends, some who have become like a sister to me (and reconnect with many old friends throughout this whole process!). If I only knew...I will find strength in myself that I never knew existed. But, that strength will never compare to the strength I see from my child. If I only knew...Our oldest son will be ok - even through four hospital stays, a host of health issues, doctor visits, and therapy all for his brother. He still goes to bed each night telling us he loves us and that his daddy and I are his best friends. In fact, the other night, he told me his brother is his best friend. If I only knew...Dreaming about his future is ok. He will have a future. If I only knew...Super heroes are real. My son proves it. If I only knew...I will eventually forgive myself for the feelings I once had.

I can tell you now that life certainly is ok. In fact, it is more than ok! Through our challenges and subsequent triumphs we, as a family, have made it through stronger, tougher, and more appreciative. Life is different. It is actually better than I could have ever imagined.

Today, Eli is 10 months old. He recently started sitting, and two weeks later started commando crawling. Now, he really enjoys standing. His strength and determination impress us on a daily basis. After so many health challenges, he has proven to be a total rock star. His smile lights up a room, and his laughter is infectious. Watching our two boys play together completes me. I don't know what I was ever afraid of. Life is perfectly what it was supposed to be, and our hearts are overwhelmed with pure joy.

~ Melanie, Eli's mom; 36; Washington, United States

Blogging @ Our Journey Through Life at www.mellbugg.wordpress.com

{Bryleigh}

My pregnancy started out like so many others. I took a pregnancy test (and then two more), and once the double pink lines were confirmed, I started anticipating the exciting months that would soon be ahead of me. My husband and I weren't actively trying for a baby at the time, so it took us both by surprise, especially this being our first. He was in the middle of a big career change -- balancing school and a part-time job -- so timing wasn't exactly ideal for us.

My routine doctor's appointments began shortly after finding out we were expecting. I remember seeing my little raspberry-sized baby for the first time on the ultrasound, and hearing the steadily beating heart; each beat causing my own heart to skip. I felt so

connected to this tiny baby inside of me, and it brought so much joy to me. It was little moments like that when I really understood the sentimental connection between mommy and baby.

When I went to the much-anticipated appointment at 20 weeks to find out the gender, we were elated to be told that we were having a girl. I remember that day more clearly than most and the ultrasound lasted close to an hour. It didn't take my husband and I long to start the celebrating and name-deciding upon finding out. Our fingers couldn't type out the text messages to our families fast enough, and just when we thought we were in the clear and could begin the necessary preparations, we were told the earth-shattering news that only three of the four chambers of her heart were visible on the ultrasound. All color drained from my face as I intently listened to everything the doctor was trying to explain. My first concern was, of course, whether this baby would make it. After I learned that she was fine while she was in the womb, I sighed out of relief, but I immediately knew this was certainly not the typical pregnancy. . This unknown heart problem resulted in us being referred to a specialist for a detailed ultrasound. I left the doctor that day with tears in my eyes and a script in my hand that read "Atrio Ventricular Canal Defect."

I wasn't able to grasp the severity of the heart problem for quite some time. A lot of questions went unanswered as more and more filled my mind. As weeks went by, I went through any and every message forum and blog that I could find relating to the topic. My husband and I were overcome with emotion, but we just kept on trusting in God, that this is His plan, and deep down we knew that everything would work out. After going through the motions of the ultrasound with the specialist, it confirmed what we came to accept by that time: our child's heart was flawed and would need surgery. What I soon found out was that it didn't just end there. Another curveball was being thrown our way, and not only was there a heart problem, but now our child could potentially have Down syndrome.

This was one thing I had not prepared myself for. All the other soft markers that they look for on ultrasounds seemed to be normal, so I had already ruled that possibility out of my head. I never pictured being a parent of a child with Down syndrome. I never knew or met anyone that had Down syndrome. Surely, there was a mistake. I couldn't even tell myself that this was an option, because it was too large of a burden to bear -- or so I thought. We decided to have testing done to determine whether or not this would be the case, and I opted for the less-invasive MaterniT21 over the amniocentesis. I wasn't worried; after all, I was a healthy 25-year old, and my chances of this actually happening were 1:1400. The doctor called about a week and a half later with the results, explaining that the blood work came back positive for Trisomy 21, which meant that our baby girl would in fact have Down syndrome. Looking back, I remember that day being the most difficult of them all; I was at work when I found out, and I wasn't able to reach my husband for quite some time because he was in school. I cried until my head throbbed and my vision blurred; it lasted for hours.

I felt that the emotional connection I previously had with my baby had been lost. My co-workers tried to console me, but I couldn't wrap my mind around it. It felt like I was living in a bad dream that I couldn't wake myself up from. I was ashamed, depressed, upset, angry, and feeling completely helpless and alone. I prayed so many times for God to change my situation. I was ready and willing for Him to intervene in any way -- as long as I wouldn't have to go through this.

Weeks passed, and I very gradually came to a place of acceptance. I still cried and felt sad at times, but I knew that the outcome wasn't going to change. On the outside, I held it together, but inside I was losing hope; doubts continually crept in. My family really came through for me during the rough times. They listened. They cried with me. They also reminded me what kept me grounded, and that was my faith in God and his sovereignty. Why did I think God would only be present if I had a "normal" pregnancy? In my weakness I had to rely fully on Him, and He gently reminded me of that. He chose this baby for us. This wasn't a mistake. My husband was really there for me too, and he also struggled with envisioning our future, not sure what our life would look like. In the midst of the tears, he was my rock and it really comforted me knowing that he was by my side through it all.

When it came time for our first pediatric cardiologist appointment, I remember the nerves rushing back up to the surface again. The stark white walls of the building and fluorescent lighting had been everything but consoling upon our arrival. I had my first echocardiogram that day, which is basically an ultrasound of the baby's heart. I was always so excited to see my little girl moving about on the ultrasound screen, and I became happy knowing that I still felt so much love toward my baby throughout all the tears I had endured. When we met with the doctor and came face to face for the first time, we were so relieved to have someone with a very gentle and wise demeanor. She thoroughly explained to us about our child's heart condition, and what this would mean post-pregnancy. I felt confident in knowing that she would be the one overseeing my baby and that to me was a godsend.

Many appointments and countless echocardiograms later, I had a scheduled induction date at 39 weeks. By this time, I felt more confidence in having a child with Down syndrome; I was ready. At 38 weeks, our baby decided to make her grand debut, and on October 24, 2012, my sweet Bryleigh Kai came into the world and changed our hearts forever. Immediately following her birth, my nerves were still a mess, because I wasn't sure what her condition would be, but I had an unexplainable sense that it would be okay. In those first moments after she arrived, my husband kept kissing me and telling me how beautiful she was. I was able to hold my baby for a mere few seconds before the nurses rushed her off to NICU. But in those seconds, my world was pieced back together. My nerves vanished. My Bryleigh opened her precious almond-shaped, twinkling blue eyes and for a split second stared deep into mine. I couldn't help but feel remorse for every bad thought I had of her. She was a beautiful, angelic baby all along, and I was so worried about my own insecurities and couldn't see past them until that defining moment. I was so proud to be her mom, and couldn't wait to be with her.

Bryleigh's NICU stay was exactly five weeks long. During that time, we struggled with feeds, irregular oxygen levels, and various heart issues. It was certainly a trying time that seemed to last forever, but alas, there was an end to it. We took our sweet girl home and loved on her with all we had.

Just before she turned four months old, she had her scheduled open heart surgery to repair the two holes in the upper and lower chambers of her heart. Since then, she's had an amazing recovery; she is still on heart medication and is being followed by her cardiologist. There are still so many obstacles to be faced, but we wouldn't trade any of it for the world if it would mean not having our miraculous, beautiful daughter, extra chromosome and all.

~ Melissa, Bryleigh's mom; 25; Florida, United States

{Olivia}

Our story starts on the most highly anticipated day in my pregnancy, the 20 week ultrasound. This was going to be the day we found out if our baby was a girl or a boy! I was so excited that I had planned ahead to take the entire day off from work just so I could shop for all of the gender appropriate clothes and baby items I could get my hands on after we found out the sex. I would be lying if I said I remember completely what happened next, and in what order, so I will start with the good news -- we were having a girl! My excitement didn't last long, because as the ultrasound continued, we could tell that something was not quite right. The ultrasound tech just stared at the screen. He

tried over and over again to get a different angle. My stomach began to sink, and I began to feel nervous. My husband asked what he was looking at, and all he would say was he was looking at the heart. For the details, he said we would have to speak to the doctor. So we waited. Our doctor came in, and told us what we both feared. There was possibly something wrong with our baby's heart. He told us that the left side of her heart looked much smaller than the right. He wrote a referral to see a perinatologist for a level two ultrasound, for possible hypoplastic left heart syndrome (HLHS). I went home from the doctor that day with tears in my eyes. How did something that was supposed to be one of the happiest moments in my pregnancy turn into one of the worst moments in my pregnancy?

I was so upset, even the idea of shopping didn't sound fun. I didn't want to buy anything for the fear that she wouldn't be okay. The week long wait until the next appointment was one of the longest weeks of my life. At first I cried... and then, I did what I do best. I researched! I scoured the internet for anything and everything I could find about HLHS. I learned that HLHS was one of the rarest and worst heart defects. It required a series of at least three surgeries, and if this was not successful, a heart transplant. As scary as this all sounded, by the time my appointment rolled around, I had researched out the best hospital in the nation to handle HLHS, and was confident that no matter what, we would do everything in our power for the baby.

The day arrived for us to get answers. As we started the ultrasound, the doctor confirmed our worst fear: yes, our baby had a heart defect. He told us that our baby had an unbalanced AV Canal Defect. What?! That is not HLHS -- our baby had a totally different heart defect, one that I hadn't researched, and knew nothing about. But that was not all. The doctor then informed us that she also had a "double bubble", which he told us is usually caused by duodenal atresia, an intestinal blockage. Not only would both defects require surgery shortly after birth, but because our baby had both defects, he thought there was a high probability our baby had Down syndrome -- 1:3 odds, to be exact. We were shocked... devastated, really. We had gone into the appointment prepared for one problem, and we left with two confirmed defects and the type of odds I would play the lottery on for having a baby with Down Syndrome. How did this happen?

Our doctors gave us information, facts really, into the health risks and probabilities. Our family was great, saying that no matter what, we can handle it and we will love her. But not knowing for sure was just not an option. We needed to know. So we agreed to have an amnio. For two days I cried so hard that even my dogs weren't sure what to do. I cried because I was scared of the unknown, because of the fear of our baby having Down syndrome, because of the fear that our baby would need multiple surgeries. It just didn't seem fair! Why us?! I was so careful. I didn't even touch a drop of caffeine my entire pregnancy.

Finally, the amnio results came back. Our baby girl did in fact have Trisomy 21.

After we found out that there was a chance our baby would have Down Syndrome, I would be lying if I didn't say there was a moment that I thought, could we even do this... could we actually raise a child with Down syndrome? That thought, and the thought of any option of termination, didn't last long though, because all I could think of was that little life inside of me, and how much I loved her and would love her no matter what. The turning point in my grief really occurred when my brother put things in perspective for me by saying that raising all children presents challenges, and that this was just a different set of challenges. From that point on, I stopped worrying so much about my baby being born with Down Syndrome, and more about her heart. Olivia's heart defect was still very serious. The left side of her heart was much smaller than the right side, and we wouldn't know until she was born if the left side would be large enough for a biventrical repair. My fear completely shifted from the fear of raising a child with Down Syndrome to whether or not my baby would survive, and if her heart would be fixable. And so we had no choice but to wait until her birth.

You never think your pregnancy is going to be super stressful and eventful. Miserable and exhausting, yes, but the former, not so much. My pregnancy was easy as far as sickness goes. I pretty much didn't have any. That is where the easy part of my pregnancy flew out the window. After finding out about our baby's heart defect and intestinal defect, along with her Down syndrome, my entire pregnancy plan changed. No longer could I give birth at the small hospital near my home. We needed a level three NICU now. This also meant that my planned delivering doctor now could not be my delivering doctor. Additionally, not only did I have to continue to see my OB/GYN, but I also had to start seeing a perinatologist, in conjunction with a cardiologist. Suddenly I had twice the amount of doctor's appointments, and tons of ultrasounds and scans.

My main concern, and my doctor's main concern for the remainder of my pregnancy, was to keep Olivia healthy and in the womb for as long as possible. You see, Olivia was diagnosed with a more complicated than normal AV Canal Defect because she had an unbalanced AV Canal Defect. The most concerning part of Olivia's heart defect was the unbalanced nature -- that the left side of her heart was much smaller than her right. The cardiologist explained the implications of the size of our sweet baby's heart -- that if there is enough tissue and size, she will be able to undergo a biventrical repair. If not, the only option is a single ventricle repair, which according to our cardiologist, was not often successful in Down syndrome babies. This was my greatest fear, and the worst possible scenario that I prayed daily would not occur. The most stressful part of my pregnancy was the fact that we wouldn't know until she was here exactly how big the left side of her heart would be, and what type of repair she would be a viable candidate for. It was for this issue that I scoured the internet for hours researching, trying to find answers to my questions, trying to find hope. Due to this fact alone, as soon as I found out about the heart defect, I decided that we would do everything in our power to ensure that our baby received the best health care possible to overcome this hurdle. I researched heart programs, and was ready to travel all the way across the nation if need be in order to save my daughter.

I happen to be a person who believes that everything happens for a reason. So when we found out that the cardiac surgeon who works closely with our local children's hospital cardiologist was also the very highly thought of and nationally recognized surgeon to whom I was recommended by a pediatric doctor in our family, I knew that this doctor had to be our daughter's surgeon. This meant that now not only was I going to have to deliver in a different hospital, by different delivering doctor, but in a whole different city, over three hours from home.

If the stress of extra doctor's appointments and changing birth plans was not enough, my body decided to throw another curve into my pregnancy. Around week 31, I began to have high blood pressure. I had to be monitored even more closely from that point on, if you can even imagine. This meant more doctors appointments, more labs, more urine tests. It was critical at that point to ensure that my high blood pressure didn't turn into pre-eclampsia. If this were to occur, then the doctors would take the baby early, which may or may not give the baby -- and particularly her heart -- enough time to grow strong enough and big enough for her impending surgeries. No pressure, right? In addition to high blood pressure, I had more amniotic fluid than normal due to Olivia's duodenal atresia, which was not only uncomfortable for me, but also required close monitoring as it could cause premature labor. By this point in the pregnancy, I was being followed by three doctors: my obstetrician, my perinatologist, and my new delivering doctor in Dallas. All three doctors were monitoring me very closely and threatening to put me on bed rest, something I was dreading, as I work as an attorney with a high volume practice. Who has time for bed rest? I managed to make it a few more weeks, but when my blood pressure continued to persist, the doctors made the call that I had to be put on strict bed rest.

From this point on in my pregnancy, I moved up to Dallas, where I stayed with my parents for the remainder of my pregnancy. Strict bed rest did wonders for my swollen feet and ankles, and managed to keep my blood pressure somewhat under control. In fact, I was able to make it all the way to 37 ½ weeks!

It was November 24, two days after Thanksgiving, when in the early morning hours, my water broke. We called the doctor, and were told to head up to the hospital. I was almost in shock... this was really happening. On the way to the hospital, the contractions began. Of course, this early on in labor, the contractions I was feeling were child's play. Once we arrived at the hospital, I began fourteen hours of labor, which culminated in pushing for two hours, and a baby who refused to move down the birthing canal. Can you say stubborn? Finally, my doctor, who was showing some concerns about the baby's heart rate, told me that we could either move to trying out forceps or prepare for a c-section. Ultimately, although either choice had risks, I felt that the best option was a c-section at that point.

Literally five minutes after entering the OR, we heard the wonderful, loud screams of our sweet baby girl, Olivia Grace. She was born with an Apgar score of 9 -- I always joke that Olivia is the healthiest baby who ever had multiple defects -- a super high number for a baby with both an intestinal blockage and what turned out to be two heart defects. That's right -- I said two. It turned out that not only did Olivia have an unbalanced AV Canal Defect, but she also had a coarctation of her aortic arch. The latter heart defect was one that required more immediate surgery than the AV Canal would have by itself. In fact, if Olivia had not had the intestinal defect and surgical repair, she would have had the heart surgery even sooner than she did.

Olivia was a fighter from the day she was born. She underwent intestinal surgery on day two, and her heart surgery at two weeks old. Luckily, her heart surgeon felt that she would likely be a candidate for a biventrical repair, and he was going to go in and repair both conditions at once. This surgeon, Dr. Joseph Forbess, is a doctor that I can honestly say performed a surgery on our daughter that, from my worried research, not many doctors would or could perform on such a small baby. In my eyes, he performed a miracle, and he allowed my little miracle to recover and flourish. We stayed in the NICU and the hospital for just over six weeks before we were released on New Year's Eve. I couldn't have asked for a better way to start the New Year than to be able to go home with my family!

I am not going to say that undergoing several surgeries and spending day after day in the hospital was easy or fun. Day after day we endured ongoing labs, blood draws, x-rays, tubes, wires, echocardiograms, and that incessant beeping. We had to hand over our child to essentially perfect strangers numerous times to have her rolled back to surgery, where she was put under and came out looking like a completely different child. If I hadn't seen numerous pictures beforehand, and mentally prepared myself for what Olivia was going to look like immediately after surgery, it probably would have been even more difficult.

In my mind, I had pictured my baby being born around the holidays and having a wonderful Christmas with family and our new baby. I had never imagined that we would be spending our baby's first Christmas living in a hospital -- never in my wildest dreams. I learned from this experience that life happens, and while you can make all the plans in the world, you really have no control. I am so thankful and grateful that we had my family nearby to support us and to be there every step of the way, and that we were able to receive such wonderful healthcare.

On our return home to central Texas, we embarked on our new journey of struggling with feeding, weight gain, and yet more appointments. There were in-home nursing appointments, cardiology appointments, pediatrician appointments, occupational therapy appointments, ECI evaluations, and more. There were so many appointments, and all while struggling to get our sweet baby to take her bottle and transition from the feeding tube. If we couldn't get her to successfully transition, the next step would be a g-tube, not something I wanted to occur, as it meant yet another surgery. Luckily, our little fighter was strong, and as it turns out, loves to eat. After a couple of months, she finally made the transition successfully to bottle feeding, such that we were able to pull the feeding tube.

Olivia is 8 months old today, and she is doing wonderfully. Her scars have healed, she is holding her own bottle, eats anything and everything we give her, and is the sweetest, best natured baby I could ever have asked for. She has always slept through the night --

one benefit of NG tube feedings was that she didn't technically have to wake up to be fed. Everything about her development thus far has been on par with her typical, non-Down syndrome peers. If I could go back now to the day I found out about Olivia's diagnosis, I wish I could have better comforted myself and saved myself some tears. I wish I could have told myself what a smart baby I would have, how alert she would be, and how downright adorable she would be. I wish I could have told myself how just seeing her smile and hearing her laugh would erase any of the fears I may have had about her future. My daughter is perfect just the way she is -- extra chromosome and all.

~Julie, Olivia's mom; 31; Texas, United States

{Noah}

Perfect. That was what we had expected to hear on that rainy summer afternoon. We had decided beforehand that we did not want to know the gender this time. The 20 week ultrasound felt more like a formality. We joked about whether we would be able to tell the gender or not. When things became quieter in the room, that's when I knew we were about to be hit with some news. "There is a shortened femur. In comparison with the head size, there is a small chance that your baby could have Down syndrome." That was all it took to push me to tears. My husband stayed strong, and we made plans for a level two ultrasound in a larger city. The last thing I remember being told was, "I'm 99% sure you will be back here in a few months telling me that I had you worried for nothing."

I spent the rest of the night researching anything I could find about shortened femurs and other markers for Trisomy 21. A week later, we had another ultrasound that showed basically the same thing. There was a disparity between the head size, which was measuring a little bit ahead, and the limb length, which was measuring a little bit behind.

There was also a choroid plexus cyst in the brain. We were told the cysts were typically inconsequential, but are more common in a child with a trisomy. Afterward, we met with the genetics counselor, and were given lots of numbers and probabilities. I was just 25 years old at conception, so the chance that our child

would be born with Trisomy 21 was minute. The risk of complication from an amniocentesis was higher. We had declined all testing in both of my pregnancies, because we were solid in our beliefs that life is a gift from God. We declined the amniocentesis and moved forward. We opted for closer monitoring to ensure that if the baby had a trisomy, we could catch any organ anomalies and be prepared. Following an ultrasound at 34 weeks that showed a more round head shape, we opted for an amniocentesis to give a definite answer. The risks were less severe to the baby at that point.

We told ourselves that the outcome didn't matter, but it was a long weekend waiting for the results. On Monday, I called the genetics counselor. Our child did indeed have 47 chromosomes. I couldn't have expected how it would feel in that moment. I tried to pull myself together to make the call to my husband. I can't remember exactly what I said, but I do remember breaking down, wishing so bad that we were together instead of hours apart. We talked for a short time about how resilient we are, and that our love for this child far exceeds any other challenges we would face. As I drove home that day, I did a lot of thinking. I thought about the changes that this meant for my family and my life. How would this impact my daughter, how would it impact my marriage? I also thought a lot about how fiercely I loved this child, and that I would do whatever it took to make sure that we would be okay. After my husband got home, there were more tears, a lot of hugs, and even a few laughs. We did our best to go along as normally as possible for the sake of our daughter. After we talked to our parents, it really sank in for me. This was real. This was not happening to someone else, it was not a dream, this was our new reality. We talked to our close friends, and there were more tears shed. For me, the sadness was not that my child would have Down syndrome. It was about the fact that as a parent, your job is to make life easier for your children, and be able to protect them from the cold, cruel world. We didn't know anything about raising a child with special needs. I think that we were terrified that people would treat our child differently, or even that we would treat our child differently.

We met with the genetics counselor to discuss a few things and ask some questions that we had. On the way, we discussed whether we should find out the sex of the baby. In our meeting, we decided that we wanted to find out the gender. It was a BOY! We were absolutely overjoyed, and we both started crying. We were so excited, and the rest of the information went right over my head. All I was thinking was about this boy growing inside of me, and I felt more love for him than I ever had. I felt so connected to him and on the way home, we began thinking of a name for him with a new mindset. We focused on being together as a family and dreaming about our newest addition. I can't say that my mind didn't fool me in to thinking that we couldn't handle this more than once. It was hard, there were a lot of tears, but beyond it all was hope and joy. Knowing the diagnosis

before he was born meant
that we could just be happy
and focus on our son after his
birth. We couldn't wait to hold
him. Perfect is no longer a
word I use to describe people.
Not one of us is perfect. The
love I have for my son,
however, is absolutely
perfect.

~Jenny, Noah's mom; 26;
Wisconsin, United States

{Ethan}

My husband and I have been married for seven years. We have a four year old little boy Eli. We had been trying for two years to become pregnant, and had a miscarriage very early during my second pregnancy. In December of 2011, we found out we were pregnant again   and would have an August baby! The first 14 weeks were very exhausting with extreme nausea/vomiting, near syncopal, or fainting, spells, a subchorionic hemorrhage (bleeding hematoma inside the uterus), low lying placenta, and then a heart abnormality noted on my 16 week ultrasound. I received the   phone call at work that my unborn child had a heart abnormality. Unfortunately, my regular physician was out and another physician triaged the call, and a nurse called me with this information. I was   frantic. What did this mean? I met with my regular   OB/GYN, who referred to a specialist at Riverside Maternal Fetal Medicine (FTM) to see Dr. Minginone

in Columbus, Ohio. Unfortunately, we had to wait a very   long three weeks. I clammed up immediately after receiving the news. I just knew something was not right. I remember sharing the news with my husband, and he assured me that everything was going to work out just fine. Our baby was going to be just fine. I just could not see past this. I lived in a box for the next   three weeks. We only shared this news with our immediate family.

On Tuesday, April 3, 2012, we had a very long one hour drive to the city where we met Dawn, who would perform the level II ultrasound.   She was very kind, reassuring, and soothing. She asked us if we knew the reason for the referral. My husband spoke up and said, "Yes, a problem with our baby's heart." I was about 20 weeks gestation. We had decided we did not want to know the gender of the baby. As   Dawn started the anatomy scan, the first pictures popped up between his legs, and there it was! We were having a boy. I asked, "Is that what I think it is?" Sure enough we were having another BOY! I had a huge sense of relief, watching him wave and kick around. He sucked on his fingers a lot and blew bubbles. Once she was finished, she let us know the doctor would be in soon. Then I got a huge knot in my stomach. I started shaking. My hands were sweating. My heart was beating out of my chest. My husband was so calm.

He held my hand tight as Dr. Minginone came in through the door to greet us. He did a quick scan, and then he proceeded to tell us that he was certain our baby had Down Syndrome. He had three markers for Down syndrome: the heart defect, which accounts for 40% of Down syndrome, the flat nasal bridge, and hypoplasic mid phalanx of the fifth digits of the hands. Everything else checked out fine -- ventricles in the brain, bones, abdomen, etc. We opted for an amniocentesis. This would give us 100% confirmation of the diagnosis. They needed to do the procedure anyways due to increased fluid, and could not see all of the organs clearly. The procedure wasn't bad at all. I've had worse menstrual cramps and those last a lot longer!

My heart stopped. I felt like I was living a nightmare. This could not be true. I asked him over and over   if he was certain, and he told me that he was 99.9% certain. He told me he did not need to do any further testing unless I wanted it.   He also said under the Ohio state law, I had to make a decision if I wanted to abort the baby before 22 weeks. Even though I had my fears and unanswered questions, abortion was not an option for us. I proceeded to have an amniocentesis for my peace of mind. I needed the confirmation for my sanity. He sent me out the door with lots of resources. We received the FISH results in five days, which confirmed Trisomy 21. Exactly 14 days later, we received the final confirmation that our little boy would have an extra special chromosome.

I cried the entire way home, and I cried for weeks. I found myself in a deep depression. I felt selfish. I knew they could repair his heart. But we could not fix Down syndrome. I feared how society would accept him. How would other people accept us?   I feared what he would look like, what his facial features would look like. Would he look like us, and like his brother? I found myself not wanting to get out of bed for days, but I had to continue with my life. I had a family and needed to care for my unborn son. I knew it was not going to be the end of the world, but it certainly felt like a piece of me died that day.

On August 17, 2012 at 38 weeks, my water broke at my weekly appointment. My labor went very smoothly and quickly. Once my contractions started with the Pitocin, I delivered a beautiful baby boy at 6:56pm named Ethan Matthew Wolfe. I was numb. The cord had been wrapped around his neck twice, but they got it off quickly. The NICU nurse was ready, and checked him over. He was doing great. It was hard to believe he was doing this well. Everything seemed like a nightmare, and now we were floating in a dream. I got to spend the first hour with him. I breastfed him, and he latched right on to my breast. The tears were flowing down my face. I still felt no emotion. I could not shake this feeling. They took him away to the NICU where they could monitor him more closely. He required oxygen and a feeding tube by the second day. He was very red from the high red blood count, which is common with babies born with Down syndrome. Even though he seemed like a mess, I wanted his big brother to see him. I kept thinking that I could not live with myself if something had happened to him. So that evening, Eli came to visit. I was holding Ethan, and Eli was very quiet and nervous. But he gave me a kiss and a hug, and then leaned over and gave his little brother a kiss. Then it hit me. Eli did not see Down syndrome. He did not see the oxygen tubing, feeding tube, heart monitor, IV lines, or wires. He saw his little brother, Ethan Matthew. I then started to see Ethan through Eli's eyes. My heart melted. No words will ever describe this feeling. He is a true blessing!

~Renee, Ethan's mom; Ohio, United States

{Reuben}

My husband Carl and I had been blessed with three amazing boys, but we felt there was one more child to come, so we were happy to find ourselves expecting baby number four in the August of 2010. At 10 weeks and six days gestation, however, I was shocked to find I was bleeding. The general practitioner I saw told me I'd "had a mis", as she put it,

and sent me to have a scan to confirm this. Thankfully, we heard a beautiful heartbeat, and the scan showed our little one was fine. We went home relieved.

At 19 weeks and five days, we expectantly went to our major anatomical scan, hoping to find out the sex of our baby. The sonographer told us we were having a boy (surprise!), and then went to get the senior doctor who examined our little fellow. "Is everything all right?" I asked anxiously. "Baby has some markers of a chromosomal abnormality called Trisomy 18 or Edward's Syndrome," she said. "The outcome for these little ones is not good." At that point, my heart dropped to my stomach. We were completely shocked. Our little boy's hands appeared to be clenched, he had chorio plexus cysts in the fluid of his brain, a heart defect, and fluid around his heart. We left feeling devastated and lost.

After getting home, I started searching for a name for our son. I said to Carl, "If he's not going to be with us long, he needs a name, and he needs one now!" We found Reuben John. Reuben meaning "Behold, a son" and John meaning "God is gracious".

At the High Risk Clinic of our hospital, a compassionate obstetrician spoke to us about Trisomy 18 and our options of termination or birth. We were also offered an amniocentesis, which we accepted, as we wanted to know what we had to prepare ourselves for. We decided we would continue the pregnancy -- that we would love him and hold him close for as long as he was with us.

We had to wait for the results of the amnio for nine agonising days. Finally, a nurse rang and gave us the results. "Well, it's not what you were expecting. There are two dots beside chromosome 13 and 18, and three dots beside chromosome 21, so that means Down syndrome," she said. "Oh, ok... thank you," I managed to reply. Everything went very still, like I was in some kind of limbo-bubble. We were thankful that Reuben was not going to die soon after birth, but in a 180 degree change, we were suddenly facing a life of long-term care for our son. "It's Down syndrome... he has Down syndrome," I heard myself say to Carl, but it didn't feel like it was me speaking about our son.

The next day we asked the neonatologist and obstetrician about the medical conditions associated with Down syndrome. As the doctor quietly listed them, Carl slid lower and lower in his chair. A termination was offered, and then we were left alone for a moment. "How will we cope?" he asked slowly. The prospect of dealing with extra medical issues and trying to juggle the needs of our other boys was overwhelming.

Carl went back to work, and I went home and Googled every image of children with Down syndrome that I could find. I sat at the laptop with tears streaming down my face, looking at pictures of so many beautiful children, and searching for families that looked something like ours. I wanted to see them doing normal everyday things... I needed hope that the future would be ok.

That night, when Carl came home to a teary wife, he said he had been thinking and praying about what to do and felt strongly that it was not our call to make. We didn't know what Reuben's destiny or purpose would be. So we decided that Reuben was not going anywhere. Our parents, while shocked, were supportive and encouraging.

We invited our senior ministers from our church to come the next night to tell them about Reuben, via text message. That night, a friend named Annie told me when she had read our text, she heard the words "Angel Unaware". She knew this was a book written in the

1950s about a father and his child who had Down syndrome. Hearing this brought me great comfort, and confirmed to us that Reuben was meant to be here. I figured that if God had told Annie that Reuben had Down syndrome to prepare her to help us, then He knew what was going on, and I could trust Him with Reuben's future and the future of our family. Annie encouraged me to be very gentle with myself with the emotions and grief I was experiencing, and to allow myself to accept all of it, without self-judgement. We later told our extended family and a few close friends, many of whom sent words of love, acceptance, and encouragement.

As the days passed, the feeling of numbness lifted, but the emotions of shock, anger, guilt, and fear came. I just could not believe this had happened to us. I grieved and released one dream and tried to embrace a new one. And fears, I had so many fears... fears of the future, fears of the medical issues we'd face once he was born, fear of leukaemia, fear of him dying, fear of rejecting him just because of how he looked. I shed many tears and asked many unanswerable questions, yet I still wanted to believe that everything would be alright. I kept reminding myself to trust God, and to love Reuben. When I focussed on these two very simple things, peace came, and I knew we would be ok.

Reuben arrived early at 36 weeks (yet another surprise!) on March 24th, 2011. He was born naturally, weighing six pounds and one once (2.765kg), and was 45cm long. After some suctioning and a little oxygen, I was able to hold him. He was pink and soft and velvety, and had a beautiful little round face. His hands were fine, and a later scan showed no signs of any cysts in his brain. We were relieved and grateful he didn't have to go to the NICU or special care, and was doing well. I knew I was concerned about a great many things, but I also knew that without a doubt, I loved our Reuben-boy.

The next few days were a blur of family and friends visiting and check-ups including heart, brain, and hearing checks, blood tests, a visit from the hospital physiotherapist to show us how to position and wrap Reuben, lactation consultant visits, and phototherapy for jaundice. We were able to go home after four nights in the hospital, only to be called back in twice due to Reuben's high bilirubin levels for more phototherapy. It was an unsettling time for us all. All I wanted to do was settle into being at home and love my boys! It turned out Reuben was only just getting enough breast milk from me to sustain his weight. His body could not flush the bilirubin out of his system or put weight on, so I started expressing breast milk for him.

A day after being discharged from the hospital for the third time, we were sent to Melbourne to see the paediatric cardiologist at the Royal Children's Hospital. Travelling by myself with a 15-day-old baby, born a month premature, was certainly an experience! I got some interesting looks from older ladies who saw me bottle-feeding my baby boy. It was my first taste of fixing my eyes on Reuben and declaring in my heart that it didn't matter what others thought about what I was doing... I had to do what was right for him!

The visit to the cardiologist went well His oxygen saturation levels were good, and to my great excitement, the Patent Ductus Arteriosus (PDA) that hadn't closed at birth had now closed. That meant no operation to close it! All in all, Reuben was doing well, and we were sent home to return in a month.

After trying to breastfeed and express for three weeks, I decided to stop breastfeeding and continue full-time expressing. Trying to do everything and still be Mum to my three other boys was becoming overwhelming, and the anxiety from trying to breastfeed added to the mix. While I was upset about not being able to feed Reuben, I realised it was nothing either Reuben or myself was doing wrong... he simply did not have the oral muscle tone to take what he needed from me. Being premature with a heart defect also caused him to tire more easily. He was happy drinking expressed milk from a bottle, and I was more relaxed knowing how much he was getting each feed. The expressing also served two purposes for me. It continued to build the bond between him and myself, and it gave him all the nutritional benefits of breast milk. Holding him and looking into his eyes as he fed were beautiful, often teary times for me.

We were told Reuben's prolonged jaundice was possibly an indication of hypothyroidism, so he had a nuclear imaging scan at three weeks of age. This showed no sign of any thyroid gland at all. So we found ourselves yet again grappling with a new diagnosis. This involved giving him daily doses of thyroxine, for life.

At seven weeks of age, Reuben and I went for his second visit to Melbourne, which showed the small Atrial Septal Defect (ASD) had closed, leaving the small AVSD. The cardiologist was happy with Reuben's growth, and to our relief, the remaining defect was not hindering Reuben's heart function.

We returned six weeks later to find out more good news – the ventricular part of the AVSD had spontaneously closed, leaving a four to five millimeter ASD. The cardiologist said we didn't need to see him again for another year, and that we could see him in our hometown, so that meant no more 6:00 am flights! We were so grateful.

Slowly life began to settle, and in between doctors appointments, we began our fortnightly visits to early intervention at eight weeks. We both benefited from attending these sessions — Reuben got all the necessary monitoring and help with his development from his teacher, a physiotherapist, a speech therapist, and an occupational therapist, and I felt "normal" going there. I got to meet other parents with children with special needs, and a few with Down syndrome. I also got to talk about how I was processing the new journey I found myself on.

While going to early intervention was great, I found I struggled with comparing Reuben's development to the other children there who had Down syndrome. In fact, in the early months, without realising it, I also compared his weight and height to typically developing babies his age. I did this until I realised it was utterly pointless doing this. He was running his own race, and would be the weight and height he was, and would do things when he was ready, and that was ok.

To help Reuben communicate, we were all encouraged to begin using AUSLAN signs (Australian Sign Language) with him. I have always loved watching people signing, so learning some basic signs to teach Reuben was fun. Reuben watched and watched, until one day, about a year later, he signed "dog." We cheered, and he looked so proud!

Reuben loves to sit on my lap and read books. I remember an incredible moment when he was 14 months when I said, "Turn the page Reuben," and he did it! I realised he understood me! Tears flowed, and I felt incredibly relieved. From then on, I started asking him questions, and giving him choices, and waiting for a response. Something as simple as asking and seeing him turn the pages of a board-book became cause for celebration. These seemingly little things became encouraging moments of hope.

As time went on, I began to find going out with Reuben less challenging. Initially, I used to tell most people I talked to, be they strangers or friends, that Reuben had Down syndrome, but then I realised that was like me introducing myself by saying, "Hello, I'm Elisa. I have a cold." I realised it was unnecessary. He was simply my son and I found the more at ease and smiley I was with strangers, the more at ease they were with us.

The remaining ten months of his first year were full of paediatrician appointments, monthly blood tests checking his thyroid function, hearing and eye tests, and more early intervention sessions. We also negotiated the chicken pox at six months, started solids shortly after, had problems with constipation, and saw a dietician to monitor Reuben's nutrition levels at 11 months. We also celebrated the milestones of smiling, giggling, rolling over, and sitting unassisted. Reuben's smile was, and still is, amazing! His auntie says he has rainbow eyes and sunshine smiles!

We also went to our first Buddy Walk with Reuben at seven months, and our first Down Syndrome Tasmania Family Camp with Reuben 11 months old, both of which were confronting and wonderful all at once. Meeting so many beautiful families was incredibly encouraging, and so good to know we were far from alone on our journey. On returning from camp, I realised that Reuben would not suddenly turn into a 20-year-old man who had Down syndrome, but that he would gradually grow into becoming one, and that as he grew, so I would grow also into being his Mum. I had to remind myself to not look too far ahead and become overwhelmed, but to focus on today and the coming week, and to just keep loving my little boy.

To my great excitement, we discovered World Down Syndrome Day (WDSD) occurred three days before Reuben's birthday, March 24th, on March 21st, so we decorated the house and celebrated many things that March. I watched WDSD videos like 'Will you Let Us In?' and 'Ordinary Miracle' from the International Down Syndrome Coalition with tears streaming down my face, incredibly thankful to find ourselves part of a global family, with all of us somehow connected by the extra copy of chromosome 21.

On the 24th of each month, and at the time he was born, we always remembered Reuben's arrival day and sang him Happy Birthday, and so to finally celebrate his first year birthday was wonderful. We rejoiced that he was here and was so well, and that we had gotten through an incredibly tough year. We had Reuben dedicated at our church on his birthday. To be able to say thank you to God for the gift we never knew we needed, and to acknowledge again that He truly does know best, was emotional and so very beautiful.

Every night, after getting Reuben ready for bad, I put on his sleep-time CD, and would hold him close, often cheek to cheek. Most nights I found tears would begin falling as I told him how much I loved him. I would say through my tears how I trusted God's plan for the future, that I knew we would be ok. Those times were, and still are, times of healing and acceptance. They are times of bonding and of love. It was during one of these times, when Reuben put his head on my shoulder for the fist time, that I realised Reuben knew I was his Mummy. Knowing that was incredible!

When Reuben was about 18 months, I remember a friend asking me if I was doing ok after me telling her I'd been feeling a bit low. She said she wondered if I was still in shock about Reuben's diagnosis, and I burst into tears. Even with a prenatal diagnosis at 20 weeks, I realised I was still in shock about it at 18 months! To acknowledge this was a turning point in my journey, and helped me to move forward. The ever-present fear of the unknown, the "what-ifs," and the feeling of treading water, slowly began to ease. I could finally say my son had Down syndrome without my heart aching. I saw Reuben as perfect because he is. He is not flawed in some way just because of the way he looks sometimes, or because of what he cannot do or say.

Not so long ago, I realised a wonderful thing. I realised that Reuben has helped me to become the woman and mother I always wanted to be. He has helped me to be more accepting and less critical and judgmental of differences in others, more compassionate, more playful, patient, and loving. He has enlarged my heart, and has changed forever my idea of perfect. Perfect is not a beautifully-dressed model or an immaculately-styled room in a magazine. It is life, with all its joy and grief, it is happiness and it is pain; perfect is God's plan for our lives, and perfect is our son Reuben, our gift.

~ Elisa, Reuben's mum; 37; Tasmania, Australia

{Zarilya}

From the moment of conception, the princess was mine. There was no doubt in my mind, no second thoughts, no hesitations -- she was planned and very much wanted. From the moment that second line appeared on the pregnancy test, faint as it may have been, the unconditional love was there.

We were given a 1:3 chance that our baby had an abnormality. For the lottery these odds seemed great, but not for the baby lottery. Every parent hopes for that 'perfect' baby, with twenty three pairs of chromosomes, ten fingers, ten toes, and society's expectations of what a child should be. Down syndrome: the words rang in my ears for the longest of moments, deafening me, paralysing my every thought, my hopes and dreams. It felt like someone had punched me in the heart. Would you terminate all because of an extra chromosome, and what exactly does that really mean? To some it may

mean the end of the world, but to those of us who know better, it is the beginning of a whole new one. Faced with the prospect at the time though, is not a decision to be taken lightly and definitely not an easy one. A life commitment to the well-being and development of a child who has Down syndrome requires courage, and at that particular moment in time, I remember feeling very weak and insignificant as my world caved in around me, my courage and strength failing me.

Our story began on a sunny Wednesday morning, arriving at the hospital for a twelve week scan. My husband parked the car and took our toddler while I went up to wait. To my astonishment, they called me in very quickly, and my husband still wasn't there. We waited for what seemed like a lifetime and the sonographer said we had to start. I was so excited, I couldn't wait. She started, and immediately, I could see something wasn't right. Having worked as a midwife had given me some insight into what a "normal" scan should look like, and mine was not one of them. I felt the tears welling in my eyes, and the knot in my heart. Hubby arrived somewhere after that moment. He took one look at me, and one look at the ultrasound as I could see his heart breaking. Our princess had a thickened nuchal fold and no visible nose bone. The sonographer made some phone calls, sent off the results to the genetic lab, and organised for us to meet with the genetic counsellor. My tears would not stop flowing, and my heart was breaking. We were in too much shock to even communicate with each other. We waited and saw the counsellor, and the results of our combined scan and my blood tests were rushed through. They came back at 1:3, so she offered us a CVS, or the option to wait four weeks and have an amniocentesis. I am unsure as to why we chose to have a CVS, but thinking back, I believe it was for 100% clarification. However, we knew the picture and the odds were there in black and white. The counsellor organised a CVS for later that day. I now had something else to fear -- that needle looked mighty big, and I was not happy about where it was going to be placed. But the procedure went without a hitch, and we went home to await the results.

Thursday came and went with no phone call, while our hearts ached and my eyes were bloodshot and cloudy from all the tears I had shed. Somehow, through all these tears, I had decided that there was no way I would terminate, but feared that my husband did not feel the same way. We were still finding it hard to share our feelings. Friday came, and late in the afternoon, the phone call finally came. Our princess had Down syndrome. I cried again, but this time I think it was relief. Confirmation had come, and now we could get on with life.

So life was about to take a major turn onto what would probably be a bumpy road. Little did we know at this point in time exactly how bumpy it would really be. At our twenty week ultrasound scan, there was more bad news. Our princess had a major heart defect, known as Tetralogy of Fallots. This meant my precious baby girl was going to need open heart surgery. We took this information, prepared ourselves, and kept soldiering on, eager to meet our precious bundle. Then, somewhere around thirty weeks into the pregnancy, my placenta started to deteriorate. Monitoring increased, ultrasound scans were more frequent, and by thirty four weeks, I was in hospital. At thirty five weeks, it became critical, and our princess had to be delivered early. This scared me even more, as I knew being premature as well as having a heart condition was not a good combination. As they lifted my baby up for me to see over the drapes, my heart melted and I fell in love. She was so tiny, so beautiful, and so precious. She was quickly whisked away to be stabilized for transfer to the Royal Children's Hospital. It seemed like forever that they worked on her in a little room next to the operating theatre. I couldn't hear her crying, and I just wanted to hold her.

Eventually, they wheeled her into the room. She was wrapped to keep warm inside a transport cot, and had a breathing tube in. Tears streamed down my cheeks as I got to

hold her hand for about a minute before they whisked her away. I sent my husband to stay with her so she would not be alone, but it was several days before I could even go to see her. It was extremely hard being on a ward and hearing other babies cry while my baby was somewhere else, sick and without her mummy. Three days after she was born, I finally got to hold her. She smelt so sweet and felt so soft. Her breathing tube had been taken out, and she was doing really well. Surgery was to be when she was around six months old. Only a few days more in hospital, and we were allowed to take her home.

Since the moment we knew our baby was a little girl, we were calling her our princess. Trying to name all our children had been hard, as we do not like conventional names. Our oldest daughter we named Kiarra, our second daughter we named Jamayka, and our little man we called Jaspa. So her name had to be special, and while searching for names, I came across the name Zahlia, which it meant princess. We didn't like the spelling, so we changed it to Zarliya, and we had a beautiful name for our princess.

If I were to write about all the in between stuff, it would literally make a whole book. So I will skip through the six hospital admissions for respiratory problems, including a six week hospital stay for bronchiolitis, RSV and pneumonia. With each admission, her symptoms and stays were less and shorter. At four months of age, Zarliya started having blue spells from her heart condition. She was admitted, but due to complications, the surgeons could not perform her full repair. Instead, they inserted a shunt. After that, there was fairly smooth sailing through her first Christmas, her first birthday, and growing, learning, and surprising us every day. Every single second spent with her was a miracle, special and cherished. A month after her first birthday she was admitted for her open heart surgery. The wait was excruciating, with eight hours of trying to keep busy and not think about what was happening. In intensive care she looked so tiny, even though she was one year old. Our little hero recovered miraculously, and was discharged six days after this major surgery, and was soon blossoming and thriving.

Since her surgery, our princess has thrived. By sixteen months, she is sitting independently, commando crawling, rolling everywhere, talking and babbling, playing, smiling, laughing, kissing, hugging, and loving just like any other baby. We don't see her as delayed, and she is accepted for who she is. In some ways, she still looks like a baby about half her actual age, but after what she has been through, it's no wonder. Each day I give thanks for the blessing that she is, and could not imagine my life without her. Children with Down syndrome are not burdens, but blessings.

~ Samantha, Zarilya's mum; 38; Victoria, Australia

{Josephine}

At 5:15 pm, my cell phone rang. I remember because my cell phone never works in my office. It was the genetic counselor from our perinatal office. I already knew what she was going to say; nevertheless, I held my breath and answered.

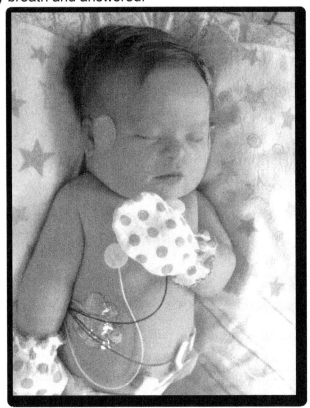

"Stephanie, we've received your MaterniT21 results back. It was positive for Trisomy 21. I'm sorry because I know this isn't the result we were hoping for." I calmly responded, "Well, it's what we were told to expect." She replied, "Please let me know if I can be of any assistance to you during the remainder of your pregnancy."

I worked in a zombie like state for another 30 minutes before I said goodnight to my coworkers. I barely made it to my car before the tears started.

This was our first pregnancy, and like most first time mothers, I relied on my doctor to guide me to the ways of being pregnant. When my obstetrician strongly suggested I decline any prenatal screening – because "they only create more stress in an already stressful situation" – I agreed. I distinctly remember sitting in her office at eight weeks pregnant, when she asked if we would terminate if our baby had Down syndrome. My husband and I immediately responded no. At that time, they were just words. We never knew we'd be putting our money where our mouth was.

Our 20 and 24 week ultrasounds were textbook, except for a baby that refused to sit still long enough to have her heart examined. "It's no big deal," the tech said. "This happens. Just to be safe, let's send you to the high risk perinatal center to get better pictures". As I waited for them to make the appointment, I overheard the tech say to my obstetrician, "I believe that the baby has a heart abnormality." At 25 weeks, the perinatal center confirmed what the original tech had suspected – our baby had an AV Canal Defect. After our ultrasound at the perinatal center, we were placed in the waiting room to speak to the genetic counselor. I used that wait time to Google "AV Canal Defect". I was scared, more so because no one wants to hear that their unborn child has a heart condition. Was this survivable? When the words "Down syndrome" appeared in every article, I remember leaning over to my husband and saying, "We might have a bigger problem here." We were offered an amnio during our genetic counseling session, but declined for various reasons -- fear of needles, the late stage of pregnancy, and our very active baby.

At 26 weeks, I found myself having another ultrasound done, this time at the pediatric cardiologist's office. I had already researched to death how an AV Canal Defect would be handled, and felt somewhat more at ease with the situation. Unbenounced to me, the cardiology ultrasound tech was actively looking for Down syndrome soft markers while he took pictures of our daughter's heart. I remember him pointing out that kidney function was great, and that the stomach and bowels were functioning perfectly. I thought this was odd for a cardiologist tech to mention, but was happy to have the information.

"Your Daughter has a complete, balanced AV Canal Defect," our pediatric cardiologist would go on to say. "It's completely repairable, but she'll need open heart surgery when she's around four to six months old. The survival rate of these surgeries is higher than those of a boob job." My husband and I laughed at that comment. He paused. "I do need to tell you, there's a 90% chance that your daughter has Down syndrome."

That was the news I wasn't expecting. My research had all pointed toward a 33% chance, not a 90% chance. 90% odds weren't great odds. I remember sobbing in the elevator on our way home.

I had to know – for sure – what our situation really was. I knew I couldn't get past this part of my pregnancy, couldn't be happy again about our baby, until I knew. But I was still very uncomfortable with the idea of an amnio. After doing more research, I discovered the MaterniT21 test. I called the perinatal office to ask if they offered it. I would be the first person in their practice to have the test performed.

The three week wait for my results was excruciating. I read every blog written by parents of kids with Down syndrome. I googled things like "Down syndrome child ruined my life", looking for the flip side to special needs parenting. But the more I researched, the more I found out it wasn't a parenting death sentence to have a child with Down syndrome. Sure, their lives weren't always rainbows and butterflies, but their lives also looked pretty darn normal to me. Unfortunately, every time I came to the conclusion that we could raise a child with Down syndrome, this little voice that said "she may not have it" would slip in and ruin it all.

The day the test results came in, I was angry with myself about my reaction. I had spent three weeks going through the acceptance cycle –- denial, anger, bouts of uncontrolled crying -- and I was finally coming to terms with it all. So why was having a confirmed diagnosis so upsetting? Why the tears? Why did I feel like I was back at step one?

I called my husband to give him the news from my parked car. I remember apologizing repeatedly, feeling that I was to blame for this. It would take us several more weeks to find peace in our new situation. We went through a range of emotions, and had those

hard conversations that you never expect to have to have with your spouse. But we always came to the same conclusions: no one was to blame for this. This wasn't the path we would have willingly chosen, but it was the path we'd been given to travel for a reason. It wasn't always going to be easy, but we'd be in it together. And, come hell or high water – we were going to be awesome.

The last 10 weeks of my pregnancy went by with absolutely no commotion. We painted the nursery, attend baby showers, and did all those last minute things you think you have to do right before you bring a new person into this world. We had been receiving weekly ultrasounds beginning at week 33. Each ultrasound showed that our baby girl was growing, but very slowly.   I questioned if the "growth algorithm" they used during these ultrasounds took into account that our daughter would be born with Down Syndrome - a condition that lends itself to short "long" bones.   At our 38 week appointment, we were told that we would be lucky if she broke the 6 lbs. mark.   I would be induced at 39 weeks and 5 days - a week longer than my obstetrician wanted -but a week I knew my baby needed, so I fought for it.

Named after her great-great aunt, Josephine was born on the evening of a very beautiful September day. I remember laughing in surprise when the nurse announced that her official weight was a whopping 7 lbs. 12 oz.!! She would spend exactly one week in the NICU of our local children's hospital, mainly for oxygen saturation issues (a common side effect of babies with heart conditions). Once her oxygen levels had stabilized on their own, we were happily sent home. Approximately four months later, we would be back at the hospital, only this time Josie would undergo open heart surgery to correct her AV Canal Defect.   She was a superstar during the entire process – recovering so amazingly well that we were released from the hospital exactly one week post-surgery!

Since then, our lives have been remarkably normal. Josie attends a typical day care full time – where she's in a room with 7 "typical" kids.   She's developed a beautiful and hilarious personality. She looks like her Daddy – but has her Momma's stubborn streak. We have play dates, take swim lessons, attend church regularly, and make all attempts to get out of the house every chance we get. We also attend weekly therapies to help Josie reach important milestones, and we proactively see various medical specialists throughout the year to ensure that we're monitoring Josie's overall health and catching any pesky medical concerns before they become issues.   Most importantly – we celebrate. We celebrate milestones, we celebrate life, we celebrate knowing that this wild ride isn't as scary or as untraveled as we originally thought. And when we're done celebrating – we eat animal crackers, because life really is – normal.

~Stephanie, Josephine's mom; 32; Tennessee, United States

{Eli N.}

The story of our family journey began in 2010, when my husband and I became pregnant for the first time. We had been married for five years, bought a house, had stable jobs, and we were ready. Our pregnancy came easily, and we were blissfully happy with our little secret.

A cold reality closed in on our excitement when only a week later, our pregnancy ended in miscarriage at ten weeks. We felt lost, crushed, and abandoned. No one seemed to understand our grief, and nothing filled the void we felt. It was one of the darkest moments in our marriage.

Although our hearts had not completely healed, we began to try again. This time, our efforts were fruitless. We tried for six months before seeking help from my obstetrician. She asked us to be patient, and continue to try for six more months. At the end of a year, we had been through three doctors, and still had no answer as to why we couldn't get pregnant again. I had begun to believe that we were not meant to have a family at all.

My husband's cousin recommended one last doctor. He was far from us, but we felt like we had to give this one more try. After a battery of tests, we were told that I had a rare blood clotting disorder called MTHFR and a thyroid issue. My husband was informed that he had male-factor infertility.

That feeling of defeat returned. We had so many questions, no answers, and no baby. But our new doctor had a plan: IVF. It was hard to take it all in: miscarriage, fertility struggle, infertility and now IVF.

To put it into perspective, my husband felt responsible for our fertility struggles, while I felt inadequate as a woman, and we were both worn down by the year-long ordeal. But we trusted our doctor and his plan, so we decided to go through with it. IVF is a costly procedure -- financially, physically, and emotionally. We had to raise $20,000, drive back and forth to the doctor's office almost daily, and we were filled with anxiety and fear. This was it; this was our only shot at a family.

I self-injected hormones daily, underwent surgery, and my husband was, for lack of a better word, debased. During the egg retrieval, they were able to get ten eggs, of which eight were mature and seven fertilized. We had seven little embryos, and our life was about to change. At the implantation procedure, our doctor selected two embryos, which were transferred back to me. The result was two pink lines on a pregnancy test just 14 days later. Finally, we were pregnant!

The pregnancy was wrought with fear, complications and cautious optimism. At around nine weeks, I was admitted to the hospital for bleeding. I was put on bed rest for four weeks until it resolved. I was very highly monitored -- I literally have an unltrasound picture for every week of the pregnancy -- because we had already miscarried, and we had been through a unique process to get pregnant. At 12 weeks, the bleeding vanished and we had our nucal translucency scan. This scan is combined with bloodwork to help determine a baby's risk for chromosomal abnormalities. The nuchal translucency measurement was 1.2, and we were told we had a 1:1200 chance of having a child with Trisomy 21. We were no longer considered high risk, and began to see our doctor as any other pregnant couple would.

At our 20 week anatomy scan, my doctor requested a thyroid panel for me. A week later, he called to tell me that there was a lab error -- the lab had actually run AFP bloodwork, the results of which gave us a 1:243 chance that our child will have Down syndrome. This is considered a "screen positive" for Down syndrome.

At this point, our doctor was not convinced that our son would have Down syndrome, nor did he have any markers on the ultrasounds. But he did offer us a new test called MaterniT21. Houston was one of the first cities to gain access to the test, and because it was a simple blood test and posed no risk to our pregnancy, we had it performed. The results take two weeks to return, and while we had not confirmed a diagnosis, I knew in my heart that our child would have Down syndrome. Call it a mother's intuition, but I just knew.

Two weeks later I got a call that I will never in my life forget - the test had come back positive for Trisomy 21. Even though I "knew", confirmation was a hard reality to accept. In that moment, I realized how many expectations we had placed on our unborn child, of

things we wanted, and plans we had for their life. At the same time, I bitterly realized that I had deemed our family "untouchable"; we had been through so much that a diagnosis of Down syndrome wasn't something that could happen to us.

Because the MaterniT21 test was so new, my doctor insisted that I follow up with an amniocentesis. We were in such a severe state of shock and disbelief that we agreed to the procedure. Thinking back on it now, I only went through with it hoping that the MaterniT21 test was inaccurate... and in my darkest moments, that perhaps the amnio itself would end my pregnancy so I wouldn't have to worry about anything else.

Two days later, my doctor called with the news: our son would come to us with Down syndrome. I was 22 weeks pregnant, and we had just found out that we were having a boy.

To say that I fell on the floor and sobbed for days wouldn't be far from the truth. Graceful was not in my vocabulary, clearly. Once I got off the floor, I began to throw myself into researching and gathering all the knowledge that I could find about Down syndrome. Slowly, my heart began to feel joy again, as we waited for our son to arrive. In retrospect, I feel like it was a blessing to have a prenatal diagnosis. We were able to prepare our hearts, learn, share with our family and friends, and prepare with our doctors and hospital for our son's birth. His birth was a celebration, and his life has been the biggest blessing on our family. I know -- corny. You will read that everywhere, but it's true, because he is ours, and he's perfect. Having Eli has been exactly what we imagined being parents would be. Our son is more than just statistics, more than what medical journals describe, more than a diagnosis with negative stereotypes, and we feel blessed because we've done nothing to deserve him. Eli, this is for you. Mommy and Daddy love you, and we love our special journey into parenthood. Thank you for making me a mommy.

When we decided on the name Eli, we joked that it stood for "Extra Light Inside", not knowing how true that would be. God had a special plan for him and our family. It was scary at first, but he really is that extra light in our lives. His name really means "Ascend my God", and that is our prayer of blessing over him: that he would come to know God, and that he would bring glory to Him, that he would be able to use the unique gifts God has given him to bless others, and that his light would shine brightly, reflecting God's love and grace.

~ Ashley, Eli's mom; 27; Texas, United States

Blogging @ www.barryandashley.wordpress.com

{Dominic}

My journey began   during my pregnancy. The day I went to my first ultrasound appointment, I was 13 weeks. The doctor saw several soft markers for Down syndrome, and she told me to go for a level two ultrasound. I went to my obstetrician again for one of the new non-invasive blood tests. That came up positive for Down syndrome. At the time, I was not accepting it. I just did not understand what was really happening. I asked to do the amniocentesis just to be sure. I prayed the whole time, "Lord Jesus, please give me a normal baby."

Three days later, I got a call. I was all alone at home. The doctor said, "We got the results, and it's positive for Trisomy 21." I felt like someone dropped the world right on

my chest. I could feel my heart shatter. I cried, screaming and cursing God.

I called my grandma. I couldn't even get the news out without crying harder. I wanted to crawl under a rock and never leave. My pregnancy was ruined! And so is my life. Why God? Why me? What did I do? I'm only 19 years old; this doesn't happen to people like me.

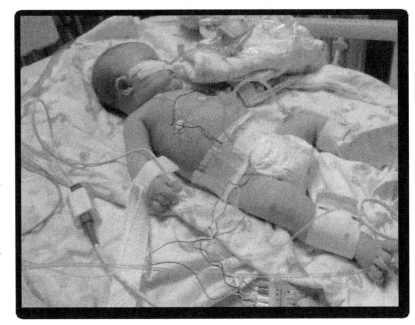

The doctors told me every bad thing will happen. They said your child will never function normally. He will be retarded for the rest of his life. Through the pregnancy, I still felt alone, but somehow I found a way to move on.

On September 11th, 2012, I went to a routine check-up for the baby's heart. After looking at his heart, the doctor advised me to go downstairs; I would be delivering the baby today. He had fetal hydrops. The doctors warned that my baby would be born very sick. He may not be breathing when he was born. He may die within 24 hours. He was five weeks early. At 9:12 pm, Dominic came into the world SCREAMING. They took him away to the NICU before I could see him. Later, I was able to see my tiny four pound baby boy. He had tubes all over him.

The very next day, the neonatologist came into my room, sat down beside me, and said that his blood work came back, and it didn't look good at all. They found leukemia cells. Dominic had Transient Myeloproliferative Disorder (TMD), or transient leukemia. I couldn't help but scream. Why? She told me this is just one of those things that happens; it's rare. She had me sign a paper giving consent to treat my two day old with chemotherapy. I never heard of such a thing. He was born so very sick, and on top of that, he had to do five days of chemo.

My heart ached for him. I just wanted to shut down. All of it just hit me like a ton of bricks. I would argue with God, and then cry and pray for my son. He was on chemotherapy for five whole days. He was so tiny and soft. He was just so sick. He had to get multiple blood transfusions. His platelets were very low, and so were his white blood cells. This all made him at a greater risk to catch any little bug going around. He was kept isolated for weeks.

As the weeks went by, God answered my prayers and Dominic's health seemed to be improving. He got off the oxygen. We were working on feeding. After weeks of trying, I agreed to have a feeding tube put in. After God's healing, Dominic finally came home after three months in the NICU. For a while, I believed he would never come home to me. But he did, just before Christmas.

He was only home for just a few weeks, and then his feeding tube site started getting red and he had fevers, so I took him to the emergency room. When they checked his oxygen, it was low. They admitted him into the PICU, and when they handed me my parent badge, I just started crying.

I had faith he would come home in a week or so. But his breathing continued to worsen. About a week after being there, he went into respiratory distress. They hooked up the ventilator to Dominic, and now the breathing machine was breathing for him. My faith in God was, and is, strong. I knew my boy could get through this. I checked into the Ronald McDonald house so I could take a shower and get at least one night's sleep.

Dominic did great, and they took him off the vent, but he was still on the oxygen. Every morning, the doctors would do their rounds. I hated to keep asking them the same question: "Do you think he will be able to come home soon? When?" But I never got an answer.

Days went by, and we had a plan just to keep him there for a few more weeks to fatten him up for his heart surgery. Two weeks later, we scheduled a heart catheter. We were transferred to the fifth floor, to the CVICU. Dominic wasn't doing well. He developed fevers as high as 106 that caused seizures. His breathing was getting worse. The doctor came in and told me that she was amazed that he was still actually breathing, and that this does not look good.

He had to be intubated again. They also paralyzed him, so his body did not have to work so hard. I was so scared. I was alone. I had no family there -- it was just me.

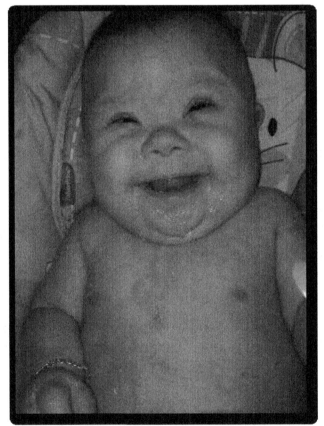

I called my family that lived about an hour away, and told them what was happening and to just pray. I couldn't even look at Dominic without crying. He looked lifeless; he was white as a ghost and colder than a ice cube. They had to give him a blood transfusion to see if it would help his oxygen and body temperature. I never left my son's side.

I prayed to God. I blamed myself. What did I do, God? Why is this happening to us? Please God. I don't think I can take anymore.

Dominic was intubated for six weeks. I was not able to hold him for so long, I would crawl up with him in his crib. I felt like I had been robbed of my baby boy. We waited until he was healthy and strong again to extubate. He still had a fever that always seemed to be there. Many specialists came to find out why, but nothing ever came back. We finally decided to do the surgery and see if that would help.

He went into surgery on April 9th. He did wonderfully! He had no more fevers. He was breathing just right. After five long, long months, Dominic was able to come home. Dominic had become like a celebrity on the fifth floor. Everyone knew us. He changed my life, and still is. I knew there was always hope.

I love him so much, and he truly is an amazing, strong little human. I still don't understand why I was chosen to mother a special needs child, but I believe God has something in store for me and Dominic, even as a young single mom.

~ Dayna, Dominic's Mom; 19; Florida, United States

{Aiden}

After two miscarriages, we made an appointment to do a procedure to soften the lining of my uterus. The Friday before my appointment, I took a pregnancy test -- and the results were positive!

Our first prenatal appointment was super scary; my age was a huge factor, along with the two miscarriages prior. We were so excited, but the doctor was so negative. He talked about all test I would have to take and he kept talking about how high risk I was... ugh!

At our first sonogram, we were told about how thick my baby's neck was, and it was right at the measurement to cause concern. Again, they took away the joy of our first child together, the child we so desperately wanted.

We did the blood test, because that's what the doctor said to do. My doctor kept referring to me as a "high risk pregnancy". No, I thought; my name is Bonnie or Mrs. Scott. His office ended up losing my blood work results, so he did an ultrasound in his office to see if he could see anything, and to show my daughter that was visiting from college her baby brother or sister. At that ultrasound, he started talking about how big my baby's head was, and it was a sign that he had some kind of birth defect. "He has Down's," the doctor told me. I walked out of his office that day and never planned on going back. I was so offended! He made my baby sound like an alien in front of my other baby.

I started seeing a perinatologist, and she was a dream; her voice comforting and soothing. We talked about my age, the sonograms, and all the other visits to "that doctor". She did an ultrasound, and it was a boy! It also showed some markers for Down syndrome, and she recommended an amniocentesis. My husband wanted to know; I didn't. We were never going to abort my one and only son, I dreamt of him. I prayed for him. I was so in love with him. I named him!

We got the phone call with our results; my son had Down syndrome. My world went black. I hung up the phone, and cried and cried and cried. I called my husband, and he was not answering... and I started to panic.

What will I tell my family and friends? How will he look? What will happen to him? How would he grow? This can't be happening to me. I don't know how to raise a child with Down syndrome! I don't know anyone with Down syndrome. What is Down syndrome? My husband came home, and I finally told him the results. We sat there together and cried. I was hysterical and he was calm, as always, but I could see the look in his eyes.

We looked up Down syndrome on our computer, and that made it worse. There were no African-American faces. What was in store for us being so far away from our support system and family? My mom would never understand -- she lives in Jamaica. What would our friends and family think? My oldest called to find out the

results. I told her the news about her brother, while sobbing. All she could say was, "That's just my brother and this makes me love him even more."

The next two weeks were full of quiet and tears and just telling my core people, a select fifteen, listening to their feedback and words of love, encouragement and support. I mourned the ideas and my dreams of a "typical" son. His dad was calm like always, but deathly quiet. We took it one day at a time. There is no preparation for Down syndrome, I felt so alone. Our world was going to change. I was not looking forward to it. I couldn't handle it. I was not strong enough for this. I'm not one of those kind of moms!

~Bonnie, Aiden's mom; 38 Iowa; United States

{Charlotte}

This is the story of our third child. And I'm going to start at the end. Charlotte is now six months old. She is beautiful, and perfect, and oh-so-loved. Her arrival has changed our family dynamics yet again, and she is a perfect fit for this family.

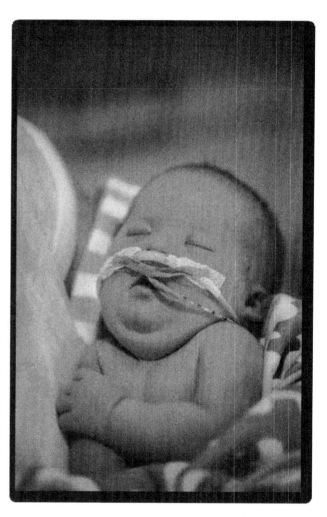

We had always talked about three being the magic number for our family. For a while, we toyed with the idea of staying at two, probably somewhere in the never-ending sleepless nights that we had with Bailey. But we made the decision, and yet again, we were blessed in falling pregnant first shot.

The first trimester passed slowly, with constant nausea and exhaustion, but we hit 12 weeks, and things sped up. All of a sudden, we were having our 19 week morphology scan. We took Alyssa, who was very excited to see the baby. Everything looked good to our eyes. But then the sonographer said she wanted to get the doctor, who came in for a second look. The nuchal fold measurement was larger than it should be. An obstetrician was called in, and she told us that the nuchal fold was around the nine millimeter mark, when it should be less than six millimeters. And within the nuchal fold was something called a cystic hygroema – a pouch of fluid from the lymphatic system. There were a few things it could be caused by, and we were referred to a maternal-fetal medicine obstetrician. But we couldn't see her until Monday morning. It was Wednesday afternoon at this point.

We spent the weekend stunned, and trying to stay away from Dr. Google. Monday morning, we met the lovely MFM doctor. It could have been a number of things, but the front runner was a chromosomal abnormality, with the main culprit being Trisomy 21. I went from having a risk of 1:900, to being high risk at 1:57.

We discussed, but declined, the offer of an amniocentesis. We would not act on the results, and so felt it was not worth the risk to the baby, something our doctor fully supported us in. She arranged frequent monitoring and extra scans. We had weekly appointments with her for the first few weeks, and by week 24, we had been given the all clear from an echocardiogram scan of the baby's heart. Another scan showed that the cystic hygroema seemed to be reducing in size. Everything was looking great, and with Christmas upon us, it was decided that we would not have our next scan and appointment until 28 weeks.

A couple of days before our appointment, I started to get a little bit worried. The baby's movements didn't feel right, and were quite reduced. As we had the appointment scheduled, I let the thought sit at the back of my mind, and hoped that the scan would show that I was worrying about nothing.

I went along to our 28 week scan, and again had a feeling something wasn't right, despite the reassuring presence of a heartbeat. I sat down in the doctor's office, and she told me that she wanted to deliver my baby... the very next day. I was only 28 weeks and four days along. I knew that it wouldn't be good. I burst into tears, and after a hug from my lovely doctor, she briefly explained why. The baby's lungs were full of fluid. She sent me home to get Daniel and pack my bags, and we arranged to meet her later that afternoon, when she would go through everything.

But our baby must have a guardian angel watching over her, because whilst we were gone, the doctor decided to ring a colleague at the main birthing hospital in the city, who referred us to the head doctor in the maternal-fetal medicine department there. I got a phone call from our doctor telling us of a change of plans. This doctor was expecting us that afternoon to see if he could drain the fluid off whilst the baby was still inside me, and hopefully buy us time to keep the baby in for longer.

We met the new obstetrician, and he took us straight to an ultrasound room. He didn't waste any time in taking a closer look at what was going on with the baby. He explained that the main reason our doctor at the first hospital wanted to deliver was due to a lack of blood flow back through the cord to the placenta caused by the pleural effusion (the fluid on her lung). The baby's left lung was so full of fluid that her heart had been pushed way out of position, so the aorta and arteries at the top of the heart were being pushed out of line, which was pinching them, and the heart was having to work harder than it should be. At that stage, the blood flow around the body was ok, but she was showing signs of heart stress. He didn't want to deliver –- if we delivered, her lungs would not be able to inflate because of the fluid in the cavity and she would not be able to breath, and they would have trouble ventilating her until the fluid was drained. He felt that if we delivered at that moment in time, it wouldn't have been a good outcome for our baby.

As scared and upset as we were, there really was no choice but to drain the fluid to try and save our baby. The procedure took less than 10 minutes, and the relief on the baby's heart was immediate. He removed 80ml of fluid from her left lung. He also suggested that he do an amnio whilst he was doing the procedure and we agreed: it was already invasive, so we might as well try and find some answers to what had caused the buildup of fluid.

I was admitted to the antenatal ward that night for the foreseeable future. I was given two doses of steroids overnight to help mature the baby's lungs, just in case we still needed to deliver.

Our new obstetrician arrived early the next morning to do another scan and see how things were looking. The bad news was the fluid had accumulated a lot quicker than the doctor would have liked. The good news was that the blood flow through the cord had improved. The doctor commented that she must be tough and pretty resilient.

It was decided that, rather than drain the fluid with a needle like the previous day, he would place a stent into the baby's lung cavity to drain the fluid continuously into the amniotic sac to prevent it building up again. The procedure had an even higher chance of causing me to go into pre-term labour, or for the baby to go into distress, so it was carried out in operating theatre under sterile conditions. I was prepped and ready for a caesarean, just in case they needed to put me under and get the baby out quickly. I was freaking out on the table, praying that the procedure would work.

They tested the fluid, and it was lymphatic fluid, and the pleural effusion was classed as a chylothorax. Her lymphatic system was immature, and so not draining the fluid itself, which was causing it to build up in the lungs.   The most likely cause of this was a chromosomal abnormality, so we waited for the results of the amnio.

I spent another six days in hospital, as things with the baby stabilized and her blood flow through the cord returned to normal levels.   I was scanned each day, and each day, I was grateful that we had gotten that little bit further with the pregnancy. For the remainder of my pregnancy, we had weekly scans.   I drove around with a bag packed in the back of the car, and each time we met with the doctor, I expected that to be the day he told us he wanted to deliver the baby.   And each week, she was stable.   There was no more sign of fluid, and she was growing nicely.

At week 30, the amnio results came back. The baby was most definitely a girl.   And she had an extra copy of chromosome 21.

Even though we were high risk (1:57) and I felt like we were prepared for this result, it was still a shock.   I felt like I had been hit by a bus.   I kept telling myself that my world hadn't ended, it had just changed the angle it was rotating at. I phoned Dan, and after a minute's silence, he said "Well, now we know."   We were both stunned and unsure.

I later texted a very good friend, who told me that it would be ok, and that our baby would be perfect. Another good friend overseas told me that this baby would still bring joy and love to our lives, and would still be perfect.

Dan processed and came to terms with the karyotyping quicker than I did.   I felt like I was grieving.   I was upset that I wasn't getting the baby I thought I was, and for the future that I thought I had lost. I didn't know what the future was going to look like for us now.   I was scared of the challenges she would face, and I was scared that I wouldn't be good enough.   I didn't want this diagnosis, but I worried that the baby would think that I didn't want her, which was never the case.

As the weeks went on, my fears began to fade, and whilst every now and again, I would catch my older two children doing something, and wondered if this baby would do the same, I began to believe what my friends had been telling me.   It would be ok, it really would.

By week 33, both the doctor and the sonographers were having difficulties finding the stent.   But she was lying deep down on that side, and so it was assumed to still be there, as there were no signs of fluid building back up.

During week 34, we met with a neonatologist, who went through some likely scenarios. They were pretty certain we were in for a NICU stay, but it could be anything from weeks to months.   The best case scenario was that the chylothorax would resolve in utero; worst case, they would have to put a more permanent drain in once she was born whilst they waited for it to clear.   She would most likely need breathing support, which could be just through nasal prongs, but there was a possibility that she would need to be on a ventilator.   We had already toured the NICU at 29 weeks, and had some idea of what to expect. Both the neonatologist and our obstetrician were very keen for her to stay put as long as possible, as it would mean less complications associated with prematurity.

At our scan in week 35, the sonographer finally found the stent – our little monkey had managed to pull it out, and it was floating in the amniotic fluid, up near her face.   But the good news was that no fluid was building up so our doctor was happy for us to continue with the pregnancy. Just over 36 weeks along, I woke up in the night with what I thought was pre-labour. I was in denial that it was real labour right until I hit transition... which just happened to occur when I was sitting on my mum's toilet, an hour away from the main birthing hospital. Even then, I was still thinking I could drive in to get checked over, but it was quickly apparent that an ambulance was needed.

Because of the potential problems with the baby, we had a second ambulance meet us on route and follow behind us.   To begin with, the plan was to still take us to the city hospital, but after about ten minutes, a decision was made to divert to the nearest main hospital.   We would have been no more than a couple of minutes away from the hospital, when all of a sudden I couldn't fight my body any longer, and in one push, my waters broke, the head was out and then there was a baby lying on the bed.   The paramedic had no time to put down her notes and catch the baby -- all she could do was yell, "Pull over!!"

Charlotte Rose came out crying at 9:45 am.   She was quickly placed on my chest, and Dad got to cut the cord.   As we were so close to the hospital, I got to hold my baby for the two minute drive. We were met by a NICU team, who triaged her.   Whilst she was breathing, she still needed some oxygen support, so once they had done a quick check over, she was off to NICU, and I went to labour and delivery.

After I was checked over and had a shower, I was wheeled round in a wheelchair to meet our baby properly.   By then, she had been hooked up with all manner of wires and tubes. Charlotte spent just over a week in intensive care, on hi-flow oxygen to help her lungs inflate.   A chest x-ray showed remnants of fluid, but her chylothorax had cleared up in utero.   An echocardiogram showed that she had a PDA, but they weren't too concerned.

We quickly realized that in the NICU, it was often a case of a couple of steps forward, and then a step back.   But slowly, things began to improve.   By the middle of her second week, she was moved to special care, and by week three, she was taken off the oxygen support.   Her only issue then was with her feeding.   She wasn't tolerating her feeds very well, and she went backwards and forwards from hourly tube feeds to three hourly, back to hourly, and back to profuser feeds.   But by the end of week three, the doctors decided to challenge her with three hourly feeds, and she began to tolerate them more.   Her growth was still an issue, as was establishing suck feeds.

By week four, she was well enough to come home, but her feeding continued to be an issue.   A doctor mentioned the possibility of her coming home on a naso-gastric tube, and I clutched that idea, asking the doctors every day if we could do that.

In the end, she spent 30 days in the NICU. Given what we had been told during our pregnancy, she far exceeded all of our expectations, and we really feel like we had the best possible outcome. All the same, an extended NICU stay really hurts the whole family. The day I was discharged and drove home without my baby, I sobbed for what seemed like hours. And each day, I would walk out of the hospital with the nagging feeling I had forgotten something. I was exhausted from the drive, pumping three times hourly and trying to continue a normal life for our other two children. I was torn, because I couldn't not go to the hospital daily, but I felt guilty for not being at home with the other two. My eldest daughter couldn't understand why our baby couldn't come home, and for the first week, didn't want to touch the baby.

At home, Charlotte seemed to be thriving on a mix of breastfeeds and NG tube feeds. But at eight weeks old, she was losing weight, and starting to work harder at breathing. She was readmitted to the NICU, and then transferred to the PICU, where she was diagnosed with laryngeal-tracheal malacia, and this was causing her breathing issues. It's something that she will grow out of eventually, and in the meantime, she is on home oxygen support to ensure she's getting enough oxygen through her airways.

Being the youngest of three and having compromised airways means she's since had three hospital admissions for bronchiolitis. A cold for the other kids has seen her end up in the PICU. She's also still got the NG tube, as it's been a struggle to get the weight on her, and to keep it on. The constant worry about keeping her out of the hospital, and getting her to grow has been the hardest thing for me to deal with. The older children don't give the tubes a second thought these days, and have adjusted to Charlotte and I being in hospital on a monthly basis. It's just the way of life for us right now. But I will be so happy to lose the NG tube and the oxygen. And I'm hoping that spring will mean no more illnesses.

These days, Charlotte having Down syndrome doesn't really factor into things. We're just starting therapy, and attend an early intervention play group. For us, her health issues have overridden our initial reaction to the diagnosis. When we were faced with a sick baby, we stopped caring about that extra chromosome. We just wanted her to be born as healthy as she could. At times, I do wonder if we've dealt with her diagnosis properly, or whether we've filed it away in the too hard basket whilst we focus on her health. But I don't think that is the case. We're ok with the diagnosis. It's part of who she is. But so is her determination and resilience, and her gorgeous smiles and attention-seeking personality. She is perfect just as she is.

Charlotte is almost 6 months and things are getting easier. She lost the NG tube last week and is going beautifully on the bottle. She's had her first taste of carrots and is loving them! Her weight gain has been slow but she's finally got some gorgeous fat rolls, and is finally out of newborn nappies. She loves attention, and gets quite vocal if she feels she is ignored. Her smile is beautiful and she gets quite chatty. She's beginning to roll, and trying to sit up unaided. She is totally adored by the whole family, and by most people who know her. At times, the future still scares me, but then I remind myself to forget about what may happen, and focus on what is happening now. Life with Charlotte is beautiful and awesome.

~ Samantha, Charlotte's Mom; 31; South Australia

{Kate}

I remember being pregnant the first time with my son. Every time I went in for an ultrasound, I was terrified -- terrified in the beginning that there wouldn't be a heartbeat, terrified later on that there would be something wrong with the baby. Every ultrasound went off without a hitch. I was delighted when he was born absolutely perfect.

My husband and I were ecstatic when, seven months after our son was born, we found out we were expecting our second little miracle. I was given the choice to follow with the same perinatalologist that I had with my son. I decided I would have all the prenatal testing offered, the same that I did the first time. I remember going for our nuchal translucency screen in the first trimester. It was so different this time, because I had such a sense of calmness and excitement to see our baby. That appointment went great, and the doctor said our baby was doing wonderful. A few weeks later, my husband and I went back at 15 weeks for our second trimester genetic screening. We were so excited for the possibility to potentially tell the gender. We kept prodding at the tech to tell us if our son would have a brother or sister. I remember watching her face really focusing and concentrating. She told us she was

done with the scan and was going to grab the doctor to come in and speak with us, like usual, to go over the results. When the doctor came in, her face was solemn. She proceeded to tell us that there were a couple of abnormalities viewed on the scan. The baby had an echogenic intracardiac focus, the bowel was also echogenic, and lastly and most concerning to the doctor, was that the amnion had not fused to the uterus. This apparently is done during the first trimester, and I was well beyond that. I asked the doctor what this indicated for our baby. She had replied that the baby likely had a chromosomal abnormality, and was in danger of not surviving the pregnancy. The unfused amnion posed a grave threat, and it was likely that the pregnancy would not go full term. I was at risk for miscarriage at anytime. We had my blood drawn that day to check my hormone levels for the second part of our sequential screening. I remember going home and crying in the car with my husband. He was trying to be positive and kept saying we knew nothing for sure and we couldn't stress.

We talked a lot over the next couple days while waiting for the blood work. I was terrified of a Trisomy 18 diagnosis. I kept saying that Trisomy 21 was fine with me. "I can do Down Syndrome," I told my mom. "My baby will laugh, learn and love. I can handle that. I can't handle my baby dying inside me or right after birth." I remember spending those days feeling like my world was knocked upside down. I felt like God was punishing me for being too greedy and wanting a baby so soon after we had our son, as he was only ten months old. My biggest concern was losing the pregnancy and miscarrying more than receiving a diagnosis.

The blood results came back and the doctor called me at home. She said she had the results of the sequential screening, and it came back positive for having a baby at high risk for having Trisomy 21. I remember I let out a sigh of relief. The doctor was unsure of my response. I explained to her that I never had a fear of Down syndrome. I'm pretty sure I'm the only patient who ever responded to the news that way to her. We were given 1:16 odds of having a baby with Down syndrome. That day, I knew in my heart our baby would be born with Down syndrome.

We went back and had an amnio at 16 weeks. The results came back that our baby girl would be born with Down Syndrome. I can say that I was not surprised by the results, and felt ready to hear them out loud, as I had already known this in my heart for some time. I spent hours and days prepping for that moment by reading and learning as much as I could about Down Syndrome.

I spent plenty of time on BabyCenter and downsyndromepregnancy.org. I also read books, blogs and websites. I joined our local Down syndrome support group. There, I met so many women who have now become dear friends. I accepted her diagnosis and saw it as an opportunity to learn. I can honestly say that I was at peace with her diagnosis shortly after receiving it. I was able to enjoy my pregnancy.

Kate Gianna was born at 37 weeks and six days, just two days before her scheduled induction. She came out fast and furious at eight pounds, ten ounces, and 21 inches long. I remember the neonatologist coming in to see  her and whispering to me that her heart and lungs were great, but that she had Down syndrome. I remember thanking him and smiling, telling him I knew that she did. I cried tears of happiness as they put her on me for skin to skin. I cried as I proclaimed to my husband how beautiful she was. I was, and still am, such a proud mommy of how my daughter was so truly perfect.

~ Janessa, Kate's mom, 30; Florida, United States

{Conner}

As I sit here and think back on our diagnosis, it seems just like yesterday... but at the same time, it seems like it was a lifetime ago. It all started out as a very normal ultrasound at twenty weeks -- or at least, I thought it was normal. Nothing was said, and there was no indication from the tech that they noticed anything wrong. So after the ultrasound, we went home and put our picture on the refrigerator. The excitement was growing in the home. Here comes our precious baby number two! I guess when I look back I should have followed my motherly intuition, because from the moment I thought I was pregnant, I had this feeling something was not quite right. I kept telling myself that it was just because I was so sick the first sixteen weeks, but I just couldn't shake this feeling that there was more.

Two weeks later, we were scheduled for our monthly visit to the obstetrician. I had written down the wrong day on the calendar, and so in the end, we had to reschedule for the next day with a doctor we had never seen before. I was upset that I would not get to see my doctor, but I figured it was just a regular appointment, where we would hear the heartbeat, do a measurement and be sent on our way. When we arrived, the doctor walked in, and very quickly our appointment turned scary. First, he said that he tried to call us two weeks ago but they mustn't have the right number, so I was frustrated. He very quickly said that they saw a few things on the ultrasound that appeared to indicate that our child may have Down syndrome. My heart sank. What did this mean for us? I was so confused and worried. He scheduled us for a level two ultrasound the following week to check the baby again.

He said we had to hurry, because I was twenty-two weeks pregnant and we are running out of time to make any decisions. What did he mean? What would I do? I knew from day one that this baby was meant to be. That didn't mean I didn't have any worries. Would we be able to handle everything we would have to deal with? What about our baby's future? How would I care for this baby? How would we care for him as an adult? Both my husband and I are older parents, and we do not have much family support. I was so terrified he would be alone when we were gone. How would this affect our older son? I wanted him to have a sibling that he could grow with, and now he would have extra burdens of taking care of his sibling. I kept thinking, what did I do?

For the next week I lived in denial. I went about my business, and I was convinced that the ultrasound tech was wrong... until the day I drove the hour and half to get my second ultrasound. That was such a sad and lonely drive all by myself, because my husband had to stay home with our son. I remember laying there, watching the ultrasound and seeing this little baby just kicking and moving so much in my belly. I kept wondering how something so perfect could be so wrong. Afterwards, the doctor quickly came in, and said again they couldn't see a nasal bone, and there were possible kidney issues. My husband and I had talked about it ahead of time, and decided if they again saw soft markers, we would go ahead and do the amniocentesis. If our baby would have health issues, I wanted to know and prepare as much as I could for his delivery. My stomach was in knots, but I never cried. Not yet.

It was exactly one week later that we got the phone call. That phone call changed my life forever. It was so early, and I thought I heard my phone ring, but by the time I found my phone I had missed the call. I waited a few minutes, got my son settled with breakfast, and then called the doctor back. I remember thinking, why did I have to miss that appointment those several weeks ago? Now that OB that I didn't like was my doctor of record for the test, and he was the one calling me with results that could change the future I imagined. He quickly came to the phone, and was very abrupt. Who knew it would only take 30 seconds to change someone's life? He very quickly stated that he had the results and they were positive. WHAT? Next, I was asked if I had any questions. What?? I was in shock, and so overwhelmed. I quickly said no. I hung up the phone and just cried. It was the first time I cried since this all began, and all those questions started racing through my head again. Then the guilt came. "What did I do?" raced through my head. I quickly tried to call my husband, but he was in a meeting. I decided to proceed with my day as best as I could.

We had to take the dog to the vet 45 minutes away. I cried the whole way there. I again tried my husband, and received no answer. I needed someone, so I went to visit a woman that I had worked with for years. We were talking and catching up, when I quickly blurted out that we were expecting another child, and the baby would have Down syndrome. It was the first time I said those words. She quickly grabbed me and hugged me tight. All she said was that it would be okay, and that if anyone could take of this baby, I could. I needed someone to tell me I could do it. Later that afternoon, I finally got in touch with my husband, and had to tell him the news. There was silence on the phone, and it was deafening. Finally, after what seemed like forever, he just said, "I love you and we will get through this together."

As the day went on, I cried off and on all day. I would see another woman with a baby, and I would cry. I lay in bed all night and cried. I knew I loved this baby no matter what, but I worried for his well being. Would he be healthy? Would he be ok? What if I delivered and he was ill? The next day, I woke up, and I started to learn all I could. I needed to be prepared for the worst case scenario, but hope for best. In the early days of the diagnosis, I had a great amount of guilt, because I felt it was my fault due to my age. I thought I needed to do everything I could to be ready and prepared to take care of this little baby that was going to need me so much. At some point, I had to step away from the computer for a week, because it was all just too much information.

Some days, I was so sad that I just didn't want to deal with anything. Then I would be mad and have those "Why me?" days. I even worried that, with all this crying and stress, the baby would think I did not love him. Quickly, those days began to become less frequent. It started to become clear that I wasn't sad about the diagnosis, but over the fear of the unknown. I wasn't mad about the title of Down syndrome, but I was scared for this baby's well-being. What I realized in those early days is that through my anxiety and stress, I can't control everything in life -- but I can control how I handle the life that I was dealt. This little baby growing inside of me was the same little baby that I dreamt about. He was the same baby that I felt kicking in my belly each night. He was same baby that I would read to each day. He was the same baby that I would talk to about all the fun things we would do together as a family. With all that was going on I realized that this little baby was just like any other baby. He needed love, care, and someone to always be his protector, just like his brother before him. He is our blessing. Life may not always turn out the way we envision, but it turns out the way it should.

The rest of my pregnancy was filled with appointments and complications. I developed polyhydramios as I did with my first, which meant bi-weekly non-stress tests and weekly ultrasounds. Sometimes, though, God works in mysterious ways. There was a nurse at the hospital that would sit with me during my tests and talk to me. She told me about her sister who had Down syndrome, and what a blessing she was. It was so comforting to me at that time. As I reached my 32nd week, my amniotic fluid actually stabilized, so that was not a huge concern anymore. I also developed gestational diabetes with this pregnancy, so I had to poke my finger four times a day, and watch very carefully what I ate. They also had me go for a fetal echocardiogram to check the baby's heart, because I would be delivering in a small hospital. Overall, there were issues and obstacles during my pregnancy, but it was a little smoother than my first since I didn't have to be on bed rest for ten weeks this time.

It was December 16th, and we had two more days until we were scheduled to deliver our baby via c-section. I was looking forward to just relaxing, finishing my Christmas preparations, and just spending time with my other son, because I knew when the baby arrived, we would not have that one-on-one time anymore. As the morning was nearing an end, I began to feel uncomfortable, so I decided to go lie down and rest. Within two hours, I was having contractions every four to five minutes. Then I thought I would go rest in the tub for a few minutes -- within fifteen minutes, my contractions were coming every one to two minutes. That is when the nerves and fear started to come again. We called our friends to watch our son. It took them 45 minutes to get here. Once we got to the hospital, we had to wait for the on call doctor because our regular doctor was out of town. I was so scared, because I depended on my doctor so much, and he was always able to calm me down. Again, God works in mysterious ways. The doctor that came to deliver my son had a thirteen-month-old little girl with Down syndrome at home. She was such a blessing to me those first few weeks. I remember her and I crying in her office about the overwhelming feeling and fear that comes with little babies in the beginning. It was a long and painful day, but my beautiful son was born 7:21pm via c-section, and he was just precious.

I remember lying in the operating room, just waiting to hear that cry. Once he cried, and the pediatrician came over to me to let me know me was ok, I could finally breathe again. When I got to hold him for the first time, it was amazing. He was just beautiful. When he looked at me for the first time, I felt like he could touch my soul. There is just something about those blue eyes that made me feel such peace. We spent four days in the hospital. We were very fortunate that we did not have to spend any time in the NICU. Conner had a hard time keeping his temperature up, so we spent a lot of time under the lights. They discovered that I had an infection, so they started me on antibiotics, along with Conner just as a precaution.

Our big concern was his feeding. I could not get him to latch. We tried and tried, but we would eventually go to the bottle. When I think back on that time, I felt alone, scared, and anxious. I was scared for the unknown, anxious about the future, and lonely because I spent most of that time in hospital alone. My husband had to stay with our older son at home. I am so thankful for the nurses at the hospital. They were a true godsend, and were helpful, especially those first few days.

The first few weeks were consumed with trying to get him to gain weight. Conner had lost almost a pound before we left the hospital. I was still trying to breastfeed, and he was just not getting enough milk. We spend the first three weeks of his life going to the doctor every few days to check him. We tried several combinations of breastfeeding, pumping and bottle feeding. We realized that even after 45 minutes of breastfeeding, he only got 15ml of milk. He was just too tired, and his suck was so weak, that he was not able to get milk. I finally decided to exclusively pump and bottle feed. That has been my biggest struggle and stressor, because it is so time-consuming and overwhelming, especially with a three-year-old at home also. I am proud to say that I am still pumping, and it has gotten easier, but it is still quite annoying at times.

I feel like we have been fortunate that Conner has had some minor health issues, but overall, we have been very lucky. After we got his weight stabilized, we were able to take a moment to relax. Conner was born with low muscle tone, which has affected things such as gross motor development, and even contributed to constipation issues. At our eight week appointment, our doctor noticed a heart murmur, so we were referred for another echocardiogram. Those results showed that his murmur that should resolve itself, so we wouldn't need to check it again until he turns three. Around twelve weeks, we began to think Conner was not hearing well. We scheduled an appointment with an ENT. After two attempts, we were able to get a good ABR. We discovered Conner has perfect hearing in his right ear, and severe hearing loss in his left. The whole process took several months, but we have been fitted for and received our new hearing aid. Although hearing problems are common in kids with Down syndrome, the doctors believe that his hearing loss may be the result of an infection I had before his birth, and the preventive antibiotic they put him on at the hospital. This was another time in which my guilt flooded my thoughts for a few days. Conner continues to have feeding issues that we are working through. Starting solids has been a struggle, but he is slowly beginning to grasp the concept, and we are very proud. He started early intervention at eight weeks, and has slowly begun to increase his therapies over the months. We have physical therapy, occupational therapy, speech therapy, and a feeding specialist. I think my biggest struggle has been to juggle the appointments and therapies. On the bright side, this whole process has helped me become more structured and organized, which I have wanted to do for years. At Conner's six month appointment, we had his thyroid and eyes checked, and all is well. Overall, I am happy with how things are going, and feel very proud of my little man and how hard he works each day.

As I sit here writing this, I have realized it has been almost one year since our diagnosis. What a difference a year makes. I do know now looking back how truly lucky I am to be blessed with my little boy. There are still days when those fears and worries overwhelm me, but they are becoming less and less over time. Now our days are filled with pride and love for a little boy who exceeds my expectations every day. When I see that smile, or hear that laughter, my heart melts. When I see him conquer a milestone that I took for granted with my first child, I am overwhelmed with pride. I know in the future there will be struggles and fear, but I know we will get through it. I still have fear for the future, for his health, and for his life when we are gone, but it is my job to prepare him and us for all the possibilities that could arise.

What I know is Conner has taught me to look at life in a new way. Small accomplishments are sometimes the best things. He has shown me a new love, and he is teaching me patience. All good things come to those who wait. When we hurry, we miss those small things that many take for granted. He is showing me that I am stronger than I thought, and I can handle more than I imagined. I need that strength to be his advocate, so he has the most rewarding life possible. I have many dreams for him and his future, and I believe with my help and the help of other parents, our children can accomplish whatever they want. We can teach society all the things that our children can offer. Finally, no matter what the future holds Conner has been a true blessing, and he is truly loved by his mom, dad and his big brother. We could not imagine our lives without him.

Today, Conner is a happy and healthy eight month old little boy.   He is working on sitting unassisted, and learning to crawl. Learning how to eat solids is a work in progress. Each day, he seems to make more and more strides in these areas. We are so very proud of him and how hard he works. His older brother just loves him to pieces, and it has been such joys watching the love   between the two of them   flourish. It has been a year since our diagnosis, and it has been hard at times, but I would not trade it for the world. He has brought us so much   love and happiness. His smile just melts my heart. I can't wait to see what a wonderful man my little boy will become, all that he will accomplish, and the love he will bring to others.

~ Kari, Conner's mom, 39 Washington, United States

{Felix}

After much discussion, and changing our minds at least a dozen times, we decided in November 2009 to try for our eighth baby, and our first together. We figured that if it happened, it happened. I was a month away from turning 39, and my husband was 30 years old.

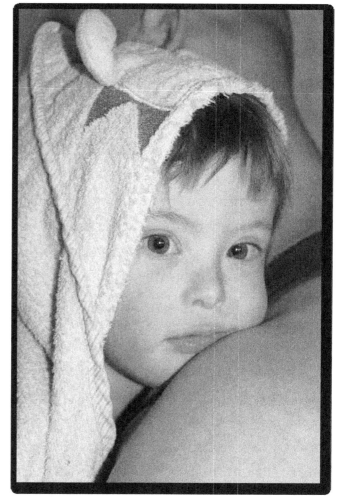

On February 16, 2010, those two pink lines appeared to confirm that we were having a baby. I was five weeks pregnant. We were extremely happy to know that, in late October, we would welcome the newest member of our family into the world.

The early part of my pregnancy was stressful. I bled off and on quite a bit, and on my husband's birthday, when I was about eight weeks pregnant, I thought for sure we had lost the baby. We went up to the hospital to have it checked out, and cried tears of joy when we saw that tiny little heart beating strongly. My husband still says it was the best birthday gift ever. The bleeding continued for several weeks, but another scan at 12 weeks pregnant again showed that strong little heart chugging along beautifully. This baby wasn't going anywhere!

At exactly 19 weeks and 2 days, we excitedly headed to the hospital to have our routine morphology ultrasound. We had 95% decided to find out the sex of our baby, but in the end, the decision was made for us when the first thing we saw on the scan was a little something extra between the legs. We were having a boy!

The scan was going so well. There was that little heart again, thumping away, ten fingers, ten toes, a little round tummy, and wriggling limbs. And there was that face... that beautiful little face! He was sucking his thumb and opening and shutting his mouth. He was just perfect.

Up until that point, the sonographer had been very chatty. She suddenly went quiet as she looked at his little face over and over again. My stomach sunk. There was something wrong. My baby was going to die. It was all I could do to keep from bursting into tears. It was then I asked, "Is everything OK?" She made a fairly evasive comment about needing to just check something with the radiologist, and then left the room.

It was then I cried. I told my husband there was something wrong. They never say they need to check something if everything is fine. I told him that if the radiologist came back in with her, then we'd know there was something wrong. And of course, the radiologist came back in with her. My husband asked what was wrong. The radiologist was not forthcoming, but said she just wanted to check a few things again. And there was his face... that gorgeous little face again.

We waited for what seemed like ages while things were checked, and then the radiologist turned to us. She said she was concerned about a couple of things. Our baby did not have a nasal bone, hence all the checking of his face. That meant nothing to us. All I could think was that our baby was going to die. "I think your baby has Down Syndrome", she said. I cannot explain the feeling of relief that washed over me. Here I was thinking our baby would not live, and all he had was Down syndrome! We could handle that! My husband shocked the radiologist by saying, "Is that all?" She told us she didn't think we understood what she was saying, but we assured her we did. We were in love with our baby from the first time we saw those two pink lines. Him having Down syndrome did not change that one little bit.

We were stuck sitting in a room being 'counselled' by a doctor from the hospital for a couple of hours. His recommendation was to have an amniocentisis with a view to termination if the results came back positive. He reinforced every negative stereotype about people with Down syndrome that I had ever heard of. It was all negative information, and the pressure to terminate was intense.

We repeated to him several times that if our baby had Down syndrome, we were OK with that. We did not want an amnio, which carries a small risk of miscarriage. We were happy to continue with the pregnancy, and love our baby regardless of the outcome. He did not want to listen, so we asked if we could leave. After making a booking for a follow-up ultrasound at 25 weeks pregnant, we left.

We had discussed Down syndrome before I even got pregnant. I was 39 years old, and at an increased risk due to my age. Neither of us had an issue with that possibility. Looking back, I remember reading a lot about Down syndrome during those first few months of pregnancy. Maybe it was a mother' instinct.

Once we got home, we read all we could find about Down syndrome, and ordered some books for us and the kids. We also contacted the Down Syndrome Society, who were a wonderful help with information. Our family was incredibly supportive, and we all looked forward to meeting our little guy... even more so than before!

What happened next crushed us.

We returned for our 25 week scan excited to see our little man once again. We enjoyed watching him wriggling about on the screen. He was an incredibly active baby and barely ever stopped moving. After the scan, we went to see our obstetrician for a check up. He looked through the report from the scan, looked at us and said, "I suppose you were told this is not going to end happily?" I was a little confused. I told him we were aware that he probably had Down syndrome, but we were happy with that, and not sad at all. He replied, "No, your baby has hydrocephalus -- fluid on the brain. He may not survive the pregnancy, and if he does, possibly not for long after that." I felt a rush of emotion, and was totally devastated. Our baby may not live after all. This active, wriggling baby moving inside of me was very ill. I found it hard to believe.

We told him that no matter what happened, all we wanted was to hold our baby in our arms. He assured us that he would do everything he could for our baby to be born alive. We were to have scans every two weeks to measure the ventricles in his brain and the size of his head, which was already bigger than normal due to the fluid. We left the hospital with heavy hearts, and shut ourselves away from the world for a couple of weeks to grieve for our beautiful baby.

Over the coming weeks, the fluid levels in his brain stayed the same: still dangerously high, but no worse. We allowed ourselves a little glimmer of hope with each passing day, and in the last couple of months, started to get a bit excited. Maybe everything would be OK.

On September 29, at 36 weeks pregnant, I rolled over in bed, and my waters broke. I woke up my husband, who nervously drove me to the local hospital. We were then air-lifted by the Royal Flying Doctor Service to the city to have our baby. My pregnancy was considered high risk, and the paediatric neurosurgeon, obstetrician and others who were reviewing my pregnancy were all on call there in case of any problems.

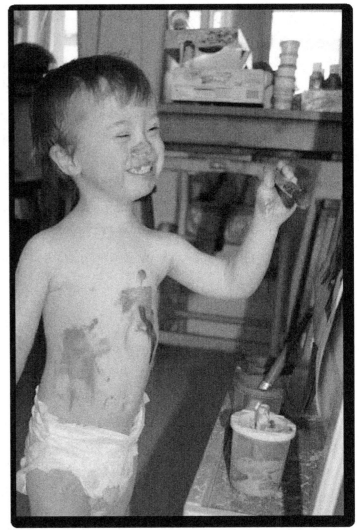

My labor only lasted four hours, and all things considered, was quite easy. The time came to push, at which time my husband got the giggles... nerves, I think. He and I both reached down, grabbed our baby under each arm, and lifted him onto my belly. Our precious little guy! I took one look at his little face and said, "Yep...he's got Down's, and he's perfect!" Our little man was alive. He was alive, and he was healthy, and to look into his eyes was one of the most overwhelming moments of my life.

We named him Felix Sawyer. He was 3110 grams (7lb 1oz), which was not bad for four weeks early. He was 47cm long, and his head measured 33.5cm.

Apart from having poor muscle tone, which is common in people with Down syndrome, he was completely healthy. He needed to be tube fed for a couple of days until he was strong enough to feed, partly because he was early, but fed like a champion after that. A brain scan the next day came back NAD (Nil Abnormality Detected). Even the paediatrician in neonatal said he was a miracle. He told us that the name Felix means 'lucky'.

After four days, we were able to bring Felix home to begin our lives together. He is the source of so much happiness to us and to others. We are thankful every day to have him as part of our family.

~ Kylie, Felix's mum; 39; Australia

Blogging @ http://felixsmum.blogspot.com.au/

{Luke}

I held on tightly and pushed my head in between my hands as I gripped the steering wheel of my parked car. I was sobbing and my body was shaking. I couldn't catch my breath. My eyes were pouring tears, and they stung from the salt. Just moments ago, I'd been in the store buying supplies for my son's first birthday party tomorrow afternoon.

While I was shopping, I'd seen two brothers chasing each other, playing. I wondered if my boys would play like that some day? I managed to maintain my composure, but when I was checking out, I caught a glimpse of a man with a disability greeting

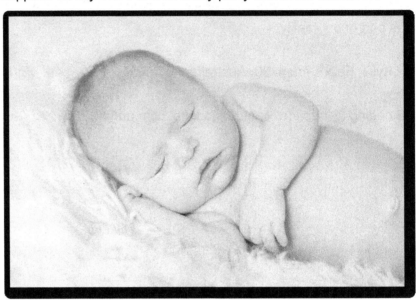

shoppers as they entered, and it was too much. Would my son be able to hold a job some day? I completely lost it. The cashier didn't know what to do with me. I shoved my money at her, exited the store amidst the heat and humidity of mid-August, and ran to my car.

I was 21 weeks into my second pregnancy, and I'd gotten the call earlier that morning. Our doctor contacted me to let me know that the results of our MaterniT21 test had come back "consistent with Down syndrome". We'd been waiting seven days for the phone call; however, when I saw the caller ID that morning list the name of my doctor, I still felt butterflies in the pit of my stomach. My husband, Dustin, and I had spent the last week preparing for this moment. The test was just a formality; our doctor had already found so many indicators.

It all started with my choosing to complete the quad marker screening, a blood test that is drawn at 12 and again at 18 weeks gestation to look for neural tube defects and genetic abnormalities. Quite honestly, I hadn't put much thought into agreeing to do the blood draw. I'd completed it during my first pregnancy just a year ago, and the assurance that came along with knowing my baby was normal and healthy felt great. I was looking forward to having the same results this time around, too. My results came back normal for the quad marker at 12 weeks. Our next "big" appointment was our anatomy scan at 18 weeks gestation. We learned that we were having another boy, and I spent the remainder of our ultrasound dreaming about how, with our boys only being 16 months apart in age, they would play sports together and rough house on the living room floor. I thought about how since they'd only be one grade apart, they'd even share a junior/senior prom!

"Ma'am, are you sure about your dates?" The ultrasound technician, Roger, broke me away from my thoughts. He explained that the baby's heart didn't seem mature enough to be 18 weeks yet, and that he thought it looked to be closer to 17 weeks. I told him I was sure of when I became pregnant, and I was confident that I was 18 weeks along. He reminded us that a lot of development takes place even in a day's time, and that he'd like for us to come back a week later when the baby was more developed, so he could get another look. Before we left the clinic, I took a seat in the oversized green vinyl chair, and made small talk with the phlebotomist as she drew my blood for the quad marker follow-up test. That was a Friday. I spent the next three days dreaming about the future in store for the wonderful family Dustin and I were creating.

On Monday afternoon, just before leaving work, I had a call from my doctor. She was new at my clinic, and for the first time in my life, I had a doctor who appeared to be about my age instead of someone gray, wrinkled, and full of experience. Nonetheless, she seemed confident. Although I wasn't an established patient of hers, when I went into labor with my older son, Matthew, she was on call, and stuck with me for the first 15 hours. Even after she went off call, she came to my room to let me know that she'd be around doing paperwork for a few more hours, and if the baby were to come during that time, she was going to see my delivery through since we'd been together all night. In the end, Matthew didn't come quickly enough, and I ended up with one of her partners for my c-section. Because of her awesome bedside manner, I sought her out for my follow-up care, and when I learned that baby number two was on the way, I wouldn't have considered anyone else. On that Monday afternoon, she was calling to let me know that the results of my quad marker had come back abnormal, showing a 1:85 chance for Down syndrome. As my mind began reeling, she reminded me that the screening was known to show a high rate of false positives, and that I shouldn't get too concerned yet; however, she was recommending that I come in later in the week to see a maternal-fetal medicine (MFM) specialist who had an opening on Thursday for what she called a level two ultrasound.

We had a different ultrasound technician later that week. She was young and blonde, and told me that she'd spend the first 30 minutes or so completing the ultrasound, and when she was finished, the MFM or perinatologist, as I later learned was the appropriate title, would come in to look at the pictures she'd taken. She told me that together, they'd take more pictures, and that he'd likely narrate to me as they surveyed the baby. The monitor was connected to a wall-mounted, flat screen TV and we could watch as they examined our little guy. When the perinatologist came in, he was polite and kind, but I was quick to notice that he didn't narrate. He concentrated hard on the monitor, asking the technician to review some of the baby's body parts two and three times. When they were finished, the technician left the room and the doctor spun his stool around to the counter behind him, found a piece of scrap paper and began drawing. Dustin and I exchanged a look. We knew that if he needed to draw a diagram, there must be very important news coming our way.

When he spun back around, I noticed that the diagram was of a heart. Somehow, even though our anatomy scan had been less than a week earlier, I didn't make the connection of the immature heart that the tech had mentioned and the diagram in front of me now. The words started as a blur, but eventually, it sunk in that he believed that our baby had a congenital heart defect known as Atrioventricular Canal Defect, or AV Canal for short. He showed us on his pencil-drawn diagram that there appeared to be a hole between the bottom two chambers of the baby's heart, known as a VSD or Ventricular Septal Defect, and another hole across the upper chambers, known as an ASD or Atrial Septal Defect. This man, a doctor who would become a very important figure in my life, also shared that our baby had a shortened femur and a six millimeter thickness of skin on the back of his neck, which, when combined the with heart defect and the abnormal quad marker screening results, led him to believe that our baby had Down syndrome. I didn't cry right away -- honestly, I didn't really know what to think. I pushed the doctor to tell us what he believed to be the "odds" of our baby having Down syndrome based upon the new findings, and he shared that although the quad marker had indicated 1:85, he believed our odds were actually higher than 1:2. Before leaving, we made a follow up appointment to see him the following week to complete an amniocentesis.

That night, my regular obstetrician called me from her home. I was struck that she trusted me with her personal cell phone number. We talked for about an hour, and during that time, she solidified my trust and respect for her as one of my medical providers. We talked about what it meant to have a diagnosis of Down syndrome. We talked about the emotions that were going around in my head. We even talked about abortion. I was confident that I could never terminate the life of another, especially a being who was growing inside my own body, but at the time, it felt important for me to be educated about the option, and the physical process of terminating a pregnancy this far into the baby's development.

The day came for us to complete the amniocentesis, and I was terrified about the possibility of miscarriage related to the amnio. We'd had a hard time conceiving our first child, and I couldn't imagine what it would be like to lose this pregnancy, especially due to us making the choice to complete the procedure. The nurse had me sign the paperwork that stated I understood the associated risks, and she got me prepped so I was ready for the amnio when the doctor entered our room. When he joined us, however, we validated that we were not going to terminate based upon the results, and because of that, he suggested that we do the MaterniT21 test in its place, which was a simple blood draw instead of an invasive procedure.

We'd waited seven days for the results, and they arrived the morning before we were set to celebrate Matthew's first birthday. We didn't want the news to take over Matthew's special day, so we kept it to ourselves, sharing with just a few important people when the party was over. In addition to keeping appointments with our perinatologist, we also began seeing a pediatric cardiologist, who we'd follow with for the remainder of the pregnancy to monitor baby's heart as it developed. Additionally, we'd meet with medical genetic counselors to learn more about Down syndrome. I spent a lot of time researching, trying to learn what to expect. Eventually, we accepted our diagnosis. As I continued to feel baby stretch, kick and roll inside my belly, I soon regained excitement about the pregnancy, and once again, became eager to meet our baby boy!

My official due date was January 9th, 2013, but because I was having a repeat cesarean, my scheduled delivery date was the morning of January 2nd, 2013. I had spent the month of December preparing for Christmas with our sweet Matthew, while also getting ready for baby's arrival. In anticipation of baby, I was completing tasks like sterilizing my nursing supplies, and working on getting our nursery together in the final few weeks of the pregnancy. I was thoroughly surprised when I went into active labor early on the morning on December 22nd, 2012. The delivery went off without a hitch, and my perinatologist even came in on his day off to deliver me. Luke William arrived at 11:44 AM, and weighed in at six pounds, eight ounces, was 18 3/4 inches long, and had a head circumference of 12 inches. His APGARs were eight and nine. The nurses cleaned him up and allowed my husband to hold him, while I lovingly gazed on as my doctor continued with the surgery. We snapped a few photos, and Luke was taken to the NICU, where he was evaluated by the cardiology team soon after birth.

The next time I saw Luke, I was being wheeled into the NICU on my way from recovery to the general nursing floor. The nurses pushed my bed in next to Luke's isolette and the first thing I saw were his feet. During the delivery, as our doctor lifted Luke from my body, I'd questioned if he could tell that the baby really had Down syndrome, and his response to me was, "It's often difficult to see physical signs immediately after birth, but rest assured that your son is beautiful."

Finally, I would get to see my baby! As my bed passed his, I saw those toes. As if it was my maternal instinct kicking in, I saw the first physical sign, a wide space between his big toe and the next one: the sandal gap. As I held him for the first time, and inspected each of those toes and his ten little fingers, and his nose, eyes and ears, my heart began to melt. The fears, anxieties and worries that I'd been carrying for the previous months began to fade. I was in love. Down syndrome didn't seem like such a big deal after all.

One of the hardest parts about Luke's arrival wasn't that he had Down syndrome; it was that he arrived just three days before Christmas, and because I'd had a c-section, I was to be admitted for four days, not to be released until the day after Christmas. As my pregnancy had been considered high risk due to Luke's heart defect, we delivered in a large hospital about an hour and a half from our hometown, which meant we hadn't seen Matthew since we put him to bed on the night of the 21st. I was aching to see my big boy, and was so sad that we wouldn't all be together for our first Christmas as a family of four. Not short of a miracle, the hospital actually granted us our wish that day, and made a special exception for us to allow our boys to meet in a private room for the first time on Christmas Day, 2012. Those short 35 minutes will forever stand out as one of the most precious memories of my lifetime.

That was nearly nine months ago, and our lives have changed as we've grown into a family with two small children, not unlike any other family in our circumstances. It may come as a surprise to some, but my life feels remarkably normal. We all play together, read books, sing and dance. My husband and I go to work, cook, clean and do laundry. We give the boys their baths before bed and dress them afterwards in cozy jammies. My life feels good! My perspective on Down syndrome has evolved from what it was just one year ago. I am not sad for Luke; he is who God designed him to be before we ever knew he was planned for our family. It's a privilege for all of us to be a part of his journey. I am not sad for Matthew; he has been blessed with a little brother – one that he adores. I know that he will learn lessons throughout his life; because of Luke, he will learn a love and compassion that many never experience. I am not sad for my husband, although I'm not sure he ever felt much sadness himself. He has been a rock and on many days, he's been a great source of strength for me. He is such a loving and involved father, we are all lucky to have him in our lives. I am most certainly no longer sad for myself; however, I'd be lying if I said there wasn't a short period of time when the reality of our situation rocked my world. I have become more than I ever knew I could be before Luke entered my life. The emotional obstacles I've overcome have led me to being more confident in my role as a mother, and also as a woman.

I don't believe all of our challenges are in the rear view yet. In fact, a big one is still looming in our future, as we are currently awaiting Luke's open heart surgery to repair his AV Canal. We are expecting the operation will take place sometime when he's around 15 months old. We know there are other medical issues that could present themselves, and obviously due to the presence of that 47th chromosome, we are expecting that Luke might have to work harder than others to achieve throughout his lifetime.

I'm not letting myself worry too much about what the future might bring. For now, I'm working hard to live in the present and enjoy our young family. When Luke smiles, his entire face lights up, and when I see him smile, my face lights up, too. The joy his soul emits is radiating and consuming, and it reaches me in a way that no other individual has

ever touched my heart. The thought of him not being a part of my world is devastating. While there was a time when I questioned if I was really cut out to be the mom of a child with special needs, I can now say with

complete honesty that I would go to the edge of the earth for both of my children – regardless of their "special child" or their "typical child" needs. Throughout this journey, I've been surprised by my own ability to stretch and grow and learn about a world that I'd never been exposed to before Luke. I am inspired in different ways by both my children, and I am confident they will make their own individual contributions to our world!

~ Kristin, Luke's mom; 31; Ohio, United States
Blogging @ www.luke-bringeroflight.blogspot.com

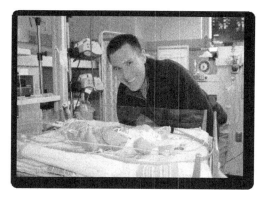

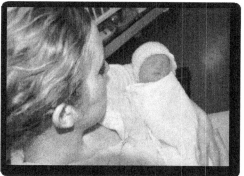

{In Due Time}

Waiting on a possible diagnosis

Waiting.

For some families, this was a conscious choice. For others, it did not become apparent that they had waited until their new little one had arrived. 'Waiting it out' is a term used by some to define parents who may have an increased risk of a chromosomal abnormality based on prenatal blood tests or ultrasounds, but then choose to not undergo any further testing for an official diagnosis. As a result of some tests, parents are given a risk assessment for some of the more common trisomies (13, 17 and 21, for example). Even with only a risk assessment to go on, many families grieve initially, very similar to those who have receive a confirmed prenatal diagnosis. There is an adjustment period that must take place. Eventually, grief subsides and hope is renewed as families begin to put things into perspective. For some, the wait can be torture. Waiting, wondering, not knowing, imagining how life could possibly change. Some may delve into research or join support groups and begin to prepare themselves for the birth and future life of a child with Down syndrome. For others, holding onto hope is enough for them to sail through the rest of their pregnancy with very little thought of the fact that they are, in fact, 'waiting it out.' Generally these families have come to peace with the idea of having a child with Down syndrome. The waiting game is hard, there is no way around it. Having so many unanswered questions, while at the same time experiencing the life of your unborn baby tossing and turning within your womb, can leave an expectant mother feeling overwhelmed and exhausted. Know, however, that when you finally give birth to your precious child, every second of the wait will have been worth it! To finally have answers ...

{Our Stories}

{Kayla}

At our 19 week ultrasound, we walked in feeling great. We were not planning on finding out the sex of our baby, so really this was just going to be a routine visit to count fingers and toes and make sure everything was developing properly. I walked into that room without a care in the world. It never even crossed my mind that they would find anything that would indicate there was something "wrong." Our little stinker was very cooperative;

she kept her back to us, so even if we wanted to know the sex I don't think we would have been able to find out. The ultrasound technician spent what felt like forever going over every little organ and feature. This was our first child, so I had no clue how long these things were supposed to take. When she was finished, she called the doctor in. He matter-of-factly looked right at us and told us that our baby had dilated kidneys. By itself, this was really no big deal. But this, combined with our quad screen results (which were also news to us at the time) showing a 1 in 99 chance that our baby could have Down syndrome was a slight "concern." At this very moment, I just froze. And then the tears started to flow. I was not prepared to hear those words. I had never even considered something like this happening to us. Things like this happened to other people, but not us. Even writing this now, I realize how ridiculous this sounds.

The doctor immediately said we needed to discuss having an amnio to confirm if our baby did in fact have Down syndrome. My husband and I both looked at each other and without hesitation declined. Even though it isn't huge, amnio carries a risk of miscarriage, and for us that was not a risk worth taking. I understand why people do it and I am not judging that decision at all, but for us, this was not an option.

I left this appointment in tears. I was terrified. I am pretty sure I cried for two straight days. Rich kept reassuring me that everything would work out the way it was supposed to, and that if this is what was meant for us, we would figure it out. A couple days later I finally stopped crying and moved on. Once I realized there was nothing I could do to change the circumstances, I let it go.

We had two subsequent ultrasounds to monitor the kidneys. In each ultrasound the kidneys kept looking better and were eventually within the normal range by our last ultrasound. The doctor's opinion was that we were, in his words, "good to go." Because we only had this one soft marker outside of the quad screen, I convinced myself that everything was going to be fine. A 1:99 chance is only a little more than one percent. I did continue to read the complications board on my *What to Expect When You're Expecting* app for anything related to dilated kidneys and Down syndrome for the rest of my pregnancy. I have no idea why. Maybe, I was curious or maybe I subconsciously knew. But I never did much research beyond that. I never even googled Down syndrome, other than the phrase "down syndrome and dilated kidneys." I never searched for pictures of babies with Down syndrome either. I still wonder about this. Was I protecting myself? Did I not believe that this was really going to happen to us? Did I not want to know and see what our possible future could look like? On June 5, 2012, I went to my weekly doctor's appointment. We decided to have my membranes stripped, which was one of the worst experiences of my life. I am pretty sure I will just let things occur naturally next time. We were told that there was a 50 percent chance that I would go into labor that night, but I was convinced that it wouldn't happen. So I went about my business, working a full day from home because I had terrible sciatic nerve pain and it was a serious struggle to walk, especially up and down stairs. I worked the full day, and really didn't think anything more about my membrane-stripping earlier that morning. On my husband's way home from work, he stopped to get me dinner. I scarfed down the three tacos he brought me like it was my job and, within minutes, the contractions started.

My contractions were painful, but I am such a rule-follower, I waited until they were exactly five minutes apart before we called the doctor. My husband told them the situation and they told him to bring me in. That car ride was the longest car ride of my life! There was nowhere to turn or move my body when I was having a contraction, so it was miserable. We finally arrived at the hospital 20 minutes later, even though it felt like five hours!

They immediately checked me and said that I was already seven centimeters. No wonder I was in so much pain! I wanted the epidural. Honestly, it was never a question. I knew I wanted it. I knew I needed it. I quickly progressed to 10 centimeters dilated, but she was not ready to come yet. They also said that I was too numb and I needed to wait so I was able to feel the push, but at least at this point I was relaxed. Several hours passed, and then they had to give me Pitocin to start my contractions again. This whole series of events was a bit bizarre, but eventually the doctor announced that it was time to deliver. I was going to meet my baby soon. I started pushing and pushing and pushing. I think we tried every position imaginable. I pushed for over three hours. I honestly didn't think I was going to be able to do it. I was convinced this baby must be at least 10 pounds, considering how difficult this was. I was also surprised that they eventually didn't say that I needed a Cesarean section because the whole thing was taking so long. They had more faith in me than I had in myself.

Finally, at 8:41 a.m. on June 6, 2012, our angel arrived. I was so exhausted from all of the pushing and crying, I couldn't even see my baby when they held her up. I just remember saying, "what is it? What is it? I can't see! I can't see!" My husband shouted through tears, "it's a girl! It's a girl!" I never knew how badly I wanted a baby girl until I heard those magical words. This was definitely a bonus for waiting to find out the sex. It was one of the most amazing experiences of my life. She was finally here, all 6 pounds, 7 ounces of her.

After I was told my baby was a girl, she was swept away to be checked out by the team of nurses. She did not cry right away and that worried me a little, but I was too exhausted to think much of it. I don't remember hearing a lot of talking or celebrating going on either. They finally handed me my baby so we could be skin to skin and it was the most amazing thing I have ever experienced. This little person was mine. God trusted *me* to be this perfect little angel's mother. She was very swollen, probably from all of the pushing. She also had a slight cone head from coming out sideways. People have asked me if I knew she had Down syndrome the first time I saw her, but I had no clue. Honestly, the thought never even crossed my mind for one second. She just looked like a perfect little swollen angel to me. Now of course when I look back at pictures, I wonder how could not have known.

My actual doctor didn't make it in time for our delivery, but he did make it a few minutes after, just in time to stitch me up. He was very quiet the whole time, which is not like him. He wasn't cheerful; I don't even know if he said congratulations. I am sure he did, but all I remember is a lot of silence. Looking back, I believe this was because the nurses told him their suspicions and he was probably sad for us.

At some point during this first day, the nurses informed my husband of their suspicions as well. I am still not quite sure why they didn't feel the need to wait and tell us together. They told him, because she was so swollen, there was a chance that they were wrong. He asked them to wait until some of the swelling went down to be sure before they told me. He didn't want me to get worked up for nothing. So I went along in my blissful state of new motherhood for another day before I had any clue.

On June 7, 2012, my world was forever changed. My husband came in the room with the doctor on duty. The doctor looked right at me, said hello and told me that she was pretty sure that my daughter had Down syndrome. At that moment, I just felt completely numb. I honestly don't even know if I replied. She kept talking, but everything she said sounded muffled. My mind was going in a million directions. I couldn't hear anything. I kept thinking that this was a dream, this could not be happening to us. Even days later, I still thought it was a dream. I do vaguely remember the doctor telling us that she too, had a daughter with Down syndrome and that, really, it was no big deal. At the time I was so distraught, that I remember thinking that it might not have been a big deal for her, but it was for me. I was not cut out for this sort of thing. And then the tears came, and they continued for a couple months.

Throughout our hospital stay, my husband was so strong. He's the type of person that can handle something like this, not me. I broke down crying every few minutes. I know now that most of my fears were all fears of the unknown. I really didn't know much about Down syndrome. Of course now I was kicking myself for not doing more research when I was pregnant. My husband kept reassuring me that we could do this and everything was going to be ok. Of course, I didn't believe him at the time.

The next couple of months were filled with many tears and many breakdowns, to the point where my husband thought I needed to seek help. I just couldn't keep it together. One minute I would be perfectly fine and then the next I would be on the floor crying. My mom even came back to stay with us to try to help keep me sane.

As I sit here now, staring at my beautiful daughter, I realize how ridiculous I acted. I wish so badly that I could go back and tell my old self, just how "ok" life was going to be. In

fact it would be so much better than "ok," better than I could ever imagine. However, I wouldn't change a thing. I feel like I had to experience those emotions to get to where I am now.

Now I am in a place of complete amazement that this is my life. That God trusted me to take care of this awesome little girl, who just turned one. This year has been filled with many ups and downs, but definitely more ups. I feel truly blessed. I look back and almost laugh at the things I was worried about. I do want Kayla to know this. Through all of the sadness and tears, it was never about you as a person. I loved you with every ounce of love I had. I was scared of the unknown, about your future. But my love for you never wavered, not for one second. I just wanted to protect you from all of the evil in this world.

This year Kayla has taught me so much about myself and about life. She has made me see the good and beauty in all people. She has taught me that every single life is precious and we should not spend one day on this Earth wasting it. She has given me a renewed relationship with God. I truly believe that this was my plan all along. When I was going on and on about how I couldn't do this and this sort of thing didn't happen to people like me, God knew better. He knew that this was the exact type of thing that happened to people like me, and I was one of the lucky ones. It may have taken me a little while to accept this new life. But now that I am here, I would not trade it for the world. Kayla has always been exactly the person she is supposed to be: the beautiful, fun-loving, sassy little angel that is absolutely amazing. I am not saying that I will not have hard days; there will be days when I worry about her future and days that I absolutely hate Down syndrome. But I accept this life and any challenges it brings, because this life brought me the most unbelievable gift: my sweet girl. Kayla, thank you for being you. I am so excited to watch you grow and see what you do with this one amazing life you have been given.

~ Amber, Kayla's mom; 33; Ohio, United States

{Angus}

I had fallen pregnant for the first time and I was thrilled at the honour of finally becoming a mum. I made an appointment to see my General Practitioner for confirmation; she said that due to my age, I should have first trimester blood screening. I knew no better so went ahead and had them done at 10 weeks. A few days later I arrived home message from my GP stating that I should call her back about my results. The worry set in as I wondered what the problem could be. When I called her, she told me that my baby had a 1:17 chance of being born with Down syndrome. She asked if I wanted a copy of these results and provided for me information on genetic counselling. I had also received a call from my newly-appointed obstetrician; at this point I felt like I had done something wrong! I wanted everyone to leave me alone let me enjoy my pregnancy. I wanted to put my hands over my ears and sing "La La La La La La La." My husband and I had discussed the procedures that had been offered to confirm diagnosis and we did not want to have these invasive tests done. If our child had Down syndrome then he/she would be welcomed into our loving home just like any child. But my head and heart were fighting a vicious battle. My head was saying no, your baby doesn't have Down syndrome. Everything will be OK. Since it was my first pregnancy, I felt like this couldn't be happening. "Why me?" I would ask through tears. Then the voice of reason would come in and remind me that I was going to be a beautiful mum to this child no matter the outcome. He/she would be a blessing and bring us much love.

Then it was time for our 12-week scan. There was the little blessing on the screen before me: strong heart, all organs good. Bub looked healthy and strong, so we carried on...

16 weeks through the pregnancy, we were on a plane to Paris. This trip was organised before we knew we were pregnant, but I was glad to get away for a few weeks. I remember visiting Notre Dame Cathedral and, despite the crowds, it filled me with a sense of peace. I believe in synchronicity and the universal laws and sometimes, a person just needs to let go. I lit a candle in the cathedral, sending a prayer to the spirits, ancestors, angels, or whoever wanted to listen to please let my baby be healthy and arrive safely. I purchased a small sculptured token of mother and child, a symbol I held onto throughout my pregnancy. On our return back to the Land of Oz, we had our 20-week scan booked for the next day. My husband and I started calling the radiologist "Dr. Charisma," as he truly lacked people skills. He measured the fluid behind the neck,

which was within normal range, and said that while our baby was small, everything seemed fine. The only soft marker was his little finger; the middle joint was missing, a condition known as clinodactyly. I was still hopeful that my prayer had been heard. Yes he/she was healthy, small, and had a bent little finger, but that didn't mean that anything was out of the ordinary. I spent the rest of my pregnancy watching the disk of the scan and looking at the beautiful little being. When you are told there is a possibility of having a baby with Trisomy 21, you start looking for things that are wrong, because people put it into your head that something is wrong. Back at the obstetrician's office we discussed that the baby was measuring small and that there was a possibility of aneuploidy, or chromosomal anomaly. Once again, I was asked if I wanted to have an amnio and I declined. "What if the baby has Down syndrome?" they asked. "Would you continue the pregnancy?" The answer was simple: YES.

I cried many times in the obstetrician's office. I always felt like there was something incredibly wrong with the baby due to the way medical staff would talk. I never thought for a second about terminating, as I felt this child deserves a full life, regardless of the perception everyone else had. Yes, my child may have Down syndrome, but he/she was a perfect combination of me and my husband's DNA. Shouldn't he/she be seen as an individual, just like a child with 46 chromosomes?

Weeks 33 and 34 I had weekly ultrasounds, as my obstetrician wanted to keep a close eye on growth, so we journeyed back to "Dr. Charisma" to learn that baby had not grown much. He told my husband and I to expect the worst, which upset me. "The worst" for me would be the death of my baby. I was also going into the hospital twice a week to have Cardiotocography monitoring, which was fine. My obstetrician wanted to transfer me to a larger hospital due to the slow growth and possibility of aneuploidy. We had an ultrasound, this time with a lovely woman who genuinely was concerned for the baby's well-being. She stated that this baby needed to come out, which left me truly worried and, yes, crying. Again.

We had a planned caesarean section at 36 weeks. When our beautiful baby boy finally came into the world, I immediately knew he had Down syndrome, but he was perfect. The Paediatrician noted a few markers, such as the single line across his left palm, the inward curve of his little finger, and the gap between his big and second toe. That evening the concerned Paediatrician told us the interim chromosome report stated that

Angus had Trisomy 21. Of course, I cried. I was totally exhausted. But regardless of this outcome, what I had been holding in my heart was true: I loved this beautiful child, no matter the number of chromosomes.

~ Angus's mum; 39; Australia

{Henry}

I was 31 years old when I found out I was finally going to be a mom. I had just married my significant other of ten years, and within two months, we were excitedly moving forward with our life together and starting our family. Shortly after our first ultrasound to confirm the pregnancy, I fell ill with the flu, including a severe fever. I was so worried about my little baby being affected by it, all I wanted was to hear that heartbeat again, to make sure everything was ok. We hadn't even chosen a care provider yet, as we were in the process of interviewing midwives for our planned home birth. I told one of the midwives that I was particularly concerned about the baby, so she offered to fax a referral for me to have another ultrasound.

I was just shy of 13 weeks when I went in for my appointment. I noticed it was a perinatologist office, but I didn't know what that meant. I was just focused on seeing and hearing my baby again so I could stop worrying. The nurse who performed my scan was very thorough and didn't say much. The time was long and the room was quiet. It didn't strike me as odd, though, I was simply happy to see my baby squirming up on the screen in front of me. Afterwards, she put me in a room and told me the doctor wanted to go over the results with me, and that he would be right in. I was mildly annoyed as I sat there waiting for well over 30 minutes. He came in and had a terribly morose look on his face, like someone had died. My heart sunk and my ears started to get hot. I heard him explain that my baby had a very large NT measurement, nearly 6mm, including a cystic hygroma, and that he didn't even need to do bloodwork. He had been "doing this for years" and could tell me with confidence that my baby had Down syndrome, if not some other guaranteed chromosomal anomaly. He looked at me with pity in his eyes and remarked, "not every pregnancy can be perfect and these things unfortunately do happen." He did not leave me with any literature or further recourse, other than to say, "you have a lot to discuss with your husband."

I felt like I had been punched in the stomach as I walked out to the car alone, ignoring my husband's text asking me how it all went. I was more worried about how I would be able to tell *him* when he got home from work. Would I be able to remember all the technical jargon? Would I be able to stay strong for him and not cry? From what I could piece together that day, they had performed a high level ultrasound on me because that's just what they do there at perinatologist offices. I had unknowingly and by chance walked into a high-risk office, only to find out that I was indeed, myself, a high-risk pregnancy. Google became my best friend and most hated enemy as I ravenously read about Down syndrome, cystic hygroma, and nuchal translucency measurements.

I grieved, my eyestrain giving way to sobbing and tears. Each day following was an eternity of obsessing at the computer. I kept staring at the little ultrasound profile, trying to discern if the doctor was correct. I kept a smile on my face to friends and family, but inside I was crushed.

I asked myself some very dark questions. Surely this was punishment for any number of sins I had committed in my lifetime. 'Why us?' was often echoed by an even lonelier call, 'Why *me*?' My husband and I each experienced a deep and personal struggle, but we also went through it and came through together, hands held. We knew we would move ahead with the pregnancy, forgoing the amnio, and just treating the pregnancy as if we knew for sure our baby had Down syndrome, as this was just prior to the breakthrough diagnostic tests now currently offered to expectant moms that carry no risk. I channelled my grief into research and educating myself. Intellectually I forged ahead, while emotionally I struggled, stagnated in anger. My own mother made it worse, upsetting me with her attempts to pray away the quasi-diagnosis. Any shred of lingering religious faith I had left as a young adult was obliterated with this experience, and it was an insult to me that she would unwittingly infer that my baby was in need of fixing. I told her that what I needed was *acceptance*.

Well, it was official; my pregnancy would not be rainbows and unicorns. I was now an outsider, a role that I actually felt pretty comfortable with in other contexts. All the same, it was hard to see other pregnant moms walking around without a care in the world when I had to wake up everyday and wonder whether my baby had Down syndrome or not, and if so, what other myriad of health issues would accompany it? It felt like never feeling the sun on my face for six months. I was walking in the dark. I wallowed in pity, lamenting that the joy of my first pregnancy had been stolen from me. My privately complicated pregnancy was made even more complicated because of my pre-existing mistrust of doctors and nurses.

I won't mince words, I detest the American medical system. Always have. I think it's a corrupt institution, right alongside the insurance companies they partner with. I have never believed [in] MDs, yet found myself feeling utterly at their mercy because of my high-risk pregnancy. I grieved the loss of my planned home birth just as hard if not more so than the actual diagnosis of my unborn child. You see, I did not yet know for certain my unborn child had Down syndrome, but I *did* know about the AVSD heart defect. We found out about it the same day we learned our son was a son. A guaranteed open heart surgery was our child's fate, and we hadn't even met him yet.

My husband and the midwife we had chosen together remained my rock as we navigated the uncertain course ahead. I "played both sides" so to speak, my midwife fully aware of the possible Down syndrome and confirmed heart defect, and my perinatologist aware that I was still seeing my midwife for prenatal care. We were told I would have to deliver at a hospital with a level III NICU or higher, as this is the standard protocol. As I filled out the registration paperwork, it felt as if I were being forced by another hand to sign a lifelong lease with the roommate from hell. The prospect of having to deal with doctors and nurses on an ongoing basis was honestly a living nightmare for me. I have since come to embrace it as my life's most ironically enticing challenge.

My son's prenatal echocardiograms were encouraging despite the hole in his heart, a beacon of hope to me already. I didn't know much about him, but I could tell he was strong, a fighter and defier of odds. When my water broke spontaneously at 37 weeks, I was rather caught off guard, but had a long labor in which to wrap my head around the fact that I was going to be a parent. I had focused so much on the potential special needs part, that I forgot I was going to be *just a mom*. Period. Hello and holy $&@#!

My son was born a healthy eight pounds with no signs of distress, my midwife and my husband by my side. I remember when my son was placed on my chest, I immediately tried to get a good look at his hands. I was looking for the simian crease. I couldn't get his palms open, because he was clutching my own fingers so tightly. I then gazed upon his face, finally meeting him, recognizing that he did have Down syndrome. It didn't upset me though, because I was completely overwhelmed with love for him. It was that simple. All the wondering and worrying that had been building up all those months sort of faded from my mind and became background noise; the loud crescendo of unconditional love struck my heart, as my son finally became real, something I could know and hold. I knew then that I was just like any other mom falling in love with her baby, and if there *were* differences that would reveal themselves with time, they could only challenge my character in the best possible ways.

His karyotype of Trisomy 21 was confirmed shortly thereafter in the hospital NICU, where he would ultimately stay for 20 days. It was the longest 20 days I have ever endured, and even more difficult than when I had lost my own father a decade earlier. The NICU ironically decided the cascade of minor setbacks that would keep him there: the usual jaundice due to being separated from me and not nursing those first critical hours, followed by low oxygen and then the beloved feeding challenges. I was helpless to fix the problems they created and forced to follow someone else's say-so regarding my child. It was awful.

Being discharged from that hospital after giving birth and having to drive home without my baby was excruciating. As if the postpartum period isn't hard enough on a new mom, I had to grieve all over again with the confirmed diagnosis and then go home without my child. That nasty sterile hospital would become our second home for a month as we drove back and forth in the Las Vegas heat every few hours to pump milk for him and hopefully get to hold him and love on him.

It was so heartbreaking to see him in that incubator, attached to monitors, alone beneath the bilirubin lights. I wanted to snuggle him so badly. Every cell in my body cried out to be able to do what mommies do. My son's own cardiologist had cleared him to go home when he was just two days old, but that evil NICU insisted he stay anyway. It was ridiculous. He looked like a giant diapered Buddha, ready to bust out of that plastic rectangle, sticking out like a sore thumb amongst all the itty bitty preemies surrounding him. They were not satisfied with the amount of milk he was ingesting, even though he lost very little weight, and was making consistent gains. His suckle was weak, so he was fed breast milk through a tube in his nose. As day followed day, I came to understand the archetype of "momma bear" much better.

At my friend's suggestion, I eventually sought assistance from the hospital's patient advocate, because I was not happy (gross understatement) with how long it was taking for my baby to be released to come home. Every hospital has someone with this job title, and they are there to help **you**, the paying customer.

Recalling it all stirs up the residual frustration of something I am so glad to be on the other side of. Going through that experience made me fully aware of the deep well of strength I had within myself, which was the silver lining of my son's NICU stay. I still have to deal with the medical concerns in my son's life as they come along, and will continue to do so within his best interests, but it's in much smaller, more tolerable doses now compared to those early months.

When our little man turned 10 months, we found out he was going to be a big brother (Gulp!). We had been going back and forth with the cardiologist about when his surgery would be scheduled, because what they originally believed to be a complete AVSD was

indeed a partial AV Canal, and did not require imminent surgery after all, which was great news. We could have waited another year or more to have his repair done, but we all decided it was best, emotions aside, to move ahead preemptively, because doing it with a new baby in tow would've been much harder logistically.

He had the hole in his heart repaired when he was 15 months old, which was very stressful, but it was stunning to witness just how resilient our little ones are! He charmed all the nurses during his recovery, and was back home in less than a week's time, completely unfazed. He was right back to cruising the furniture and had no setbacks in his development. He was doing great before his procedure, but we could tell he was doing even better afterwards in terms of growth! He is truly an amazing little guy, and I was very humbled by the swift success of his open heart surgery. I even caught myself liking his surgeon! Just a little bit…

My son is nearly two years old now, and our life is very "normal," whatever that means. I chase him around and try to keep him from incessantly sticking his fingers in baby brother's mouth! We didn't do any prenatal testing with our subsequent pregnancy either, because I wasn't scared of the possibility of more Down syndrome. It's all we knew until just recently and we feel very blessed. Not chosen. Not burdened. Not special. Just blessed.

~Leah, Henry's mom; 31; Nevada, United States

{Emily}

We chose to not do any genetic testing, as it wouldn't have changed the end result for us. We first learned that that something was amiss at our 20-week ultrasound; the doctor reported that Emily had a large kidney and we would need to have at least one more ultrasound to monitor the situation. We were told that this is common and it usually goes away before they are born; we assumed there was nothing to worry about. I had my repeat ultrasound right after Christmas, around one month before my due date.

After the ultrasound, I went to the exam room as usual, but I remember it taking a long time for the doctor to come in. I thought she must be busy with other patients or delivering a baby, but instead she was reviewing my ultrasound report. The doctor finally came into the exam room and starting discussing the ultrasound.   It's hard to recollect everything as the moment was such a blur, but I remember that the doctor told me she had a "double bubble," or a duodenal atresia, a common occurrence in babies with Down syndrome.

 I was an emotional mess, as my baby was sick. I still can't believe I was able to pull myself together and return to work. I was given a great book and received much support from the doctors in Bismarck. Now, after hearing several horrid doctor/patient stories, I feel very fortunate that I had a supportive medical team. I was also told that I would need to move to Minnesota immediately so I could be closely monitored by specialists, as Emily would need immediate surgery to fix the duodenal atresia.   I would deliver her there since there are no pediatric Gastroenterological surgeons in North Dakota and I certainly would not want to be 430 miles away from my baby girl.

I moved to Minnesota a week after receiving this news, leaving behind my husband and three-year-old son. I am very fortunate that I was raised in Minnesota and all my family is there; they were incredibly supportive and went with me to many Maternal Fetal Medicine appointments and ultrasounds. They found over four markers that indicated

Down syndrome. I remember looking at her ultrasound pictures and seeing if we could "see" evidence of an enhanced chromosome. I was offered an amniocentesis to confirm the diagnosis, but in reality, why? We were faced with pretty good odds due to all the markers. We did meet with a genetic counselor, who took notes on our family history and gave us a folder with information from the local support group in Minnesota. I thought the hardest thing was going to be telling my family, but to my surprise everyone was supportive and there was never a negative comment. Emily was officially diagnosed with Down syndrome one week after she was born.

I was initially shocked, upset, and fearful of the suspicion that my baby would be born with Down syndrome, mainly because of the unknown future. How was this going to

change our lives? I often asked myself whether or not I was capable of taking care of a child with special needs. After getting over the initial shock, reality hit me and I decided that there was a reason why I was given this gift. She's going to make me a better person and it makes me happy to imagine how many people she will positively affect in her life. Granted, there are going to be hurdles, disagreements, and setbacks, but life is short, so we need to stay strong and be positive. I need to enjoy my extra-special gift and take every day as it comes, even if we don't know where this bumpy road is going to take us.

~Ranee, Emily's mom; 35; Minnesota, United States

{Ellie}

I would assume that very few individuals ever imagine themselves raising a child with Down syndrome. Even though I had been fortunate enough to both grow up with a

wonderful friend who has Down syndrome and work as a pediatric nurse, never had I envisioned my life as a parent of a child with special needs. This was a thought that had never crossed my mind.

It was a warm, sunny day in September of 2011 when I got the call - the call that would forever change the course of our lives. I was 16 weeks along in my first pregnancy and my husband and I were counting the days until our 18-week ultrasound when we would hopefully learn the baby's gender. It

was about noon and I was just sitting down for lunch when the phone rang. It was my doctor's office: "Your quad screen has indicated that your baby is at an increased risk for having Down syndrome. Based on your age (I was 28 at the time), there is a 1:25 chance. We would like for you to go for further testing and have a level-II ultrasound done."

In that moment I was panicked, shocked, and devastated. Quite honestly, those are the only words that I remember; the rest was just a blur. Immediately upon hanging up with the nurse, I burst into tears. I realized that I needed to call my husband. I thought to myself, how will I tell him the news? How will he handle it? Will he be able to continue his work day?

I quickly dialed the phone and told him through tears, "Honey, I just got a call from the OB's office, they said that there is a very good chance that the baby may have Down syndrome ... something about there being a 1:25 risk." I was totally not prepared for the response that I would receive. "And you're calling me emergently at work why?" he said. "This is not a big deal. If the baby has Down syndrome we will still love him/her either way. Don't worry! I've got to go - I'll call you when I'm on my way home." I hung up even more upset than before I had called. What did he mean, "no big deal"!?

After four rounds of oral fertility meds, three IVF cycles, an early miscarriage the year before, and three years of waiting on God's timing, I couldn't wrap my brain around the news that we had just heard. I wondered why, after all that we had been through, this would happen to us. I cried out to God and asked for the testing be wrong. I pleaded for a perfect level-II ultrasound in the coming weeks and for us to be blessed with a "normal" baby. I immediately called my two best friends, my sister, and my mother to tell them the news. That evening, I wrote an email to our closest friends and family asking for them to pray with us. I stood by as my husband called his parents and told them what we had learned. Instantly, there was an overabundance of love and support from everyone with whom we had shared our news.

Days later, after some much needed processing, I realized that our sweet angel baby was a gift. I truly believed that we had been chosen to love and nurture this little person because God knew that we would be the perfect parents for him/her. I finally understood what my husband understood all along - this really wasn't a big deal! What fear I had quickly diminished as I became an advocate for this tiny little person growing inside of me. The focus of my prayers shifted, as I asked God to bring us a healthy baby with or without Down syndrome. Down syndrome would be the least of our worries, so long as our baby was healthy. By the grace of God, I had found peace and acceptance.

Two weeks after the quad screen, we went in for our level-II ultrasound and learned that our baby girl (Yes, GIRL!) had a condition called ventriculomegaly, where the ventricles in her brain were dilated. Additionally, we learned that the long bones in her arms and legs were behind on growth. Both findings were markers for Down syndrome, bringing our risk from a 1:25 chance to 1:4. Given our new risk assessment, we decided to not pursue further testing. We had come to terms with the fact that she would likely have Down syndrome. From this point forward, we dove head first into researching Trisomy 21 and learning all that would could to best prepare for our girl. For nearly another 18 weeks, we would "wait it out," not knowing for sure if our baby would be born with Down syndrome. Further ultrasounds would reveal additional markers for Down syndrome including a heart defect, hydrocephalus, and an increased nuchal fold measurement, among other findings. Our risk assessment was eventually adjusted to a 1:2 risk.

Our angel baby entered the world at 37 weeks, on a snowy day in mid-January. On that day, all of our fears vanished as excitement took over. The baby that we fervently prayed over had finally arrived and was miraculously healthy! There was no need for an immediate shunt placement for hydrocephalus, nor was there a need for immediate open-heart surgery. Our girl was thriving! It was about 24 hours after her birth that we

finally received the diagnosis that we had been waiting for and it was confirmed that our sweet angel did, in fact, have Down syndrome. We literally high-fived (yes, high-fived) the geneticist when she told us the news. After all that we had been through and after all of the concerns we had with regards to our baby's health, a Down syndrome diagnosis was truly the least of our worries.

Knowing that our girl could have been born with a different disorder or anomaly, some of which may not have even been compatible with life, we knew that Down syndrome really was the best case scenario. Finally, we were at peace and could totally, wholeheartedly move on with our life, with our newest addition now a part of it.

Today, Ellie is 19 months old. She is happy, healthy, smart, vibrant, and full of personality. She has been walking for two months now and is into everything - such a typical toddler. She is an excellent communicator and knows over 100 signs. Lately, she has also been a bit of a chatterbox, pointing to and trying to say everything that she knows within her environment. Some of her favorite activities include swimming, playing at the playground, rocking and feeding her baby dolls, dancing, reading books, and spending lots of time with family and friends, Despite our doom and gloom pregnancy, Ellie never needed brain or heart surgery, as we anticipated. Though she wears glasses because she is farsighted, Ellie has been discharged from all other specialists. She is an absolutely incredible little girl and is our greatest blessing. She is changing minds and hearts every day, and we couldn't be more proud to call her our own.

~Lauren, Ellie's mom; 28; Virginia, United States

{Matthew}

On Labor Day weekend of 2011, the phone rang and I heard the words, "your triple screen came back 1:5. You can call Tuesday to speak with the doctor and make an amnio appointment." 1:5? What does that mean? And I'm left hanging over a holiday weekend? The following week I spoke to the doctor, who said I need to have an amniocentesis because there was a high risk for Down syndrome. I declined the amnio. She proceeded to tell me that I had no idea what I was doing or what I could be getting myself into. That's when I decided it was time for a new doctor.

My new OBGYN was wonderful! They completely supported my decision to avoid invasive testing. I wasn't willing to risk losing my baby and wouldn't terminate in the face of unexpected results, so I just wanted someone who would take the best possible care of me and baby and allow me to enjoy the pregnancy. I was already considered high risk due to my age (43), so I was being monitored very closely anyway. Our level II ultrasound showed no markers and the fetal echocardiogram showed no issues , so we felt like we were good to go.

Fast forward to February 20, 2012 at 3:16 a.m. I got up for my potty break and felt trickling. By 4:30 a.m., my water broke! It was my birthday and I had a pedicure and dinner planned, but I was off to the hospital instead. I had to wait around for a few hours since I had to have a cesarean section, and at 12:37 p.m. my beautiful Matthew was whisked into the world. I asked question after question in those next few moments: "Is he OK?" Yes. "Is he breathing?" He answered me with a scream! "Does he have hair?"

"Happy Birthday, Mommy. He's beautiful!" they said as this gorgeous little baby was placed into my arms. "Happy Birthday to US!" I corrected them.

The next day his doctor came to see me after checking him out. She told me he was beautiful and was pleased to know he was nursing well. Then she said, "if you don't mind, I'd like our geneticist to come take a look at him. He has a few markers that lead me to believe he may have Down syndrome." I stared at her and it was like my head was suddenly in a tunnel; I wasn't hearing right. She also told me that he would have to be placed under the bilirubin lights that night because he was slightly jaundiced. So not only would he be away from me, but he might also have Down Syndrome? I couldn't breathe; all I wanted at that moment was to be alone and cry. I felt like a truck was just dropped onto my chest! But for the next few hours I had to put on my happy face for our visitors and my little girl, who kept telling me she loved her new baby brother so much she just wanted to cry!

I had read up on so much during my pregnancy that I knew I didn't care that he had Down syndrome deep down, but I was so scared at the same time. I knew he had no complications in utero, and had checked out fine so far, but the fear of uncertainty had its hold on me. Finally everyone left and I had a chance to sob uncontrollably. My friend called me that night and I could barely get the words out. "They want to check him for Down syndrome," I said. Beyond that, I couldn't speak. I just kept crying. What will this mean to our family? Will he be able to go to school? Will other kids accept him? Will they tease Zoe about her brother? All of this was running through my mind as I cried. I had to go sit with my baby and hold his hand.

The next day the geneticist (who had NO bedside manner) examined Matthew. She agreed that she thought he had Down syndrome and we needed to run a blood test. I sat with Matthew clutched to my chest as she rattled off all of the horrible things a child with Down syndrome could have. *Gee lady*, I thought, *have you noticed how healthy he is? Is there anything positive you can say?* I told her to run the test and we would talk about everything once we had results. At that moment, NO ONE was going to take away my joy of giving birth to this precious, healthy baby! Matthew had no health issues, so we were discharged on February 24th.

We had a check up on March 1st. All was well and there was still no news on the labs. But no sooner did I walk in the house from our appointment when the nurse called and asked if I could please come back, as the doctor needed to speak with me about our

labs. I was just there, so I knew what the results were if I had to go back. I felt my whole chest tighten up. We got in the car and I couldn't speak, so I turned the music up. The words "what doesn't kill you makes you stronger" came blaring from the radio and I started to laugh, hard. I saw it as a sign that I would make it through this.

When I heard the words, "Yes, he does have Down syndrome," I cried, but only for a minute. I had already shed enough tears. Now I had to be strong for my son. He failed his initial hearing test, so my only concern was if he could hear and communicate with me. I got my list of all of the doctors I needed to see immediately and took it from there.

16 months later, he passed his hearing test, his ASD has almost closed, he has seven spoken words, four signs, and eats like a piggy! His smile lights up a room and his giggles leave me in hysterics! He has his sister's stubbornness (maybe a bit of that came from me, too), and all is just as it should be!

~Melissa, Matthew's mom; 43, New Jersey, United States

{Connor}

I had my first child when I was 29, and it was the biggest, most positive thing that had happened in my life in a number of years. My first born son also just happened to have Down syndrome. Connor's diagnosis was officially confirmed in January of 2005, just after he was born. We didn't need a blood test to confirm what I had known in my heart for a long time. And I was ok with that, but we were still scared.

We had been married at the end of 2001, and after going through the death of my father-in-law and my grandmother, and losing my first two pregnancies to miscarriages, Connor was a welcome addition to our family. We didn't need to grieve, as we had already been through that process after it was confirmed that the second child I miscarried had Down syndrome as well. I felt terrible knowing that a 28-year-old could have a baby with Down syndrome (how wrong I was in my lack of knowledge), and I grieved for that child a great deal. I think the worst thing was knowing that the baby had been a little girl.

I lost my first pregnancy at 11.5 weeks and my second at 12 weeks. I'm terrible at being

pregnant, so after finding out of our so-called "genetic abnormality" in our second pregnancy, we had felt like we had to find out if we were genetic carriers of Trisomy 21 and were so relieved to find out that we were not. So with a change of towns we decided to try for our much-longed-for baby. I spotted through the beginning of this pregnancy as well, and I was petrified. Things settled down and we made it to 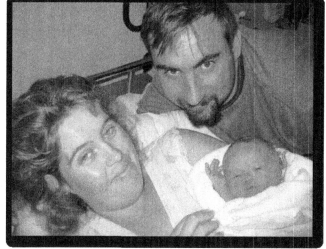 the 12-week mark, when we also had a nuchal testing. In our small town, the regional expert in this test coincidentally happened to be working on the day of our scan. He picked up on some markers that increased our chances of having a child with Down syndrome. Add that to our history and we weren't surprised to find out we had a 1:2 chance of having a child with Down syndrome. We decided that we wouldn't have any invasive tests (even though we had made a pact before we got pregnant to have a CVS) and mentally prepared ourselves that our child would be born with Down syndrome.

That night I had a heavy bleed and we were petrified that we would lose another baby. I had had half an aspirin a day with my second and third pregnancy, and stopped it when I had my heavy bleeds. After my next ultrasound showed that there was still a heartbeat, I stayed in my chair in the lounge room and didn't move for weeks. I had terrible morning sickness and could hardly eat anything, and was threatened to be put on a drip if I didn't improve. I think I was terribly nervous about every little thing.

After I hit the 20-week mark, it all settled down for me. We had a couple weeks of a perfect pregnancy without stress until my General Practitioner said he needed to be sure our baby didn't have any heart conditions or else he couldn't deliver for us. The ultrasounds were awful and showed a number of problems, so we travelled to Brisbane and saw more specialists. My parents and my mother-in-law came with us. The doctors and nurses couldn't believe that we hadn't had an amnio, and they kept saying that we had two weeks to decide if we wanted to keep our baby, as the option for a medical termination ended at 24 weeks. We were incredibly stressed and out of our depths. Since we refused invasive testing, we kept the ultrasound on me for over half an hour to see if our baby would unclench his/her hands, as this is an indicator of Trisomy 13 and Trisomy 18, neither of which are compatible with life. After what seemed like forever, our baby unclenched, and we were ecstatic.

We made an appointment with a heart specialist for the next day and, in the heat wave in October 2004, we travelled our three hours home and prepared to do the trip again the next day. That night was terrible for us. I was gutted as I was pretty sure I had seen boy bits floating around, and I didn't want to know the sex of my baby. We even decided to have an amniocentesis if the heart specialist had terrible news, just to prepare ourselves. But he said he didn't know what the other scanner saw, as our baby's heart was great. He saw some holes, but they weren't anything to stress about. On the way home from that appointment we bought a baby's cot and hid it in our spare room; we thought we could finally start to prepare for the reality of having a baby.

My General Practitioner was happy to deliver our baby and I laboured on my own all night. We went to the hospital at 5:30 a.m. and had our son at 6:36 a.m.; he was 2.7 kilograms and 2.5 weeks early. I stayed in hospital for 10 days, as it was a small country town and I didn't feel confident enough to go home. We struggled with a very sleepy baby and he wouldn't feed very well, so I breastfed him every two hours during the day, then pumped to try to increase my milk flow. I demand-fed him every three or four hours at night. I had read that breastfeeding was the best thing for speech therapy so I did that exclusively for nine weeks. In hindsight, I should have stopped at seven weeks; the community health nurse was visiting often almost labeled him "failure to thrive." We were petrified.

Connor, on the advise of our paediatrician at the time, started solids at 12 weeks. Being bottle fed, and starting the solids definitely helped him gain weight. We woke him up for a dream feed every night at nine, and eventually he started to sleep thru the night at 12 weeks. My weeks were full of appointments, early intervention, and mother's groups. Despite this busy schedule, I clearly remember someone telling me shortly after Connor's birth that we were very unlucky to have two babies with Down syndrome in a row, and that I might have a fault in my ovaries. But we certainly don't think of ourselves as unlucky at all. We finally got what we wanted: a baby.

Connor is eight years old now and I've since had two other children. Hayley, who is six, had the same due date as Connor, so they are almost exactly two years apart. Jeremy, who is three, was our "surprise" baby. Connor has mild to moderate hearing loss, so every year he goes under anaesthetic for a check on his ears since his canals are so tiny, and grommets are inserted if necessary. This year he has had his ears checked and five baby teeth were also removed in that surgery, as his teeth were overcrowded and they baby ones were wedged in. He has had a testicle pulled down, and next week

the surgeon is pulling the other one down, so this year has been huge for him. Generally he is healthy and his lack of speech is our only concern. He loves our semi-rural life, especially the tractors and cows.

~ Shannon, Connor's mum, 29, New South Wales, Australia.

{Beatrice}

Our official diagnosis for Beatrice did not come until she was three days old. It was January 21, 2011, and honestly it was more of a technicality than anything else. At that point, acceptance had already started to set in. But five months prior, during my 13-week ultrasound we were shocked to receive our first hint that something might be "wrong."

It was August 2010 and I was extremely nervous for our first trimester screening ultrasound and lab work. I was 36 years old and knew that risks were higher for my age. Having been pregnant three times before, I also had a gut feeling that with this pregnancy, something was different. The technician took some measurements and, knowing that the nuchal fold reading should be a fairly low number (< 2.0-2.5mm), I was shocked when it measured at 3.5mm, 4.0mm, and 3.8mm, over and over and over. I work in the healthcare field, and I asked the nurse if I could to talk to the doctor right away, since I knew what these measurements could indicate. I wanted some reassurance and a simple explanation of what problems we might need to be concerned about. I knew that the test results would take several days and I dreaded the thought of waiting without any information. They told me that the doctor didn't have time. The nurse came in and drew my blood and seemed very jumpy and nervous. A long, five days later, the office called. Yes, my lab work was abnormal. Yes, the nuchal fold was high. My chances of having a child with Down Syndrome went from 1 in 300 (according to my age), to 1 in 5.

I was at the local zoo with my 3 boys when they called. I tried to hold it together, but I cried and cried in my van. I was fearful of what the future would hold. I wished my husband was nearby. I wished my boys weren't with me to witness my pain. I wished the doctor could have met with me right after the ultrasound to discuss the findings with me then. Maybe then this information over the phone, in front of my children, wouldn't have hit me so hard. Maybe I could have been more prepared. The office wanted us to come in as soon as possible and advised me to "bring a support person" with me.

Later that day, the perinatologist pushed for CVS or amniocentesis, saying "we didn't have much time." My husband and I insisted the result would NOT change a thing. She replied, "That's what everyone says. No one knows how they will ultimately respond until they know the truth." We immediately switched perinatologists. Our personal OBGYNs were phenomenal. They were nothing but supportive and caring. They called to check on me. They encouraged me. They listened to me. They supported whatever our decision was--to wait it out or to ease the anxiety of the unknown and have an amniocentesis. They reassured us that we could choose to have the amniocentesis at any time for the rest of the pregnancy if the waiting became too unbearable. They were with us every step of the way. They made us feel that no matter the outcome, life would be wonderful.

After many long discussions, my husband and I decided to wait it out. We did not want to risk miscarriage just to know whether or not our child would have a chromosomal abnormality and relieve our personal anxiety of the unknown. It did not change anything for us. We would love our first daughter (after three boys!) no matter what.

Yes, the waiting was hard. But in the end, I know we made the right decision for us. Once Beatrice arrived and we received confirmation of her Trisomy 21 diagnosis, the best medicine for me was simply taking care of my baby: feeding her, burping her, bathing her, changing her diaper, swaddling her, and rocking her.   These things helped me to focus on Beatrice, the baby, my daughter, our princess. She is the light of our lives!

Beatrice is now 2.5 years old. She is just learning to walk, starting to say a few words, and soaks up signs more quickly than I can learn them and show them to her. Yes, the milestones take longer to reach, but she is still a daddy's girl, a sweet little sister, and an irreplaceable member of our growing family. We look forward to seeing what she will accomplish in life!

~ Tracy, Beatrice's mom; 36; Iowa, United States

{Ryan}

My water broke around 8 a.m. on a Tuesday, September 4th, the day I was returning to work after a much-needed, long holiday weekend. I was minutes from leaving my apartment to hop on the hot, smelly, crowded subway for a 30-minute commute to Penn Station. Not fun or comfortable for a 37-week pregnant lady.

I contemplated what to do. My husband was out with the dog and I certainly didn't want to be the one to cry wolf. Finally, I decided to text my doctor after persuasion from my mom. He was pretty certain that indeed, it was time to welcome our baby into the world. I was quite calm, which came as a surprise to me. I was TERRIFIED of giving

birth. I would have panic attacks just thinking about it. But when it came to crunch time, I delivered (literally)! We followed the instructions that we learned in class - try to remain home as long as possible. And so we did. It was 5 p.m. when I finally called my brother and told him it was time to go. He had been on standby all day to take me to the hospital. That ride up the West Side Highway was brutal. By this time, contractions were very frequent, and starting to get a little uncomfortable. Why I waited until rush hour on a rainy day, I will still never figure out.

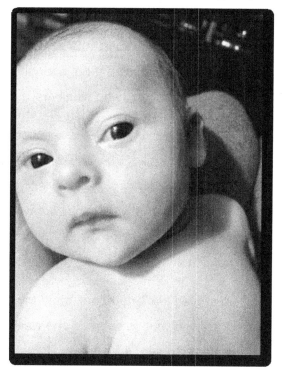

Once at the hospital, it was confirmed: I was 7cm dilated. I was so proud of myself! We were instantly whisked to a room, and so it began. The birth was relatively easy; really the whole pregnancy was. I was one of the "lucky ones," with no horrible symptoms besides occasional heartburn and a craving for ice cream (actually the craving is a lie. I just capitalized on it as an excuse to eat ice cream every day). The only minor incident we had was when our doctor called us after our 12-week ultrasound to tell us we were at an elevated risk of having a baby with Trisomy 21 due to my age and some soft markers they found. We were offered additional tests, but my husband and I both agreed there was no need. These things don't happen to us. And even if they *did*, what was the point of another test?

Everything had been perfect. And at 11:04 that evening, our Little King, Ryan, was born. He was gorgeous. He was placed on my chest, and I was in love. Instantly. It's really something you can't put into words. We celebrated, called our friends and family, cried, and laughed. We were so happy. Everything was still perfect!

At some point early the next morning, the pediatrician came around to check in on Ryan. I can remember her saying, "His ears look a little smushed, don't they?" I wasn't really sure what to say in response to that. I'm sure I gave her a blank stare. Of course instantly, my mind raced. But when she said, "it's probably just from the birth," I went on my merry way of basking in the glow of new motherhood. That afternoon when they took him for his circumcision, she came back and pulled up a chair. My heart instantly dropped. And from that point on, everything is very fuzzy. I heard a lot of "Wha wha wha...Down syndrome...wha wha wha....soft markers....wha wha...Down syndrome...."

She left, and I cried like I have never cried before. My husband held me tight, but I kept sobbing uncontrollably. How could this happen to us? These things don't happen to us. Next thing I know, we had another visitor. He introduced himself as a Geneticist. He was there to tell us that yes "Wha wha wha...markers for Trisomy 21...wha wha wha....test....wha wha...tomorrow....Wha wha...Don't Google it..." And again, more uncontrollable sobbing from me. My husband held me tighter.

My mom arrived that afternoon. I told my husband that I would put on a brave face and tell her the news, but as soon as she walked through the door, the uncontrollable sobbing started again. I literally could not get the words out of my mouth. It's like I was paralyzed, and all I could do was cry. I didn't want to cry, and I wasn't exactly sure why I was crying. I didn't know anything about Down syndrome. Was it because I was afraid of the unknown? Was it because I was afraid of what he would look like? Was it because I was afraid he wouldn't be able to play with his cousin? Was I feeling guilty for thinking these things? Was I just so in love with him that I couldn't control my sobbing? Was I embarrassed because I was crying? Was it pregnancy hormones? I'm still not sure. All I knew was that definitely, without any doubt in my mind, I loved this little man more than anything in the world. And I would do anything in my power to protect him.

Next up, another visitor. She introduced herself as a cardiologist. Again, I heard a lot of "Wha wha wha" as she was drawing something. It was a diagram of the heart, and she drew where Ryan's 4 holes were located. What? Holes in his heart? We were just told that not only does our precious baby have Down syndrome, but he also has congenital heart defects that would require open heart surgery most likely before he was 2 years old.

This is where is gets even more fuzzy. There are a few things I can remember from our hospital stay: my husband telling me that "We aren't taking Park Avenue, we are taking Madison instead;" my mom and husband holding me tight constantly, and being the ones who listened to the doctors when discussing his conditions; sobbing into my brother's arms after we told him the news; being angry at the nurse who abandoned me and Ryan after she said she would be back to assist with nursing.

We were released from the hospital after 2 days. My emotions were still unstable, to put it mildly, and remained that way for months. My husband and my family were amazing. I am so lucky that Ryan has a Daddy who can put everything in perspective, take care of his emotionally-unstable wife, rock a swaddle, and love unconditionally. On the drive home, I remember telling my Mom, "I now know how much you love me." I knew deep down everything was going to be ok. I had my baby, my husband, my family. Everything was still…perfect. And so was Ryan.

~ Mandy, Ryan's mom; 37; New York, United States

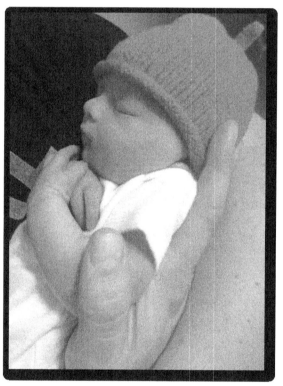

{Simply Unexpected}

Receiving a Birth Diagnosis

The birth of a child typically evokes feelings of joy, excitement, and celebration. But for many women whose babies receive a birth diagnosis of Down syndrome, the emotions can be decidedly different: sadness, confusion, fear. There is no right or wrong reaction, but many families have eerily similar accounts of those seemingly dark first days.

The baby you have prepared for so diligently is not at all what you expected. You may feel bewildered. You may have feelings of grief, confusion, and worry, yet your love for that baby—YOUR baby—is incredibly real and as strong as any bond between a parent and child.

At first, every second is filled with new thoughts, feelings, and fears. The unknown future and your lack of preparation now top your list of worries. What will your baby's life be like as they grow up? How will you handle the increased responsibility that comes with having child with special needs? And perhaps most poignant, how will the arrival of this baby, with its unexpected extra needs, affect your other children?

But those first confusing, terrifying seconds turn to minutes, then to hours, and finally to days and months passing with your baby. You are smiling again. Your baby is smiling, cooing and snuggling, and bonding with your other children—and they with him. You realize that your baby is just that: a baby, more alike than different in so many beautiful ways.

Down syndrome is now a part of your life, but it has not become your life.

{Our Stories}

{Darcy}

So many people tell you to trust your instincts; your gut feeling that says something isn't quite right. Throughout my second pregnancy I had a feeling of uneasiness that I simply couldn't explain. I made every attempt to shrug off this feeling and believe all was well, but in the depths of my existence I knew it wasn't, I just didn't know why or how. It was day two of Darcy's life when I understood for the first time, what that gut instinct was trying to tell me.

Darcy was born 5 weeks prematurely by emergency caesarean on 21ˢᵗ November 2010. When my obstetrician held up our beautiful little boy in the theatre for us to see for the first time I remember thinking how perfect he looked. He weighed 5lb 8oz and was chubbier and healthier than his older brother Charlie who was born 6 weeks early and weighed just 4lb 3oz. Mark and I held him for a short moment before he was taken to the special care nursery for assistance with breathing. My husband went with Darcy to the Special Care Unit (SCU). After a short time, he proudly came to my room and told me what a good looking little man we had. Later in the day, I was able to go into the special care unit and I marvelled at how perfect our little boy was. As I put my hands into the humidicrib and touched him, putting my finger into his tiny little hand, I was overcome with love for our little bundle. I spent the first night of Darcy's life as a loving new mother, proudly telling everyone that our second beautiful son had been born and was doing very well. Our family was complete and the world seemed perfect.

The following day, my perfect world turned utterly and completely upside down. Mark had gone to work and I had a friend visiting when a nurse came to tell me the paediatrician wanted to talk to me about Darcy. I eagerly headed off to the SCU expecting to hear news of how well he was doing and how he was easily breathing on his own. What was waiting for me was something life changing, something I never expected in a million years. In a gentle but assertive voice, our paediatrician said the words a mother never wants to hear..."We think your baby has Down syndrome." I will remember those words for the rest of my life as clearly as if they had just been spoken and my spine still tingles when I think about it.

In that moment, the world around me stood absolutely still and I felt so alone. I remember feeling a cold chill take over my body. My stomach wretched as if I was about to throw up and my ears were ringing. My legs shook and the floor beneath me felt as though it was going to collapse. The doctor proceeded to show me the line across Darcy's palm, the extra skin in the corners of his eyes, the slightly upward slant of his eyes. I could hear her talking but I did not comprehend a thing she was saying. Big, warm tears poured down my face and began dropping onto my beautiful little boy. The only words I managed were, "Are you sure?" A blood test would be done, but she was 90% sure. 90% I thought to myself. That meant she wasn't certain and there was still a chance she was wrong.

The hardest phone call I have ever made in my life was to tell Mark. To this day I am not sure how I got the words out of my mouth but I managed to say, "The doctor thinks Darcy has Down syndrome". Mark came straight to the hospital and again our paediatrician went through the physical signs. We listened but could barely speak. After a short time we went back to my room and fell into each other's arms, sobbing uncontrollably.

We wanted to believe the doctors and nurses were wrong. There had been no indicators during our pregnancy to suggest our baby had anything wrong with him and we couldn't understand how the medical fraternity could let us down so badly by missing this diagnosis. We hoped and prayed that there might be a miracle, but in our heart and soul we knew our Darcy had Down syndrome. 24 hours later, our paediatrician confirmed the diagnosis of Trisomy 21. Mark and I cried more than a river of tears in the following few days. We grieved openly and honestly together. Initially, it seemed as though the emotional attachment we had to Darcy when he was first born had disappeared and we felt completely detached, like he wasn't really ours. We felt cheated out of the chance to have a "normal" child and we had fleeting moments when we thought we didn't want this baby.

The first time I saw Charlie after Darcy's diagnosis, I hugged him tighter than I ever had before. Suddenly, my cheeky, naughty little toddler seemed so perfect and I felt the need to keep him very close to me in a selfish attempt to help ease the terrible pain I was feeling. Ironically, while Charlie was the one thing that helped me to smile at that time, he was also foremost in my mind as the tears flowed—I couldn't bear to think about the impact it would have on him to have a brother with Down syndrome. He didn't ask for a brother with a disability and it was so incredibly unfair to impose it upon him in his life.

The emotions we felt at this time were so strong and so overwhelming that I couldn't imagine ever feeling like I could cope with this news. These feelings lasted for what seemed like an eternity. In reality it was only a few days before we realised that our little man didn't ask to be born with Down syndrome and what he needed more than anything in the world was parents who would love him unconditionally. We came to a place of acceptance and from that point forward, we have loved our little boy with every ounce of our being.

Darcy was in the special care unit of the hospital for two weeks. In that time he was poked and prodded more than any poor little baby should ever have to experience. Initially the paediatrician believed that Darcy's heart was fine. Mark and I were very relieved about this, since we had been told that heart problems were very common for children with Down syndrome. The greatest immediate concern was Darcy's bilirubin levels and he spent quite a lot of time under lights to try to improve his jaundice. Every day the staff from pathology came to take his blood to see if his bilirubin levels were improving; and every day they were amazed at just how well he handled all the testing. Even at such a young age, Darcy's bravery and resilience were clearly evident and we have seen him demonstrate these characteristics many times in his short life.

Each day Darcy's paediatrician conducted a thorough review of his heath. During one of these checks, when Darcy was just five days old, she located a "non-innocent murmur" in his heart that she was concerned about. We were immediately referred to a paediatric cardiologist for further investigation. I can clearly remember that this was the moment when my very strong protective maternal instinct kicked in and I felt a sudden urge to do everything I could to make sure our little boy was going to be alright. Only days before we had wondered whether we really wanted this child in our lives. Now we were placed in a situation where there could be something seriously wrong with our baby and in an instant I transitioned from a grieving, uncertain mother, to a mother who fiercely wanted to nurture and shield my baby from harm. I was panicked and terrified and frightened and oh so protective. I held my little boy close to me as often as the special care nurses would allow in the hope that he would feel my strength and know I was fighting for him. Two days later Darcy had tests conducted on his heart and the specialist diagnosed thickening of the pulmonary valve. It was not immediately life threatening and the cardiologist was happy to review him in two months.

While in hospital, Darcy had two hearing tests conducted as his left ear did not pass. We were referred to have more tests done after being discharged. He also had an ultrasound done on his kidneys as pre-natal testing identified that his kidneys were enlarged. This also needed to be reviewed again in a couple of months. Thankfully, none of these health issues were major and we were discharged from the hospital with a list of things that needed to be reviewed, but nothing urgent or life threatening. By the time we were able to take Darcy home, I was an expert on medical terms related to his health. I educated myself so I could understand everything that needed to be watched or monitored. I recall during one of Darcy's hospital stays later in his life, some paediatric medical students were asking questions about his history. I rattled off everything Darcy had been through and one of them asked me if I was a nurse. I chuckled and said I was just a "Well educated Mummy"!

Following Darcy's release from hospital at two weeks of age, we did the best we could to "normalise" our family life. We really were at a place of acceptance and we had gone past the stage of grieving and were instead sponges for information about what the Down syndrome diagnosis meant for our little boy. We read many books, some encouraging and others that were confronting and difficult to comprehend. One such book that we found particularly hard to read outlined all the possible health problems a child with Down syndrome could have in their life. The list went on and on and on and as I read, a sense of panic and fear washed over me again. Eventually I put the book away for later reference, in case we ever needed it, secretly hoping we would never have to refer to it again.

Darcy was five weeks old when the most significant of his health problems became apparent. It was Christmas Eve 2010. We were all excited about the celebrations that were planned for the following day. Like every other day we bathed Darcy in the evening and I placed him on the change table to dress him. As he looked up at me, I saw for the first time cloudy cataracts in both his eyes. I knew instantly they were cataracts. That awful dreaded book I had been reading said that cataracts were a possible health concern for people with Down syndrome and I was certain that was what I was seeing. In an instant my whole world crumbled again and I felt that same sinking, wretching feeling that came over me when Darcy was first diagnosed. I had come to terms with having a child with Down syndrome. I had been reading about ways to help Darcy learn through visual and sensory stimulation. How was I going to cope with a child who had Down syndrome and was also blind?

Being Christmas, there were no specialists available and we had to wait over a week before we could finally see an ophthalmologist. We were immediately referred to see a paediatric ophthalmologist in Brisbane and Darcy was scheduled for surgery to have his cataracts removed. The day of his surgery was terrifying. I had to search into the depths of my soul to trust that the doctors knew what they were doing and were going to fix my little boy. Handing over my tiny little baby was painful; seeing him come back from surgery with patches over his eyes and tubes connected all over him was heartbreaking. A week after his surgery, Darcy was fitted with his first set of contact lenses and he has been wearing lenses ever since. His vision was slow to develop but he is now doing quite well. Since that time we have had two further lots of surgery to fix bilateral strabismus that developed post cataract surgery. He has also developed glaucoma in his right eye – which is apparently a common side effect of cataract surgery. We have made many, many trips back and forward to Brisbane to see the paediatric ophthalmologist who has become more than just a doctor, but a trusted friend who will never give up on trying to give our little boy better vision.

In the midst of the problems with Darcy's eyes we also had heart reviews and endless hearing tests. At three months of age the paediatric cardiologist reviewed Darcy's heart and concluded that he had a "functionally normal heart." The thickening of the pulmonary valve had corrected itself and there were no further issues with his heart. You can imagine the joy at hearing this news. After having such a tough ride with Darcy's eyes, we were so relieved to know that his heart was okay.

Darcy had his first follow-up hearing test when he was only one month old. This was the beginning of a very frustrating journey trying to find out exactly the cause of his hearing problem. It was a very stressful experience as the testing could not be done in our regional town and we had to travel each time we needed to have tests conducted. Each time he was tested he was either too congested to get a true reading or he would not sleep for long enough to test him thoroughly and we would be asked to come back again at a later date. Eventually, Darcy had a hearing test conducted under anaesthetic (during one of his eye surgeries) and he was found to have permanent mild hearing loss in both ears in the high frequency range. This really came as a shock to me and I found myself becoming very emotional when I was told the results. I think I had convinced myself that Darcy would have "glue ear", like many other children with Down syndrome and I was certain that it was something that could be fixed. I had not mentally or emotionally prepared myself for a permanent hearing loss. We decided not to use hearing aids at the time and continued to have Darcy's hearing tested every six months to check that there had not been any changes to his level of hearing and to ensure there were no middle ear problems. Following his check up at 2.5 years of age, the audiologist reported that Darcy had hearing that was adequate for him to develop normal speech and language without the use of hearing aids. That news was music to my ears and I literally jumped for joy when I got home and shared this piece of positive news with Mark.

Not long after Darcy was born, I started joking with doctors that everything about Darcy was "just a little bit not normal". He had a slightly enlarged kidney, but nothing to be concerned about. He had a mild hearing loss, but nothing to be concerned about. His bilirubin levels were just out of the normal range for quite a while, but nothing to be concerned about. He has mild sleep apnoea, but nothing to be concerned about at this stage. His iron levels were often a little bit low, but nothing to be concerned about. His eyes were not perfect, but we were working on it. We had a list of things that were "not quite right" about Darcy and we were certainly kept on our toes trying to stay on top of all the appointments, surgeries, reviews and testing. On top of these minor issues, he had recurrent chest infections and nasal congestion and was hospitalised twice for bronchiolitis and croup. There were times when it felt very unfair that one little person had to go through so much in the first early years of his life, but most of the time we were so incredibly proud of our little boy who handled all the poking and prodding with seemingly unshakable ease.

Darcy is now almost 3 years old and I am pleased to report he has been free from significant health problems for the past six months. The first two years of his life were certainly not easy. We had medical appointments and tests almost every week and quite often the results we received were not good news. It was an emotional rollercoaster. Just as we managed to get on top of one issue, there seemed to be something else come up that rattled our emotions again. There were many times when I wondered "what else" or "how much more" and I felt like I might collapse in a sobbing heap and never get back up again. Sometimes I did collapse in a sobbing heap, but somehow I always managed to get back up. I had to. My two boys needed their Mummy to be strong and they needed their Mummy to look after them. Our challenges are not over. Darcy's eyes are still a "work in progress" and more surgery may be needed to fix the glaucoma. At some stage he may need surgery to have tonsils and adenoids removed to improve his sleep apnoea. Of course, there are the unknowns we can't predict that can come up at any time.

As a family, we are stronger than ever, despite the turbulent couple of years we had with Darcy's health. Every day we are filled with joy as we watch our little boy learn and develop. He and Charlie are so interactive and Darcy watches everything his big brother does and tries to copy him – even climbing onto the coffee table and trying to be superman! We are thrilled to see Darcy reaching milestones that we thought might have been impossible for him, especially as we really had no idea what his vision would be like and how this would affect his ability to do things. Today he is a typical boy who loves his cars and trucks and the outdoors, but who is equally happy to sit and read books snuggled up with his Mummy or Daddy, or draw pictures on the chalkboard. He is charming, very adorable and has a wonderful ability to wrap people around his little finger with just the flash of his smile. Our boys are our world and I can't imagine our lives being any different. I think back to the time when Darcy was first born and I don't think I could have ever pictured back then, just how happy we would be and how wonderful our life would become. What seemed so very difficult in the beginning has now become our "normal" and we love our "normal" life.

~ Allison, Darcy's mum; 34; Queensland, Australia

{Alvaro}

My blood pressure had been high for several hours. The nurse came in, checked my vitals and read my blood pressure to me. It was high again. I made a comment about how high it was and she said, "Its okay, you've been through a lot."

She was referring to the diagnosis I received a few hours earlier. We welcomed our son Alvaro into the world on February 16, 2013 at 6:24am. At 37 weeks I was full term and induced because I was losing my amniotic fluid.

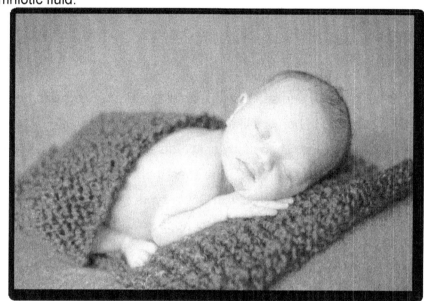

I remember pushing him out with tears in my eyes. They handed him to me. As soon as I started talking to him, this little baby boy stopped crying. It was magical.

Four hours after he was born, the magical feelings were crushed. The pediatrician, after having examined him, asked everyone but the parents to leave the room. With a shaky voice and an apologetic tone she began to explain to us that she believed Alvaro had Down syndrome. In fact, she was 80% sure. She shared with us the markers that led to her suspicions: the low muscle tone, the slanted eyes, and the crease across the palm in his hand.

While my heart was filled with dread and I felt as if the wind knocked out of me, somehow deep inside I knew it to be true. You see, the first fleeting thought in my mind when I held my baby boy was, "This looks like a baby with Down syndrome." I don't know where that thought came from. I had never seen a baby with Down syndrome before. I had only seen older children and individuals with DS. I pushed that fleeting thought from my mind and told myself it was because we had different cultures in our families that he looked different to me.

So here I found myself in the hospital room having been told my son has DS. My blood pressure was sky high for 24 hours. I was in shock. I felt dread. But above all I felt fear. The fear led to questions such as: 'What did this mean for my baby? What did this mean for my family? How could something be so wrong with such a perfect little baby?'

The next few days I experienced confusion, grief, and pain. But I also felt a fierce protectiveness over this little boy's life and body. This was still the same baby who grew inside me. The little boy we'd spent months waiting for. I had to reconcile the boy I went to the hospital to welcome and the little baby boy in my arms with Down syndrome. I reminded myself they were one and the same.

All I could see when I looked at his face was that: Down syndrome. My heart broke that I couldn't see past the diagnosis. I grieved and felt guilt that I wasn't excited and that I felt so sad inside.

A NICU nurse came and spoke with us the day after Alvaro was born. Her own four year old son has DS. Speaking to her was like sunlight shining through the clouds of my heart. My immediate fears were verbalised. Then many of my fears were dispelled. She began to educate me about what a wonderful child Ben was. She shared about her triumphs and even sorrows on her own journey as the parent of a child with Down syndrome. She was a Godsend for me. In the middle of the turmoil in my heart, the seeds of hope, joy, and relief were planted.

Despite the beginning of joy, hope, and relief, I was still processing a gamut of emotions, two of the primary ones being fear and guilt. I experienced a lot of fear and then guilt for all my "negative emotions." I had told myself for years that if I had a baby born with Down syndrome, I'd love him or her just the same. But the reality of the diagnosis stung more than I cared to admit.

I was blessed to have so many supportive friends and family. I was immediately connected with friends of friends who have children with Down syndrome. And luckily, I only received one "We are so sorry and brokenhearted for you," comment. Despite my own personal struggles to accept my life with a new reality, I did not want to be pitied. I wanted to have others love Alvaro for who he was, whether that included 46 or 47 chromosomes. I immediately joined the ranks of those who want their children to be accepted and included with their typical peers.

Equally as scary as an unknown future, was the list of possible health issues Alvaro could possibly have. His first week check-up at his pediatrician's office was met with a long list of specialists Alvaro would need to see to rule out (or find) any of the most common health issues prevalent in individuals with Down syndrome. By the time Alvaro was 6 weeks old, he had received an echogram, had a scheduled appointment with a pediatric Cardiologist, had seen a pediatric Ophthalmologist to check for cataracts, and was evaluated by a Geneticist. I started attending the appointments with my breath held. I received one positive report after another: no cataracts, no major heart condition, good muscle tone, etc. Then, of all things, his jaundice levels started to rise. I was referred to a pediatric Gastroenterologist. The jaundice tests revealed that my son's liver may not be working correctly. He underwent several blood tests and scans to verify that his liver had all the necessary components and checked if it worked as it should. To our great relief, it did. The jaundice began to recede and the possibility of a surgical procedure was taken off the table.

His thyroid levels however, were see-sawing between high and normal levels. We have since seen a pediatric Endocrinologist and he did have high TSH levels which are currently being controlled by medication.

On a social and more personal level, most of my attention was spent settling into a new routine now that I had added a second child to my family. As the days turned into weeks, Alvaro's condition became less and less a focal point. While it remained a reality of my life, it was no longer as important as who he was as a person. His personality began to shine through.

I spent the first few weeks after his birth educating myself about Down syndrome. I read books recommended by friends and the National Down Syndrome Society. I joined a Facebook group for Moms with babies who had DS. I joined the chapter of local Down Syndrome Association. I quickly learned that there were more similarities than differences with DS. Alvaro's extra chromosome just made him extra special. He was not broken. He would live a full and happy life. He may take a little longer to walk or talk, but these were skills he would master. He would be able to go to school, be educated and have a job. He may get married. His potential is NOT limited because he has an extra chromosome.

Because of Facebook and the wonderful sisterhood of fellow mothers of children with T21, Down syndrome became part of my "typical" world. I got to see children every day with Down syndrome. In fact I saw as many, if not more, babies in Alvaro's peer group with Down syndrome than without. Having the ability to share my life, feelings, fears, hopes, and thoughts with these fellow Moms was so important. The support and understanding really helped me in so many ways.

I will be honest also that the first few weeks connecting with these Moms were at times a struggle. So many were so happy and loved their children so well. I was still feeling guilty about my sad feelings. I shared this with them, and again they surrounded me with empathy, support, encouragement, and understanding.

I did have to be careful though how much I spent online. It was easy for me to get excited and scared about all the possible health issues some of the babies were dealing with. I seemed to live online looking up information on ailments such as RSV, Infantile Spasms, and other scary possibilities.

I learned though to just let go and just let Alvaro and his body be our guide to what was going on with him.

By the time Alvaro was four months old, what I thought about when I saw him was simply that he was my son, a joy and a delight. We're lucky that he has had very minimal health issues. He receives physical therapy weekly to work in areas that are physically more challenging for him. Aside from that, I had noticed very little to no difference from my typical son at that age.

Alvaro is one year old now. I have come to wholly accept who he is. In fact, his Down syndrome is just an ingredient in his makeup. Alvaro isn't "my son with Down syndrome." He is simply my son. I do not even think of him as someone with "special needs." I'm not in denial that he is in the special needs categories. It just isn't a label that defines him.

Would I change Alvaro's condition if I could? I don't know. I don't think I would. I would change any health issues that would have negative effects in his body. But I would not change my son. I love him just as he is: beautiful, happy, fun, smart, and well... mine. I am proud and honored to be his mother.

~Rosa, Alvaro's mom; 33; Florida, United States

Blogging @ www.xeeomy.blogspot.com

{Everett}

One would think when you are getting ready to have your fourth child, you would be somewhat prepared, old hat, right? I had a pretty easy pregnancy, some morning sickness but all of our testing and ultrasounds assured us that the baby was doing just fine. I was 38 weeks along

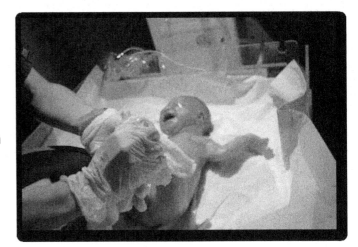

when I had my first contraction at 6am. I foolishly labored (pun intended) under the impression I would have lots of time to prepare and get ready at home. Three short hours later while my husband drove frantically down the highway going 70 mph with me trashing around in the front seat shouting profanities at anyone and anything, I remember thinking I probably shouldn't have made time to shave my legs!

As we pulled up to the hospital, the car hasn't even stopped before I had the door open and I was running to the check-in...well running as fast as anyone can when their contractions are one minute apart! They whisked me up to labor and delivery floor where I got the last open room and met the labor and delivery nurse Beth. I will always remember her lovely blue eyes as she talked to me through the pain and her patience with me as my fear took over.

They eventually were able to give me an epidural but the baby's heart rate was dropping and seemed only happy unless I was flat on my back. Not my optimal laboring position but I made do. The doctor, whom I had never met before, came just in time to deliver the baby, with few quick pushes and a cord that needed to be cut quickly, they brought him up to my chest. I remember seeing him and being in total disbelief! A boy! We finally had a wonderful and precious boy, after three girls, I guess we didn't even think it was possible!

I cuddled him on my chest, he was crying and a bit blue, I looked down at him and asked aloud "What's wrong with his eyes?" They were extremely puffy and oddly shaped but I chalked it up to such a fast and furious labor. The nurses took him to get him weighed and cleaned up a bit while Paul and I joyously called and texted our friends and family members. Neither of us noticed how quiet the room was, how the nurses asked for a pediatrician to come to our room, how the obstetrician left the room in search of one. What I do remember is when he returned.

He took the baby from the nurses and placed him in my arms bundled in his blanket and with stocking cap that all newborn babies seem to wear as a rite of passage. Paul looked over my shoulder, both of us still in amazement we had a baby boy.

The doctor looked at me and said kindly "I want you to tell me what you notice about your son." I didn't hesitate a moment. As I stared at the bundle in my arms, my eyes filled with tears and my heart began to hammer in my chest. I immediately replied "His ears are low set and his eyes are close together, he has Down syndrome, doesn't he?" The room was utterly silent as I began to sob.

Everyone was obviously shocked I saw it so quickly. "I'm an obstetrician, not a pediatrician but yes, I believe he does based on some of his features." The nurses' eyes were filled with tears.

I don't remember looking at Paul, but he tells me he just was in an utter state of disbelief because the baby looked so 'normal' to him. He did not see what I saw. Know what I already knew in my heart. He began to cry with me.

I pulled the baby tightly to my chest and said "Oh, my sweet, special baby boy, we are going to love you" as my sobs and tears grew. I will always cling to the fact this was my first visceral response to the news because what feelings came next. Feelings that I am ashamed to admit I had.

I don't know if I can ever truly describe the emotions. I went from such elation to complete and utter devastation in the space of a second. Just typing these words causes such an exquisite ache in my chest and tightening in my throat, so hard to put into words and onto paper and to be honest and remember.

My whole body was numb, I felt no pain other the searing hole left in chest where my heart used to be. Shock, pain, disbelief, devastation all blended together, the joy was gone.

My husband took a picture, as I told him we needed to have a photo of me smiling, because what would he think one day looking at his baby book if there were no smile.

The pediatrician came into the room; she was a kind lady who examined the baby. She explained she would be sending a chromosome test to check the baby for Trisomy 21. She pointed out the traits that indicated to her he had this condition. His eyes have the epicanthal folds, lows set ears that are slightly folded over, a sandal toe gap (a space between the big toe and the next). A small placenta also correlates with Down syndrome which I had. She did comment that he had good muscle tone and was pleased he seemed to be nursing well.

How could this have happened? I was furious and felt utterly betrayed the medical people who cared for me during pregnancy. I had the testing which showed my risk was normal and my prenatal testing and high level ultrasound was normal. I was only 33 when we conceived. I raged against the world, this was not real, there was a mistake. This was a horrible nightmare, this happens to other people. Not to me. Not to MY family.

What I am about to admit are shameful, despicable feelings and thoughts. I'm sure others will judge me but it is real and my truth and my story.

I vaguely remember moving from the labor and delivery suite to the mom and baby room. I was pushed in a wheelchair as I held the baby in my arms. My eyes were swollen and tears flowed down my cheeks. I kept the baby pressed to my chest; I didn't want anyone to see him. People averted their eyes as I rolled past. I saw their eyes as they looked at my face and how their glances would slide off into the distance. I was holding a baby but something was wrong. The nurses at the station all knew, I could see it.

We got settled in the new room, the baby was in the bassinet to my left between the bed and the window. I couldn't even look at him. He wasn't a baby to me, I didn't know what he was.

I was alone in the room as Paul left to get my mother at the airport, the sun was setting and the room grew dark. At that moment the vilest thoughts crossed my mind. I did NOT want him. Was there a way to place him up for adoption? But then what I would tell the girls? What if he died and I had to bury him? I didn't want him alive; I wanted a 'normal' baby, not this thing- this imperfect thing with funny looking eyes and ears. He would never leave our home, he would have an awkward looking body, he would be made fun of, as would our other kids. I would spend the rest of my life taking care of him. I would have no life of my own. He would never live on his own. He would never play basketball in high school like his dad, never drive, never go to college, and never marry. The list went on and on in my head...

I cried and sobbed for hours straight, alone in that room except for that baby. The pain and sadness exploded, my body was wracked with grief and pain- grieving for a child I had lost and despising the one had. I'm sure whoever passed my room must have thought the baby had died in childbirth by my sobs, little did they know it was just a mom who was wishing for it. As the

room became dark and my head hurt and my eyes were so swollen I could barely see, I couldn't even look at him, as I rejected him. I look back at that night and the days that followed, his NICU stay, his heart defect diagnosis and a subsequent hospitalization and I wonder how I could have had those callous, horrific feelings. What kind of mother was I?

What kind of person was I? I suppose time has allowed me to be kinder to myself. I regret my feelings, but it was the journey I took. My best role models were my three little girls who welcomed and loved their brother without any hesitation. Complete and utter lover, no reservations.

I guess I need to be kind to myself. I knew nothing of Down syndrome, I never met anyone with it. I think my lack of knowledge and the lack of information that came with his birth left me paralyzed. I had all these ideas of what it would mean, but I realize now, 19 months later, I was so wrong. He is a survivor and fighter. Everett will have a life worth living and will make an impact. He is not suffering. He is perfect. He is normal. He is thriving and teaching me every day what it truly means to love.

~ Amber, Everett's mom; 34; Colorado, United States

{Thea}

It was anything but ordinary. My husband and I anticipated this day with much excitement—having a home visit a week before with our midwife where we finalized the plan to have our little child at the local birth center. Labor started and continued quickly at home, after some time laboring at home it was time to make our way to the birth center. Upon arrival our excitement continued; we had been waiting for this day for nine long months and it was finally here: the day

to meet our first child. Plans changed quickly, very quickly when it was determined that I was fully dilated and baby was breech; to be exact our little one was footling breach. Our excitement deflated when we were transported to a local hospital by ambulance. Labor pains continued but I was instructed to ignore the endless urges to push while being inundated with endless medical professionals rambling off question after question. An emergency C-section was scheduled soon after we arrived. The sterile operation began, and I was placed in a hospital gown despite my request to remain in regular clothes; I was told it was not an option. Endless thoughts circled my brain—this was definitely not "the plan" but I was comforted with the thoughts that it won't be long and we'll be

united with our little child soon, very soon. Sure enough, she arrived. I was able to see her seconds after the delivery as a nurse positioned a mirror and my spouse announced that baby was a girl! My intuition was right – a little girl as I had expected for much of my pregnancy. I still can't explain exactly what gave "it" (Down Syndrome) away but I knew the second I saw her. Or I thought I knew; my brain was flooded. I was alone on the operating table. I was numb, completely numb, both emotionally and physically. The wait in the recovery room was the longest two hours of my life. I couldn't begin to process anything with the combination of the pain medication, the exhaustion, and the uncertainty. Physically, my body shook. I was finally reunited with my spouse and we didn't have to say anything but we wept together because we were overwhelmed. The next 3 ½ days were much of a blur—many of the events ran together:

numerous consultations, blood draws, screenings and tests, and tears both of joy and sadness. A resident gave us the diagnosis of Down syndrome the day after her birth. The resident angered me, saying senseless things by categorizing my child. I thought many, many times "give her a chance, she is unique and she is my child." Despite all the questions and worries, I had a calming moment as our baby looked up at me with her beautiful little eyes—she reassured me that she was going to be okay. She is our little warrior and she will accomplish many, many things.

During those first few days of life we learned of Thea's heart defect. We were told she had a "large" VSD. Despite the physician whom gave us the initial Down syndrome diagnosis the rest of the medical team were supportive. During the hospital stay the time of her heart surgery was unknown; but ideally the team estimated the surgery would be around 6 months of age. We had regular monthly visits to monitor her growth, heart murmur development and weight gain.

Ultimately, the team decided to surgery was better completed earlier than later. Thea was scheduled for surgery just before she turned three months; she only weight 7lbs 8oz. Still a peanut. Surgery to this day, this the most difficult thing I have been through. The preparation, the team taking her and the waiting…and waiting. Hourly updates were helpful but we just wanted to be reunited with her. She showed her strengthen, after 7 hours of surgery she had her 3 holes repaired; 2 ASDs, 1 VSD and a closure of the PDA. A warrior. I don't think anything can prepare a parent to seeing a child following OHS; it's hard, devastating, a feeling of helplessness. Recovery, happened. It was the longest 12 days

in that CICU (cardiac ICU). I didn't' think it was ever going t end. There was progress but setbacks; infection, a clasped lung, but day by day she gained strength. The warrior shined through. We have had our number of medical appointments and visits with ENT/audiologist, ophthalmologist, swallow study, cardiologist follow-ups, endocrinologist. But bless her soul; she is strong and health. Only once has she been prescribed antibiotics in her the first 17 months of her life.

Thea is now almost 18 month; and she truly is such an incredible child. Honestly, I wouldn't change a thing about my girl. Some days, I do worry; but worrying is expected for any parent. I probably worry more some days and I am okay with that. What worry me most are stereotypes and stigmas. It's time to open the world to what is the truth. I am working on it- one day at a time…everyday!
Thea is the child we always wanted. She is feisty and has a happy, hearty-soul. She makes our days brighter. I have no doubt she will be an amazing little girl and will continue to surprise us with all her accomplishments. She has already brought so much joy to our home and hearts. And she will definitely continue!

~Kate, Thea's mom; 30; Wisconsin, United States

{Zoey}

Defining moments.

When I look back over the past nine months this is the phrase the most often comes to mind. There is now a definite line in the sand. Before Zoey and after. I have long known the before - it's the after that had me scared to death.

In all honesty I did not know much about Down syndrome. I just knew it was the thing I was often warned about as a complication as I grew older at my yearly OBGYN visits. As I approached 30 it felt like this was just cause to create some urgency in starting a family.

Growing up I didn't really know anyone with Down syndrome. We had a summer camp hosted at our local high school for young adults with different developmental disabilities. Some of my friends volunteered that week and I remember really admiring them for that, personally I felt a bit

uncomfortable. I was so afraid of having anyone think I was "talking down" to them, I just didn't want to insult anyone and for that I shied away. I was ignorant and nervous about stepping out of my comfort zone.

Fast forward to present day, I was 35 years old and pregnant with my third baby. I had had a 2nd trimester miscarriage with my previous pregnancy so while this pregnancy was turning out to be uneventful I was often on edge. I frequently asked baby for some reassurance and she was always willing to oblige with some hearty kicks.

As my due date came and went I wasn't too worried. I had gone over with my previous pregnancies so I felt this was just routine. My doctor had me undergo a biophysical exam, followed my a non-stress test because baby didn't want to do her practice breathing. Two days later same tests were repeated with the same result. The reason I mention this was because immediately after I delivered she didn't cry hard - I was so worried she wasn't breathing - I must have asked a million times if she was ok. Looking back I should have known something was going on. The room was much too quiet. There were too many people there. No one congratulated us on the birth of our baby. Nobody said we had a healthy baby girl. No one was talking, the room was so quiet, and looks avoided.

The most remarkable times in my life have been the birth of my children Jack and Maya, I felt joy like I never knew existed, like my heart might just explode with happiness. Zoey's birth was different.

I had a very rapid delivery and had a terrible migraine immediately following delivery. I was able to hold her for a few moments before they whisked her away to the NICU. At this point I wasn't too concerned. She was breathing on her own after all. I remember looking at her and thought "huh ... something seems different?" But soon she was gone and my family and I were laughing and joking about that crazy delivery.

Not long after the doctor walked in and I knew something was wrong, I could tell whatever he was about to say was something paining even his heart. I will never forget those moments. I will never forget the detail. I will never forget how the doctor spoke softly but yet with concern. Down syndrome.

This must be some kind of nightmare. Please God please wake me up! This can't be happening, this can't be real. This CAN'T be happening! I felt heartache like I had never known. It was the most devastating sadness. Sadness and heartache so intense, so very intense, so cutting. I couldn't breathe, the weight was so heavy. I clung to my husband and sobbed. Still praying for this to be some kind of nightmare. We were in shock. I felt numb.

It seemed like forever till we were able to go see her. It felt strange. I was nervous to see her. How was I going to react. I mean I still loved this baby right? Yet everything felt different. I just had a baby, where was the happiness? Instead it was replaced with instructions on NICU protocol, my baby covered in wires and tubes, and immense fear. She didn't look like my baby, this didn't feel like my baby. I hurt so desperately. I looked and looked at her and touched her soft skin. "Why God?" I hate to admit I questioned 'Why us?' Why were we being punished? I feel terrible for those feelings now, but I want to add these details because somewhere someone else may be going through the same emotions – and it's okay. I know its seems so hard right now but you will pick yourself up and do this. You will find love for your little one that is more powerful then anything you could ever imagine.

Joy has returned. It was there all along but my own worry, fear and ignorance were in the way. I say "Defining Moments" because it has all changed. My role as mom has changed, my relationship with God has changed, my outlook on life has changed. Everything changed – changed for the better. I feel my own life has taken on such focus – advocate and educater.

I recently read a quote "If you believe in something with all your heart, then fight for it with all your might."* And I believe in Zoey.

~Jackie, Zoey's mom; 35; North Dakota, United States

*sevenly.org (quote source)

{Aiden}

To tell you our story I will have to take you back to the part when we decided it was time to bring a baby into our lives. I had always dreamed of being a mother, raising my children with my husband by my side. A baby was all I could think about and over the next fourteen months we discovered just how difficult it was to get the timing right. After one heart breaking miscarriage I was pregnant with Aiden. During the next nine months I day dreamed about who he might look like, I just wanted him to be perfect in every way. Than strangely on the other hand I would day dream about how I would cope if he was born with a disability and think about how that would impact on our daily lives.

Strange as this may sound I think I did this as a way to prepare myself for the unexpected. As I always had this feeling something wasn't quite right even though the midwives reassured me at every appointment that he looked perfectly fine. But no matter what I just couldn't shake the feeling. I guess you might call it mother's intuition. I remember one visit in particular with my midwives when I brought up the nuchal translucency scan. She was surprised I asked about it and reassured me that I was low risk due to my age and no family history. She informed me I had only a three day window left to get the ultrasound done. The next day I was straight on the phone calling all the scan places though no one could fit me in. I still the remember the phone

conversation I had that day with my husband. I told him I couldn't get the appointment, then I asked him, "It will be alright wont it? Like the midwife said we are too young to have a baby with Down syndrome". He responded confidently,

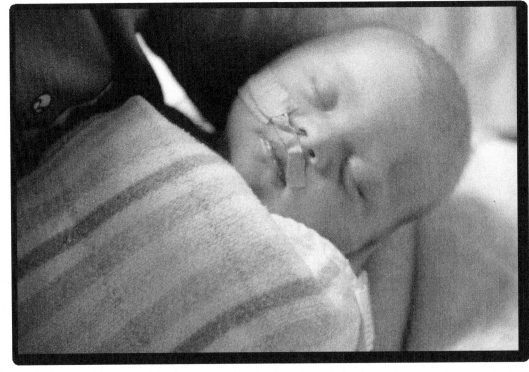

"Yeah of course it will be ok". Then that was the end of that. Looking back I believe God intervened here as we were both adamant from our previous discussion that we didn't want to bring a child with a disability into this cruel world. It would be too heart breaking to see them struggle and suffer. Little did I know that that's not what life would be like with Aiden.

Finally the day arrived a little earlier than expected at 36 weeks. I was more excited about going into labour than scared of what was to come. I called all my family while pacing excitedly and breathing through each contraction. I kept focused in the beginning by reminding myself that each contraction was bringing me closer to holding my baby for first time. After eight hours of what I described as the most horrific pain I have ever felt I finally saw my little man for the first time. Feeling his warm slippery body on my chest was surreal. I gently kissed his forehead in complete awe that this baby somehow fitted inside me and now here he is. Then they whisked him away.

Still in a daze from the birthing experience I was being attended to by my nurse while the other was looking Aiden over doing the usual assessments. Out of nowhere she announced, "I am going to call in the paediatrician because he looks a little floppy." Little did I know how my world was about to be tipped upside down and my path in life changed forever. I remember the paediatrician announcing to the room, "He has features of trisomy 21". I looked around the room at my family's' worried faces and my husband asked him what that meant. He responded with, "Down syndrome". I questioned him disbelieving his words, "Are you ever wrong?" In a cold, definite tone he stated, "No" and marched out of the room. In that moment I felt myself detach from reality and in my head all these images of what I thought Down syndrome to be flashed in my mind. The almond eyes I knew but I had images of adults not being able to walk, talk or function. Then a thought crossed my mind that this baby who will grow to be an adult will now be living with us for the rest of his life. He will need twenty-four - seven care right through his adult years. Selfishly I kept thinking I will never have a life with just me and my husband again and that's if we even survive this. I felt myself go numb and cold inside. Then it was my turn to hold him and I reluctantly did. He looked peaceful all wrapped up in his stripped hospital blanket. I stared at him thinking this isn't what I wanted over and over again. In that moment I disowned him and handed him to who ever wanted him, I just knew it wasn't me. Looking back I wished that the doctors would have let me have my bonding time first before they dropped the bomb on us that night. I couldn't help but wonder if this would have changed my post natal experience with Aiden.

That night the nurses kindly rearranged the rooms so my husband could stay with me. All night I laid in bed awake waiting for the sun to come up and for it all to be a mistake. Getting the confirmation the next morning was earth shattering. I was overwhelmed with grief for the baby I had imagined had lost and for the one who now took its place. Despite my worries from the moment Aiden was born my husband was a proud loving dad who only saw a helpless little baby who needed our love and support. He stayed by his bedside until I had the strength to face reality and visit him in the special care nursery the next morning. He was my rock through the most difficult time in my life and this only strengthened our bond as a couple.

Over the next week Aiden was transferred between hospitals as they discovered he had two holes in his heart (complete AVSD) and the doctors explained that he would stay in hospital until he either went into heart failure or began putting on weight but surgery was inevitable. As the weeks passed his condition continued to deteriorate despite the doctors best efforts. That time in hospital I spent every day with him trying to form an attachment. I bathed him, cuddled him, talked to him and when no one was around quietly sung him songs. Truthfully I felt like an actor pretending to be this loving mother but all I felt was numb inside.

I was adamant that I wanted to try to breastfeed Aiden as we all thought it would be a great bonding experience for the both of us. Despite my efforts Aiden had trouble latching due to the low muscle tone then as his condition deteriorated so did his ability to stay awake and feed. At four weeks old he was transferred to the children's hospital and three days later I reluctantly handed my vulnerable little man over to the heart surgeons. It was in that moment I realised I didn't want to let him go. I broke down in an uncontrollable sob and truthfully this surprised me. That day I prayed to God "I do want him, I will love him, I don't care that he has Down syndrome. I'm sorry I didn't realise it at the start but please help him get through this". Just in case God didn't hear me the first time I repeated it over and over again in that waiting room. The second the pager beeped my entire family all jumped up at once and raced to the door to hear the good news that the surgery was a success.

Looking at Aiden for the first time with all the wires and tubes was confronting and scary. He was swollen and looked nothing like the little man that I held that morning. Over the following week he was weaned off his medications, oxygen and began tolerating tube feeds again. Slowly his swelling went down and after a few scares and six weeks in hospital from his birth day it was time to go home. Naively I thought the worst was over but little did I know the challenges that lay ahead for both me and Aiden.

That time at home I was overwhelmed with administering his heart medications, specialist visits, therapies, dealing with his range of health issues and sicknesses plus on top of this processing all the information I could find relating to Down syndrome. It wasn't long until it was obvious to my friends and family that I was depressed and not coping. With my families support and encouragement I sought the help I needed and finally I saw the light at the end of a very dark tunnel. I remember the time when it all changed for me. Aiden was eight months old laughing and giggling in his cot. I picked him up and for the first time I felt a surge of love inside me. In that moment I fell in love and began to feel again. I finally began to feel proud to have my little man and began to see him as a baby first and his diagnosis second. Overtime I no longer saw the Down syndrome when I looked at him and I eventually stopped thinking about it constantly. To us Aiden is just Aiden.

We feel so lucky and blessed that he chose us to be his parents. He brings so much joy and laughter to our lives. He means the world to our families and we would never wish to change him or our journey. I know our future will be challenging with many ups and downs but now I am not scared. I am excited to see him grow and develop into a young man. We are just thankful to have him here with us and whatever the future holds we will face it together as a family. If I could go back in time I would tell myself back then that life now with Aiden is difficult at times but most of all it is full of happiness and laughter. He is perfect and exactly what you wanted plus more, you just don't realise it yet.

It has taken me four years since his diagnosis to write my story. This is the first time I haven't cried reliving those painful memories of our first year. I used to feel guilty about my feelings in the start and how I reacted. I found it hard to share these deep dark feelings with anyone but now I have realised it's not about where you start, it's about the journey and where you end up that's important….love and acceptance. Now instead of feeling a great sense of burden that I will always have to care for him I feel lucky that he will always be close by perhaps even out the back in the granny flat. But whatever the case I hope he is never too far away.

Aiden is a thriving, cheeky, strong willed four and half year old little man. His fun loving personality is infectious with not only family and friends but strangers we meet on our daily journeys. He starts at special needs school next year and is talking two to three word sentences. He loves exploring outside and being overly rough with his younger brother. This year he has been healthy with no trips to hospital or sicknesses. All the specialist visits have slowed right down and life finally feels normal. It's been a tough journey but he is definitely worth every minute of it.

~Michelle, Aiden's mum; 25; NSW, Australia

{Eden}

When I think about the day we got Eden's diagnosis, there is no one word to explain it. It is like a million tiny air bubbles, each with a different emotion or thought, effervescing to the surface of reality. Some thoughts sting, some are sweet, and you just cannot take them all in at once.

We received her diagnosis at birth, but to understand the place I was in, I have to provide a little background of my pregnancy first.

I met my husband in a whirlwind of romance in 2009. In 2010, we lost our first child to an early miscarriage. But in 2011, I found out I was pregnant again just after our 1 year wedding anniversary! We were so ready to do everything right, and that included taking any options offered to us such as pre-natal testing, even though I didn't exactly know what that was at the time. After my 12 week ultra-sound/NT scan and first trimester blood tests, I sat alone in the waiting room filled with every confidence in the world. After one miscarriage, I figured this was my turn to have the perfect pregnancy! I've rarely ever been sick. I like to think I take good care of myself. And I'm pretty lucky most of the time—that's just how my life works. Everything was falling perfectly in place.

After quite a long time of fumbling with the blood test numbers, the doctors at the testing center were able to present me with first trimester screen that just cleared the "normal range" for someone my age [for a Down syndrome pregnancy]. (1:336) They wrote down some dates I could come in for an amnio, but invasive testing was never in my plan. So I opted just to come back for the Quad Screen (to complete the sequential screening), hoping to set my mind at ease. Weeks went by. My pregnancy stayed right on track. And I called to check the results of the Quad screen at about 18 weeks. "1:560" the nurse let me know. This pregnancy was now officially "normal."

Our 20-week anatomy scan looked great, and we found out we were having a baby girl! My only complications were nerve-related pain, but everything with our baby girl checked out perfectly every time. She had a strong heartbeat, and she even used to kick the heartbeat monitor they put on my belly—which prompted the nurse practitioner to tell me that meant she was "smart". Ten days before my due date, on the weekend of a full-moon (just as I had predicted), my water broke at on a Saturday morning. By 10pm we were at the hospital, and labor was on!

Our sweet baby girl was born at 4:56am on a Sunday. She was placed on my chest with wide-open doe-eyes, flanked by long lashes, and she looked right into my eyes with tiny expression of wonder. In those first few moments, I will admit that I had a sense that something about her was *different*. But I had certainly never seen a baby that brand new, so I quickly pushed any uneasy thoughts to the back of my mind. I kept her close to me for a few minutes before I

relinquished her to my husband who carried her to the nursery with the nurse.

When my husband returned, I started to get up to get myself together, and that's when the pediatrician on call stepped in. He said he wanted to talk to us "about the baby," but the tone in which he said that was off. I was already feeling horribly guilty for taking the pain medicine, and I was expecting to get a scolding for that. But he began to go through a list of her features and finally said, "It looks like we have a Downs baby." I just stood there, part of my brain thinking that he *must* be wrong because that was not what the tests said and part of my brain already knowing that he just verbalized what I went through my mind earlier that morning. I was sad, scared, angry at the doctor, apologetic to my husband—I felt like I had failed him. But that's when my husband hugged me and said, "God must have thought this little girl needed some awesome parents."

We hugged a little while longer, and he asked me if I wanted to stay in the room a bit more. But the next thing I remember saying was that I was ready "to get dressed and get tough." She needed us. And we didn't know if yet, but we needed her too.

~ Sheri; Eden's mom; 35; Tennessee

On Twitte:r @xinefly

{Henry}

I came home worn out from the long week of work. My ever-growing belly was now at 38 weeks, and I was slowing down. I woke up Saturday morning, feeling rested and refreshed. We went about our day, going for groceries and taking our dog for a walk through the winding streets of our neighborhood. The weather was beautiful and the contractions started coming, with Charlie studiously timing them.

As the night came and went, time got fuzzy and the pain intensified, until we decided to go to the hospital at 6:00am.

The triage nurse then checked me for dilation, and I was at a 9, so was immediately wheeled me into L&D to start pushing. My OB materialized, and no more waiting! I could feel the baby moving, and I changed positions until I found one that worked.

I caught my breath one more time and pushed as hard as I could, screaming the whole time. "Fire, fire, fire!' and then relief, as his head, then shoulders came out. He was here at last! Our Henry. I listened desperately for his cry, which came loud and clear and mad. I heard Apgar scores of 9's in the background and sobbed with happiness and relief. We were safely on the other side.

The nurses put him right on my chest, wide awake, with deep, dark blue eyes. His poor head was coned from all the pushing but I didn't care. He was perfect. He looked right at me almost curiously, studying. I gingerly touched his spiky tuft of blonde hair, his narrow shoulders, and kissed him. He was so warm. I held him to me, bringing him to my breast. He looked up at me and tried to suck. He was just a little small, still, to latch, but he licked and tried. Proudly, I exclaimed "My smart baby, you know what to do!"

The nurse later asked Charlie if he wanted to hold his son, wrapped up in the pink- and green-striped swaddling cloth. He took Henry from me nervously, and leaned down to him. "I'm your daddy, do you know me?" I cried again. We grabbed our iPhones and I snapped a picture of Henry with his dad and we started texting and calling, getting the news out. The room quietly emptied out.

We moved to the comfortable Recovery room, which already had 'Welcome to the world Henry Joseph!' scribbled on the whiteboard. The sun shone and we couldn't stop staring at our boy. Henry loved cuddling with both of us, but we were still struggling with breast feeding. I asked for a lactation consultant to come in because he still wasn't latching, but I'd read somewhere it would take practice and time for my milk to come in. The University of Michigan basketball game came on at noon, and Charlie watched the game with Henry sleeping in his arms. He was the happiest I'd ever seen him. I slept for the first time since he was born.

The pediatrician came for his rounds at 2pm. He greeted us and took Henry gingerly from Charlie's arms, and laid him on the examination table. He moved Henry's limbs, checking for flexibility. He picked Henry up to see how strong his neck was. I looked at my firstborn being handled and then impatiently at the doctor, just wanting my baby back.

He quietly handed Henry back to me and I was only half listening as he began to talk. I already knew what he was going to say, that Henry is perfect, and focused all my attention on my baby. "Did you know Henry was going to be a boy?"

"Yup!" I said proudly. "We could tell right away at the ultrasound."

"You had an ultrasound?" he asked, almost sharply.

Cluelessly, I answered again happily, looking only at Henry, "Oh, yes. We had one done at 19 weeks."

He cleared his throat and started speaking again.

"The nurses noted some characteristics that led them to believe there is a possibility that your son has Down syndrome..."

I finally looked up at him, holding Henry protectively as he continued.

"Henry has smaller, lower set ears, and his tongue protrudes somewhat. There is a gap between his big toe and his other toes and he may have folds on his eyelids. I've looked at him and can't quite be sure, though. Usually babies with Down syndrome have low muscle tone and he doesn't. There is often a single crease on the palm of the hand, but I don't see that with him."

"Babies with Down syndrome may have heart issues. I didn't hear a heart murmur at all, which is a good sign, but in order to confirm he's okay we'll need to do an echocardiogram on him right away. The most common defects are ASDs and VSDs, and there are ways to fix them if Henry has either of these."

"Again, it's hard for me to tell. The nurses noticed it but I don't see it so clearly. The only way to know for sure is to get a sample for a karyotype to count the number of chromosomes. I just don't think it's fair to take this without telling the parents. In case it is positive they should be prepared."

My mind raced and I was very still as I was taking this in. The important thing was not to scare Henry - or the doctor. I wanted to handle this well. I thought quickly...The nurses are who noticed first. They see so many babies, they usually are right because they have all that experience... Still, Henry probably didn't have any heart problems. The doctor even said so.

I held Henry tight and trained my eyes on the doctor. He was uncomfortable. That wasn't a good sign either. My stomach started to feel dread. Still, there was only a possibility. Maybe just a ten percent risk. And I'm so lucky. There's no way this will turn out bad in the end. I'm so very lucky. Very soon I'll be out of the hospital and remember this as a scare.

I didn't speak, but eventually heard Charlie's clear voice, behind me. God, I was so relieved. I couldn't even think to ask any questions, and was so thankful he could.

"When you say 'a chance', what does that mean? What percentage would you give it?"

The doctor cleared his throat and said, "Fifty-fifty, maybe."

I stopped breathing, and remained very still, as my mind flew. ...Fifty-fifty is too big. No. No. It's just too much of a chance, a flip of a coin for my son's future? It's not that maybe he has Down syndrome anymore, it's that maybe he doesn't...

I looked down at Henry, trying to shut the doctor out. The room grew, the doctor seemed to retreat, and Henry and I shrank together, everything seeming too massive. I heard Charlie's voice again, far behind me this time. Not even a second had gone by but the world was completely different.

"This conversation doesn't feel like fifty-fifty. Would you put money on it?"

The doctor paused and looked at us, assessing. Then, simply:

"I'd put money on it."

The conversation continued, quietly, with us grilling the doctor. What did ASD and VSD stand for? We needed to research. And then it was over, the sun was setting in the warm winter. He promised to come back tomorrow, to check on us. On his way out, our pediatrician stopped.

"The most important thing right now is that you treat him just like you would for any baby. He needs the same food and care and love that any other baby does."

Well duh. Of course I would treat him the same. Still, it was a relief to hear.

We were alone now. The room started out silent, with me on the hospital bed holding Henry and Charlie in the father's corner, both researching furiously on our phones. We both stared at Henry, trying to reconcile him with the images of babies with Down syndrome on the Internet. I found the statistics, that about 1 in every 750-800 babies born to women my age have Down syndrome, and started scanning everybody that I knew who had a baby. I was the only one. A new parents guide online had a question on if the assessments from doctors were ever found to be wrong once the karyotype was back. The answer was no, that it was incredibly rare. So, that was it then. No more denial, it wasn't a 50-50 shot. It wasn't even an "I'd put my money on it." It was pretty much a certainty. Even in the dusk, looking down at Henry in my arms, his ear was a little too folded. Everything else I could explain away, but the ear. All of it together just added up. And why wouldn't it be me, us? It only makes sense. Statistically someone will be the one out of 800.

Charlie was over in the father's area coming to the same conclusion. I had family friends that had a daughter with Ds, so the questions started, raining on top of me. How much did I know? What were her limitations? Could she play sports? Read? Talk? Then came the most important questions. "Is she happy? Are her parents happy?"

I thought about it honestly. Well, yes, she is happy. I used to go to her basketball games. She could talk, and walk, and play sports. Her parents are very happy, still in love after all these years. I looked at Charlie and firmly stated "This is not a tragedy. This is just something we didn't pick." He agreed again, and we changed Henry together.

Charlie said he was going to talk to the pediatrician tomorrow, to tell him that we understood what it all meant and that we were fine. At least that way we could get our cards on the table without being patronized.

After feeding Henry and gently placing him in his bassinet, I got a heavy heart again. I crawled out of the hospital bed and over to the father's futon area, near the window. It was dark now, and we clung to each other, crying at times. He was hooked up to wires to check his heart and too small and tired to breastfeed. Everybody would know. All of our friends, everybody at work, would find out and pity us, gossip about him.

I deserved this, somehow. I was so proud of myself the whole pregnancy for giving Charlie a healthy baby. I crawled into the shower and as it started to warm up, my insides ached and I began wracking with sobs. I went from having everything I'd ever dreamed of and lost it all, all within hours.

Why did it have to be my son? He's innocent, perfect. He didn't do anything to deserve this. Why is it him and not me?

I racked my brain stupidly, trying desperately to offer something that would help. A trade. I'd offer myself for him to be normal. I knew even as I was thinking that it was useless. I couldn't give anybody anything that could help. I was completely helpless. I had absolutely nothing to offer. Charlie wouldn't want us anymore. He would be ashamed of us.

I stayed in the shower a long time, willing the water to wash away my grief. My routine helped, shampoo, conditioner, face wash, body wash, towel dry, lotion. My nice clean warm clothes in place of my bloody robe. It was a first step towards normalcy.

And after this, Henry slept soundly, curling into me, trusting me. Suddenly I was ashamed. I had to protect Henry from the world, even me. He is my baby, and I wasn't going to let him down ever again. He was healthy and handsome and just the baby I asked for, and we vowed not to ever take him for granted. I climbed back in the oversized bed, cuddling with Henry again to soothe me, and Charlie soon joined us both. When we were with him it was all so much easier. He was just our son and we were his mommy and daddy.

Today Henry is a happy, thriving 19 month old! He is standing all by himself and already taking a few steps! He toddles around the house holding my hand looking for his doggie and eating Cheerios off the floor. He breastfed until he started solids at 6 months old, and his favorite foods are avocado and pasta. Every day he kisses and tickles his mommy and daddy, plays with his elephant and ring toys, stacks his blocks, and helps us play music and read books. He uses about 15 signs with us, showing us trees, fish, and telling us when he wants food or is 'all done'!

He is handsome, smart, loving, and wonderful, and best known for his white blonde Mohawk and his amazing smile. He is truly the most fun little boy I could dream of having, and I wouldn't trade one moment with him for the world. We were made to be his parents and Henry to be our son, and the more we grow together the more I realize how lucky we are! He's already taught me more about life, love, and happiness than I ever thought possible!

~ Shawn, Henry's mom; 32; North Carolina, United States

{Camden}

I was walking to Starbucks at work with a friend and I was talking about my 20 week sonogram coming up. "I can't wait for this appointment because I have been worried about Down syndrome". I don't know why I said it, but it was true. I declined all prenatal testing even though with my first I did them all. Fast forward to being 28 weeks pregnant and I'm in the hospital. My water had broke and I was on bed rest hoping to wait it out until 34 weeks. A perinatologist comes in to do a detailed sonogram. "Did your OB ever mention anything about Down syndrome?" I kind of froze and just answered "no, why? Do you see something?" She said she saw nothing in particular and it was not discussed further. I would stay on bed rest in the hospital for approximately three more weeks before Camden would make his appearance. I never thought about Down syndrome again. I put it out of my mind.

At 31 weeks a c-section was scheduled since baby boy decided he was ready. I remember that Monday as if it were yesterday. It was November 26th at 7:00 am. The nurse who would

accompany me would be the first nurse I had at admission three weeks earlier. I hadn't seen her since then. This was my first c-section so the nerves were high. I remember my husband sitting by my side holding my hand still because I was shaking uncontrollably. It took only minutes and I hear the doctor say, "Here he comes". I start whispering "Please let him cry, please let him cry" over and over

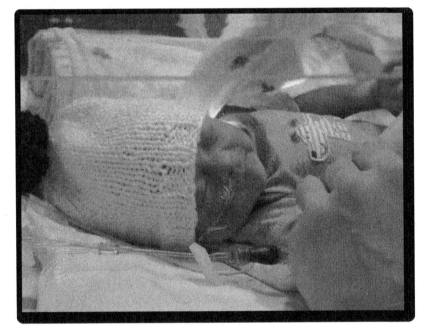

again. He's not supposed to be here this early and I just want to hear him cry. In the next few seconds I hear the angelic sound of my baby boy's cries. Sighs of relief and tears come soon after. I get a glimpse of him before they wheel him away to the NICU. My husband would accompany him while they finish up with me in the OR. After what felt like a lifetime I was taken to the NICU to see my boy. He was perfect. He was breathing on his own and doing fantastic. They put him on my chest and I just closed my eyes and held him. The next few seconds would shatter my perfect moment with my boy. The doctor came over to explain what wouldl happen during his stay in the NICU. Then he said, "We are sending off some tests because of his dysmorphic facial features". Huh? I was still in a bit of a haze due to medications and I didn't

even think to ask him anything else before he disappeared. So I then turn to the nurse and ask her what he was talking about. She tells me that they suspect he has Down syndrome. It still didn't register in my brain. That couldn't be right. Everything has been fine up until now. She told me it would take a week to get the results back and not to worry. I have heard when a physician suspects a newborn has DS that they are right about 90% of the time. This was so different because it was more like 50/50. I'm half Korean which means Camden is a quarter. So a lot of the nurses (and even doctors) thought it was just the Asian features. One doctor even told me not to worry because she doubts he has it. So, I didn't really worry about it. In fact, my husband and I put it out of our minds because it didn't seem possible.

Exactly one week later on December 3, 2012, I heard the words that would change our lives forever. "I'm sorry mom, he does have it". I can't describe the pain that goes through you. It's as if she told me my child was gone. I couldn't see because there were so many tears. I remember putting my baby boy back in his isolette and walking out of the NICU broken hearted. I called my husband since he was not with me. He was two hours away back at home working. I don't recall much about the conversation as we were both devastated. We didn't even talk the next two days. I will always remember when my husband came to see us after those two days and the first words out of his mouth when he pulled up were, "I'm excited. This is gonna be good". That was the moment I knew we would be okay...more than okay.

Camden is a healthy, happy, thriving and stubborn 9 month old today. All the medical appointments have slowed down and we are enjoying each and every moment with our sweet boy. His personality is really starting to shine through. His whole face lights up when he smiles and he lets you know (very loudly) when no one is giving him any attention. He is definitely a daddy's boy as daddy spoils him rotten. We are working on sitting, rolling, and crawling. We just started using sign language videos and he seems to really enjoy them! We are excited about what the future holds and I can tell you that this amazing boy has changed our lives in the absolute most positive way!

~ Diane, Camden's mom; 33; Texas, United States

Blogging @ www.mycsinthecountry.blogspot.com

{Asher}

I am the mom of three boys. My second son was born with a birth defect called Spina bifida. It is a defect of the spine and can often be diagnosed via ultrasound while the baby is in utero. When we decided to have a third child we asked to have periodic ultrasounds so we could look

for any signs of Spina bifida. This was just so we knew how to proceed in plans for the birth. We were always sure we would have this baby.

At 20 weeks we had an ultrasound done by a perinatologist. At the appointment he told us there were no markers for Spina bifida and the baby looked to have a completely intact spine but there were several markers for Down syndrome. My heart felt so heavy I thought it might fall out of my chest. I had been so focused on Spina bifida I hadn't even thought of any other possibility. I was in shock. The doctor offered several different tests but they all had risks to the baby and we wanted the baby regardless of the results, so we refused them and went home.

Over the next weeks I felt in a panic. I talked to family and friends who had similar markers, a spot on the heart, enlarged kidneys, advanced maternal age, whose babies had turned out perfectly fine. My fears began to diminish. I was just sure God was not going to give us two babies with special needs.

At the 32 week recheck the spot on the heart had disappeared. So, with only the two other markers our odds of having a baby with Down syndrome went down significantly. Both my husband and I relaxed completely, sure that this meant the baby would be fine.

At exactly 38 weeks I went into labor. It was a fast labor. I had a planned homebirth. My midwives made it in time to guide the baby out, within 20 minutes of their arrival Asher Riley was there.

Right away the midwives knew something was not quite right. He never opened his eyes. He never cried. It was like he was sleeping, through the entire birthing process. The midwife started to do mouth to mouth on him hoping to perk him up and wake him. His color pinked up, he had been very blue, but still there was no sound and no eyes looking around.

We decided to transport to the hospital.

At the hospital we learned that Asher weighed in at 10 pounds, 2 ounces and was 22 inches long. We also learned he had many markers for Down syndrome. As soon as the pediatrician said we think he has Down syndrome the tears started falling. This was not supposed to happen again. I was not supposed to have another baby with special needs. I was supposed to be cuddling my new baby at home, on my bed, surrounded by my loving family, with my husband cooking me French toast in the kitchen! What kind of rotten joke was this?!

I remember at some point my husband whispering in my ear that he looked just like our first born and they must be mistaken. I remember grasping on to that last thread of hope, willing him to be right. The next two weeks Asher was in the NICU of our local Children's Hospital. He had to be tube fed for the first week and a half because he didn't want to wake up and do it himself. We were told of the test results, that Asher did indeed have Down syndrome.

I felt anxious, scared, angry at my body for 'messing up' again, angry at God for not fixing things. But the more I held my new baby, and smelled him, and touched him the more those negative feelings started to wash away. Asher didn't open his eyes for the first four days of life and the first time he looked at me I thought not just my heart but my entire body would melt from sheer joy.

Moments of joy just kept coming. Watching his older brothers with him was amazing. Their unconditional acceptance and love for him was a testimony to me. When my middle son whispered in his ear, 'It's okay, Asher. I'll protect you,' I realized that this was a great place to be. This was our normal. This was where I belonged. It may not look like what the world portrayed as the perfect, typical family but this place was incredible and so much more than that cookie cutter image!

I have learned through my second son and now with Asher that there will be moments of sorrow and grief, moments where I will wish things were different, where I will be sorrowful that things are so hard for Asher. And I must allow myself to embrace these times, allow myself to grieve. That is part of the process. But I also must force myself to let those moments go because if I hold on to them I will never get to experience the incredible gift it is to get to be Asher's mom.

And he really is a gift. Our family has been changed because of his existence. We are all better people because he is in our world.

~ Kristin, Asher's mom; 35; Minnesota, United States

Blogging @ http://countitalljoy.blogspot.com/

{Isabel}

In June of 2011, at ten weeks pregnant, I went in for an ultrasound and found out that our baby's heart was no longer beating. I was devastated. We had lost two babies prior to our oldest child and now a third? My husband Mike and I decided that we should be content with our two healthy daughters and made plans for him to get a vasectomy. We just couldn't bear the thought of losing another little one and going through that incredibly painful experience ever again.

Despite our intentions, time passed and we never got around to scheduling Mike's procedure. It was December and I was extremely busy getting ready for the holidays. Our baby's due date had been December 24th and I couldn't help but feel sadness that the one Christmas gift I desperately wanted would not be arriving. A few days later I realized that my period was late and quickly ran to the store to get a pregnancy test. I took the test and two pink lines showed up and I couldn't help but feel joy where there once had been sadness. God was repairing my broken heart and giving us this unexpected chance to add another blessing to our family.

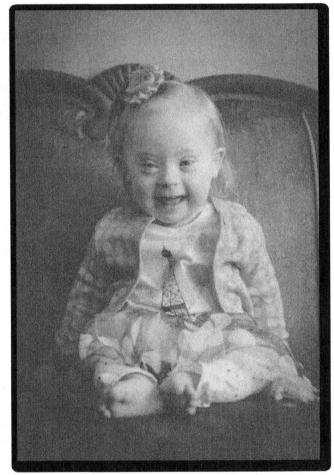

My pregnancy was fairly uneventful. I declined all genetic testing despite being considered at risk due to my "advanced maternal age" of 36 years old. I figured any major health problems would be apparent on our ultrasounds. We found out that we were having another girl and decided to name her Isabel.

My c-section was scheduled and on August 17th, 2012, we headed to the hospital to meet this new little one. Isabel arrived much like her sisters, getting pulled out of me, cold and crying. I was relieved at the sound and couldn't help but cry my own tears of thankfulness that she appeared to be healthy. I impatiently waited to get a close look at our new daughter. It felt like an eternity but when they finally brought her to me, I immediately noticed that she looked quite a bit different from our other daughters and for a moment I felt a tinge of worry. I quickly brushed it off as nothing and relaxed while they whisked her off to our recovery room with Mike.

While they were sewing me up, Mike had some time to get a further look at our new arrival. He couldn't help but notice that her neck looked a little different in addition to her facial features. Although neither of us had any experience with Down syndrome, he immediately felt that these features pointed in that direction. He wasted no time in expressing these concerns to our nurse, who quickly dismissed his questions as silly. When I arrived in the room, the nurse finished cleaning Isabel up and handed her to Mike so she could get me situated in our new room. It was then that Mike asked for a third time if she may have Down syndrome. After an uncomfortable period of silence, our nurse quietly approached us and told us her suspicions that our baby did in fact have Down syndrome. In that instant it felt like the world had collapsed all around me. I felt numb as she showed us all of the physical markers that Isabel displayed. Our nurse went on to tell us that our little girl could have a hard time nursing due to something called "low tone".

Breastfeeding was something that was so important to me that I immediately felt a need to prove her wrong. Surprisingly, Isabel latched on beautifully and nursed like a pro. I felt comforted in this fact and rejoiced in Isabel's success.

Somehow Mike and I were able to hold it together in these first moments. There were no tears, no sadness and no anger. After we were transferred to our permanent room we knew it was time to allow our parents, siblings and girls in to meet our newest addition. Despite Isabel not being what we expected, I did not want there to be sadness. I also felt that the news should be relayed to our family before they came to the room. I knew I would break down in tears if I was the one to say something so I asked Mike to tell them in the waiting room. When our family finally entered our room, we received congratulations, love and joy over our new little one and for this I will be eternally grateful.

Our plan had been for Mike to return to our home with the girls for the night. I knew that, like me, he was hurting on the inside and desperately needed time to himself to process everything before we could talk together. Thankfully his parents agreed to watch the girls and he was able to have that alone time.

That night, while in my room with Isabel, I finally allowed myself to grieve for the child that was not to be. Desperate to talk to someone, I called my dear friend Val. Through my sobbing and tears I told her the news and shared my fears. My biggest fear was that I could not be the mother that Isabel needed. I could barely handle my two girls, how could I handle a child with special needs?

Despite my grief, I shared my belief that Isabel would be good for our family. I knew that she would shape us into better people. But would we be able to give HER the love and care that SHE needed? Adding to my fear was the very scary list of possible medical issues she could have that the pediatrician had shared with us earlier that afternoon. I poured my heart out to her and like always, she told me exactly what I needed to hear.

With our older girls with our parents, Mike and I spent the next two days in the hospital together with our new little girl. She seemed to be doing remarkably well. Despite this, we were fearful that Isabel could have a serious heart problem and our pediatrician arranged for her to get an Echocardiogram before we were discharged. Thankfully, there were no serious defects found and we were free to go home.

We couldn't go home without a middle name for our baby. Initially we had wanted her to be Isabel Sophia, but that just didn't seem right. Despite our concerns, we could already tell that she would bring happiness to our lives and there really wasn't any other middle name that could fit except "Joy".

After we arrived home, we struggled to get our little girl to stay awake and eat. Although she did well at breastfeeding, she continued to lose weight due to her sleepiness. I eventually started giving her pumped breast milk with added calories and finally she was able to gain weight. Isabel also had another Echocardiogram and thankfully that did not show any areas of concern.

When Isabel was six weeks old, we had our first meeting with the "Help Me Grow" Early Intervention Program. They thought she was doing great but were a little concerned with her vision as she had not started to track things. While we waited to see the Ophthalmologist, I almost convinced myself that she was blind. After a thorough eye exam, we found out that while she did have clogged ducts and nystagmus, Isabel's vision was completely fine.

These first two months were consumed with worry over immediate feeding concerns, therapy questions and uncertainty about her health. I spent a lot of time online researching feeding techniques, therapy, vision questions and learning as much as I could about life with Down syndrome. I bonded fiercely with Isabel. I also clung to God. I filled the room with praise music to help me stay awake during our night-time feeds but also to fill my spirit with hope.

We finally made it past survival mode when Isabel was 2 1/2 months old. We had gotten into a routine and she was growing and healthy. It was then that the diagnosis really hit me. I started to realize all of the ways that she was going to be "different" and I entered into a dark place. What eventually helped pull me out of my depression was the adorable

smiles I started to receive from our little girl. I also joined a Facebook group for moms of babies born around the same time frame that offered support and encouragement.

Isabel is about to turn one and is doing remarkably well. She is sitting up, pulling to stand and signing new words every day. She has been a healthy baby and our life is normal. As I reflect on our first year I am amazed at how much a little baby can affect change. I still feel inadequate as a mother, but I'm learning to give it all to God and let Him work in me. I will do everything I can to ensure Isabel is confident in her identity and knows that she is an awesome creation.

Although my period of depression was difficult, I think it was in my brokenness that I was able to let go of the plans that I had for my life and come to a place of acceptance. I had to come to terms with my ideas of what constitutes a meaningful life, what beauty really is and face the reality that we are now "that" family. Of course there are days that I still struggle, but I can see the good in this and see the gifts that she will give us... Patience, compassion, humility, kindness, joy and most of all, love.

~Heather, Isabel's mom; 36; Minnesota, United States

{James}

It seems fitting that our story began at the base of Hope Pass in Leadville. I didn't know it then, but that was the first week of my first pregnancy. It's a 3,000 foot climb filled with dreams and adventure, but also full of doubt and challenges. It is here that people's dreams soar and people's dream are crushed. I had no idea what it would mean for me to stand on top of that pass a year later and how different my life would be.

A few months later I was having a healthy pregnancy and received my quad screen results for Down syndrome which were 1in 8500. I knew there was still that slight possibility, but there were no other soft markers and it really didn't matter to me so I opted out of further testing. At 33 weeks, my baby was diagnosed with intrauterine growth restriction (IUGR). He was tiny, not growing and my placenta was failing. We decided to induce him at 37 weeks to give him the opportunity to grow better.

Megan Newton PHOTOGRAPHY

It was the scariest 41 hours of my life. James wasn't tolerating the induction well; his heart rate kept dropping really low. We would back off the pitocin, wait for his heart rate to stabilize and start again. Finally my OB said we could try one more time, but it was time to start talking about a c-section, which I desperately wanted to avoid. I guess James didn't want a c-section either and he finally made his appearance into this world.

We had decided to be surprised by the gender and my husband was literally speechless when he saw our baby was a boy. What we didn't expect was we were about to get another surprise. James was my first so I didn't really know what to expect, but he was blue and not crying, so I was definitely worried. They got him on oxygen and I was finally able to hold him for about 30 seconds before they rushed him down to the NICU. About 30 minutes later the neonatologist walked back into my delivery room, sat down and said, "I have some bad news". All I could think was my tiny baby is in the NICU I don't know what's wrong with him, but apparently it's something pretty serious. I had just endured a long, stressful labor and I wasn't sure how much more I could handle. "He has Down syndrome," were the next words out of his mouth. I'm not sure what I had expected him to say, but this wasn't it.

I was a mix of emotions, not sure what to think or do. My mind raced as I ran through a list of possibilities, but I realized there was only one option. I was going to be the mom of a boy with Ds. I didn't know if I could do it, I didn't know what it meant and tears streamed down my face as I realized all of this.

My heart ached wondering what this new life would be like, wondering what had happened to the little child I had spent 8 months dreaming about. The runs we would go on, the mountain tops we would view the world from. Was any of this going to be possible? My heart still aches sometimes wondering if he will ever get to experience falling in love. To me this has been one of the hardest emotional hurdles. I know James may find the love of his life and fall madly in love, but he may not and that breaks my heart to think about.

I was so scared seeing him on the warming table in the NICU that a nurse had to tell me it was okay to touch him. I lightly touched his hand and he grabbed my finger fiercely as if begging me to let him know it was okay and that I still loved him. In that moment I knew not only would everything be okay, but everything would be better, not necessarily easier, but definitely better because James had now blessed my life. Tears welled up again.

James had a short NICU stay to help regulate his body temperature, stabilize his oxygen saturation, for jaundice and NG tube feeding. Within an hour of James being born they scoped his digestive system and performed an echocardiogram. We were told everything looked okay and we were encouraged that our little fighter was at least healthy.

We never got that moment where we left the delivery room and they played a lullaby through the hospital for James, I never got wheeled out the hospital with a little baby in my lap. I think that was one of the most heartbreaking things for me. Somehow I felt like our baby wasn't worth that picture perfect moment. But when we did get to break James out of the NICU it was so much better than the picture perfect dream I had imagined. We were taking our little boy home to be a family.

Once we got home we had to take James to his pediarician for weekly weight checks and oxygen saturation checks, he came home on oxygen due in part to us living at 9,000 feet in elevation. At his one month check-up his pediatrician noticed a heart murmur and asked about his echocardiogram. He asked me to wait while he called the cardiologist who reviewed his echo while we were in the NICU. He came back and explained James had two holes in his heart and we would need to see a cardiologist about a potential heart surgery. My own heart sank and it was all I could do not to break down crying. A couple days later we were at the Children's Hospital for the first time to meet our cardiologist. After his echo and chest x-ray he explained James had a PDA, ASD, VSD, pulmonary hypertension and pulmonary stenosis and would likely need open heart surgery by the time he was one. I was numb, no thoughts, no emotions, nothing. I was pretty sure I wasn't hearing this doctor correctly. He must have looked at the wrong results. We left being told we were waiting for James to go into heart failure. There were a lot of sleepless nights after that. When James was almost 4 months old he started the initial phases of heart failure. We started him on medication to clear the fluid from his lungs and continued to wait.

And then we got our Christmas miracle. Just before Christmas we went for a cardiology follow-up and were expecting to schedule heart surgery. But instead James no longer showed signs of heart failure. His cardiologist said we would continue to monitor him, but the chances of open heart surgery were now 50/50. As we have continued to monitor his VSD it has started to close and the chance of open heart surgery has decreased.

When we first took James to meet his pediatrician he told us "James is complicated and is going to scare us from time to time." He was right on.

Twenty-two months after bringing him home from the NICU he's still on supplemental oxygen. He has had multiple surgeries to: place ear tubes and eye stents, remove his adenoids, fix his epiglottis and heart and check his lungs. James' medical journey has been a wild ride; an endless stream of appointments, tests and trips to the Children's Hospital. There are days I just feel completely overwhelmed by it and there are days I just take it all in stride. I am grateful he hasn't had any major issues, but it's still frustrating that his little body is fighting all of these other things when other kids get to focus more on their therapy. I know the day will come when I'm just worried about James breaking an arm playing soccer, we just have a ways to go to get there…he's complicated.

James has a smile that melts heart, eyes that light up a room and a giggle that never leaves your heart. In the time I have had to get to know James he has taught me patience, acceptance, selflessness and hope. It's been a hard journey. There are days where I wonder how this is my life now. And there are days where I wonder how I got so lucky to have James as my son. I love my little guy so much, his eyes hold so much promise for his future, so much joy and love that I know I can handle this and I will. With each mile of trail I ran after he was born allowed me to work through and accept his Ds diagnosis and to deal with the medical issues that have come along with Ds. With James there have been hills, more ups and downs, and my unsure footings, but the most beautiful views are after the massive climb.

Three months after James was born I stood on top of Hope Pass for the first time. As I stood there, in the dark, I looked back at where I came from and ahead at the miles that lay before me and I smiled. I have stood in that same spot many times since, always with a smile and always remembering the journey that has led me there.

~Siobhan; James' mom; 33; Colorado, United States

Blogging @ www.co-running.blogspot.com

{Jasmine}

We had everything planned. My husband and I planned to have two kids close in age and we were blessed to conceive both times in my first cycle. My older daughter was just six months old when I got pregnant of our second baby. My doctor had alerted me about the risks of Autism with my pregnancies being so close together but I was certain my baby would be born perfectly healthy. Besides my aches and pains, I had an uneventful pregnancy. All tests and ultrasounds were okay and my doctor even joked that I was in "cruise control". I was not too worried about the baby's health when I went to the hospital on February 18, 2013 for a scheduled c-section. Baby seemed healthy, had 10 toes, 10 fingers and she was in breech position.

At 39w and 3 days, our baby Jasmine was born measuring 8lbs 3oz and 20.5 inches. Right after the surgery she was brought to my arms. She seemed perfect, she was beautiful. They brought her to me, we did skin to skin, I fed her and they wheeled us into our room where my parents and my in laws anxiously waited for us. It was a real birthday party! We took lots of pictures, sipped on champagne

and even had Surf and Turf for dinner. A real treat at my hospital for the new parents!!

That night, after everyone had left the hospital, my husband was sleeping in the couch, baby was in the bassinet, I had nurses coming in and out of the room and for some reason I felt alone, I felt alone like never before. It was 3am…I was awake and worried of what I was seeing in my Jasmine's sweet little face. I could not help but wonder, did they see it too? Up to that point, no doctors or nurses had mentioned Down syndrome to us. Baby was over 12 hrs old when I started crying compulsively and woke up my husband. I was in shock; I could not believe my eyes or my thoughts. I could not share my worries with my husband. It was almost as if I said them out loud, they somehow would become real. I had spent the last few hours holding my baby in one hand and searching the Internet with the other hand. I had checked my baby's delicate body for all Down syndrome's marks: she certainly had the almond shaped eyes, the flat small nose, the small ears, rounded face, flat profile but she was still so much alike my older daughter. She was beautiful, just perfect! She did not have the single crease across her palms, the short stubby fingers, and the larger gap between her toes, nor any apparent heart condition. When I finally calmed myself down and was strong enough to first say out loud the two words 'Down syndrome', my husband's first reaction was to deny it. He had not noticed her almond shaped eyes nor suspected anything wrong with our perfect baby girl. He hugged me and let me cry for a very long time. I don't think I ever cried so much in my entire life. Since the beginning he has always assured me things would be fine and that he would always be the best husband and father he could be.

Next morning, when the pediatrician came to exam our baby for the first time, I could not wait to ask her about my suspicious diagnosis. She mentioned about Jasmine's low muscle tone and almond shaped eyes, but she was not very sure of the diagnosis. That same day, I could not stop wondering how we did not find that out during our pregnancy. I thought all the tests indicated a normal baby. I was devastated. I was pissed at my OBGYN. I had trusted him. Why did my baby have Down syndrome? Before getting pregnant my husband and I had talked about a possible termination if we were to find out our baby had any disability. We had no choice. Jasmine was here, she was in my arms, she was perfect and needed our love.

The next morning, right before we left the hospital the nurses collected her blood sample and I was told the genetics results would take about 2-3 weeks. Two entire weeks? How would I survive the unknown for two entire weeks? I wanted to stay at the hospital and run all sorts of tests on her, but the doctors said she had a clean bill of health and was ready to go home. She did not have any medical issues common with kids with Down syndrome, no heart defect, no vision or hearing problems, no thyroid issues.

We decided to write a letter to inform our friends of her syndrome even before receiving the official diagnosis, I could not imagine having to tell and explain all of my friends and family in person that she was not perfect, that she has an extra chromosome. All I did for the first two weeks was cry. I read many blogs, books; so much was going through my mind. I was afraid I would lose my friends; that they would slowly distance themselves from us. I am glad I was wrong, they have been really supportive. Most people were surprised like we were at first, but everyone said we had been blessed and that God gives his harder battles to his strongest soldiers. I joined several local and online support groups. I started going to church again, started counselling and have created a great support team.

In the first 36 hours of life, there was a whirlwind of emotions and I was completely overwhelmed. I had no idea what the future would hold, and I was scared to death. While there is still not a day that I do not worry about the future, I can honestly say that our journey has been much more enjoyable than I could have ever imagined. Jasmine is a wonderful baby and I pray that our future together continues to be surprisingly normal. I was, and still am, worried about her differences, but the unconditional love for her I have in my heart is still unbelievable.

~ Juliana, Jasmine's mom; 32; Florida, United States

On Facebook @
https://www.facebook.com/PrincessJasmineSchallert)

{Lilly}

One night I had a dream where a man told me I was pregnant. We had been trying to conceive for 5 months. I felt suddenly excited and knew I had to take a pregnancy test. However, it was a work day. I was meeting my first client at the local shopping mall at 9:30am. Before our appointment I quickly purchased a test and waited anxiously for my client to arrive. Much to my delight she didn't appear, so in a public toilet of our local Westfield Shopping Centre I found my self staring back and forth at the results, "Am I reading this right, could I really be pregnant?"

I called in sick for work and went straight to the local medical centre for confirmation. The results were positive and I was feeling really nervous about telling my husband. He had wanted to wait a while to have children but had agreed to start trying, as he thought this would lower the chances of a disability. He was happy with the news in a calm, male sort of way. I however, was over the moon. We were offered the blood test to check for trisomy 21 at 8 weeks but declined for two reasons. Firstly, abortion was not an option for us and secondly, we didn't think we

would have a child with Down syndrome; after all I was only 27 and healthy. However, at my 20 week scan things were about to get very real. My ultrasound lasted for 3 hours and I was contacted the next day by my GP asking me if I could go straight to the hospital as there were some abnormalities presenting on the scan. I burst into tears and fear started to flood my body. I had no idea what to expect. However, there was a part of me that always knew something wouldn't be "quite right".

As a Christian I spend time praying and reading my Bible. Just before I became pregnant I felt directed to read a passage in Matthew 6. This section talks about not worrying and seeking God first and he will meet our needs. One part of the scripture says;

"Consider the lilies of the field, how they grow: they neither toil nor spin; [29] and yet I say to you that even Solomon in all his glory was not arrayed like one of these."

I felt God saying, "Do not worry, Lilly is going to be okay," We had decided to not find out the sex of our child but I had a strong feeling I was going to have a daughter and if this was so I was to call her Lilly. A friend had also contacted me before I knew I was pregnant saying she had a dream that I was going to have a baby and she was to pray for me throughout my pregnancy.

When I was summoned to the hospital it didn't come as a shock but I did feel very apprehensive. The doctor told us that our baby didn't have a nasal bone, she had an echogenic bowl and her spine seemed to be fused incorrectly. We were told she could have cystic fibrosis, spina bifida, Down syndrome or none of the above. We were sadly offered an abortion (which we declined straight away), and where also asked if we would like some further testing. My husband and I took some time to think and decided not to get any further tests and asked the doctors not to mention it anymore.

I felt confident that everything would be okay. After all why would God tell me not to worry, that I am having a girl, give me her name and guide my friend to pray for me? I went through the rest of my pregnancy praying daily and honestly believing that my baby would be born "normal." In hindsight I can see the message 'not to worry' was not only for the 38 weeks and 4 days of my pregnancy but for Lilly's whole life.

On the 5.4.13 I was admitted to hospital at 38 weeks and 3 days. My baby was small, the fluid around her was almost nonexistent and there were concerns the placenta had stopped feeding her. I was induced and after a 5 hour labours on 6.4.13 my darling Lilly Grace was born and lifted onto my chest. Filled with happiness and awe I held my perfect, alive, crying baby girl. Shortly after her birth the paediatrician examined Lilly. When they gave her back to me they said they were pretty sure she has Down syndrome but they would need to send off the placenta for confirmation. It felt like I had a huge hole in my stomach and grief and sickness began to consume me. I remained in hospital for over a week as Lilly had difficulty feeding. Through out my stay all the midwives were speaking about Lilly as if the diagnosis had already been confirmed. They were very kind, however, I wasn't ready to come on board with Lilly's diagnosis.

The two weeks before we got the official results were like a rollercoaster but not a fun one at a theme park. This was like a roller coaster through a grave yard, with zombies chasing you trying to take your life. It was very, very scary, "My daughter can't have Down syndrome I'm only 27."

"That kind of thing only happens to other people. Does this mean my chances are higher if I was to have other children?" My hormones mixed together with grief and fear, left me feeling confused and overwhelmed.

When I arrived home I received a pack from the Down syndrome association. I began reading a book called "Parents guide to raising a child with Down syndrome". This book was quickly discarded when I came to the section about all the possible sickness. I spent time in prayer and felt God direct me back to the scripture. "Consider the lilies of the field, how they grow". I felt him say again "Don't worry, Lilly will be fine". I decided to discard all negativity and stop dwelling on the 'what ifs'. My daughter is 3 months old and first smiled when she was 6 weeks old. She now lifts her head when lying on her stomach, is starting to grasp and play with her toys, sucks her thumb and rolls to her side and just started to roll onto her stomach.

I see it as a blessing that I didn't know about Lilly's diagnosis prenatally. If I had known, I would have prepared for Down syndrome. Instead, I prepared for Lilly. I prepared for a child, a family, a gift – not a syndrome. My baby girl is such a gift.

My passion now is to see many more children like my daughter given the opportunity for life. I believe it's not our right to choose to take life away. That is God's choice and his alone. Had I chosen to abort my baby I would have been destroying a beautiful little girl who deserves the chance to life just like you and me.

The bible says in Psalm 139:13-16

"For you created my inmost being;

    you knit me together in my mother's womb.

[14] I praise you because I am fearfully and wonderfully made;

    your works are wonderful,

    I know that full well.

[15] My frame was not hidden from you

    when I was made in the secret place,

    when I was woven together in the depths of the earth.

[16] Your eyes saw my unformed body;

    all the days ordained for me were written in your book

    before one of them came to be."

God designed and created my baby girl, God breathed life into her and I am very thankful and happy.

~Katrina, Lilly's mum; 27; Australia

{Elijah}

Elijah came three weeks early, born at 37 weeks 1 day. I was driving back from my weekly check-up at my doctors when somebody pulled out in front of me and I had to slam my brakes on. Thankfully I have ABS (anti-lock breaking system) so didn't hit them, but it set contractions off. Around an hour later I was calling an ambulance to take me to hospital! I honestly doubted I was going to make it in time.

Elijah was born within an hour of arriving. Straight away I knew something wasn't right as he looked like he was crying but there was no sound and he was very purple. I kept babbling about it but they rushed him straight out for oxygen all the time telling me he was ok. They then came back in and told me he was in NICU (neonatal intensive care unit).

A midwife rushed in with excitement at one point going on about his abnormalities - short fingers, his face - and I had no idea what she was on about!! I still don't understand why she was so upbeat about it either.

Elijah was born on June 12th 2012, weighing 3602g. It was three very long hours before I was able to see him. He was in a humidicrib with a CPAP machine (oxygen) and I was only allowed to touch him.

At 24 hours old, he was wheeled in for surgery for an imperforate anus. After surgery late in the afternoon I was able to go and see how my little man was going in NICU. While I was down there with my mum they broke the news about his diagnosis... He has Down syndrome. I don't remember a lot of what the diagnosing neonatologist, Dr C, was saying and I teared up, but was trying so hard to be strong. What never left me was Dr C talking about testing in pregnancy and I told him straight I wouldn't go through with it and wouldn't trust the results. His response was, "Really?" in a condescending tone.

When I left NICU I went outside to ring those close to me and tell them and broke down. I remember a stranger walking by and asking if I was okay; she was really worried to leave me there crying. I admit I was naive at this stage. I didn't have much idea about Down syndrome at all; and certainly not how it would, or could, affect his life – our life. I've since found out my thoughts were normal but I worried I wouldn't be able to continue study, wouldn't be able to work in the future, what was his future going to be, what was mine, schooling; the list goes on... I also worried if something were to happen to him would I be blamed. I've been told it's a grieving process of sorts. I had already lost my husband, though newly separated at the time, to suicide and another lady I know pass from breast cancer. And here I was being told I would go through a grieving process for the third time in less than 12 months. And grieve I did... for the 'ideal' baby I thought I was going to have.

But, you know what? How wrong I was!! He is perfect, and special, just the way he is. I can study. I can work if I choose to. His future is bright. Sure we'll have people look at him differently, it's how we deal with it and raise him that will make all the difference. A few days after diagnosis I decided "I WANT TO REBEL AGAINST CONFORMITY"... If people are going to judge my little boy, they'll have to judge his mum too. So eventually I did colour my hair, shaved some of it, and that's the way it's staying :) It's actually quite liberating!!

Elijah is 14 months old. He's now started the bridge pose and we are working on walking. The physio is so impressed with his strength we aren't 'focussing' on anything at the moment. I have started simple signs with him and he has his ENT surgery this week, otherwise healthy. Adored by all our family & his sisters can't leave him alone. Even on my darkest of days, just seeing him smile brightens my day; he's brought us so much joy & inspiration.
I'll finish this post with a quote from my friend. "It's like the kids song "going on a bear hunt". You can't go over it, you can't go under it, you can't go round it, you've got to go THROUGH it."

~Kat, Elijah's mum; 32; Australia

{Ari}

Several hours after the lovely water birth of our son, Ari, our nurse took him to the end of the bed to take his measurements. Everyone seemed very quiet and I assumed it was just because it was early in the morning after a long night.

I remember everyone leaving my room and then our midwife and nurse returning and telling us they needed to go over some things. Our Midwife began by saying that they had found some things while doing Ari's checkup. He had low ears, short fingers, a gap between his toes, single palmer creases on his hands. I listened in a daze, wishing she would get to the point, not having a clue what that point might be. Before she got to it, Tim interrupted and said, "does he have Down syndrome? I was shocked to hear him say it, like he had been suspecting it all along. I found out later he had thought his eyes looked

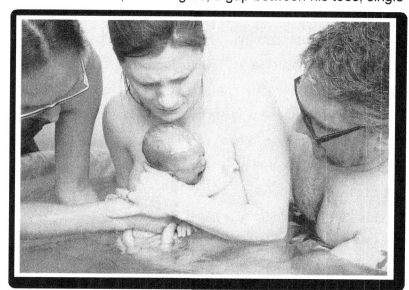

funny and had gone to the restroom and googled images of babies with Down syndrome. I couldn't see anything different in him, so I was taken off guard. Laura answered by telling us that she can't tell us if he does have Down syndrome, and only a genetic test could confirm that, but that the markers they found all point to this being the case. Both her and Melissa cried and tried to comfort us by telling us that he was going to be the most loving and wonderful child. They told us that we need to be transferred to the hospital to check his heart and that an ambulance would come to transport him. I don't remember crying, just staring into nothingness and feeling completely numb except for the burning knot in my gut. The ladies left the room and shut the door and Tim and I hugged and cried. I remember very clearly that all he said to me through his tears was, "I love you so much."

The ENT's entered with a cart to take Ari out in. Tim and I were to drive over separately while Ari went in the ambulance. I remember someone saying how handsome Ari was and I feigned a smile and didn't go to him before he was wheeled away. I didn't recognize him as mine at that moment and it felt so awful.

We were directed to Ari's room in the NICU and I was propped up in a chair by one of the nurses, who handed me my boy, hooked up to a million wires. She helped tuck him inside my shirt to warm up and told Tim and I to try to get some rest. She turned off the lights and closed the door. I remember closing my eyes and leaning back in the chair, willing myself to sleep. I was convinced that when I woke up, this nightmare would be over, and I could go back to the time before he was born. Eventually they found a room for us to sleep in and we decided to leave Ari for a short bit to try to rest. Tim wheeled me to our room and we each took a hospital bed and curled up in balls. I began to fall into sleep, but Tim was sobbing and I couldn't sleep without trying to comfort him first. I curled up behind him and we cried hard together. He told me that he did "not want this." He didn't want to be a "special needs parent." I said I didn't either, but what could we do? He told me his heart was broken and it broke me to hear that. I had thoughts in that room, thoughts I don't like to admit. We felt at times that our life was over. But I told myself that he was my baby and I loved him, even if it felt like he wasn't mine, or at

least he wasn't the baby I had expected. I told Tim that he was just a baby and he needed his parents. All we could do was be there for him and love him.

I believe the grieving was a very necessary part of our experience and inevitably led to healing. We got the final word on his genetic test results, and though we were expecting it, it was still hard to hear.

One of the first mornings I recall, I was holding Ari after a feeding and in the NICU room alone with him. I sang to him and cried. I whispered to him that I was sorry. I was so so sorry that I couldn't give him a better life.

Several weeks later, once we had been home for awhile, I sat on our bed holding Ari and I started on again about how sorry I was and that he wasn't going to have a very good life, when it hit me – he was going to love his life! And we were going to give him every opportunity. He may not have the exact life that was in our heads, but it wasn't about us anymore. It was about him and his happiness. 99% of adults with Down syndrome report being happy with their lives. I can't imagine that number would be anywhere near as high in the general population. This was just the beginning of my acceptance of our situation and the rest of our story is still unfolding. What I can say right now is that I couldn't love my son more if I tried. He brings me joy tenfold and brightens my days. I truly believe that he will do great things in his life.

Ari is almost 18 months now and is doing amazingly well! We haven't had any additional health issues. He is taking steps and so close to walking! He keeps us entertained all day because he is so silly. We are constantly in awe of just how smart he is. He understands so much more than we might give him credit for. He is following commands and signing about 10 words. We truly couldn't be more proud of him or love him any more than we do!

~ Lacey, Ari's mom; 27; Colorado, United States

Blogging @ http://youmightgetlost.blogspot.com/

{Alaina}

I knew all along – good ol' mother's intuition I guess. I think friends and family got tired of me saying over and over again, "I just want the baby to be healthy." I remember sitting on my husband's lap in our office, after getting out of the hospital for pre term contractions, looking at the 3-D ultrasounds photo of our baby's face. "Squirt (what we lovingly nicknamed the baby since we didn't know the gender) looks different – like it has Down syndrome." Where did those words come from?? I didn't even know anyone with Down syndrome…why would I say that? I knew. I had such anxiety about having her. Not about becoming a first time parent, but the actual birth…I knew something was not going to be right.

When I went to my last doctor's appointment at 36 ½ weeks and he told me I could go off the pills that were keeping my contractions at bay, all I could think about was the date of the following day and I thought…any day but that day, it holds so many sad memories. September

11th. But inside I knew it would happen.

I woke up in the middle of the night not feeling well. By 5 am, I knew I needed to get Bryan up. We called the hospital and were on our way. I said we'd see how I handled pain before I said

yes to the epidural. Apparently I don't do pain well! I asked for it by the time we got to a room. I wasn't even 5 cm dilated yet, but I couldn't relax through the contractions. I think I dilated fully with half an hour after receiving the epidural! I pushed for 2 hours and at 9:25am, Thursday, September 11th, 2008, our 6 pound 12 ounce Alaina Marie entered the world. I had no idea what to expect. She came out crying like any baby should. It so ironic to me that I said those words about her ultrasound picture just three weeks prior, because when I looked at her, I didn't notice anything. The only thing I thought looked different were her ears, but our doctor even made mention that it was probably because she was early – I don't know if he knew and just didn't want to say anything at that moment or what. We did all the normal newborn things with her. We called family and spread the news that she was here. It was a couple hours later, our doctor came in the room and told us both he had a suspicion that Alaina may have Down syndrome, but he wasn't sure. She had some of the markers, but not all. So that left us feeling - should we worry or not? They would take a blood sample and send off for testing. The results could take weeks to receive. I'm not even sure what I was feeling at that moment in time. Shock maybe? Uncertainty? Yes. I can't say I was really scared or worried...I didn't know what to think. The doctor didn't seem certain – why should we jump to conclusions and worry if we didn't have to? We didn't tell our families of his suspicions.

By the next day, she was having a little trouble with her sat levels and keeping her temperature up. So she was spending a lot of time in the nursery. I still didn't know what to think at this point – I think I just wanted it to not be true, and it would probably turn out okay. I worry over nothing sometimes. I was sitting in my room talking with my parents when our doctor stopped by. I quietly asked if they had any results from the test yet. He said no, but at that point he told me it was a test just to confirm the diagnosis. He said she has Down syndrome. That was my turning point. After he left the room, I sat on the bed speechless. I lost it. My parents didn't know what to think. They had looked at her in the nursery just minutes before and had no suspicions, so they were shocked at my tears. I told them the news. From there on out, it became real. She had had some feeding issues, so we were finger feeding, she was jaundice and still having some temperature and oxygen level issues. Nothing major, but just not the first time parent experience one imagines in their mind. She had an EKG of her heart, which revealed a bicuspid aortic value and a small ASD, but nothing that was causing her any medical issues and didn't cause her any from that point forward. We were so blessed with her good health.

We were in the hospital with her for six days. I remember the fear most. Fear of the unknown. All I knew were stereotypes. All I could do was replay my pregnancy in my mind, questioning everything I did. What did I do wrong? I didn't understand how it really worked and I didn't want to. I felt like I had let my husband down, everyone down – I didn't produce this perfect, healthy baby. I felt a sense of paranoia. Were people disappointed in me? Feel bad for us? I felt like they were always looking at me to see if I was holding it together....I was the only one I really saw cry - everyone else seemed to be able to hold it all together, or they just accepted it much better than I did. I felt such guilt. I know others had the same feelings as me, sometimes I wish someone could have said, "Forget being strong" and just cried it out with me. What happened to that baby I had carried for nine months? The one I was expecting to have? Where did that baby go? There was grieving. Telling people was hard. Everyone wanted to be positive and say the right things. I felt like I couldn't be sad. I had a healthy baby (she really was healthy compared to issues we could have faced) and everyone was saying how grateful I should be. But I didn't feel that way. I loved her because she was my child, but I didn't feel that mother-newborn connection you always hear women talk about. I didn't know her – especially this baby that I wasn't expecting. Then you feel the guilt on top of it all for feeling like you're not in love with your child the way you are supposed to be.

The nurses were wonderful. We live in a rural area, so our hospital was relatively small – sometimes you are the only patient in the hospital. We got some amazing, personalized care. One nurse went to town printing off article after article about Down syndrome and put it all in a black 3-ring binder. I couldn't bring myself to open it. It was enough to just do the day to day things. I didn't want to read about everything we could be facing raising her. It was too scary at the time. I never did open that binder. I put on blinders to so much those first few months. Being a new mom was enough – I couldn't face the what-if's.

There were lots of tears. I had more tears and fear then I care to admit looking back, but at the time that's how I felt, and a process I guess I had to take. But we took care of her and loved her like you should and things slowly changed over time. I still have hard days, I wouldn't want to go back and tell myself then to not cry or not be scared, but I wish I could have gone back and told myself about all the smiles, laughter and normality we would have too. Things that my naïve self didn't think was going to be possible.

So here we were at home…with a brand new baby and a whole different normal than we were even expecting. Alaina was 2 months old when the "Birth to 2" program came to visit the house for the first time. What a nerve-wracking event that felt like at the time. I already had this feeling of failure, now someone wanted to come "evaluate" my baby. Of course it was always worse in my mind than in real life! Little did I know how important those people would become to us – like family.

For three years, they came into our home every week for an hour and got to know Alaina – and me too. They were my sounding board, my reassurance, my information source. They were invaluable for Alaina's sake - and mine. The first few months I kind of coasted. I thought it was better for me to stay home. I didn't want Alaina to get sick, and honestly, it was hard to connect with others at that time. We had so many friends who were pregnant at the same time as us – it was like a club or something! And hearing of all their births, seeing their babies, hurt more than I could have imagined. We shared the same dream, shared pregnancy stories, shared congratulations…but our story ended much differently. While they were showing off their baby to family and friends and getting into a routine and thinking about going back to work, I was doing lots of the same things, but included were evaluations, cardiology visits, blood draws…things that didn't seem to be on any other parent's radars. I felt so different being in the same situation with someone else as I could possibly be. Yet looking back, things were obviously more normal than I realized. We did all the baby stuff everyone else did. It just felt so incredibly different at the time. But we were finally getting to "know" her. She loved her daddy – and still does. She was a super smiler and seemed to capture attention where ever we went – it was impossible not to. Once she learned how to wave, you were hard pressed to get by her without a wave and a smile! Besides being a big spitter, she was a pretty good baby. Best sleeper out of our three kids – so that's puts her in a little extra special place in our hearts, too! ☺

When Alaina was 6 months old, I got pregnant with our second child. I don't think anything more terrifying could have happened. I was excited, but scared you-know-what-less! Pregnancy no longer sounded enjoyable and exciting…it sounded like 9 months of worry. And it was – right or wrong. Everything was deemed normal for my first pregnancy and look what happened… If everything was "normal" for this pregnancy too, what kind of peace of mind does that give me? There was no peace of mind until Aubrey was born – I'm embarrassed to admit I couldn't look at her when she was born. I just told Bryan "just tell me she's ok….I can't look until I know she's ok." Our doctor was such a kind, wonderful man and had been with us since the beginning…he came into the room hours after Aubrey was born and I was alone and sat on the bed beside me and told me how proud he was of me – as he knew that day would be hard for me. If I wasn't already, that endeared me to him forever. He will probably never know how much those words meant to me and still bring me to tears to this day.

By the time Aubrey was born, we had settled into a good routine with Alaina. She had met so many of her milestones – sitting up at 6 months, crawling at 11 months and was cruising along furniture and walking behind push toys by the time she was 15 months. She nicely transitioned to eating table food and seemed to have no aversion to any of it. She had tubes in her ears when she was 9 months old and a week after, she started babbling up a storm and never really quit! I remember the first word we could distinguish for her was "ba-pa" (backpack on Dora! Kids aren't supposed to watch TV, right?? I could care less if it got her to talk!) It was true….life didn't seem as different as I feared it would. One of the big differences for me was the schedule of therapy. We started doing physical therapy with her before Aubrey was born, so we had occupational therapy, time with her early childhood special educator every week, and physical therapy every other week. Not to mention well baby visits, cardiologist checkups, ENT appointments and trips to specialized pediatricians who could give us evaluations and make suggestions on therapy for her. It felt like a full time job just keeping appointments straight and working around them sometimes. At that point, we were so thrilled with her progress and she was a bundle of personality that still attracted lots of attention and we were so proud.

I remember still feeling sadness some days – especially when we would get together with friends who had babies around the same time. It still kind of stung. Even though she wasn't at all, or at least not far behind those babies, discussions seemed odd. While they were talking

about what their kids were doing, just like I was, the rest of the conversation was filled with our therapy schedule and what she was working on or needed to try to work on…it's those things that made everything still feel different and brought sadness sometimes.

There were some wonderful mothers in the area who had kids with Down syndrome that reached out to me. I tried getting together with them a few times, and not because of anything they did at all, it wasn't working for me. It should have been a good support system, but it was hard to see the things their kids struggled with – it made me panic that Alaina would struggle with the same thing at some point – which there was no validity to that thought at all. At the time it seemed very valid though. It wasn't my time to join these groups yet. As she has gotten older, it's gotten much easier for me and I've come to very much appreciate their support, insight and experience. A heartfelt, "I understand" goes a long way when you've hit a rough spot and are frustrated. And, "That's wonderful – way to go Alaina" at her accomplishments is so appreciated! They were a tremendous support when we had issues with services in our school district, too. Their encouragement and support meant a lot during that time.

As Alaina has gotten older, some things have gotten easier and some things have gotten more difficult. I'm not going to deny that I still cry, still have sad, hard days and still have so many questions – some days I almost feel no different than I did almost 5 years ago in terms of knowing the best way to help my daughter. I bring up the sad days so often because I do want mothers to know that it's okay to have sad days – no matter what age your kiddo is. Doesn't mean we don't love them to pieces, it means we're human. We love our kids fiercely and sometimes that means we feel their challenges and struggles, too. And I think that will always hurt for a mother.

Easier is the medical schedule…as we were blessed with her amazing health. Cardiology appointments have been stretched out to every 2 years, we don't see the specialized pediatricians anymore. We just go to the doctor when she's sick or for yearly check-ups. But therapy still remains a constant. We run more than we have to, and that's by my choosing. Any time someone can give us a different perspective or different activities to do with her, I'm all over it. I seek input from anyone who will give it to me. She's going into her third year at school – which she LOVES – and gets her weekly services there. But we also do additional physical and speech therapy at children's therapy clinic that's over an hour away. This summer we started hippotherapy with her, too. She rarely fights therapy – she so interactive and loves to play that she does pretty well – that doesn't mean that stubborn side doesn't ever come out though! ☺ And a stubborn side she can have – believe me! Now, my worries come more from thinking about her life long-term. What skills can we help her build and achieve to give her the best chance possible of having an independent and fulfilling life-however that may look for her? We still work on specific skills – cutting, writing, etc – but now we have lots of social skills to throw in the mix. The kids she goes to school with seem to adore her – which makes my heart happy. But I worry about her building friendships, being able to navigate social situations and helping her integrate into her classroom and peers as best we can.

But just like when she was first born, some days it seems so unnatural –our schedule. Spending so much time in therapy and driving to and from therapy. It consumes enough of our weekly routine that sometimes I don't feel like doing other things. Mommy guilt is tough as I feel like I neglect my other two kids to do all these activities with Alaina. But her brother and sister love her so. Their relationship is so heartwarming – to see Down syndrome through a child's eye is to not see it at all. They just see Alaina – wish it was that way to the whole world. She is one of the biggest bright spots in our family. Her smile, laugh and upbeat attitude is contagious. We couldn't be prouder of her hard work and all she has accomplished. It is true that every milestone seems so precious and is so celebrated. And we do lots of high fives and celebrating around here!

~Lauren, Alaina's mom; 29; Minnesota, United States

{Liam}

I had nine miscarriages before I finally got pregnant with our third child. I was under the care of a specialist at our hospital and had been for 2 years. From the earliest days of my pregnancy I was monitored and scanned, each ultrasound filled me with a sense of dread, but also excitement – wanting to see a heartbeat, but daring not to hope. I had opted to have the 12 week nuchal translucency scan, despite my fears, because it was another opportunity to make sure my baby was alive. I went alone and as soon as the sonographer placed the hand piece over my belly I could see the little heart beating away – pure relief! The scan went without a

hitch, it took a little longer, but everything looked great. At the end of the appointment I was told that they needed to speak to someone senior and asked me to wait in "the room".

My heart instantly sank. Something must be badly wrong because no one went into that room for good news. Alone, tears sprang to my eyes and the panic set in. It seemed like forever before someone came back and told me that, because it was now after hours, there were no senior staff available and I needed to go downstairs straight away to speak to a doctor in women's assessment. I was led to an empty room, my legs practically crumbling from fear and two doctors sat down and told me that the scan had shown my baby had a 'slightly increased nuchal fold'. That, plus my age (42), meant my child was a high risk for Down syndrome. I fell to pieces in the chair. I was immediately offered a CVS the next day or told I could wait and have an amniocentesis a couple of weeks later to give a definite diagnosis. The female doctor was very reassuring, but I found myself asking if I would be forever judged by the medical fraternity if there was indeed something wrong with my baby and I had refused the testing. The pressure to test felt great, but for me, the risk of miscarrying this very much wanted baby was too high and the 1:200 risk of losing it meant there was no way I could agree. I suddenly felt trapped and needed to get out of there. We agreed that they would continue to monitor the pregnancy closely and use ultrasound to determine if there was indeed anything further to worry about.

I'm not sure how I drove home from the hospital, I was in no state to drive. When I got home I Googled 'Down syndrome' on my computer. Through the blur of my tears, lots of stereotypical images shot back at me, making me cry even more. I eventually stumbled on a blog about someone's child with Down syndrome and, as I read, I realised it was kind of positive. The more I read, the more I thought that maybe this wouldn't be the end of the world. My actual words to my husband that night were, "After reading that, I will almost be disappointed if this baby doesn't have DS!"

We talked a lot that night about how there are no guarantees in life, that our other two typical children could be struck down at any point and life could change. I relaxed as my husband spoke because I knew *I* could handle whatever we would be given, but I didn't know about him. It was reassuring to hear he was on the same page.

Our morphology ultrasound at 18 weeks was uneventful. The sonographer searched long and hard for 'soft' markers for Down syndrome, but there were none. I breathed a sigh of relief and we were overjoyed to find out we were having a boy!

At 20 weeks, I took the first photo of my pregnant belly and finally acknowledged that we were having a baby. There were more growth scans and a review at 32 weeks to check on a low lying placenta. It was at this scan that the sonographer brought me to tears when he flicked a button and there was a 3d image of my baby's face! He took some photos for me to take home and I proudly shared them with everyone. At my next antenatal appointment I showed my specialist the amazing pictures of our boy. Her words to me, "Well, he definitely doesn't have Down syndrome!"

The next five weeks were exciting. I felt pretty relaxed, despite still being scared of losing him. I was really starting to think that this dream was going to come true! It would take his birth to bring the world crashing down again. We could see it straight away. Our baby had Down syndrome.

Liam was born via planned caesarean section, due to my history of previous sections and being an insulin dependant diabetic, and as soon as he was delivered there was a silence in the air. In the photo taken as he was lifted out of me, you can see the two doctors looking at each other with frowns. When I held Liam I started asking straight away if he had Down syndrome. No-one replied. I asked my husband what he thought and he agreed with me. I asked my student midwife friend and she said the paediatrician would have to have a look. Despite the resolute silence, I was still filled with an overwhelming sense of joy at the birth of a live baby, nothing else mattered. At this point I didn't realise my husband wasn't coping. While I was in recovery our boy was taken to see the paediatrician on call who agreed that Down syndrome was evident from the physical features that presented themselves – epicanthal folds to eyes, low set ears and sandal gap between toes. The official results from genetic testing confirmed the rarer diagnosis of Mosaic Down syndrome two weeks later.

The news was conveyed to me that Liam's DS had been confirmed, but I seemed to be oblivious to everything else in my little bubble of happiness. Liam looked amazing to me! Back in my room, there was excitement as my parents and older two children came to join us. My husband however sat in the corner of the room, stony faced, silent and with his arms folded as if he was about to explode with rage. I have one photo of my husband holding his new son during the first two weeks of his life and it was taken at this moment when the midwife made him hold Liam while she checked my wound. My daughter took it, I remember her saying, 'Come on dad, smile'. It was painful and the tension in the room was palpable and that is when I realised my husband wasn't okay with this. I haven't been able to look at that picture since.

For me, the first week of Liam's life was a roller coaster of emotion. A visit from my husband would reduce me to tears and then a friend would come to visit and I would be optimistic and happy. I felt like I was keeping up appearances with a genuine sense of happiness, but an overwhelming fear of the unknown and the imagined. On the second day a nurse asked if I wanted some information on DS. They brought me in some black and white photo copied pages with horrible, dated pictures and the worst case scenarios. As I started to read it I burst into tears. I hadn't realised there could be so many potential medical problems! I thought it was just DS. There were so many people coming and going – doctors, nurses and social workers. It suddenly dawned on me why they were taking him away all the time – for testing. I felt so bad that I hadn't gone with him when they checked his heart. I felt like the worst possible mother he could have and that was compounded by the fact that I couldn't get Liam to breastfeed due to his low tone. I felt like such a failure and blamed myself for everything that was 'wrong'. I kept the paper work tucked away under his cot so no one else could see it when they came to visit, I wasn't ashamed of him, but I didn't want that paperwork to define him. I cried every day that the hospital photographer would come and ask if I wanted to buy a photo package. I don't know why I cried. I thought he was beautiful, but I didn't want them to capture the DS, almost like I thought he might grow out of the look later on. They would skulk away from my room and I'm sure they thought I was crazy. They stopped coming after the third time. I was offered a visit from someone from the local DS Society, to which I agreed, but the social worker wasn't able to reach them and left their number with me to call – which I wouldn't do for another 11 weeks. I wasn't ready to enter 'that' world yet.

On the fourth day I received my Foundation 21 (a local DS charity organisation) pack. It was modern and colourful and the kids looked healthy and happy and I read, 'Welcome to Holland' and I cried, but I smiled too. That pack gave me so much hope. It's funny, but I was so proud and excited to share Liam with others, but so scared of saying the words 'disability' or thinking about the future. I thought I was going to have to give up things in my life that I took for granted before. I was studying at the time and my immediate thought was that I was going to have to quit that, and my job. The social security paperwork for disability payment application was so hard to complete. I worried what it would all mean for my other children – the burden later on, would they be embarrassed? I cried again when I read that all males with DS are considered sterile. I worried about when the time came for school, where would he go?

On the fifth day, Liam was cleared of all congenital conditions linked to DS. While I had already announced his birth to the world via Facebook, I had only told those close to me about the DS. I finally had my way to acknowledge Liam's something extra, when I sent a message saying , 'So happy to announce that after lots of testing, Liam only has DS, thank God!' and I meant it. I knew there could be a lot more things worse than DS.

When I finally left the hospital after six days, some normality to began to return and, in our home environment, my husband started interacting with Liam until one day he asked to hold him. I took a photo of that and I look at that one all the time.

While I can't speak for my husband, I know during the first year that he struggled at times with Liam's diagnosis, but the love that he has for him is always evident. They are the best of mates and already seem to enjoy the same interests. It has been three years now since his birth and Liam has, without question, transformed our lives in a way that we could never have imagined.

There is a richness now that wasn't there before and it is hard to describe the love and learning we have experienced without resorting to clichés.

Liam has struggled with some respiratory issues related to his low tone, but I was so happy when at 6 weeks of age he breast fed for the first time. I only just managed to wean him at 3 years old! We have certainly had a number of hospital visits, a few surgeries and medical appointments along with all the usual therapies. I couldn't have imagined how I would manage that before, but somehow you do. It becomes part of your life and I don't hate it. We have been welcomed into an amazing little community of families with a similar journey and have been shown inspiration and the beauty and meaning of life on more occasions than I can remember. Our little guy seems to bring with him all that is good in the world. He attracts people and animals and we now enjoy the smallest of milestones that we missed in our 'typical' children.

So, after Liam was born, I returned to work part time, I continued to study full time and I didn't have to give up a thing. Our direction changed slightly, but it was probably always going to, and I couldn't be happier with where we are at the moment. I still sometimes worry about the future, but I realise now that it will never be worse than what I imagine, so I might as well just face each day as it comes. My main fears are for how Liam will be treated by others in the future and to counteract this I have made it my mission for as many people as possible to know him now. Thanks to his older siblings, Liam has been exposed to hundreds of people through school, sports and different clubs. He has always been loved and accepted and for that I am truly grateful. The downside however, is it now takes twice as long for me to do things like the food shopping.... now that we have to stop and smile and chat to people all the time

~Sue, Liam's mum; 42; South Australia

{Preston}

My husband and I were very excited to start a family in April 2011. We got pregnant within one month and were ecstatic! The pregnancy was so easy. I considered myself lucky since I had no sickness and felt great. Even with feeling so good, I still always had a feeling something was off.

My husband and I declined genetic testing because we both agreed we would never terminate. We also thought we had no genetic issues to even worry about (I was 27 and he was 28). We had our 20 week ultrasound and the doctor said she saw a few things but she was not concerned. She said there were some spots on the brain and a bright spot on the heart. She said this is somewhat common and we did not have to worry. She said we needed to have a

level II ultrasound because there was a less than 1% chance it could indicate Down syndrome. Again, she emphasized not to worry and that this ultrasound was just protocol.

After the level II ultrasound was over, my husband and I were nervous as we waited for the doctor. I asked my husband, "What if it really is something?" My husband reassured me there would be nothing wrong. The doctor came in and said the spots on the brain were gone. She went on to say the spot on the heart was "just a freckle." All of the measurements were normal, and given my age, she did not suspect Down syndrome. My husband and I were relieved. Even with that news, I still felt in my heart that something wasn't right.

As great as I felt, things started to change at 35 weeks. It was the week after Christmas and I was dreading stepping on the scale at my regular appointment. I went nuts on all the holiday food, a pregnant girl's dream! I stepped on the scale and saw I lost a few pounds. The nurse and I both thought that was strange, especially with how much I ate the last week. I went to get measured, and I measured small. The doctor was not too concerned but said she would keep an eye on it.

At my 36 week regular appointment I was measuring even smaller. My doctor said it was time to do an ultrasound because I was continuing to get smaller. She also was concerned the baby's heart rate was lower than normal. I was hooked up to a monitor and the heart rate kept changing from normal down to the low 100s. It was very scary, and that's when I really knew something was not right. The ultrasound showed the baby was measuring small. His femur was especially small. My doctor diagnosed me with intrauterine growth retardation. The baby just wasn't growing, and there was no explanation. I was put on bed rest to try and keep the baby in until as close to 38 weeks as possible.

At my 37 week appointment I was still measuring small and the doctor told me that I might need to be induced by the end of the week. At my 38 week appointment, my doctor told me to go to the hospital to be induced. I remember having a complete nervous breakdown on the way to the hospital. I was nervous about having a baby for the first time, but I kept thinking something would be different.

Labor was not too difficult. When it came time to push, my son came out in about 5 pushes (I was lucky). After he came out, I just wanted to see him. The nurses took him to measure and weigh him. Then they gave him to me all swaddled up. As soon as I saw him, I knew he had Down syndrome. The facial features were not evident at the time, but I knew. No one said a word about it, but I knew 100%. My parents came in the room and I asked them, "Does he have Down syndrome? He looks like he does." They reassured me he did not. Even today they still say they did not think he had it. I asked my husband and he said no. After getting the diagnosis he admitted he did think our son had Down syndrome as soon as I said it, but he didn't want me to know that at the time. I tried to keep Down syndrome out of my mind during the hospital stay. I never talked about it, but I kept thinking about it and knew it would become a reality.

After my son was born, the nurses and doctors at the hospital said my son looked great. The next day the pediatric doctor came in and said he was a little concerned with his muscle tone. I had no idea that was connected to Down syndrome. Before we were discharged, another pediatric doctor came in and said the doctors wanted to "check for chromosomes." I knew exactly what that meant, but not one doctor or nurse every said the "D word." I cried and said I didn't want anything wrong. The doctor assured me she thought nothing was wrong and the other doctors that suspected just wanted to know for sure. Everyone was reassuring me there was absolutely nothing to worry about.

The seven days before we got the blood test results were the most emotional and intense days of my life. I was already grieving because I knew. Everyone else was convinced he didn't have Down syndrome. My parents, who are both in the medical field, told me over and over again they did not think he had Down syndrome. I continued to grieve despite everyone's reassurances.We got the call from the pediatrician that the results were in. We went to the office and she told us the blood test showed our son had Down syndrome. That is when our journey in the Down syndrome world began.

I knew the moment I had my son that he had Down syndrome. No matter how many times my husband and parents told me he didn't, I always knew. When the blood test results were in, the pediatrician came in the room and told us she was sorry. She did not have good news. She said Preston had Down syndrome. I remember feeling blank. I knew all along, but the true words were so difficult to hear, so very difficult. My husband and I kept it together until we got in the car. That is where we both lost it. We cried hysterically. I remember repeating over and over that I didn't want anything to be wrong with my son. My husband cried and said he just couldn't believe it. Why us? I told my husband we have to call our family right now and tell them. I called my parents and they left work and came straight over. My husband called his family and cried as he told them. It was the absolute worst day of our lives. We both had no idea what to expect. We just knew he had Down syndrome and that couldn't be good. I am a special education teacher and I have worked with high school students with Down syndrome. I knew how amazing the kids I taught with Down syndrome were. I don't like to stereotype but in my teaching career I always said I loved teaching students with Down syndrome the most. Out of any disability, those kids were the best to work with. I just couldn't get over that MY son had Down syndrome and I did not think about him being fun or how he could be just as wonderful as the kids I taught. This was different. I was not supposed to have a child with a disability. This was not supposed to happen to *me*.

After we got home from the pediatrician and my parents came over, I cried and cried. I texted my girlfriends that I needed to talk. They could tell something was wrong. They all came over and I told them. They cried with me. They told me it would be okay and I was strong and would be the best mom ever.

That night after getting the official diagnosis, I thought horrible things about my son. I didn't tell anyone. I told my husband that I wanted to try for another baby right away because I wanted to make up for my son. It was awful. The more I thought horrible things, the worse I felt as a mother. I cried so much. I felt like I was dying inside. I was physically hurting everywhere on my body.

The entire first year of my son's life was extremely difficult. Everywhere I went that I had been while I was pregnant the year before, I always thought about how innocent I was at that time the last year. I thought about how I had no idea the baby growing inside of me had Down syndrome. I wanted to go back to that world. I wanted to be innocent again. I wanted it all to go away. To try and deal with all the negativity I was feeling, I read as much as I could to educate myself. Even as a special education teacher, I felt totally lost since this was *my* child with a disability. Reading books and being involved in therapies really helped me feel in control while I was in a world where I had no control. My son and I did not bond as well as I wish we would have. I was not in a good place for that entire year. My amazing husband bonded with my son like crazy. My son looked at my husband with stars in his eyes since the moment he was born.

Finally, after my son turned one, I didn't feel sad anymore. I didn't worry about what other people thought, and if strangers knew he had Down syndrome when they said he was cute. I felt proud of my son. I felt proud to show all my friends how having a child with Down syndrome isn't what it would seem. We are a normal family. Yes, my son is very physically delayed and not doing things typical kids are yet, but it doesn't really matter. I know hands down he is way cuter than all my friend's typical kids (a little biased but it is true). I post pictures on Facebook as much as possible to show everyone how my son is so much fun and how we live a totally normal life. I now love how I can show off our amazing life with our amazing son!

I decided to write about my son's health issues separately. The reason I did this is because he did not have any major health concerns. He did not spend any time in the NICU and came home with us from the hospital. After he was born, the doctors and nurses were not concerned about anything with his health. There have been health issues we dealt with a few weeks after my son's birth.

My husband refers to our son's health issues as, "maintenance on a car." There has not been anything major, but there have been a lot of little things. Even though there has been nothing major (hospitalizations, heart surgeries, things like that) his health issues have taken a toll and left us exhausted many times. We live about 30 minutes from St. Louis, MO where there are two amazing children's hospitals. We have driven to and from the hospital we chose a lot and spent many hours there with all the appointments. We decided to go to St. Louis Children's Hospital because they have a Down Syndrome Clinic. The other hospital does not have this. I would advise any parent of a child with Down syndrome to choose the hospital that has the clinic if there is one close to where you live. The clinic is absolutely amazing and the doctors understand Down syndrome better than anyone. The clinic has the geneticist. We saw that doctor one time and have then seen the genetics nurse practitioner. The way she explained it is they are the "quarterback" that runs all the doctor appointments our son needs at certain times. They know what to check for and when (based on health issues of the general population of people with Down syndrome).

The first two appointments after the geneticist were about my son's hearing. He did not pass his newborn hearing screenings. He had to get a sleep ABR test. This is where the audiologist had wires hooked up to my son's head and ears. My son had to fall asleep and they recorded brain waves and how he reacted to certain sounds. The first time the test wasn't so bad because my son was only a few weeks old so he fell asleep easily. The next test it seemed like it took forever for him to fall asleep. My husband had to hold my son the entire three hours it took for him to fall asleep and have the test. It felt so long sitting in the testing booth! I remember being so terrified he had a hearing impairment. It ended up he had fluid built up in his ears which was causing him to fail hearing tests. After finding this out, we decided to have surgery to put in tubes. We wanted to do everything possible to help with his hearing and speech development. He had to have two sets of tubes put in by the time he was 16 months. The first pair ended up becoming infected and fluid was again building up. Those were two quick surgeries but we combined them with other issues that needed to be taken care of.

One surgery we combined with tubes was not necessarily Down syndrome related. My son had undescended testicles. This surgery seemed rough but he bounced back quickly. The urologist suggested the surgery because the testicles needed to be descended to help decrease cancer risks in the future. My son had this surgery at 10 months.

When my son was 14 months, he had to be put under anesthesia to have a sedated ABR hearing test. This was to check his hearing. Even though it wasn't technically surgery, he was being put under which was nerve-wrecking and a long visit to the hospital.

The other surgery that was combined with new tubes was tear duct probing. We started noticing when my son was a few months old that his eyes would always get goopy and crusty when he slept. It was horrible trying to wipe his eyes every morning. We saw the eye doctor at our yearly genetics appointment (the Down Syndrome Clinic has babies with Down syndrome go to the eye doctor to make sure there are no vision problems which are common). The eye doctor said our son had clogged tear ducts which is common in people with Down syndrome. He said it would require surgery. They go through the nose and open up the tear ducts. This surgery was the most painful for my son. The doctor said it would feel like he broke his nose for a few hours. The evening of the surgery, my son was really upset. After that though, he slept through the night and was acting normal the next day.

My husband and I thought our son was having seizures around 12 months. He started doing weird movements with his head and his eyes. We went to the neurologist (with video documentation which was very helpful) and he said he wasn't sure they were seizures. One of my son's therapists mentioned it could be a self-stimming behavior. He was doing it because it felt good or different and he liked doing it. Just to be sure, we wanted to see the doctor. Since the neurologist did not know for sure, he said we needed an EEG. My son had an hour EEG test that showed normal results. After that appointment he continued the behavior and did it for longer periods of time. We decided a 24 hour EEG would be the best way to determine if it was truly stimming or really seizures. Thankfully, the results showed no seizure activity. We were so relieved.

Currently, we are still having to get my son tested for hearing since his sedated ABR still showed hearing loss (which we are pretty sure is because his tubes had fluid built up). He will have a behavior hearing test soon (he will not have to be sedated).

The only health concern that has been serious is hypothyroidism. My son was tested at 6 months (standard testing by the Down Syndrome Clinic/geneticist). With hypothyroidism it is very important to treat because if left untreated, it can lead to many health problems. With this being our only real consistent concern, we are lucky. My son has to take a pill every day for the rest of his life possibly. We just crush the pill up in his food and he eats it with no problem. He has to get a blood draw every three months to make sure the pill is the correct amount. Since he will gain weight and that will be changing as he grows, we need to keep getting his blood tested. It gets annoying to go the hospital to get the blood draw, but I always tell myself it doesn't take too long and it is definitely worth it.

So, it's obvious to see we have made many trips to and from Children's Hospital. After the appointments I think how it wasn't that bad but it I still dread going every time. It's hard to take off work for appointments that are fairly often. We are so lucky and thankful to not have had major health concerns.

Today, Preston is 19 months old. He is a very active little guy! He isn't quite crawling but can get anywhere by scooting, climbing, and rolling. Preston loves giving hugs and kisses. It is so cute! He absolutely adores his daddy! They are best buddies and love doing "boy stuff" together. I will

be having a baby next month and can't wait for Preston to have a sibling because he will be the best big brother. We celebrate each milestone with so much excitement. Preston works very hard with therapies to reach those milestones. We are so blessed that Preston is healthy and very happy! He is just the cutest and most lovable little guy!

~Lisa, Preston's mom; 28; Illinois, United States

{Jacinta}

It was my birthday when I first started to really wonder if I was pregnant. It had been a crazy time, moving house with two small children and a husband living interstate Monday to Friday, so I started to realise that it had been a while since my last period. My husband and I had decided the day we moved that we would definitely go for a third child. We had two girls already, out of four pregnancies. It was exciting to think that we might be pregnant again finally, particularly since I had thought I might have been pregnant earlier that year but despite having a very long cycle never managed to get a positive HCG result.

I did a home pregnancy test one weekend a couple of weeks later when my husband was home and it showed positive. I didn't get around to going to the Dr straight away and then I started bleeding. It wasn't a lot all at once, but was enough to be significant and was every day for about a week. I did another test and it showed a fainter positive. This got me thinking that I had probably started to miscarry. At this stage I thought I must be somewhere between 8-10 weeks. I went to the doctor a day or so later. He sent me off for an urgent ultrasound. There was a heartbeat, which was such a relief, though the embryo was measuring 6 weeks 2 days - I couldn't believe I still had half the first trimester to go!

At that point I kind of did a deal with the embryo. In my mind I told it that I would do everything possible to keep its environment healthy if it would agree to hang in there.

We declined any genetic screening since we're not the sort to act on it and didn't see the point in worrying. We did have a 20-week scan, which according to the radiologist was all normal. My home situation got complicated at this point and I didn't go back to the Dr to collect the result for the hospital clinic. About 30 weeks I started measuring big for my weeks. This continued and I had a scan about 36 weeks which showed a 7lb 13oz foetus (slightly larger than the birth weight of my eldest) and upper normal limits for amniotic fluid. The person doing the scan asked me if everything was normal in my earlier ultrasounds. I said 'yes', but I had an uneasy feeling...

Later that day I went to the Dr for my blocked ear and thought I'd get the 20 week results while I was there. I read it and saw that it there was dilation in the kidneys that should have been followed up in the third trimester....oops! I told them at the next visit and had another scan the following week to check both things. Both were still at upper normal limits. The person doing the scan was sure it was all fine and said they were both things that usually sorted themselves out soon after birth. I still had my uneasy feelings. I started talking to my husband about 'what if there is something wrong with the baby?'.

I took these two things and thought I'd google them together since it seemed to me that if there were two slightly odd things, it made sense that there would be one cause. After lots of searching I found one medical article which talked about these two things together being 'soft signs' (or soft markers) for Down syndrome. This stopped me dead in my tracks. This is the kind of thing that happens to other people and I couldn't imagine it. The thought scared me. I asked my husband what we'd do if the baby had Down syndrome. He said that we would give it every chance with all the tools we had at our disposal. This wasn't enough for me. The thought lingered for days. I finally realised that it would affect the rest of the pregnancy and taint the delivery if I didn't do something about it. I worked out that I needed something I could be sure of, that wouldn't change regardless of the outcome. Then I realised that she would be beautiful no matter what and I would focus on that and everything else could work itself out. This was the best decision I could have made.

At Christmas time I thought she was coming. She didn't. She didn't come and didn't come for a couple of weeks. Eventually one night, she started again. It wasn't convenient for her to come at 5am so I slowed it all down and I had to get her moving again later that day when we were ready. She was so ready all of a sudden we barely made it to the hospital. I was calling and calling and no-one was answering. Eventually I made the decision to just leave and the minute I got there I was onto the bed and started pushing!

45 minutes later she was out and on my chest and I couldn't work out which of my other two children she resembled. She was all scrunched up and slightly blue, looking upset. I snuggled her into the blankets and she settled down and got pink. It was when I thought I'd put her on the breast and reshuffled the blankets that she got upset and a little purple again. I handed her to my husband while I got organised and the nurses whisked her off and into the resuscitation crib and got her on oxygen. They took her to the special care nursery and I sent my husband along too. I had no idea what had just happened, but knew she couldn't be that bad. I still had to deliver the placenta so I wasn't going anywhere. I've never seen any other placenta than that one, but it was the size of a football - apparently that's large! I was exhausted and in a mystery.

Eventually I was allowed to the Special Care Nursery in a wheelchair. There she was already with an IV in her foot and she was on a glucose drip. It was out of my control. All my best intentions to give her the best start with my milk, as little pain as possible, no drugs, it was all coming unravelled. The Paediatrician had been called in and she looked over our new daughter and told us the situation. She had trouble breathing, enlarged liver, enlarged spleen, heart murmur, suspected heart defect, low platelets and dodgy white blood cells plus physical features that were consistent with Down syndrome. She needed a CPAP machine and an echocardiogram, neither of which they could do there so she would need to be transferred to another hospital as soon as possible that night.

I was possibly the luckiest mother ever to receive a diagnosis of Down syndrome. I had not only prepared myself to think of my daughter as beautiful above all else, which she still was and that hadn't changed, but I also had a friend whose son had been born 6 years earlier with the same condition. This friend of mine had searched the world and found some brilliant therapies to help her son develop in many ways as well as any other child. The last post I'd seen from her was a celebratory post saying that he was ok to go along to a normal everyday primary school the following year. I knew that she'd spent the previous 6 years working very, very hard. I knew also what results were possible. Because of this I had no fear for our baby daughter. My only thought on hearing those words was that we were writing off any other plans for the next few years because our daughter's therapy was going to be the priority.

I had to go and have my stitches and I asked the nurse to show me how to express manually and get my milk going. They told me how to store and label it so that it could be used at the hospital she was transferred to. Eventually, my husband and I had time to talk. We're not the crying type really, we tend to look at what can be done. So we decided on a name, Jacinta, and we decided to ring my friend, Kristen, and find out what could be done straight away to help as soon as possible.

The other question was what to tell people and when. My family was all gathered at my sister's place celebrating two other birthdays. They knew I had been in labour so we had to call them. My in-laws also knew we were in labour since they'd picked up our daughters from my sister earlier in the day, and of course you tell your parents! We decided to tell them that she was born, weight, time, and that she was in the SCN and would be transferred for help with breathing. I'm not sure about my parents in law but my family didn't buy it, though they didn't say anything on the phone. As soon as I got off the phone they started wondering amongst themselves what it could be.

We told Jacinta what was happening, that she was going to another hospital and Daddy was going to follow behind and that I'd stay in this hospital to get my milk going so she could have milk to drink. The transport people were lovely and as they put Jacinta into her travel unit a nurse said, 'look, she's waving'. Sure enough, little tiny Jacinta was looking right at us and opening and shutting her little hand. So we waved goodbye and she was off, 6 hours old and had already left home. Having older children who had been separated from me many times before definitely helped with this. I called the hospital after a few hours to check how she was, feeling like a crazy obsessed mother ringing at 1am. They didn't mind at all.

It was strange being in hospital alone. The photographer came past the next morning and asked cheerily, "no baby?". I was glad that I actually had a baby somewhere since that was a really insensitive thing to ask! I felt like I had no business being there, but used the time to get my expressing down pat. My husband and daughters came and picked me up the next morning and we went in to the other hospital. The other hospital welcomed my tiny expressions in their little syringes and made sure they were numbered to be given in order. They looked after us so well. They kept us informed of every little thing and were really pleased when I said we planned to just give expressed breast milk and no formula. Despite all the hope and positivity we felt, I still had strange feelings when I looked at Jacinta in the crib. We hadn't been able to hold her yet and she looked just like a person with Down Syndrome. It was hard to look beyond those physical characteristics and see who she really was.

Expressing in the middle of the night with no baby to wake me was hard work. It was both hard to wake up and sad to be alone at night expressing for my baby who wasn't there. It was a little easier in the hospital since my baby was in front of me, but not really awake.

At the end of that first day my husband and I realised that we had to tell our family the whole story and begin telling friends. We didn't want to spread the diagnosis far and wide in the beginning because we wanted to give her the same welcome our others had, but wanted to be up front with our family. My sister had arranged to come to the birth hospital where I was due to return that night to see me for a cuppa and I thought I'd better break the news before then, so I emailed around to my siblings telling the whole story and letting them know it was ok. I think the usual grapevine of "have you read the email???" went around and they all had within about half an hour. The responses were so lovely, lots of congratulations, thanks for the explanation, we're here if you need and when can we visit.

My husband had a different experience. He went over to his parents' house for his Mum's birthday. His mother's little sister has Down syndrome and she has been living in a group home for about ten years now since her elderly mother moved into a care facility. She is the classic picture of old school Down syndrome. From what I've been told, when he told his family the reaction was explosive. There were some choice words and some sentiments expressed that weren't carefully thought out. This was a huge shock for them. Amazingly though, the one person we all know in common and have a mutual high regard for is the mother of Kristen, my friend whose son has Down syndrome also. My husband told his parents about them and that he had arranged for them to see this lady the following day. This was the best thing he could have done.

We had visitors the next day which was both exciting and heartbreaking. It was lovely that our Jacinta got to have visitors like any other newborn - and this was the first of our children to be visited in hospital. At the same time, having our family there made it real and having them see her stuck in the crib barely awake with tubes everywhere was not what we had had in mind. There were tears for me that day and for several days afterwards as I felt sorry for myself and her, being robbed of our newborn experience. It was wonderful though, when my parents in law came that day. They had been to see the lady and had see how fabulously well her grandson is doing. My mother in law had fire in her eyes and she said she was on board and they were going to do whatever it takes to help her reach her potential. There are some moments in life that cement people together in a bond that cannot be broken. This was one of those.

My husband and I got working on treating however we could. We had some ideas on supplements and therapies that could be started by me straight away. We read and read for those first few weeks. I was discharged from hospital and began commuting daily to the hospital in the city. We were given an elastic two weeks as the date for her discharge. It was more like four. Her platelets took quite a while to sort out. It also was noted that she did have a heart defect, a complete AVSD with a couple of other holes, plus her aortic arch was narrowed and we were told that she might need surgery imminently. We found something we could try to help that, and it was avoided thankfully. She was kept in for four weeks in total until that surgery was ruled out.

The time in intensive care then in special care was frustrating. Expressing 6-8 times a day while looking after two other children and travelling in and out, remembering to wake myself at least once a night nearly drove me up the wall and I'm sure contributed to the torrents of tears that flowed in secret while driving myself in or while looking the other way.

The hospital looked after us so well, but they couldn't magic everything better. The day we could finally try breastfeeding was such an emotional day. It was so good to be feeling like her mother, really properly. Anyone can change a nappy or do a nasogastric or bottle feed but no-one else could breastfeed her. Turned out even I couldn't that day, but she took to it well and in a couple of days was giving it a go. The first feed changed everything for me. It was like meeting her for the first time and I finally could see her beyond the face she was wearing. The mask of Down Syndrome started to melt away from that point as I got to know her through our interactions.

However, in NICU and the SCN, it's often two steps forward, one step back. When you come off the CPAP machine it's no guarantee you won't be back on it tomorrow. Feeding was a bit stop and start because it was too difficult with the CPAP hat on. Her bloods all sorted out though and eventually her oxygen too and she was moved to special care. After another week, when it was evident she wasn't keen on the bottle and wasn't feeding around the clock (despite my middle of the night visits for feeds) she was discharged back to her birth hospital. These nurses were very mothering and it was lovely to be back with the nurse who looked after her the night she was born.

It was much easier to get feeding established with her closer to home. I could pop in and out and do 4 or more feeds a day, rather than a maximum of two. I could even pop back at 10pm without too much trouble. We tried a couple of overnight stays to see if we could get her off her nasogastric tube, but she would not wake for love nor money. People would normally kill for a baby who sleeps all night, but it turns out that in a newborn that's not such a great thing!

In the end we were so over the hospital stay that we all agreed she'd be better off at home, with us doing all the nasogastric feeding.

We were discharged into the care of the Cardiologist and to a daily routine of expressing, breastfeeding and nasogastric feeding every few hours until it was time for her heart surgery.

Regardless of the effort involved, though at times the round-the-clock intensity of the routine almost drove me mad, it was worth it to finally have her home. Our family was together at last.

Jacinta is now 14 months old. She had her AVSD, AV valve and PDA repair with a surprise MAPCAS thrown in at 4 months and then hit the ground running with breastfeeding and lost the nasogastric tube within about 4 weeks. At 5 months she was assessed as normal or above for everything except mobility, so that's what we were focusing on until about 11 months. At about 9 months she started showing signs of bleeding and bruising and since I was made aware that transient leukaemia can lead to leukaemia in early childhood, I had her tested. She's now undergoing chemotherapy for leukaemia and her prognosis is very good. Jacinta is so sociable and beautiful, she gets comments wherever we go and her sisters love her to bits. Her arrival has added a new dimension to our lives and we are all better people for having her in our family. We couldn't imagine life without her!

~ Peggy, Jacinta's mum; 36; Victoria, Australia

{Amelia}

My pregnancy with Amelia was pretty uneventful, moderate to mild morning sickness, lots of carb cravings. We were excited to find out it was a girl to add to family of two mischievous wonderful boys. We had never done any extra testing during a pregnancy because at the time of Amelia's birth tests like Harmony and Maternity21 were not available and tests for abnormalities were prone to high false positive rates. I didn't see the point of putting myself through extra worry when I knew no matter what I would choose to keep the baby I was carrying.

At 32 weeks we had a 3d ultrasound and saw our little girl up close and personal. When the tech printed off the pictures from the ultrasound the side profile seemed odd to me and made me slightly uncomfortable. My midwife came in after what seemed like a long time and asked us if the baby in the ultrasound looked like our other two children. I thought this was a rather bizarre question considering it was an ultrasound. She then mentioned that the tech had noticed that the distance on the nasal bridge was rather small rather than a "scoop" making her profile somewhat flat. She told us she almost didn't bring it up, because there were no other apparent markers, but it could be a sign of some kind of syndrome. She suggested that it was most likely just a familiar trait and that she probably looked like a great aunt or grand parent. 'It could be nothing,' she told us.

When we left I cried in the car, Caleb my husband drove home with his arm around me. He seemed confident that it was most likely nothing. For the next few weeks I looked at children as they passed me, examining their nasal bridges. My Dad, an epedemiologist did what he does best and sent me all the research on nasal bridge markers. He gave me the odds of 1:50 with my age and one marker.

(My odds with just my age were 1:832, we had not had any quad screening done to calculate other odds)

Amelia arrived at 37 weeks, after a very quick 3 hour labor. She was very purple upon arrival and when they pulled her up beside me I immediately recognized her diagnosis. With the adrenaline of the moment, and the relief of the labor being over I felt immediate acceptance. I asked the midwife about her nose and she commented that it was a little flat. The pediatrictian examined her but didn't find any other markers. We asked him about it the next morning, and he commented that her eyes were a little close together and her nose was a little flat, but again made the comment that it might just be family traits.

Amelia was the best newborn ever, she was so calm and peaceful, and seemed to smile at us with her eyes. Her bright spirit and spunky newborn nature calmed any fears that anything was "wrong" She didn't eat well, but that is not uncommon for a newborn. I erased the idea of DS out of my mind. At her follow up appointment at 9 days the pediatrician asked us if we wanted to pursue testing, and I agreed since the question had been raised. We got the test ordered when Amelia was 2 weeks old and got the results when she was 4.5 weeks.

As we waited for the results my family kept on asking me if I was anxious about them, and honestly I wasn't really. I was convinced the result would be negative. The moment we got the result will be forever burned in my memory. I was out by myself, a rare moment, and was about to stop in at a Salvation Army store. I had texted my midwife earlier with the question, "Any news on the results of the test for little girl?" and saw that she was calling me back. I answered excitedly ready to put this lingering question behind us. When my midwife said, "We got Amelia's results back and she did test positive for Down syndrome, so she does have Trisomy 21," my heart froze. I remember my voice breaking as I asked in a weak voice, "Really?" not really knowing what else to say. I was shaking. I don't remember what else she said beyond that, probably how sorry she was, and that there were lots of good early intervention programs around. I think she also said something about, "Maybe it will be very mild," which of course in my experience now I realize is like telling someone they have a mild case of pregnancy,

I got home and got out of the car, my husband asked me what was wrong and I just sobbed. I went inside and he held me as I got the words out, we were both in shock. I was hyperventalating and shaking again. I went into our room and picked up Amelia. She looked up at me with her big blue eyes and I felt my heart sigh in relief, it was still her. She hadn't changed, it was still the little girl I had just put down to a nap, still the little girl that at just 4 weeks old had completely stolen our hearts. I felt angry that something had "happened" to her, and that it was something that could never be changed, these feelings would come and go over the next several months, year as I learned to accept this unexpected turn of events.

After her diagnosis I let myself finally start doing research on Down syndrome, on the things that it actually meant, and the things that were just myths that I had believed. I realized that i had been introduced into a new family, a wonderful community of other mothers with children that had this little bit extra to love. Moms that told me that everything was going to be okay, and that the tears would eventually stop and this love that I was already feeling would overcome the sadness. They told me stories of amazing accomplishments,  and unexpected outcomes. They told me of adults leading "normal" lives in spite of this 'disability" and how their children were constantly amazing them. I found comfort in these stories and comfort in snuggling my little bright eyed girl, whom I wouldn't trade for the whole world.

Amelia is now 15 months old, crawling all over the place and getting into mischief. Even at her busy age of 15 months she will still sit and snuggle with her momma, melting into me like she is a part of my soul that was always meant to be there. I can't imagine a moment of my life without her.

~ Rachel, Amelia's mom; 32; Kentucky, United States

{Carl}

The day my son was born, my life took a very unexpected turn. My pregnancy was normal, everything was "great," my ultrasound looked fine, his heartbeat sounded perfect, nothing out of the ordinary. We never had any genetic testing done because we always said, "It wouldn't matter." To be honest, I never thought it would happen to us. I was 31-years-old when my son was conceived. We had no family "history" of it and already had a "typical" daughter. Down syndrome was something, I didn't even think would be a possibility.

My water broke at 2:30 in the morning and we left for the hospital three hours later. The

delivery was quick and easy; soon I was holding my beautiful baby boy. He was smaller than his sister was, weighing in at 7 lbs. 3 ozs. Before I knew it, I was being wheeled off to my postpartum room and my little boy we named Carl, was wheeled off to the nursery to be examined and stabilize his body temperature.

As my husband and I waited for our little guy to return, we were beaming, we were on cloud nine. We brought another little healthy human being into the world, we had no idea….

Next thing we knew a strange doctor walked into my room and quickly introduced himself. He started by saying, "Your son is looking healthy, but...". "But what?" my husband and I said at once as my body went numb. He went on to explain that our son was showing a number of signs that he has Down syndrome. His muscle tone was low, his eyes looked slanted, there was a fat patch on the back of his neck and a large gap between his big toe, all hallmark signs. I looked at my husband, he was kneeling on the side of my bed with his face buried in his hands, my mouth was hanging wide open, I was in too much shock to even cry at that point.

Then it hit me, guilt, it was my job to carry this baby into the world healthy, happy, and perfect. I must have done something wrong. The tears started, I remember looking at the doctor barely able to say, "I did this, I must have." He assured me, Down syndrome is something that just happens and is out of anyone's control. My husband then looked at him and told him to get our son.

I remember hysterically saying over and over, "Oh God," and, "I want our son." Looking back, I was probably screaming it. My little guy was finally wheeled back to us after what seemed like forever as I sobbed hysterically in my husband's arms. He looked perfect, we thought how could this be possible? Over the next few hours we tried to wrap our brain around all this. What would this mean for our son? For us? Our future? His future? Could I really handle a child with special needs? Why us? Why him?

I slowly started telling family and close friends the news. Our family, like us, were devastated. We all clung to the hope that there was a small chance the doctors were wrong. None of

the pediatricians that examined our son could make a definite diagnosis, we would have to wait for the genetic test. I texted a handful of close friends who responded wonderfully within minutes. I begged them not to feel sorry for us in the text. I couldn't muster up the strength to call any of them, a text was all I could handle at that point.

I wanted so badly to go back into the delivery room where everything was okay. We had no idea there. We were the smiling happy couple holding our baby, posting pictures on Facebook and sending out picture texts. Having to then tell everyone there was a problem seemed overwhelming. This was the birth of our son and felt like I had been hit by a truck. I didn't want to celebrate anymore. The sight of the "it's a boy" balloon made me want to vomit.

In the meantime, we were assigned a social worker to help us cope. Not only were we dealing this news, but we were still grieving the loss of my father-in-law who passed away just three weeks before the birth from cancer. It was all too much. We were once again mourning,

mourning the loss of the little boy we thought we were going to have.

Day two and we hit rock bottom. The cardiologist was worried about a valve in his heart and wanted to transfer him to a children's hospital for monitoring. If the valve was to start narrowing more, surgery would be needed. Suddenly the Down syndrome didn't seem that big of a deal, we just wanted our little boy to be healthy. Our son was transferred to the Children's Hospital of Philadelphia (CHOP) by ambulance. I demanded to be discharged early, there was no way my son was leaving without me. The transfer team loaded our baby into the transfer crib that looked like an incubator and we were wheeled out together. My husband and I sobbed as we drove behind the ambulance, it was awful, just heart-wrenching awful.

Day three and my son needed an IV put into a vein in his head. It killed me to see my little guy all hooked up to monitors and tubes. However, that day we finally got good news, his heart was ok. We would end up staying at the hospital for another four days. My husband stayed with him every night while I went home to take care of our daughter.

A few days later, it was confirmed, our son did indeed have Down syndrome. We were pulled into a tiny room with tissues on each end table. In the days leading up to this, I had come to accept the fact that my son had Down syndrome. A few of the nurses and doctors at CHOP made a few comments to us that our son did not "look" like a child with Ds. Those comments gave my husband and I some false hope, but deep down, I knew. Still, the emotions started all over again once it was confirmed. The genetic counsellor looked at us and asked, "What did they say about his heart?" We held each other and cried, then my husband said, "Let's go see our son." We dried our eyes and walked out hand in hand. I remember walking back to our son thinking, that's it, no more tears, we're just going to love our little man so much.

~ Sara, Carl's mom; 32; Philadelphia, United States

{Reece}

It wasn't until 16 weeks when I felt the baby move for the first time that I truly felt like I was having a baby, and I started to get excited. This was the same week that my doctor's appointment included a blood test known as the quad screen. My husband and I had debated the merits of the test as we knew that no matter what the results we would continue the pregnancy. In the end we decided to test, mostly because my husband thought it would be better to know, and be prepared if we were going to have a baby that was other than typical. I got the call a week later, and the nurse said everything was great with the blood test.

Everything continued with my pregnancy in a picture perfect way. The baby was growing and moving around like a banshee. I felt good. Yes, there were leg cramps, and I couldn't go to a gas station for 8 months without getting a raging headache, but it was so much easier than I ever

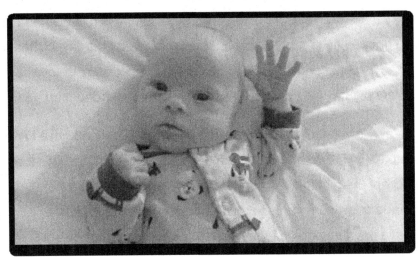

imagined. I have always been an active person and I was able to maintain that throughout my pregnancy. I played volleyball until my 33rd week (when the season ended for the year), and I played tennis until the very end. My husband and I had not been able to agree on a name for our son, so we jokingly called him starfish (given his propensity to stretch both arms in legs at the same time) or simply the hooligan. He didn't become "Reece" until he was 4 days old.

At 34 weeks, his movement slowed way down to the point where I was concerned and went to my doctor's office. They monitored Reece, and felt that his heart rate was strong and that he might be running short on room, or reacting to the cold I was trying to get over. They sent me on my way, telling me not to worry, but scheduled an ultrasound 10 days later to check on him. The next 10 days included Christmas, New Years, and the busiest time of the year for my work, but it took an eternity. Reece was moving, but it just didn't feel right. At the ultrasound the technician did some measurements, but based on the position couldn't get a good look at the whole cord, but what she could see looked good. I pushed her to keep looking- I just knew something wasn't right. After the ultrasound I met with my doctor, she said that everything looked ok, but at 36 weeks she didn't think we should take any chances. She thought there might be a kink in the cord and recommended a C-section, but as I was 3 cm dilated and soft was willing to discuss induction. In the meantime, she wanted me to check into the hospital for monitoring and to wait until 6 that evening for my stomach to be empty and her to be done with her appointments for the day.

At the hospital they put me on a monitor and discovered that what I believed to be Braxton Hicks were real contractions, and my sons' heart rate was decelerating with each contraction. So less than an hour after being in my doctor's office I was wheeled down for a C-Section. As they were prepping to do an epidural my first painful contraction hit, and his heart rate went down to 60 and stayed down. They switched to an emergency procedure, out went my husband and they knocked me out. When I woke up I was in the recovery room with a bunch of nurses, my husband and the most adorable, squishy little baby ever.

The next hour or so was a blur. I kept asking what happened, was the cord kinked, what was his APGAR, had they figured out what was wrong. Everybody kept saying he is great, it's fine etc, but I distinctly remember a nurse looking at him and saying, "I've been a nurse a long time, and his eyes don't look right." Just then the pediatrician on call came in. I found out later that she had just graduated from medical school and had only been practicing for a few months. I asked her what was going on. Is he ok? She talked about his APGAR being 6 and 9 and that his initial blood test showed that he was in distress. She was holding my son and showed me that he had low muscle tone. My thought was "duh, he hasn't moved much in the past two weeks", I didn't realize at the time that it was an indicator for T21. She quickly went on to say that the cord looked fine and they wanted permission to do some other testing including a repeat blood gas (as his first was not in the normal range) and a genetic test to rule out any issues. I felt like a genetic problem was not probable as it felt like everything went wrong suddenly, rather than being present all along.

The repeat blood test showed that he was still having issues so they took him to the NICU for IV antibiotics. Once there, they had him on oxygen monitors and found that he wasn't circulating oxygen as he should. The next 6 hours the pediatrician on call sat with us as we did chest x-rays, echocardiograms and blood tests, not to mention trying to learn how to breastfeed a tiny, exhausted newborn around a plethora of tubes and wires.

It had been the longest night of my life, and after taking 30 minutes to shower, eat and take some pain medication, my husband, Will, and I returned to the NICU room to check on Reece. We quickly realized that in our absence the night shift had turned into a day shift and our beautiful son had a new nurse. He introduced himself to us and as he handed us a copy of "Babies with Down Syndrome: A New Parents' Guide" as he said, "oh yeah, the neonatologist left this for you before he went home." He might as well have punched me in the stomach. I couldn't breathe, I couldn't talk. I distinctly remember Will asking, "Wait. What? I thought they were just ruling this out with a bunch of other things? Do they think he has Down Syndrome?" The look on the nurse's face answered the question better than any words, but the nurse quickly backtracked telling us they didn't have any of the test results back yet, but that it was a possibility.

I was in shock, but even more so in denial. Reasons that Reece could not have Down Syndrome kept running through my head. I could tell you the day that things started to feel off with my pregnancy. It was at 34 weeks and 2 days that Reece's movements slowed down, he stopped reacting to things that had always caused him to move and he stopped growing. Genetic conditions like Down Syndrome don't happen at 34 weeks 2 days, right? Besides if after treating my son for 8 hours, that neonatologist didn't say it to my face, surely he wouldn't just leave me a book. A doctor surely wouldn't be that much of a coward, right? Wait, I had a prenatal test and 4 ultrasounds and none of them found evidence of any genetic or congenital conditions so it can't be Down Syndrome. The neonatologist had spoken with us about a possible heart condition creating the issues. Heart problems are fixable, Down Syndrome is not. I want it to be the heart condition. It didn't have to be logically, it just had to mean that they were wrong.

Shortly after our conversation with the nurse, our pediatrician showed up. Reece was our first child, but Dr. Bob had been my pediatrician throughout my childhood. He looked me in the eye and said the words I needed to hear, and that the doctors and nurses the night before didn't have the courage to say. "I believe your son has Down Syndrome. " He then proceeded to go through a list of indications, like the low muscle tone, the probable heart condition, a single crease on one of his hands. These were all things that doctors or nurses had pointed out, but they had never made the connection to Down Syndrome, and I didn't know what they were hinting at until after the fact. At this point, I doubled over crying. Will was immediately behind me rubbing my back. I don't know what else Dr. Bob said that day, but I know he talked for a while.

We were in the hospital for four days. It turned out that Reece did not have a heart condition. The placenta had failed at 34 weeks and 2 days and he was just starving after a 2 week drought of nutrients. I am not a girly girl. I don't cry, or shall I say I didn't before Reece was born. I can honestly say that I have never felt so much, or as strongly as I have since Reece entered the world. Tears flowed freely for about three weeks. I have never felt such overwhelming fear; fear for the future, fear of the unknown, fear that I wasn't cracked up to be a mom let alone Reece's mom. I have never felt such irrational and disproportionate anger before. I had to abandon a shopping cart to avoid confronting a pregnant Mom with a small typical child in tow, chain smoking in the parking lot of my grocery store. Why is her child typical and mine is going to have to struggle? I don't deserve this, and Reece certainly doesn't. Sadness would hit me in waves. I would think about how easy school, friends or sports had always been for me and then I would think at how hard those will probably be for my son and I'd feel like I got kicked.

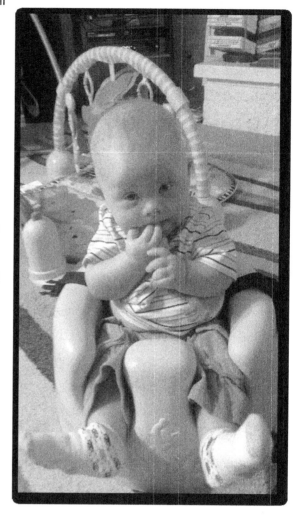

Getting the call a couple weeks later, that Reece's diagnosis of Down Syndrome was official as the genetic testing results showed the presence of an extra chromosome was anticlimactic. It felt like closure for the uncertainty, but we had already moved into the "living with it" part of life. I found community and solace with a group of women online, and now at 9 months into our journey I no longer feel like we are living with it. Yes, there are still moments that I hate his 47th chromosome, like when I had to pin him down to get blood drawn recently, but for the most part I think about it less and less, and those gaps are filling with love and wonder. I delight in his big gummy grin, and his baby giggles. He is Reece, and he is perfect.

~ Tami, Reece's mom; 32; United States

{Jacob}

Jacob was born at 2:10 am after 36 hours of agony! His birth was induced at exactly 37 weeks after an ultrasound revealed a lack of amniotic fluid. We had a very average pregnancy and birth with no complications. Jacob's nuchal fold was 3mm but put together with my age (27) there was a 1 in 1767 chance of Down syndrome. A high chance is considered to but 1 in 200. We had decided against further testing if offered it as we didn't want to terminate under any circumstances. 3mm was considered high by our local doc so we were sent for our 20 week scan in the big city. We were told it was to check "for a heart problem, as you have no chance of Down syndrome." The 20 week scan took a long time as Jacob didn't cooperate but it was all fine. They found nothing "wrong" with our baby and we relaxed again.

After he was born, they passed him to me and told me he was a boy. This shocked me greatly as I had convinced myself I was having a girl even though we had decided not to find out the sex. My second thought was I would do it all over again happily to give this little boy a brother or sister. Then I started to look at my little newborn. I remember staring in to his cute little "gnome eyes" (tiny little slits) and thinking he looked different to other newborns I had seen in photos. But I thought maybe every new one looks like this when they have just come out. As I tried to move him around to set him up for breastfeeding I remember thinking he was very floppy but to me this made sense because they had to wiggle out of their mummies so floppy was surely a good thing?

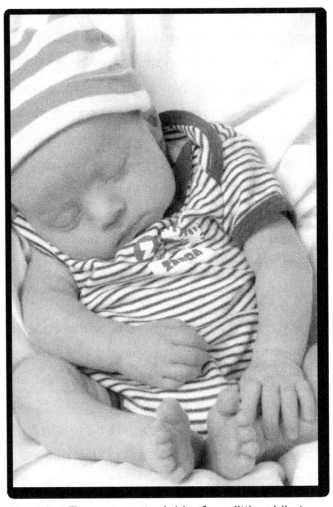

I had a lovely long cuddle with him in the delivery suite. The nurses took him for a little while to do his APGAR tests; they were 10 and 9. Which to me were like all the other tests you have while pregnant and somehow meant I had done right and my baby was healthy. I was a proud mum. I asked the nurses about his "Gnome eyes" and his floppy body. They avoided my question and told me about a cyclone storm named Yasi in Queensland (another state) that was really bad and asked if I had seen the news reports? The OB/GYN saw me the next day and questioned, "Did I have a good support network?"

Three days later still wondering about my "floppy" boy with "gnome eyes" a paediatrician came in to our room unannounced. He told us he was here to do the baby check. I thought the GP did this but mine was due to have her baby in two days, so I thought he was being helpful. He unwrapped Jacob and started to pick his limbs up and drop them, not saying a word to us. My GP randomly showed up at the same time to really do our baby check. She was preoccupied with finding the right room for her to have her baby in but asked why he wasn't filling out the forms for the check. They had a disagreement about completing the forms and my GP said she would be in to check on us.

Jacob was left unwrapped and the doctors walked out. I felt intimidated by this unfriendly doctor who was poking my child and treating him like a rag doll. He came back and said we needed to sign a form for testing.

"What testing?!" we asked.

"Genetic testing." was all he would answer.

He left the room.

I said, "What genetic testing?" to my husband.

He replied like a dictionary "Down syndrome is the most common genetic condition." I nearly slapped him!! How could he accuse my son of having that just because it was most common? This is our perfect baby boy you are talking about! How could he be so matter of fact?

Doctor Hell (the shortened version of his name) came back. I asked him three more times what the tests were for. He eventually muttered," Down syndrome" to us. I asked why he thought that. He said Jacob had low muscle tone (the floppiness) and low set ears. I agreed that he was floppy, but my mum had ears that are lower than her eyes and she doesn't have it!! He left us and just walked off with nothing else to say.

It was late that night after visiting hours, my newborn was having his first bad night that it all hit me. I had been very calm all day. I don't like the world to see me emotional. Benjamin Button of all things was on TV (what a cruel TV programmer) I realised every nurse who had popped in, to see how cute my baby was had come to see the freak show. A Downs baby on the ward for the first time in 18 years!!

That was the day my world fell apart.

I had spent the whole day hoping they had got something wrong and he was ok. How can they put a label on a three day old baby? It wasn't fair! He was perfectly healthy and just had minor temperature issues. How can his floppy legs and low set ears condemn him to being so different forever? He was my little man and he was perfect!

I had chronic fatigue syndrome since I was 15 years old. I had been in pain and always very tired for the last 13 years. Many people said I shouldn't have kids as I couldn't look after myself enough. But through all those years, I was always stronger and had more energy when I was with children. I was a childcare worker because I felt kids didn't care if I was sick, they just wanted me to play. Somehow I could always muster up energy if there was a child to play with. I didn't care what people thought. I knew I was strong enough to handle anything. You have to be strong to even drag yourself out of bed with chronic fatigue. It's like having a bad case of the flu everyday. I still had doubts and was worried about raising a "normal" kid. How could a give a baby with additional needs what he needed? Had I given this too him because I was so useless? I felt the pregnancy was the only thing I'd ever been ok at? Now I'd messed up my baby?

But I never stopped loving my little man for one moment, I was mostly worried that the world would never love him as much as I did.

It was three days before we got the 99% confirmation he had Ds with the FISH test. I still hoped somehow they had got it wrong. By the time we received the official result in 1 month, we had come to terms with it and already been through a lot with him. We didn't need confirmation. We had done the research and understood. We had come to be proud of his little differences and were even starting to show him off to total strangers. This is our baby; he has Down syndrome!

Jacob was five days old when we left hospital. On the way out, there was one more surprise. We were given a mandatory government survey to fill out before we lift because our child had "a genetic defect at birth." This form went on to ask us questions about lifestyle choices (such as alcohol and drug taking) work and home environment (such as chemical expose, age, weight). This form would be used for statistics. It might seem like a small thing, but when you have just been told two days before that your baby was "disabled," you are already looking for a way to blame yourself 100 times over. This form seemed to be a list of things we had potentially done wrong. A very long list! I have never had alcohol or drugs and tried to be very healthy for my pregnancy. I thought I had done everything to ensure my child had a good start. Now I had a list of every way I had potentially ruined his life! My husband has worked with many chemicals and was a normal young man who liked to party, so I had plenty to blame him for too. Being singled out and asked such intrusive questions at such a hard time was like rubbing salt in fresh wounds!

We got home on a Saturday. Family had come to visit so we had all three gandparents around. It was a lovely time of first baths at home and lots of snuggles. The whole time we had the possible DS hanging over our heads. I had a few tears but kept telling myself they had got it wrong. That "low tone " and "low set ears " meant nothing. He was fine. We decided not to tell anyone else until we knew for sure. I kept looking at him wondering if he looked strange? Was I the only one who thought he was adorable? How could a baby who the doctors thought was a freak of nature look so cute? Maybe I was crazy and he wasn't cute? I felt so bad for being so superficial I hated that it mattered how cute he was. But he was super cute!! I was so proud of him no matter what just worried too much what others thought.

On Monday we went to our doctor for results or the FISH test which would tell us to a 98% accuracy I believe. I told myself the results would be negative and if they were positive we still had a 2% chance he didn't have it so no need to worry yet. Our doctor was having a C section for her own baby tomorrow so she came in on her day off and told us the results. She said it was hard as she knew the results on Friday but had to wait for the appointment over the weekend. Chances are he had DS. I held it together and tried to be calm. I don't like to be emotional in public. She then introduced us to her fill in doctor. Not the time you want to meet someone new! I held it together until paying on the way out and then stood in the corner face the wall and cried my eyes out while my husband sorted the bill.

After five days at home and trying to figure out breastfeeding, Jacob had a very bad night. I tried everything but he just wouldn't feed. He wouldn't stop screaming either. I called an online breastfeeding helpline twice but the lady was grumpy and not helpful. Then I called the hospital and I was yelled at for not calling earlier and if he didn't feed to go in. He fed a little eventually. So first thing the next day the midwife brought an expressing kit and I was able to feed him. Again that night he wasn't settled and I couldn't get my usually sleepy boy to sleep . Finally at

1am I put him to bed. 10 mins later he let out a blood curdling scream. My husband decided to change him as he liked a fresh bottom. Then my husband yelled "HE'S PEEING BLOOD!!!" I ran over to see and he was right.

We took him to our local hospital. Once the nurses saw the nappy (diaper, they sent us off to drive to the bigger hospital an hour away. They said it would take too long to get him help here, if he was their son they would drive him right now. At 2am we drove for an hour. Once we got there it was a crazy they checked his last jaundice test. It was higher than one older nurse had ever seen. They did tests and it was revealed he also had a urinary tract infection, blood infection and kidney infection. Combined with the jaundice, he was very sick. We were in hospital for 14 days and had to get lots of fluid in to flush out the jaundice. We were forced to feed him with a feeding tube. When we finally got him home, we were on strict instructions to mix feed him to fatten him up. This was very hard for me as I was obsessed with breastfeeding. I felt like a failure. I hated buying formula. I felt the world was judging me for being a bad mum.

We got the official test back when he was a month old. By then we had done our research and chatted to medical staff and we knew our boy had a little extra and we were proud of him. I didn't know how to tell our friends. It felt like a shameful secret, but I knew it shouldn't be. I started by telling total strangers as I wouldn't get emotional with them. Once I got comfortable, we started to tell friends. When I finally got to post it on Facebook, I was so proud by the positive response I got. I have never had a negative word from friends or family. They love him like we do!! They are proud of him too!

After that we had ups and downs with medical issues. The only other major one was his heart.

At 1 month old we took him for a routine check, being assured that he only had a little murmur and wasn't sick as they had seen how strong he could cry. We went in to the appointment very confident. This changed as we watched the doctor's faces as they did an ultrasound on his heart. We were told he had a VERY LARGE VSD and he would need open heart surgery.

Again our world fell apart. He had a hole so big in the wall of his heart. It was like he had the wall removed to make an open plan kitchen! They said he would die without surgery.

Three months later we watched him drink less and less. He was getting so skinny; he was a skeleton. Our baby boy was dying before our eyes.

The hospital we needed to go to was full. Three times our date was moved, until eventually we drove 5 hours and flew another hour to another state to get his operation. He needed it 6 weeks earlier. On the day of the surgery he was too tired to cry even though he had to fast all day. Handing him over was the hardest thing I've had to do. I thought they would let me hold him as he went to sleep but they wheeled him away fully clothed, awake and staring at me.

Tiny. Lying in the middle of a big cot. Six big male doctors pushed the cot away.

After hours of tears, they rang to say he would be ready to see us in an hour. We rushed to the hospital. Two hours later we were still waiting… eventually, after what seemed like days, a doctor came and told us they were still working on him. I froze and didn't get to say anything before he was gone. Later we were told that they were having trouble starting his heart. Eventually we got to see him.

The next nine days were some of the hardest and best times of our lives. We made lifelong friends with our roommates and had our hearts broken once more when we received news that one of the babies we shared those nine days with lost his life after five weeks of fighting after birth. We learned the true meaning of survivor's guilt as we came home with our son and cried for our now close friend as she went home without her son. We entered a world where babies sometimes die, but miracles happen everyday. We were there as two very special children went home for the first time after many months in hospital. One child breaking the record books for being the first to survive and go home with her condition.

We feel we handled the heart surgery well because of the support from other parents. Before we left we had four months of survival stories and hope from our local Heartkids support group. We saw before and after photos. We met crazy daredevil kids with heart scars (zipper scars) that were so healthy and full of energy it scared us. We learned it would be okay! We learned to stop and smell the roses and never to take or little man for granted. He is our hero! I wouldn't change a moment of the hard times. Except, of course, to bring back the beautiful children we have lost along the way. Each one we have learned something from and we will never forget!

Since then, apart from re-occurring urinary tract infections, Jacob has been very healthy. At 2 and a half he has just started walking and became a big brother to baby Isabella who he adores! He signs over 100 words and is starting to talk. We wouldn't change our little man for the world, but we would change the world for him! We hope this book helps change the world even just a little!

Jacob is 2.5 years. At 1 month old he had an accidental drug over dose when the doctor put the decimal point in the wrong place on his diuretics for heart failure. Because of my quick thinking

and slightly paranoid mum qualities he was fine 24 hours later. He had open heart surgery to repair a VSD at four months old and was out of hospital in less than nine days. He has also had over a dozen urinary tract infections. other than that we have had a good run with his health. He is signing over 100 words and signing 2 word sentences. He loves singing, dancing and

making noise. He is obsessed with The Wiggles. He has just started walking in the last month and has also became a big brother to baby Isabella who he adores. He is a great big brother and helper. He amazes us everyday and we think he's perfect just the way he is. We wouldn't change our little man for the world, but we would change the world for him! We hope this book helps change the world even just a little!

~Rachel, Jacob's mum; 27; South Australia

{Tobin}

As I reclined on the recovery room gurney, I thought about how physically difficult this pregnancy had been. How I had reached a time in my life I never imagined possible; the point that I felt satisfied with this being my last pregnancy. And I was overjoyed at this giant 10 pound baby nestled against my bare skin. I was weary from the worry that plagued this 5th pregnancy and 5th c-section. Quietly, I chided those statistic quoting ob doctors that terrified me and only added emotional weight to the physical stress of this pregnancy. I wanted to marinate in this

new life; soak him in, learn his smell, nurse him and enjoy our couple time before going home to the busyness of life. I just held him; skin to skin while attempting to latch him on to nurse. We stayed like this for several hours, revelling in our new couplehood. And we prayed in thanksgiving to God for delivering us this sweet baby who was so incredibly cute and looked exactly like his big

brother Carsten. Our elation lasted into the wee hours of the morning as we were transferred to a private room to enjoy our new son. I tried off and on all morning to nurse him. He was just so darn sleepy. By 10 am, he was taken off to the newborn nursery for his bath and check-up.

Shortly thereafter, a pediatrician came to our room. She was an exotic looking woman with long dark hair, impeccably dressed and spoke with a beautiful accent. She explained that she had been taking care of our beautiful son. She went on to say that there were a few characteristics that she thought might be consistent with Down syndrome. I'm not sure if I laughed out loud or not but my first reaction was that this woman was completely mistaken. He looked just like his brother for heaven's sake. And then just as quickly as that thought entered my mind, I knew. It was if the Holy Spirit had been quietly nudging me throughout my pregnancy; maybe even my whole life. Not that I had that full realization at that moment. But for a split second, everything clicked. I remembered back to Advent when I was involved with 40 days for life, the pro-life prayer vigil that is during advent and lent. I learned of the staggering percentage of babies aborted that are diagnosed prenatally with Down syndrome. Repeatedly throughout my last trimester; I kept thinking, "Please God, I do not think I can handle a special needs child". I do not know what lead me to have those thoughts.

Then the pretty lady who had so beautifully expressed that my son may have this completely unfamiliar condition explained that she had requested the genetics team from the children's hospital next door come to check on him. We agreed, thanked her for her kindness, (she never once said "I'm sorry but your son may have Ds), and then spent the next hour flabbergasted. Kyle thought this doctor was out of her mind. Although I kept agreeing with him; **I knew**. Once someone verbalized it, it made sense like the last piece being slide into the open place on a jigsaw puzzle. I told Kyle that I thought they were right and he still just couldn't see it. I waivered between thinking that everything would be fine and that our world was changing in a way we could not fully realize. When a small group of people entered our room about an hour later, pulling in chairs accompanied by the pretty doctor, my heart began to ache. The geneticist was very matter of fact but her words were measured and kind. I heard only a little of what she explained would lead her to believe Tobin has Down syndrome. As tears streamed down my face, she asked where my tears were coming from. And honestly I just didn't know. Mostly I felt selfish for feeling sad. Why was I sad? I still ask myself this today and still haven't quite figured it out fully. Dr. Zackai did a wonderfully thorough job of explaining the diagnostic process and asked if we had any questions. I asked her how certain she was. She said, "I wouldn't be here talking to you if I wasn't certain".

When they left, I requested my boy be brought back. I needed him close. I needed for him to feel my love. And I grieved. I wasn't sad that he wasn't the baby I had expected. I grieved over the mom I was challenged to be. I had felt like such a disappointment, in the prior months, to my kids. I was looking forward to moving forward and having more time to be whom they needed from me. And I was so afraid that I wouldn't be able to meet this challenge. This fear gripped my heart for 3 weeks. I told only a handful of friends because we wanted people to love our son; not our son "with Ds". When I told them, I asked for their prayers that God would equip me to be the mom that Tobin needed and deserved. I couldn't read any "feel good" stories about children with Ds or families that loved them. My fear caused me to be very cynical. One day, while I was absorbed with a combination of self-pity and worry about my son's future, I heard a voice stir inside of me. Not an audible voice but a feeling. Suddenly, a very clear realization came over me. God did not do this **to** us. This is our life and it happened. How we choose to move forward is what defines us. Fear is not of God. And that was the moment that was a game changer. I felt like I could breathe again. The weight of fear and doubt lifted. I stopped the daily tears. I could look at this beautiful child without thinking about Down syndrome every time. I realized, too, that this baby was mine, just like my other four. He was mine. God didn't give him to me because I am special. I am being challenged to rise to the occasion.

Months after Tobin was born, my dear friend Sabine told me this story. Nearly 4 years ago when she was 20 weeks pregnant, she chose to do the prenatal blood work test. Before receiving any results, she said she would want an amniocentesis because of her advanced age (39). She's a very concrete, intelligent and determined person. So when I challenged why she would consider such a risk to her long anticipated son, she admitted her fear in a baby with Ds.

I remember our conversation but not exactly what I said. Apparently, I told her "Sabine, if your baby has Down syndrome, I'll raise him". To this day, she calls and asks how her son Tobin is and if I am taking good care of him.

Recently, in an online community of moms with children with Ds, us moms were accused of being all "rainbows and unicorns". I think the reason it comes across like that is because the overwhelming fear that we experience in those first days now seemed so completely unnecessary. It's shouldn't be surprising that our children with 47 chromosomes are not much different than those with 46. I cannot say with 100% certainty that Tobin's extra chromosome is what is teaching me some beautiful lessons or not but I am learning lessons that I have been working on my entire motherhood career. A mentor mom I knew in TX used to say, "The laundry will wait." I would think, "It's going to multiply while it's waiting." But you don't have a choice but to let it wait when your infant takes 45 minutes to nurse because he has low muscle tone in his mouth. And when the grandmotherly type would say, "Enjoy the baby years because they go too fast," I am trying my hardest to treasure the fact that my stubborn 17 month doesn't want to walk. I think I have felt the true power of prayer throughout the past year. I am not a perfect mom. But I have become a better mom to all my children. God is equipping me to be the mom they all deserve and I owe it all to Tobin.

Today, Tobin is a healthy 17 month old whose cheesy smile can make anyone laugh. He is working hard at walking. He is cruising on the furniture, taking 2-3 steps between his siblings and practically running if he is holding someone's hand. We are working on sign language (we did with all of our children) and he consistently signs 4-6 words. We are anxiously awaiting his first spoken words. He fills our home with laughter, activity and milestones that seem monumental. We are beyond blessed that he is a part of our family.

~Troy, Tobin's mom; 39; New Jersey, United States

{Kayleb}

Coming up on Kayleb's first birthday a lot has been on my mind. I have been thinking back to the day he was born a year ago today. There is still a twinge of pain there, but it is good. When I got pregnant with Kayleb I was very overwhelmed of how in the world we were going to make it because Klohie was just 7 months old! But after the initial shock excitement set in. It was a pretty uneventful good pregnancy compared to blowing up like a balloon with Klohie. About two weeks before Kayleb was born we were in church. Just a normal Sunday. People went up to the choir to sing. Standing there watching I saw a middle aged man with Down syndrome that I saw every Sunday go up to sing like usual. This time was different for me though.

As I watched an overwhelming joy came over me. Tears filled my eyes as I watched him sing. He was getting more out of worshiping God than anyone else up there. You could tell in his eyes that he loved what he was doing. Then I thought how could someone not see him as a blessing? Something I had not really thought about before. A quick thought rushed through my head "If I had a child with Down syndrome I could do it". No more time than this thought had popped into my head, I pushed it out quick. No no no don't think that. Almost like if I

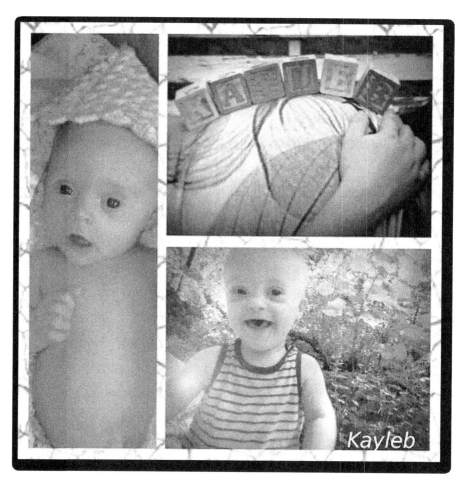

Kayleb

thought it than I was giving God permission, which I did not want to do. Fast forward 2 weeks later to a very quick labor. The pain was gone as soon as he was put on my chest. I picked him up looked into his eyes. Crying I said his name. He was beautiful. I finally got to meet him and felt intense love immediately. My boy. And then "I knew". Down syndrome rushed through my head. That day at church rushed through my head, but I shoved it out quickly. God had tried to tell me. I didn't say anything thinking if I did it would make it real and true. Everyone left the room while Kasey was holding Kayleb and I was getting cleaned up. The doctor came back into the room. I knew. It was slow motion the room was huge and dark taking him forever to get to the side of my bed and sit down. Smiling he took my hand. I knew. Most of this is blurry to me because in my head I was repeating "Don't say it. Don't say it," my mind was going crazy and my stomach lurching. He said Kayleb has some physical characteristics of Down syndrome and that they would do a blood test to make sure, that would take 7 to 10 days for results. He said it. We cried and said it doesn't matter because we love him anyway. It hurt bad. I was numb. I stuffed my feelings down.

Family came back in knowing nothing. Smiling we took pictures. It was hard to say, making it even more real, but we told wanting to get it over with. They cried. I was numb. I thought my dreams for him were shattered, my hope for him shattered. I just wanted to protect him. We went up to our room. More visitors, more gut wrenching, when all you wanted to do was celebrate your baby. More sorry eyes when you just want happiness. I didn't cry telling people, I did not want them feeling sorry for us. I didn't feel anything I was, so numb like a wall I had to put up to get through. At the end of the day I finally got to shower, with no one around it came and came. I had to let it out somewhere, but when I got out I stuffed it all back inside putting the wall back up and carried on. The next couple days were a roller coaster going from denial back to "I knew". Two doctors saying yes he does. Two doctors saying no he doesn't. We were given a long list of the health problems he is more likely to have. No parent wants to hear that there child will have a harder time with life. We had to test a lot of stuff to make sure he was okay. It was very scary waiting to see if his heart was okay. 50% of babies with Down syndrome have to have open heart surgery. We were very lucky. We came home the fourth day. And waited for the results. Inside I knew, but was in denial. The seventh day the doctor called back with his test results. It felt like we had waited forever. By the end I just wanted to know for sure either way so we could move on. Positive for Trisomy 21 (Down Syndrome) I let it out then after I told Kasey that the doctor had confirmed his diagnosis. Then we moved on and haven't looked back.

Some days are hard, but most days are great. We are just living life now. We have had a lot of doctors' appointments, this past year with more to come. Blood draws every 6 months for now to check for thyroid problems and to make sure his blood counts look good because of the increased chance of leaukemia. Checked ears, eyes, swallow study, lung doctor, sleep doctor, immune doctor. Having problems with his eyes that glasses or surgery cannot fix, where his vision could be anywhere from 20/50 to 20/200. We have physical, occupational, and speech therapy. He cannot crawl or walk yet, but works so hard! We go up to Kansas City to the Down Syndrome Clinic yearly. We are so lucky though that he is a pretty healthy little guy.

I do wish that I could make it easier for him, but more than that I wish I could change the way the world views him. I wish people were more excepting. We have met a lot of great people with kids with a little something extra also. All in all it has been a great year! I have renewed hope for my boy. He is the best baby. He is pretty laid back most of the time, but sure can let you know when you tick him off. I love his personality! He melts my heart daily. He dances like no other! I am a different person because of him. Growth hurts, but it is good. I wish I could go back to that moment and tell that terrified mom that it is all going to be better than okay and that life will turn back to a new normal and that your heart will be so full of happiness it feels like it might burst! One year ago today I was so excited to meet my baby boy, but that day will always have a little sadness to it because of how scary it was. I do not feel like I actually got to celebrate that day because of the huge shock that came along with him.

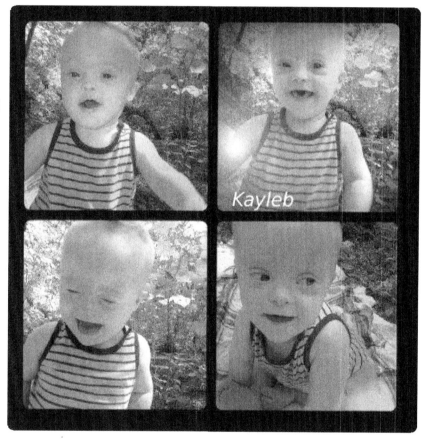

I am so excited to celebrate his birth today! The way it should have been a year ago. All life is precious no matter what extras may come along with it! Kayleb has taught me so much that I needed to know about myself, about God, about life! My boy came with lots of extras. Extra worries, extra love, extra chromosomes and I would not have him any other way! I have learned to find the beauty in the unexpected! Even though he was not exactly how I thought he would be he is still an amazing and perfect gift from God! Happy Birthday to the little boy I never knew I needed so badly!!!

~ Brittney, Kayleb's mom; 21; Missouri, United States

{Emilee}

I was blissfully ignorant. Not in a bad way. In a completely naïve, care-free kind of way. That's how I felt about my pregnancy. I was 43 years old and I was pregnant! I was thrilled, excited, and a little scared. Scared of all the what- if's.

I refused any and all genetic testing. Nothing. At my age I knew the statistics, and they didn't matter. At least I thought they didn't, but at the time, I didn't feel the need to know. Not one time during my pregnancy, did I suspect anything was wrong with my child. Thinking back, I realize that there were moments that could have pointed to a concern, like the high level

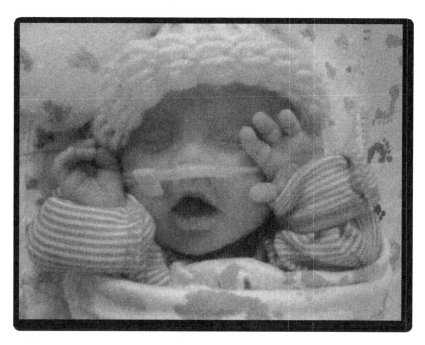

ultrasounds looking specifically at the baby's heart. She's a wiggler I was told. They were unable to get a good image of her heart so they kept bringing me in. I didn't suspect a thing. I was SO happy to be pregnant. The only hiccup I experienced during my pregnancy was hyperemisis. I was extremely sick to my stomach for the first 5 months of my pregnancy. I lost 40 pounds and barely could lift my head off my pillow at times. It was a horrible experience.

My water broke about 6 weeks before my due date early in the morning. As surprised as I was, my body had been trying to tell me something, just a few days prior. I was calm, but excited at the same time. As early as the baby was coming, I still didn't worry. I'm an experienced mom with two sons, 18 & 14. I had been there, and done that. This was going to be great.

One of the first things that struck me odd was the size of the medical team waiting for me at the hospital, when I arrived early that morning. I know that delivering a premature child can be risky, but again I wasn't aware of any problems that the baby would have other than maybe needing a little oxygen. I checked in at 3 centimeters and according to the Doctor, the baby was definitely coming. I started losing track of time soon after, I was having real contractions and beginning to experience hard labor pain. Time was moving too fast. They tried 8 times to get an IV line in.

Apparently I was dehydrated, and now the hospital wasn't offering me pain medication. I was starting to get very upset. I had zero intentions of having a baby without pain medication, and there were so many doctors and nurses. This is when things "got real".

In walked 3 people from NASA. At least I thought they were astronauts, or pilots, minus the helmets. My mind wrapped around itself, I felt like I was in a Stephen King novel. They had come to take my baby. She/He would need to be flown the closest hospital with a NICU. HOW DID THEY KNOW THIS ALREADY? No mention of heart issues, no mention of trouble, just an urgency to get the baby out.

It was in that moment, that I said No. I would not let them take my child without me. Everything that was protective, motherly, I refused to go any further. Labor stopped, everything stopped, so they sent the helicopter back and began magnesium sulfate to stall the contractions. An ambulance was called to get me to the next hospital before I delivered and the team from NASA hitched a ride, along with a midwife, and the 2 ambulance drivers. It was a tight fit.

Fast-forward 10 hours and a bigger hospital. Great birthing room, NICU at hand, I was happy. They even gave me drugs, and I was very happy. The first time the anesthesiologist gave me medication, it was a little too much and it made me numb from the neck down. I wasn't able to feel my arms or legs, or even move them. Instant anxiety attack, but everyone calmed me down and I fell asleep for about an hour. It's now 11 pm and I wake to real contractions. I can feel my legs now, and everything else down there. I ask for more meds, and they refused, stating I could go numb again and the baby was coming. I was NOT HAPPY. I had NO intention of having a baby with NO pain medication! But it happened, my worst nightmare. And the pain was bad. The baby was coming out transverse and it felt as though my spine would never be the same. I said some mean things, but in the end, I delivered the girl I had always wanted. She came out screaming and it was the sound I longed to hear from my premature miracle!

She looked like her daddy, blonde hair, blue eyes, strong German genes. Dave and I were in awe of her beauty. Perfect in every way. I was in love with her, and my dreams of pink frilly dresses, pony tails and giggles filled my mind. We were blessed.

I was told they were going to take our little girl to the NICU to be monitored and I didn't mind. I was so tired. Back into the world of pure bliss. The next morning when I woke, I called the NICU to see how my beautiful little girl was doing and instead of getting the nurse who was in charge of her care, I was accidentally connected to one of the neonatologists. I'm not sure how the cross connection occurred but when I came on the line, he thought that he was on the line with another neonatologist. He began talking about my daughter, medical terms I didn't understand. Something about a Palmers crease, a sandal gap and that he was getting ready to go see the parents because he suspected that she had Down syndrome. When I heard those words, I stopped breathing. I was in shock. I looked at David asleep in the lounger next to my bed. He was exhausted and sleeping so sound. I hung up the phone and sat there in complete shock. I didn't wake him. I couldn't wake him. My daughter had Down syndrome. When the doctor came in, he was so very gentle. I watched as the color drained from David's face. I couldn't breathe. I felt as though my entire world was crushing me down and I would never get back up. Every emotion imaginable ran through my mind. Every hope and dream that was my daughter, was gone. When he left, David and I embraced. We cried for what seemed like hours. We cried for every typical moment we would never have with a baby with Down syndrome. We were utterly lost.

When we went to the nursery, everything was different. Everything I had hoped and dreamed for, in a typical child, was lost. At least that's how it felt at the time. The nurses were so kind and gentle but in the back of my mind I felt as though they simply felt sorry for me. I was angry, VERY angry. Angry for being handed this deck of cards. Angry for every typical child in the nursery. Angry for every new mom walking in the door that didn't know my pain. I was more angry then I had ever been in my entire life. I was also sad and afraid, and confused and lost. So very lost. I didn't know one single solitary soul that had Trisomy 21. Not even a friend of a friend. I was now "that mom", "those people", "that family". The people you see in public, the ones you smile at but secretly feel sorry or pity for. On top of the Trisomy 21 diagnosis, we were told that she had several heart defects that were going to need open heart surgery. It was almost too much to bare. I didn't cry in the NICU, I didn't want the nurses to think less of me. I cried every time I went back to my room to rest, and I cried a lot. Probably the entire first day after she was born was spent crying. I didn't know how to feel. On one hand I had the daughter I had always dreamed of, on the other, she was nothing I had asked for. The first 24 hours after she was born, was probably one of the hardest days of my life.

It was on the second day that things began to turn around. Every time I looked at her I was amazed and in awe of her beauty. She was NOTHING I imaged Down syndrome to be. She didn't even look like she had Down syndrome. I went through many periods of doubt. Even after the blood test that confirmed the diagnosis, I still caught myself thinking it was all a mistake. Acceptance did not happen right away. It came gradually.

I left the hospital two short days after she was born. We named her Emilee Ember. I hated the fact that she had to stay when I was leaving but she was very sick. She was on high flow oxygen, a heart monitor & feeding tube. So many machines, there was almost always an alarm sounding. It can be a difficult place to become accustom to.

The NICU was very difficult for me, for many reasons. The hospital was an hour away from where lived but I came EVERY single day to be with her. I left in the morning after my boys went to school and came home in the evening to have dinner with them. It was very hard on them as well. My oldest was a senior in High School and my youngest was in eighth grade. They became latch key kids, taking care of each other while I was away. I worried for them almost as much as I worried for Emilee. I was under a lot of stress and in turn had difficulty producing milk. Having two teenage boys at home makes pumping extremely difficult. Then you add the stress of being on the road for several hours a day with not eating well and post-partum depression, it was a recipe for failure. I had to learn how to remove and insert a feeding tube into her nose and down her throat. I had to learn how to use home oxygen and a heart monitor. By the time we brought her home 40 days later, I felt as though I had been through a year of med school. The plan was to allow Emilee to come home and gain weight for about 6 months, then have open-heart surgery to repair her heart defects.

We had to see her Cardiologist the second day after coming home. We thought it was a routine follow up from the NICU so we decided that it would be okay that I went alone. It was an hour drive, but Dave had already closed his business for quite some time and was working extra hours to try to make up for it. She was given a high level echocardiogram during this visit and when we met with the doctor after the echo, I was completely unprepared for what she told me. Emilee's heart condition was worse than they thought in the NICU. She needed to have heart surgery in the next ten days. I couldn't believe what I was hearing. How could she need surgery already?

Emilee went into heart failure four days after that appointment. I was feeding her a bottle and she choked, then she began to cough. She started to turn blue so I rushed her to her doctor's office and they instructed me to drive her right to the hospital that was going to be doing the heart surgery. These were the longest weeks of my life. She was in heart failure and all I could think of was that she was going to die. I loved her so much and the Down syndrome diagnosis didn't matter to me anymore, only her well-being. This was my daughter and nothing, not a label, not a diagnosis, nothing, could make me feel anything less than pure love and adoration for her. I wanted her. I wanted her to live. I wanted to bring her home and do everything I had imagined I would do with a little girl.

Even though the sadness lasted much too long, I fell in love with Emilee immediately. Maybe not the diagnosis, maybe not her heart condition, but she really was the daughter I always wanted. I finally stopped asking what I did wrong to deserve this diagnosis, and started asking what I did right to deserve a child like Emilee.

Emilee is now 11 months old and the light of my life. She continues to amaze me everyday. She crawls everywhere even though it's a leap frog crawl, she is still in high motion. She's been sitting up for several months now & she loves music, it's part of our everyday life. She loves to hear us whistle and sing. She loves to dance. She signs four words and is very vocal. She adores her big brothers and they love her just as much. I love her disposition and how gentle she is. She adores her daddy. They have a very special bond. I never knew such love was possible but I'm living it every day.

~ Jennifer; Emilee's mom, 43; Pennsylvania, United States

{Seth}

I am now 40 years old, and I have been pregnant 9 times, with 8 live births. We have always opted to be as natural as possible. My first two were natural hospital births, but they came with "complications" that should never have happened, so after our first two, we decided on birthing with a midwife, to ensure our "natural birth plan" was followed. We did have an ultrasound with almost every baby, and Seth's pregnancy was no exception. At 20 weeks gestation, at which

time I was 38 years old, the ultrasound technician found nothing out of the ordinary, except for the fact that we were expecting our seventh son! We named him Seth. The pregnancy continued with no complications until I was about 34 weeks, at which point my pre-labor contractions were getting pretty strong.

The midwife checked me and found that I was dilating, so she put me on modified bed rest, no lifting and lay down as much as possible, for at least three weeks so we could get to the safe zone of 37 weeks gestation. It was pretty difficult to do, since we had just come through the holidays, and my husband was traveling a lot, but our 7 children stepped up to the plate and helped with the household duties. A week later, my favorite and last living grandparent, Byron Forbes Phelps, a WWII Veteran, POW and my fraternal grandfather, passed away. My parents were both out of state attending to the family's needs in Utah and Colorado and I was distraught. I was the only one who couldn't attend the funeral. I wept.

At 37 weeks pregnant, my husband was getting ready to leave for another trip, so we wanted the midwife to give us a prognosis on how soon our little man could be coming. She said she wouldn't recommend "Dad" go anywhere! Sure enough, the next morning, on January 24th, I was having regular contractions, 5 minutes apart. As we drove the 20 minutes in to town to the birthing center, I started doubting that it was real, but by the time we got to town, the contractions were pretty hard and long. I knew it was the day. I also realized that it was exactly two weeks after my grandfather has passed away. While we waited for the midwives to prepare for us, and got settled in to our room at the birthing center, the contractions became very difficult.

By 1pm, I was very heavy into labor, and I distinctly remember looking at the clock and thinking, there is no way he will be born in 15 minutes, which was what time 2 weeks prior, my grandfather had died. I remember thinking, "The Lord giveth and the Lord taketh away, Blessed be the name of the Lord!" Yet Seth had other plans. He literally pushed himself down the birth canal by pressing his feet against my side and pushing his head down. Fifteen minutes later, he was born into the water, and promptly brought up onto my bare chest, skin to skin, heart to heart. He was born exactly, to the minute, two weeks after my grandfather had gone to be with his Heavenly Father.

I started crooning at my new little man, and stroking his wet, black hair and saying, "I love you, Seth!" We got moved onto the warm bed, with heated blankets over us and snuggled in for recovery. He weighed 7lbs 11oz, tying for my biggest baby with two of his other brothers, but he had been 3 weeks early! I remember thanking God that he hadn't waited longer and been even bigger! We gave him the middle name of Byron, after my grandfather.

As we lay half dozing in the warm blankets, I would open my eyes and look him over. I remember thinking there was something in his eyes that was a little different, but I thought surely the midwife would say something if she was thinking the same thing I was. Four hours later, as they were going through the discharge papers, and nothing had been said, she asked if I had any questions. I finally got up the nerve and said, "Does he look a little Down-ish to you?"

"Oh, no, I don't think so! He is SO strong, and I don't see the signs!" She got out one of her books and went through all of the "signs" of Trisomy 21 or Down syndrome. "If you are still concerned, you can ask your doctor about it when you take him in."

On the way home, I ask my husband, "What if he has Down syndrome?"

"What if he does?" he said. "If he does, he does."

I couldn't wrap my head around it like that. All I knew about Down syndrome was the couple of 20-something year olds at Taco Bell, and that scared me. I got home and looked things up. He had 3 of the 20 signs and the page said if they have 6 or more, the baby should get tested.

We made an appointment with our family doctor for Seth's eighth day of life to get him circumcised. In the meantime, I went go back and forth between thinking he had it, and thinking he didn't, crying out to the Lord to heal him before his appointment, if he did indeed have it. I didn't think I could handle it.

On his eighth day, we took him to our long time family doctor who had circumcised most of our boys and seen our family grow up. I finally asked him toward the end of our appointment.

"Does he look to you like he has Down syndrome?"

"What? No!" He started looking at him closer. He looked at his hands, his feet, his neck, his head. "No, I really don't think so. We can do the blood test if you really want to, but I don't see any indication of it."

"SHOULD we do the blood test? Would you recommend it? It doesn't matter to us, but how important is it to KNOW?"

"Oh, VERY important! There are a lot of tests that need to be done if he does have it, heart, ears, eyes, etc."

"Ok," we said. "Let's do the blood test." I didn't really want to know... but I did, too.

Off to the lab we went. They tried sticking the poor little lad twice, and couldn't get it, so they sent us to the hospital lab where they are better trained for babies. On the way there, I started wondering, "Am I doing the right thing? The doctor and midwife don't think he has it! Maybe we should just go home and forget about this!" Craig was thinking the same thing, so we came to the decision that we would let the hospital staff try to stick him ONE TIME! If they couldn't get it that once, we would just go home. They managed to do it on the first try.

One thing I learned about the eighth day...there is a reason the baby boy gets circumcised on the eighth day, because his vitamin K levels are at their highest they ever will be in their entire lives, so the blood is really thick and clots very quickly. Minimal blood loss for the circumcision!

In other words, DON'T TRY TO DRAW BLOOD ON THEIR 8TH DAY OF LIFE!! The blood came out, but it was V.E.R.Y S.L.O.W. Drip. Drip. Drip. But they got it. His blood was on its way to the lab to be tested. It was done. I don't remember for sure, but I think we just held hands in silence on the drive home. I was SO scared.

We had to wait for two weeks for the test results would come back. The office called me on my cell phone while I was out running errands, wanting to have us "come in and go over the blood test." I knew right then that it was positive. I remember telling the nurse, "You're scaring me."

"Oh, don't be scared. It's okay. We'll talk about it when you come in."

I called Craig and told him he had to come with me. He said, "Of course."

Craig had to fly out the next night, so we made arrangements for the kids to be taken care of overnight, and then we arrived at the doctor's office the next afternoon. We were taken into one of the rooms to wait for the doctor to come in. Finally, he did. He had a paper in his hand. Seth's DNA. He showed us what it was, and pointed out the three little lines on the 21st chromosome and said, very solemnly, "So, now you have a special needs child." I think he was shocked that it was positive.

My husband just looked at him and said, "We ALL have special needs!"

The doctor lined out what tests we needed to have and went off to get them ordered. Then, I broke down. I cried and cried. The nurse came in and tried to be encouraging, but I just needed to mourn, and cry. My husband held me. They arranged for Seth to have an Echocardiogram for his heart the very next morning. I was a nervous wreck.

We drove to Anchorage, the major city in Alaska and spent the evening together. We went to Barnes and Noble, and while my husband browsed, I went to check out the special needs section. It was pathetic. A LOT of books on autism, but hardly any on any of the other issues. I selected "Babies with Down Syndrome: A New Parent's Guide" third edition and bought it. I dropped my husband off at the airport and went to a friend's house to spend the night. I confided in her and we cried together. I spent most of the night reading the book. I felt better, if only because we have an amazing church and a large family. Seth has six brothers and a sister who all adore him, and I KNOW he will always be taken care of. That seemed to be the scariest part for most parents. "What happens when we can't take care of him any longer?" *I* didn't have to worry about THAT!

I went to the city hospital pediatric cardiology unit early the next morning. The doctor quickly reassured me as he passed the wand over Seth's chest, that everything looked REALLY great! There was one slight thing that he thought he caught a glimpse of every once in a while that usually closed up a birth, but that should be closed up for sure within six months, so he scheduled us for a follow-up appointment in six months. I was ESTATIC!! I told my little boy that we were going to go treat ourselves to a coffee downstairs! I was SO relieved!

After that, he had an eye test and the doctor was super happy with his eyes too! The ears were another matter. He had several hearing tests, and though he wasn't deaf, he couldn't hear quite as much as she would have liked, so we keep following that, but at his last appointment, he did wonderfully.

Seth's sister had some pretty major kidney issues, so we had Seth's checked and he didn't have any problems there either! He HAS been in the ER twice for croup, and we've battled it out a few times at home too. Some days I feel like we hit the jackpot with Seth's health. Some days I feel guilty that he IS so healthy, but I know he has and will have his own struggles too.

But, he is my delightful, funny, inquisitive little boy, with a little temper, and a gift from God to our family and our church. My husband says we know God put him in the right family because only *I* knew he had Down syndrome.

Seth is now 19mo and a feisty young lad who likes to make his opinion known, but *LOVES* to kiss, snuggle, read books, watch Signing Time, play with balls, drop everything, (we think he's trying to figure out gravity already), and play with his cars making the appropriate boy noises of course! He eats almost everything he can get his hands on, but prefers if I tell him what he's eating first, or he'll spit it out to look at it. He babbles all kinds of noises, some of which are discernible, such as up, please, dog, dada, mama, and some of his brother's names when he sees them, although they all sound SO much alike right now. He is right on the verge of crawling (and CAN if I hold my hand under his chest), but much prefers his method of sliding along the floor on his belly, pulling himself by his hands. He can also "walk" around the house holding my fingers. He adores his 4 year-old brother and hugs and kisses all over him, all the while patting his head and rubbing his face affectionately. He is an absolute joy to our family, and as one friend who has a 4 year old with T21 shared with me, he is our "baby" just a little longer than usual. With seven older children, I am not complaining that he still wants to snuggle up and sign "milk" as we rock and nurse to sleep at night together. God has truly blessed our family and church.

~Grace, Seth's mom; 38; Alaska, United States

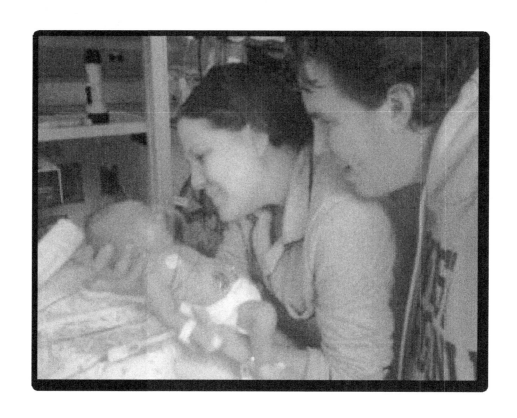

{His & Hers}

Diagnosis through the couple's perspective

Our Stories

{Samuel}

California, United States

{Cathleen, Samuel's Mom}

Looking back, I think the universe was trying to prepare me for Sam all along. Down syndrome was never something horrifying to me—more a mystery than anything else. And although I didn't understand much about Down syndrome, I had compassion for people with it. There was a guy in my junior high and high school who, in retrospect, I think probably had DS—perhaps mosaic, since he didn't show *all* the signs, and perhaps with a dose of something else thrown in, as he had some anger issues in addition to his obvious cognitive delay. He was in the special-

ed class, but we would cross paths on campus, and he was often lurking near where I was. He had a crush on me, I think, and I'm pretty sure it's because I was one of the few people who wasn't nasty to him. He scared me a little, because of his temper, so I can't say I befriended him, but I also wasn't mean to him. If he spoke to me, I

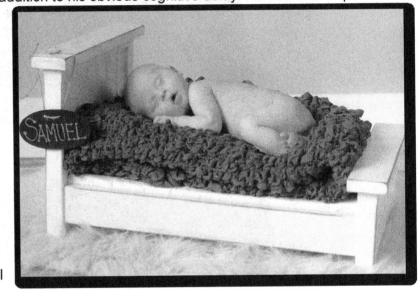

replied to him. And I guess that was enough, because he spent the better part of six years hanging out in my general vicinity whenever our paths crossed.

Years later, I was talking to a friend about children with Down syndrome, as my friend was interested in Reece's Rainbow. And we talked about how, as odd as it sounds, we sort of felt like the universe (or God, if that's your belief system) should give *us* babies with Down syndrome instead of giving them to people who didn't want them, because we knew we would love any baby with all our hearts—disability didn't matter to us.

That's not to say I *wanted* to have a special-needs child—like anyone, I hoped for a "healthy" baby. It's just that I knew if I had a child with special needs, I was capable of loving that child as fiercely as I would love any child, and I was up to the specific challenges that go along with having a special-needs child.

My husband, Chris, and I had our first son, Theo, when I was 34. Theo turned out to be a bit of a handful—he was very colicky and eventually was diagnosed with high-functioning autism, among other things. But in many ways, he's a very typical little boy, and we love him dearly and decided to try for a second child. And when I was 37, we conceived our second baby.

It was a slightly harder pregnancy than my first—just a few more aches and pains, and it felt a little different. I loved feeling Theo move inside of me, but the first time I felt Sam move, I felt a little sick, and my first thought was, "Ugh, it's like I'm growing an alien in there!" I was aghast at the thought and immediately reminded myself that this was my *baby*, who I had wanted so desperately! I brushed aside the nagging feeling of something being slightly "off," and I soon grew to love the feeling of him moving inside of me, just as I had with Theo.

When I was seven months pregnant, I was at Target one day and picked up one of their "Target Picks" recommended books. It was *Expecting Adam*—a memoir about a woman who finds out her unborn son has Down syndrome, and she decides to continue her pregnancy despite a tremendous lack of support from her Harvard University colleagues and community. I mentioned to Chris, "I probably shouldn't read a book like this while pregnant with my own son, but what the heck—it looks good, and it's not as if our baby has Down syndrome."

And then, when I was 37 weeks pregnant, I took Theo to the library in our new town to try to get a library card. I left without a library card due to a paperwork mixup, but I wasn't sorry because I was absolutely furious. As we waited in line to get the card, the man in front of us was trying to settle an issue of overdue books. He was maybe in his thirties, and clearly he had Down syndrome. He was polite, but it was taking him a while to try to figure out the overdue books and fine. The librarian, a woman in her sixties, was unforgivably rude to him. She acted impatient as he tried to settle his fine, and she rolled her eyes at me as if to say, "Can't he just *leave* already?" She was plainly disgusted with him, and I was appalled. This man, whoever he was, was obviously *trying* to be independent and handle his own library books, and she acted as if he wasn't worth the time of day. I was furious…and still with no idea that my baby, who would be born just days later, was affected by the same chromosomal anomaly as this man.

On our way out of the library, I picked up a community-activity guide for Theo, but when we got home, I realized I had picked up a special-needs booklet. I laughed at my mistake when I showed my husband later and said, "I didn't even know they *had* a booklet for special-needs activities. Guess we don't need this!"

Two days later, I almost missed my 37-week OB appointment. Theo had, unbeknownst to me, turned on the dome light in my car the day before, and effectively killed the battery. My pregnancy had been mostly trouble-free, so I thought about just skipping the appointment. But when AAA arrived and jumpstarted my car in time for me to get to the appointment after all, I went.

Our medical group provides only two ultrasounds per pregnancy—one at around 8 weeks and one at 20 weeks. But for some reason, at this appointment that I nearly skipped, the doctor cheerfully announced that she felt like doing a quick ultrasound, just to ensure that the baby was head down. "We know he is, but let's just check!" she said. And as it turns out, he wasn't—he was breech. And what's more, my amniotic fluid was low.

After a whirlwind couple of hours where the doctors debated performing a C-section right then, they decided I had enough amniotic fluid to continue the pregnancy, and they sent me on my way with strict instructions to return in two days for a fluid check and non-stress test (NST).

So Fridamorning I was back, dutifully getting my fluid check and NST. The fluid looked okay, and the NST was fine. The ultrasound tech called in a doctor just to be certain, and he spent a very long time staring at my ultrasound and making notes and calculations. Endless minutes ticked by. He finally cleared his throat and said, "Interesting."

"What?" I asked.

"Was your first child small?" he asked.

I laughed. "Hardly! He was born at 38 weeks, and he was already 8 pounds 3 ounces!"

The doctor looked at me and said, "Interesting. This baby is measuring very small. I estimate five pounds."

But he said nothing more. And I thought nothing more about it, even when I Googled "low amniotic fluid" and saw that "chromosomal abnormality" was one cause. In fact, when Chris asked me what might cause low amniotic fluid, I laughed and said, "Chromosomal abnormality, apparently! But we don't have that, so who knows." I had declined all prenatal testing, since abortion would've never been a consideration for us anyway, but I just assumed that because my 20-week ultrasound had showed nothing amiss, our baby was developing typically.

Later that very night my water broke, so I went in for my C-section 16 days earlier than planned—at 37 weeks and 2 days gestation. The doctors on staff wanted to wait to perform my C-section until morning—both so they could get some rest and because I had eaten dinner and still had food in my stomach. But the baby had other plans. After two hours of labor (and still four hours before the planned C-section), I was hit with a *monster* contraction that wouldn't end. I was near tears with the pain, and then suddenly alarms started going off, and people swarmed into the room.

"What's happening?" I asked, terrified. Alarms everywhere. People everywhere, yelling at me to roll this way and that, turn over here and spread my legs there. An oxygen mask slapped on my face. I looked at the fetal monitor and saw that the baby's beautiful heart rate of 150-ish had plummeted to 34. Yes, 34. And it wasn't coming back up. Someone turned the monitor away from me as I began to sob, "Get him out! You need to get him out safely!"

The next thing I knew, we were racing down the hallway. "Code C in Labor and Delivery!" was being announced over the PA system. "Code C!"

"Is he okay? Will he be okay?" I kept asking. No one would answer. Finally, someone said, "That's what we need to find out. We're going to need to put you under full sedation for an emergency C-section." I wept.

But when they slid me from my gurney onto the operating table, a little miracle happened. The fetal monitor started picking up—that beautiful heartbeat was back! I wept in relief. They were able to do a standard C-section at that point, and within about 20 minutes, I heard the lusty cry of my newborn son and the doctor proclaim, "He's a bald one!" And I wept as I heard "APGAR of 9." He was safe. He was healthy.

And then the doctor attending the baby came over and bluntly announced, "I need to tell you this because you're scheduled to have your tubes tied. I'm concerned about some issues of tone with the baby."

"What? You mean jaundice?" I asked, thinking she meant *skin* tone.

"No," she replied bluntly. "Muscle tone. Your baby shows the signs of Down syndrome. So I need to know whether you still want your tubes tied."

Shock. Anger. This woman was acting as if my baby was somehow "broken," and I'd want to keep my tubes intact to try again for another "non-broken" baby. What did she mean: "Whoops, this one's no good! Want to try again for another?" My protective instinct came out in full force, and I said icily, "Yes, please go ahead and tie my tubes. This is the baby I was meant to have."

Tears leaked out of my eyes as I lay there, my insides spread open for the rest of my procedure. They brought me the baby, and my heart soared and ached all at once. He was alive, and he was beautiful and precious and mine! But this thoughtless woman had just treated him as if he were less than perfect, and I knew in my heart that she would be only the first of many people to treat him that way. I knew the world could be a cruel and unaccepting place, and I had just brought a beautiful new life into a world that would likely be hurtful to him. I loved him with all my heart…but I couldn't help but wonder, was I selfish to have ignored prenatal testing and brought him into a cruel world? Would I have been a better mother *not* to bring him into the world? I felt confused and overwhelmed—brimming with love but battered by confusion.

And how *dare* this doctor mar the moments after my son's birth that way? I realize she was doing her job, but I still ache to this day when I think about it. She didn't even take a moment to congratulate us or to tell us he was beautiful. It was all about his disability, immediately. My beautiful, sweet baby was secondary to an ugly term called "Down syndrome." Was this how everyone would see him—as a disability or condition first, and a baby second? The thought overwhelmed me. I saw him as a beautiful shining light, and I wanted everyone else to see him that way, too.

Waiting for the baby to come back from being bathed and checked out was the longest 90 minutes of my life. I lay there in the recovery room, alone and with tears leaking down my face, Googling everything I could about Down syndrome on my phone. Not my best idea—the Internet can be a scary place if you're looking for information on Down syndrome! But when Chris (who I had sent with the baby) wheeled him into the recovery room 90 minutes later, I forgot all my fears. He placed the baby in my arms, and I held my sweet little sunshine for the first time. He snuggled right down into me contentedly, and I felt peace along with my confusion. My son might have an extra chromosome, but oh, how I loved him already!

We named him then—we hadn't chosen a name before he was born. He is Samuel, which means "God listened." Because God *did* listen. I'm not a religious person, but I threw a prayer up to God when Sam's heartbeat was dangerously low, and He listened. And 18 months later, that name is even more appropriate, because God really, *really* listened. He gave us a baby who changed our lives for the better. He gave us the baby we never knew we wanted, but who we absolutely cherish and could not live without. Confusion and shock about his diagnosis are long gone, replaced with the brightest love I've ever felt.

People sometimes accuse us in the Down syndrome community of painting the condition with rainbows and unicorns—making it seem like something wonderful and special, and ignoring the concerns that go along with it. Truthfully, I don't think *any* parent of a child with Down syndrome ignores the concerns that go along with it. We're all well aware that yes, there are medical issues we may have to face—heart problems, digestive issues, higher incidence of leukemia, and so on. Believe me, we worry every time our child gets a funny rash or unusual blood-work results. And yes, we worry about people treating our child unfairly, due to his perceived differences. And yes, we wonder what effect our child's cognitive delays will have on his life long-term. But *every* parent worries—that is not unique to the special-needs community. Perhaps we just worry about different things.

And the truth is that along with the worries come joy and beauty. Sam has taught us so much already. He has taught us how to celebrate the tiny joys and triumphs—the ones that we never even stopped to consider before having a child with Down syndrome. *He took a bite of solid food—rejoice! He finally pulled to standing at 17 months—celebrate! He picked up a cup of water and purposely dumped it on the floor, then set the cup back down—what awesome fine-motor skills!* He has taught us how to slow down and simply go with the flow, rather than focusing on the next big milestone or goal. *He'll walk someday—when it happens, it happens.* He has taught us that there is no one-size-fits-all approach to life and that the best-laid plans are meant to be torn apart and scattered to the wind sometimes. He has taught us to love unabashedly and freely, without reserve—who can resist a toddler that gives any random stranger a full-body smile, complete with million-dollar grin, waving arms, and kicking feet? Sam greets everyone as if he's just met his biggest hero—it's completely awesome. And having Sam has introduced to us a whole world of fascinating, diverse, and wonderful people—both those with Down syndrome and those who love them.

If a future pregnancy were still an option for us, would I do prenatal testing this time around? Yes, I would—only to be prepared in case the baby had a serious medical condition at birth. We dodged a bullet with Sam—he was physically healthy from birth, but that isn't always the case in babies with Down syndrome. But do I wish I'd had prenatal testing when I was carrying Sam? Not for a second. I am *so* glad we chose to skip it, because if I had known I was carrying a baby with Down syndrome, I would've spent my pregnancy terrified of the unknown. In the abstract, I knew I could love and care for a child with Down syndrome, but when it comes down to real life, I would've been scared out of my mind as I waited for him to be born. Instead of enjoying my final pregnancy, I would've been a nervous wreck, because I didn't *really* know what Down syndrome was like. Now I do—and I know there's nothing to fear about Down syndrome itself. There's concern about the related medical issues, but most of those can be dealt with—even heart surgery is somewhat routine now. But when you talk about Down syndrome itself, I now know that it's not scary; rather, it can be beautiful in ways you never imagined, and your life can be so very enriched because of it.

Sam is now 18 months old and the light of all of our lives. Chris has commented on numerous occasions that Sam has made him a better father to *both* of our sons. I am happier and more content than I have ever been in my life, and Sam is a big part of that. And Theo—well, Theo has just blossomed as a big brother. My impatient, volatile, brilliant little five-year-old slows down and becomes a tender, compassionate, patient teacher for his little brother. He delights in Sam, and Sam is the first person he wants to see every morning and the first person he wants to share things with.

And Sam himself? He's a happy, silly, sweet, and, yes, temperamental little boy. He is a determined little monkey who aspires to steal anything he can find and throw it into the toilet. He loves music and will dance like crazy if Theo puts on the Spice Girls. He's fascinated by our dogs and a big devotee of *Baby Signing Time*. Oh, and he hates therapy. He will attempt to pull every clever ploy in the book to get out of physical and occupational therapy, whether that means flirting with his therapist to try to distract her with hugs, crawling away as fast as he can, or sticking out his lower lip and throwing a full-blown tantrum. He's a master at avoiding what he doesn't want to do. In other words, he's a very typical toddler!

Thank you, Samuel Ames, for opening our eyes…and continuing to open them every day.

{Chris, Samuel's Dad}

It's difficult to revisit the moment my son was diagnosed with Down syndrome. Or, at least, the moment the doctors told us they were concerned about some "tonal issues." You see, the moments before that one were joyous and full of relief, as we'd witnessed the birth of our son after a harrowing delivery. The moments when most parents start to wonder about their child's future, choose his name, or figure out whose eyes he has. Typical moments.

Birth...

My wife had always told me that if she was going to have kids, she wanted to do it before she turned 40 because the risk of DS was so much higher after that age. When we conceived our second baby, she was 37; it looked like we were in the clear. We even opted out of genetic testing because the odds of DS were low and the miscarriage risk was comparatively high. (She was showing signs of early menopause before the pregnancy, so we didn't want to risk losing what might be our last chance to have a baby.) It's not to say we went into it blindly—we discussed the possibility of DS, and we were clear that we'd love our child no matter what. Not that we *expected* anything to happen, mind you.

That night, we drove to the hospital around midnight, after my wife's water broke and contractions started. The baby was breech, so we were looking at a C-section. After about an hour of waiting in the prep room, though, Cathleen had a really long, odd contraction, and the baby's heart rate plummeted. The doctors and nurses intervened quickly, whisking her away to the operating room. No one knew what was going on, only that they were both in danger. All I could do was stand out in the hallway and pray for their safety. Soon enough, everything stabilized. A nurse took me to my wife's bedside, and a few minutes later we listened as the doctor announced we had a healthy son.

The nurses carried our son into view, and then over to various machines to weigh and measure him. He looked just like the 3D ultrasound image we'd had taken a couple months earlier—

much like his brother, in fact—and had this quivering little cry. As my wife was getting stitched up, I went over whispered to him that it was OK and held his hand. He settled down when he heard me, and I breathed a huge sigh of relief, knowing my son was safe and everything was indeed OK.

Diagnosis...

I went back to check on my wife. The doctors were preparing to do her tubal ligation, which we'd arranged well in advance because we considered our family complete now. But one of the doctors suddenly interrupted and said she had concerns about some "tonal issues," so we might want to reconsider. We weren't quite sure what she meant until she clarified that he had "markers for Down syndrome." Our life changed in that instant, and we had to start making decisions immediately. We simultaneously responded that we wanted to go ahead with the ligation, rejecting the doctor's implication that we might want to keep our options open because this baby was damaged, and telling those in the room that DS didn't matter—that our son was a welcome member of our family, perfect as he was.

But that was on the outside. On the inside? I hurt—terribly. I tried to put on a good face, but it was an empty gesture. I just hurt. And I was afraid, of what I knew about DS and what I didn't know. The bottom line was that for five minutes, our son *was* typical to us. I don't mourn what he would have been—I mourn what he actually *was*, in my mind. That child was real—I talked to him and held his hand—and he was pulled away as soon as I met him. And so much of me still hurts for that loss. But when I remember we almost lost him, it hurts a little less.

That night, we named our son Samuel because it means "God listened." He did that night. He has all along.

Now...

Sam is 17 months old now and recently appeared in his first commercial for Gymboree. Yes, a commercial. We certainly thought he was cute, but how many babies have a modeling contract and work permit before they can crawl? The other day, he pulled to standing on my wife's knees, cackling as he fell back on his bottom and babbling "ma-ma-ma-ma-ma" in my wife's direction. Sam is a true joy, and he's made me a better husband, father, and person in so many ways. And for him, that's typical.

{Ella}

South Australia, Australia

{Mandy, Ella's mum}

I thought I was ready for it. That's the main thing I remember about the day I received the news that would change my life. I had said to my husband Leighton, about an hour before that I was fairly sure that our newborn did have Down syndrome, and felt like I was ready to hear that. But as it turned out, I wasn't. When the midwife said, "We have the preliminary results back, and I'm sorry, it's positive for Down syndrome", I felt like the whole world stopped. I looked down at the floor, and said something like "OK, thank you", and as soon as she left, I cried like I have never cried before, standing over the plastic hospital bassinet, clinging to Leighton, and feeling more broken than I've ever felt in my life.

I recalled sitting at my pre-natal appointment a few days after my 20-week when the midwife read from the ultrasound report "A tiny echogenic focus is noted in the left ventricle, which in the absence of any other abnormality is of doubtful clinical significance". The Doctor explained that it could be a soft marker for Down syndrome, but they saw it quite often in ultrasounds and almost always meant nothing. My 12-week NT scan had been fine, as had been my bloodwork at that time. It did concern me a bit though, and at my next appointment, four weeks later, I asked the Doctor whether I should be having further tests. I felt like if my baby had Down syndrome, I could cope with that, but I would prefer to know now. He said that it was extremely unlikely that it meant anything, and wasn't worth having further tests. I felt comfortable with this, but never quite forgot about it through the remainder of my pregnancy, and even on the day I was in labour, decided to take a really good like at this baby once she arrived, to make sure there was nothing I could see which might indicate Down syndrome. Even though it was in the back of my mind for those months, I never really believed that it might happen. After all, I, and my family, lived inside that golden circle, protected by the fact that those sorts of things happened to "other people".

The day of Ella's birth, the day before her due date, arrived. After a relatively easy labour and delivery, this beautiful baby girl was placed on my chest at 8:58pm. Yes, she was beautiful, but she didn't quite look the way I had expected. I remember staring at her with amazement, joy and love, as I had stared at my other children upon their arrivals, but there was another feeling too, an uneasy, something's-not-quite-right-here type feeling.

Once the Doctor arrived (about half an hour after Ella), he checked her over and I mentioned to him about the 20-week ultrasound report, and asked whether he saw anything which might indicate Down syndrome. He told me that there were a few things he was concerned about, but nothing worth worrying about tonight, and that we'd talk more tomorrow. I told Leighton about this conversation when he came back, but he felt that this baby was perfect, and that I was worrying about nothing.

The next morning, the Doctor came back to check Ella out, and when the midwife brought her back, she said that he did think she might have Down syndrome, and that they needed to take some blood samples and send away to find out for sure. They said we would have the results in the morning. We were very calm then, just nodding and saying "Yes, OK, no worries". Not long after, Leighton's parents came in and as soon as we told them, I started to cry, as though saying it out loud made it real.

The following morning was probably the longest morning of my life. We waited and waited and waited some more. Eventually I went to the nurses station to ask whether the Doctor was there, and we were told that he'd been and gone. One of the midwives came to our room shortly after, and delivered the news that we'd been dreading.

So here we were, in a hospital room, and trying to comprehend that news that life as we knew it would never be the same. I felt like all the plans I'd made, all the dreams I'd had for this baby were gone, and had been replaced by some scary and awful future. I was very scared, sad, angry and overall, felt ripped off. I'd had a plan for how this was all supposed to go, and this was not part of my plan. I heard a newborn in the next room crying and wondered why hadn't that baby been born with Down syndrome. Why my baby, why me?

Gradually, in the days, weeks and months that followed, we began to heal. The most important factor in my healing was the beautiful girl in my arms. I could certainly see that in some ways, a pre-natal diagnosis would have meant that I could have processed a lot of the grief and anger and pain before Ella's arrival, but I feel fortunate that in my darkest moments, I could look at her, hold her and know that everything was going to be all right.

{Leighton, Ella's Dad}

Late in the winter evening of June 18th, 2009, in a small country hospital in regional South Australia, my family was to change in a way that we never anticipated nor planned for. On the arrival of a large, gurgling and healthy baby girl, a mother's intuition requested verification that her baby was OK. The response from the doctor was measured, yet we could sense the trepidation in his voice, "Just enjoy your beautiful daughter tonight and I will see you all tomorrow morning". Both my wife Mandy and I thought that she did look a little different. Not much was said on that night, but Mandy and I reminded each other, that her scan at week twenty through the pregnancy, revealed a minor shadow on her heart. At the time we questioned the doctor, who indicated that they see this many times, and we should not be concerned; this opinion was supported by a 1 in 700 chance of our daughter having Down syndrome.

Throughout the pregnancy we had decided that our daughter would be named Lily, but this baby did not look like a Lily and somehow, Lily just did not feel right, so we settled on Ella. As Mandy and Ella settled into the night, I returned home, very concerned for my new daughter and the unforseen changes that a potential diagnosis would have on our family.

Arriving home I jumped straight onto the computer and googled, images of new born down syndrome, and an image of the baby I had just left appeared on my computer screen. With little sleep I returned to the hospital the following morning after a harrowing night to find my daughter in Mandy's arms.

Mandy and I discussed our thoughts about our baby having Down syndrome, prior to family and friend visiting to hospital. In our minds we believed that our daughter may have Down syndrome.

She was not the daughter we expected, yet we loved her from the minute she was born. The daughter that we expected was no longer, the baby we had was not Lily; tears were shed as we mourned the loss of our daughter. Yet we had this beautiful baby, Ella, requiring our immediate attention and love.

As our other children and family came to visit the hospital on the Friday morning, Mandy and I showed little emotion and kept quiet on Ella's possible diagnosis. We could feel the whispers in the corridors of the hospital grow as we waited for the return of our doctor. Midwives and nurses would visit throughout that morning, as we would question them whether Ella had Down syndrome and when we would expect to see the doctor. We learnt that to confirm Ella had Down syndrome, that blood test would have to be transported to Adelaide's Women's & Children's Children Hospital 3 hours away and tested. Our family had started to suspect that something may be wrong with Ella. My mother and father, who had driven from Adelaide to see Ella that morning took the blood samples to Adelaide immediately for testing, as these results would provide Mandy and I with the necessary confirmation over the weekend. I don't think we could have waited over the weekend and into the next week without knowing.

It was not until the afternoon on the Saturday that we were informed that preliminary results had indicated that Ella had Down syndrome. And it felt that our world had crashed around us.

As Ella's father, I felt that now was the time to step up and inform all family members and friends, as Mandy was struggling with coming to terms with not only losing the daughter that she expected, but now having a baby with Down syndrome. People reacted in different ways, with statements like "special kids go to special homes" and "kids with Down syndrome are great, they are always happy". Although well intentioned, these perceptions and statements failed to alleviate our loss of the daughter we were expecting. Mandy and I did not feel special in any way; we were normal people living our normal life, and now I question the word normal and it's meaning.

Once we had our diagnosis, immediate my thoughts raced to, will my daughter have friends, will she go to school, will she play sport, will she walk, will she talk, will she be teased, will she get married and on and on and on. Only fathers in my situation can understand what I thought and how I felt.

Prior to leaving the hospital, we were provided with the contact details of a family who lived 45 minutes from us, who had a 3 year old daughter with Down syndrome. I spoke with this family and asked if she would visit us with her daughter when we got out of hospital. The day after Mandy & Ella came home from hospital, Sam and her daughter Dakota came and visited us. Dakota was bright, responsive, she walked, talked, had selected her clothes for the day and Mandy and I could see a positive future immediately - it was what we exactly needed at the time.

By the time Ella was six weeks old, we had joined a support group two hours away in Victoria and were attending a fortnightly early intervention program at the South Australian Down syndrome association in Adelaide. The people we have met through these groups have now become our closest of friends as we all now belong to a new family.

Ella is truly a inspiration to me, our family and friends, I witness the positive effect that she has on others and the better person she has made me become. I am under no illusions that her having Down syndrome will result in issues presenting themselves at times, but we are becoming increasing more capable to handling these issues.

Down syndrome does not define Ella. More importantly she is a four year old girl that is funny, moody, affectionate, canny and manipulative, much the same as her three sisters and brother.

Ella had just turned 4 and has loads of personality, a fiery temper and a sweet, loving side. She goes to child care three days a week, and will start Kindy very soon. We have been lucky in regards to Ella's health; while she's had a few extended hospital stays with respiratory infections, it's nothing like what some of her little mates have dealt with.
Ella continues to surprise us with what she's capable of, and she continues to challenge to myths & stereotypes about kids with Ds. She has taught me many lessons in the past four years, and I think we have many more to come!

{Gianluca}

Illinois, United States

{Jenny, Gianluca's Mom}

When I found out I was pregnant with my second baby, I was ecstatic and surprised! We had been trying for a year, and recently decided not to focus on getting pregnant since we were just so busy. But there I was, pregnant!

I was 36 years old, which they called advanced maternal age, and I joked that I was an elderly pregnant lady. We knew we wanted prenatal testing; I was a planner and wanted to know everything! I had to go to great lengths to get the quad screening approved through my insurance company, and eventually we had the results that we had a reduced risk for Down syndrome (1:538).

Three days after the testing, a series of complications began. At 13 weeks I almost lost my baby due to a 6 cm tear in my placenta and spent 6 weeks on bedrest. At 22 weeks my baby was diagnosed with an atrial septal aneurism. At 36 weeks, I failed a biophysical and was hospitalized for observation.

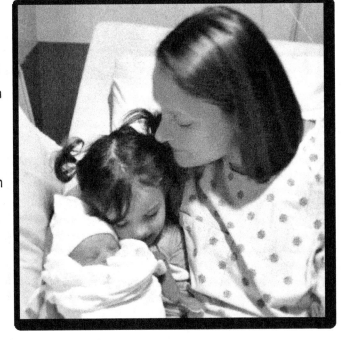

At 39 weeks, my water broke and I was so relieved. It was time to have this baby and put the stress and worry behind us. Well, as much as you can do that as a parent, but it seemed the big stuff would be behind us.

After a quick and easy labor, my son was born and I was ready to feel relief. But he wasn't crying so of course I was worried. They assured me that he was fine, his APGAR scores were great, and there was nothing to worry about. When they handed me my son I was instantly in love and so relieved that he was here. They took him away for the usual pediatrician evaluation, and we sent out messages to friends and family that our perfect son had arrived. I could finally exhale. My parents arrived with our daughter and we were so happy to see them all as we'd been looking forward to Luca meeting his sister. Our family would be complete.

Shortly after the nurse returned Luca to us, the doctor came in and abruptly asked everyone to leave the room. He sat down on the bed and told us that Luca exhibited soft markers for Trisomy 21, Down syndrome. I was in shock. He showed us the palmar crease on his hand and said it could be a sign, but could also just run in families. We immediately studied our own palms and willed our creases to merge. He showed us the sandal gap and we ripped off our socks and swore we had a big gap between our toes as well. He explained that the shape of his eyes and his lower tone were also soft markers, but he really could not make the diagnosis. He said that in some cases, he could tell the parents with confidence in this conversation that their baby had Down syndrome, but he didn't have that confidence in this case and would need the results of a blood test (FISH test) to be sure. The results in 3 days, our first day at home, so they would call us sometime that day. I immediately panicked about how we would keep family away until we heard the news because I was so emotional and unsure and scared, and just didn't want anyone to know until we were certain. I snapped out of it when he told me not to worry, that we would love our baby no matter what. Anger surged up in me at him for saying this to me. I never doubted that I would love my baby. It just seemed like such a cavalier statement to make at the time. I think he was trying to reassure us, but it stood out as rude.

Our heads were spinning. At some point in the conversation my mom forced her way into the room. Later she told me she suspected Luca had Ds from the way he felt when she held him. She's a retired nurse, so I knew she was right, even though I didn't want to believe it. She knew that when the doctor kicked them out and looked so serious that something was up. I was glad she came in because I was in such shock that I didn't know what to say or do.

My mind flashed back two years prior, when we were at a birthday party and there was a little boy there with Down syndrome. As my friend shared that his diagnosis came at birth, I remember thinking- that would be the worst. To be told at birth that your child has Down syndrome. And here I was, sitting in this hospital room, facing a Down syndrome diagnosis. I wanted to know why this was happening to us. How could this be our story? At some point, in the quiet of the night, as I held my son in my arms, I knew why this was happening to us- we were the right parents for him. We could do so much for him and others with Down syndrome. Suddenly this fight roared up within me and I knew I just wanted to be his proud mother.

When my daughter came into the room, she climbed right up into bed with Luca and me, demanded to hold him, and gave him the biggest hug. My heart melted. Holding back the tears,

I knew in that moment I had so much to learn from my kids. She showed me what true love looked like and I held them both so tight at that moment.

We weren't able to go home as planned because Luca wasn't maintaining his body temperature. As we waited to find out the results, my husband and I spent all our time with Luca. We would stare at him, pray over him, snuggle him extra long and just let our hearts connect with his. I wavered between believing he had Ds, and believing he didn't; exploring both sets of emotions. We bonded with him in such a special way those early days which was very important.

While we were sitting by him in the SCN one night, an overnight nurse started up a conversation with us. When we shared that the FISH results were not yet in, she blurted that her friend was a genetic counselor and it was unbelievable the things they find in those tests; all sorts of chromosomal anomalies that you wouldn't believe; stuff that kills babies. Our hearts sank and we were scared. She was behind a computer and couldn't see the terrified looks on our faces. It was in that moment I realized I didn't care if he had Down syndrome. I just didn't want to lose him!

It was a Friday morning, I had just gotten out of the shower and was blow drying my hair when our pediatrician came in. She had a serious look on her face so I stopped with half a head of wet hair, and sat down on the couch next to my husband. She then told us she had the results of the blood test, and Luca tested positive for Trisomy 21, Down syndrome. That was it. She asked if we had any questions. Just as she finished talking, my mom called and I started crying as I spoke. She told me everything would be ok and that we can handle this. I'll never forget that confidence and immediate support.

As the news spread about Luca's diagnosis, we were overwhelmed by the love and support that came our way. Our families, close friends, coworkers, friends we hadn't spoken to in years, and friends who were already part of the special needs community all reached out to share their love. I was welcomed into a Facebook group of moms who have kids with Down syndrome born in 2012 or 2013. It was an incredible comfort to be able to connect with moms with children around Luca's age, who were in the same stages of processing as I was. I learned quickly that this was going to be a place I could share some of my deepest, darkest, and brightest thoughts without judgment. That group was, and is, a lifeline to me.

In the beginning, I was fixated on the potential medical issues children with Ds may develop. Since the birth diagnosis was such a surprise after a rocky pregnancy, I had this creepy feeling of constantly waiting for the other shoe to drop. I read about everything from reflux to leukemia. There was so much to learn and be aware of and I did not want to miss a single cue.

It took me a solid three months to process Luca's Ds diagnosis. In those months, life felt like a rollercoaster. Not only were we grappling with what Ds would mean for Luca and our family, but we were trying to adjust to life with two children, in the midst of sleep deprivation. That was a tough few months!

For the next 2 months, we sorted out some early medical issues. Everything was very benign- Luca had reflux, laryngomalacia (floppy airway) and plagiocephaly which earned him a cool "space" helmet. I learned quickly what being my son's advocate meant as I had diagnosed each of these ailments and pushed my concerns forward to the doctors. I felt good that I was doing right by my son.

For the next 3 months, we enjoyed our son!!! Yes, it was finally at 5 months of age that we were starting to hit our stride! We had been working with a wonderful Early Intervention team for 2 months, and we were starting to think about his 6 month goals. That was when some worry started to creep back in.

Luca had been developing very close to the typical milestone timeline. Our goal had been to try to keep him as close to the typical timeframe as possible. At 6 months he was sitting up, rolling over from front-to-back and back-to-front, working on supporting himself on all fours, babbling, smiling and laughing all the time. But it seemed like he was starting to plateau. He started putting his hands in his mouth quite a bit, which prompted us all to suspect he was teething. I thought this seemed a little odd as I had read that kids with Ds may teethe late. And my daughter did not break her first tooth until she was 9 months old. I figured he was starting to feel those teeth early, and this would be a long teething process We started to have to move therapy session times around to try to catch him when he was more awake and not as bothered by his teeth.

Teething aside, we were about to go on vacation with some friends, and looking forward to introducing them to Luca. We were excited to get away as a family to do something "normal" and enjoy the beach together! Luca was so unusually cranky, I wanted to be certain he wasn't developing an ear infection, and took him in for one last check-up. The pediatrician cleared him and said there was no reason not to go on vacation!

Three days into the vacation, our world changed once again. Only we didn't know then quite how significantly. Luca started demonstrating an odd movement. He would throw his arms up and roll his eyes back. It was all very quick, like a startle. My stomach was in knots. I had watched videos about Infantile Spasms in those first few months because I wanted to know what to look for if Luca developed them. By the end of the trip, Luca was experiencing clusters of spasms. I was on the phone with his pediatrician while we were at the airport returning home begging for an appointment for the next day. Our flight home was diverted to the airport in Milwaukee, which was where Luca's specialists were, so I got off the plane with a medical emergency and brought him to the Emergency Room.

My mom and aunt met me in the ER and we worried deeply about what we were going to learn. The team there was very nice and explained that we had nothing to worry about. I showed them a video of the movements and Luca also did a few himself in the moment, and they assured us that these movements were not indicative of anything harmful for Luca. They sent us home with direction to have our pediatrician order an MRI and EEG for Luca. They couldn't do it themselves due to some insurance restrictions. I felt much better that we were given such a positive discharge.

The next day, the pit in my stomach returned as the frequency of the clusters increased. I fought hard to get in to see a pediatrician the next day, and finally, at 5pm when she saw the video and Luca demonstrate a spasm in the office, she was on the phone with the Children's hospital getting us admitted for a potential Infantile Spasms diagnosis.

On June 27, 2013, at nearly 9 months of age, Luca was diagnosed with Infantile Spasms (IS), a catastrophic seizure disorder. Hallmark symptoms of IS are developmental delays, regression, and mental retardation. Within a week of the diagnosis, we saw Luca lose nearly all of his milestones. We saw our son go from a smiling, laughing baby to a silent toddler who couldn't hold his head up. Loosing Luca's laughs and smiles hurt us the most.

Typically, children with Ds respond quickly to IS treatment, and are less likely to relapse. We faced his diagnosis with tenacity and convinced ourselves this would be a blip on our medical radar. Luca, however, took his own path once again, as he broke through 4 medications and developed 2 other seizure types. He spent time in the hospital every month for the next 6 months, was ambulanced twice, went through testing for metabolic disorders and mitochondrial disorders, and developed pneumonia which earned him a feeding tube. We longed for the days when he just had DS.

A few weeks after his first birthday, Luca smiled again. We had initiated the ketogenic diet and adjusted his medications and were cautiously optimistic that he was gaining seizure control. October 24, 2013 was the last time we saw Luca experience a seizure.

I have learned through his first year of life that the Ds diagnosis is a slippery slope. I spent 3 months processing, which I certainly needed, but now wish I had spent just truly enjoying my baby. I lived my life waiting for the other shoe to drop, rather than enjoying the moment. I realized that the developmental delays and cognitive impairment associated with Ds are just not a big deal to me.

When I worry about what the future will hold for Luca and our family, I realize it isn't a Ds diagnosis or an IS diagnosis that send me spinning. It's being a parent who is head over heels in love with her son and family and only wanting the best for them. I'm thankful to have my son, no matter what path his chromosomes send us down.

With all of the worry, fear, concern, sadness, and stress that has come with Luca's medical issues, I have to share that there has been incredible joy, love, support, selflessness, generosity and kindness brought into our lives. Our families will drop anything to help us out, our friends started a campaign to raise funds for Luca's care, my Facebook moms have sent cards and gifts with touching sentiments only they can share, a former colleague and her friends ran a marathon in his honor, and I've heard from old friends who found themselves down this special needs path offering me their support and shoulder to lean on if I need it.

At the end of the day, I focus less on the superficial and more on the real now. I've learned to truly take life one moment at a time. I'm curious to see what the future holds, but I stay in the now. And I never underestimate the healing powers of a pumpkin beer and hot shower.

{Nick, Gianluca's Dad}

"How are you doing with all of this?"

That's the signal that a conversation about Trisomy 21 is starting, and it means I better change my mood and get ready for a down and dirty honest conversation about our son, Gianluca.

My wife, Jenny, usually utters the above sentence while waving her hand around like Obi-Wan Kenobi trying to Jedi-mind-trick me into switching topics in our conversation.

It usually works, but not without some resistance on my part. I am certainly not some mindless storm trooper, but eventually the façade has to crack because that's how a marriage works, and it's especially true when dealing with a child like Gianluca.

Before that, though, Jenny has to force her way through my canned responses of "I'm OK. You?" I choose to deflect the question and give a standard response that harkens back to my days as a PR guy. Jenny usually continues to push it, and I give her a real answer because she's my wife and deserves the truth, and one of the reasons I married her is because she WILL push me and not settle on something that sounds like it came from a press release.

Trust me, I have a mental database of safe answers that would sound much more fitting coming out of a coach at a press conference or a politician trying to tip-toe around a potential controversy.

Then there's the reality, and that's exactly what Jenny wants. As my wife, she deserves it ... and so does Gianluca.

So, how am I doing? It depends on the day; some are good and some aren't. However, Gianluca's smile and gut-busting laugh makes it all fantastic, helmet and all.

When I think back to what it was like learning that our second – and most likely last – child was born with Trisomy 21, I just remember how misinformed we were. We had no idea what we were getting into, and no life experience with it. We found out after birth, and it hit us hard.

We knew there would be challenges, and we knew we would be up to face them together. One thing about us; we're strong and even stronger together.

Still, it was a rollercoaster of emotions, but only if the coaster went crashing to the ground as expectations and dreams were met with uncertainty and confusion.

We knew nothing. We just knew he would be different, and the emotions I felt were some of the rawest since experiencing the death of my Dad due to cancer in June 2000. You don't forget that feeling, which was brought back several years ago after Uncle Tommy's passing.

This time, we were starting not ending, and there were a lot of questions.

We have loving family and friends who showed tremendous support from around the world. It was truly overwhelming to get calls, emails, texts and whatever other correspondences sent to us. We knew we weren't alone in this. That's something we cherish, and will never forget, and it helped drive us.

Throughout our hospital stay, I was frequently in touch with my cousin Mary Jo, who is a doctor at Mount Sinai in New York. She would go on explaining to me what Down Syndrome was, and how Gianluca was going to be great and we were going to do everything we could to make sure of that.

Mary Jo's defiance to my ignorance included a telephone call with my sister Marcella and brother Giuseppe. Marcella is a middle school Italian teacher, and she was telling me about her experience with students who had Trisomy 21.

"They can learn a foreign language?!?!?" Yeah, I was that clueless.

After Mary Jo and Marcella set me straight, the switch was flipped.

Jenny and I would have long, difficult conversations throughout our hospital stay. There were tears, hugs, kisses, anger, sadness and finally smiles.

For all the raw emotion, I was able to draw the line; "We're still his parents. We have to do everything we can to help him."

You want to know how I'm doing? That's it right there. Every day that goes by, I just look at him as my amazing son. One day, I started to wonder what life would be like if he didn't have Down Syndrome. I stared at him, he looked at me, smiled and burst out with his laugh. I just said to him, "You wouldn't be Gianluca, and I WANT Gianluca."

He's our son and I can't imagine life without him, extra chromosome and all. Just like I can't imagine being without Jenny and our daughter Gabriella, whose unique personality keeps us on our toes and brightens up the room.

I would do anything for all of them, and I do.

Trisomy 21 may be something we have to overcome in some respects, but we'll do it together as a family, and that includes our extended family and friends. It may have surprised us, as life threw us a curveball, but we'll persevere and he'll be even better for it.

We can sit around blaming things; whatever deity you prefer, the doctors, each other, the randomness of the extra chromosome. You can waste your time and energy focusing on things that don't matter because you want answers or to place blame. That's wasted energy that should be focused on him, and the family. I don't have time for self-pity, and I don't have time to worry about what brought us here. We're here, so look forward to the challenges that we need to overcome.

That determination drives me. However, I don't want to think about the future when nothing is written. When I do, I make sure to pull myself back to reality and stay focused on the little guy.

Fantasy is for baseball and football, not raising kids.

We can influence this and help him achieve his potential, and we do that on a daily basis because he's our son, and we love him very much. I wouldn't want it any other way,

I'm doing great, and there's no need for tricks.

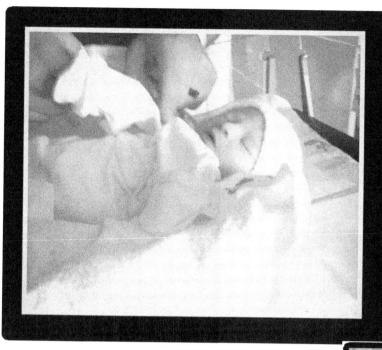

{An Added Twist}

Unique Stories of Diagnosis

In addition to not knowing about the 47th chromosome their child would have, these families encountered even further surprises as the adventure with Down syndrome began in their families.

{Our Stories}

{A Delayed Diagnosis}

When I think back on those few weeks, they seem blurry already, but what I do remember are flashes. Flashes of feeling, thought, memory, perception. There was something like a persistent tapping that only I could hear. With each of those flashes, there was another tap. *Tap... Tap... Tap...* each time it was like a marble added to a scale, getting heavier and heavier, to show me something I didn't want to see.

It started with an unplanned third pregnancy. Maybe we had successfully spun the roulette wheel twice, but that was it. I worried about miscarriage. I uncharacteristically worried about car accidents, Listeria, everything. I never told anyone how unsettled I felt. How could I? It made no sense. The quiet *tap, tap, tap* had begun.

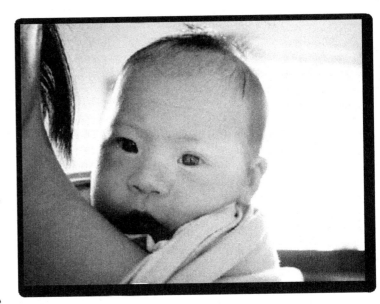

During labor, I couldn't quite place the difference, but it was there. I expected the pain, but it was as if being in labor was a one woman show, not an interplay between my body and the little life inside. When the time came to push, I felt like I was tearing myself into pieces. If I didn't keep pushing so hard, so intensely, I feared my labor would stop altogether and my baby would fade away. Later, I would learn that my baby's lower muscle tone most likely contributed to my feeling the need to push harder.

After he was born, the midwives and I peered into his little face pondering his resemblance to the family. I felt a strange pang of discomfort. Now I think that was the first time I saw a flicker of his features. There was something in his eyes and forehead that made me uncomfortable, and I spent hours staring at it. *Tap... Tap... Tap...*

He didn't gain as quickly as his sisters had. He was incredibly sleepy. It seemed that if I didn't wake him to feed him, he would just fade away. His jaundice lasted longer. Despite all this, he was all in the range of normal. But nothing felt right.

Then, I saw it.

I saw the faces of children I had seen at the grocery store, walking along the street, on pamphlets at the doctor's office. He had the face of a baby with Down syndrome.

That night I stared at pictures of hundreds of babies with Down syndrome. I learned that Down syndrome sometimes came with a set of physical markers. In the pitch black of night, I used the light from my phone to stare at his hands, his ears, trying to figure out if he had the markers for Down Syndrome. What the hell did "low set ears" mean? All babies have flattened nose bridges. If I smooshed his hand one way, it looked like he had the crease. Smoosh it another way, and the lines on his hand looked like mine.

But his face. I saw it.

The next morning, I said something to my husband. I watched closely. *Tap...* He made sure to immediately minimize it, but when pressed, he admitted, he saw it too.

I couldn't let it go. I started to read online forums, and blogs of parents who had children with Down syndrome. Each thing I read gave me a knot in my stomach. *Tap...* Even though he had no discernible major health issue, the picture they created in their descriptions somehow sounded exactly like my son. *Tap...*

I called our midwife. I felt the panic of someone standing in an open prairie, watching a storm on the horizon, with no place to hide.

Our midwife came. She said she was unsure. I held my baby and cried. And cried. That night, I went back and read my son's birth story. This was the first paragraph:

> *I think the significance of the fact that you were born in caul*
> *shouldn't be lost when I write about your birth. In fact, I wonder if*
> *you're destined to float in life with a different attitude and*
> *perspective than those around you. We will have to see.*

I found the tapping noise. All those marbles gathered their weight and tipped the scale; I saw what had been there the entire time. It was my baby, telling me that he had Down syndrome. Before we even went in to get a test done, I knew it was true.

With hindsight, I understand why no one saw it. He doesn't have many of the markers. No extra skin on the back of his neck. His ears aren't particularly low set. He doesn't have palmar creases on his hand. His muscle tone is actually quite good, but uneven.

I'm writing this now with those days behind me. I cried so much that my cheeks got chapped. The fear of potential pain gripped me. I could not bear a future of awkward moments, small and large slights, disappointments. Briefly, I regretted our choice to forgo prenatal testing. I thought about adoption. Then the guilt over being upset at all was overwhelming. Could he somehow sense my grief and feel unloved?

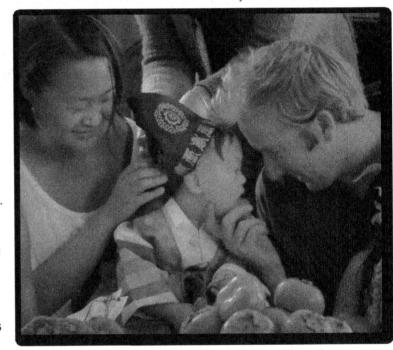

What I realized was that my grief came as a reaction to a world hostile to difference. As I scrutinized that grief, it gave way to an entirely new way of thinking. Why does our society value independence so much? Why is a person's worth measured by achievement? Why are some abilities valued over others? I had lived enough to know that independence, achievement, and ability did not equal happiness.

I can't choose all of the events in my life, but I can choose my experience of those events. I choose happiness. The choice is actually not very difficult. I have three beautiful children. An amazing husband. Wonderful family and friends. I have a kid with an extra chromosome. I know, as a mother, I must choose happiness for him now, so that he can one day choose it for himself.

~ Jisun, LP's mom; 31; California, United States
Blogging @ http://kimchilatkes.com/

{A Mosaic Diagnosis}

I have always been a very optimistic, glass half full kinda gal. I had been very healthy thus far in life and have always taken it for granted. Our first child, Makenna Grace was born in January of 2009. Motherhood was all that I had ever dreamed it would be. That was until a summer day in June when we found out Makenna had a very serious cancer like disease called Histiocytosis.

After 2 years of treatment and a clean bill of health my husband, Kyle and I were finally ready to extend our family of three. 14 weeks into my easy and somewhat mundane pregnancy I got the terrible news that my baby had anacephaly and did not survive. Kyle and I were absolutely devastated. How could this happen after all we had gone through with our girl, Makenna.

After months of mourning what was to be...we were again ready to try for our baby. This time around I was considered high risk and monitored very closely with extra testing and ultrasounds all the way up to 34weeks. My baby boy was perfect. All of our tests and ultrasounds came back clear and we were confident we were awaiting the arrival of a healthy baby boy.

Then in the middle of the night unexpectedly at 38weeks my water broke and before I knew it Kyle and I were dropping Makenna off at my in-laws and we were off to the hospital to have our baby boy.

After an easy labor and just a couple pushes my baby boy was here!! I was overcome with joy and relief. My boy was here. He was beautiful and healthy and MINE. After a couple hours of family visiting and celebrating Kyle, Colin(my beautiful baby boy) and I had a quiet night together.

The next morning I sent Kyle to work thinking "I've got this we are good, I've done this before and my boy is healthy".

After Kyle left for work Colin and I snuggled together and it was one of the happiest hours of my life. Just me and my baby boy together, all was right in the world.

About an hour or so after Kyle left for work the on call pediatrician came in and in one sentence changed our lives forever.

I was all alone and he came in making small talk and with no warning at all as if we were chatting about the weather or last nights Cubs game he said, "Some of Colin's characteristics lead me to believe he probably has Down Syndrome".

Immediately my world was changed. Did he not know he scored a 9on his Apgar...twice???

How could this be? Didn't he know all that my family had already been through? The rest of what he began to say was a fog. After a couple minutes I cut him off and said, "I'm sorry I don't mean to be rude but I can't do this right now. I need to call my mom". He said he understood and left the room.

The door closed and I was left alone with my boy. I had no idea what to do. I couldn't call Kyle. He had been through too much already and was out making calls. It was as if my world had been turned completely upside down.

I ended up calling my mom who was on her way down with Makenna bringing me lunch. I broke the news to her through hysterical crying and she said she would be down jus as soon as she could drop Makenna off with another family member. I sent Kyle a text asking him to come back to the hospital as soon as he could. I assured him we were ok but couldn't bring myself to call him in fear I would lose it on the phone. My father in law had just been at the hospital and was a medical sales representative and was going to make some calls around the hospital when he had left our room so my next call was to him. He was the first one to make it back to the hospital and I was so thankful he had come back so quickly. Shortly after my mom and Kyle returned and all three of them were dumbfounded. They didn't understand and were as caught off guard as I had been.

A while later the on call pediatrician came back and explained his concern once again for Kyle. My mom and my father in law. This time there was a great deal of uncertainty in the doctors voice. With every characteristic he explained to us that he had suspicions abut he would then back pedal and comment on how unpronounced they were. One of Colin's hands had a Palmer crease but the other did not. His nose was kind of flat but not really....bla bla bla. I was so angry! Had this man just put us through hell and now was he changing his mind? Towards this end of the conversation he made the comment "well if he doesn't have Down syndrome....he will always look kinda funny". I was beyond done with this man who had a thing or two to learn about compassion, and bedside manner.

The rest of our hospital stay was filled with tears, great sadness and guilt. I was sad for my child. Sad he might not have the full life I had wanted for him. Guilt that I wasn't happy during this time that was supposed to be full of joy. It was as if a black cloud had hovered over us and kept us from rejoicing and celebrating this wonderful gift we had just received.

The next few days as we waited for Colin's blood tests to come back from Mayo Clinic to tell us for sure he had Down Syndrome were so very difficult. I felt like I had been robbed. I wasn't able to enjoy my new baby boy because I was mourning the baby I had planned on. I was grieving the loss of the baby I had dreamt and day dreamed about, the healthy "normal" baby boy.

When the test did come back assuring what I already knew in my heart of hearts...Colin indeed had Mosiac Down Syndrome. I spent the entirety of my maternity leave transitioning into our new reality. I spent late nights researching and learning all I could about this "thing" (DS) that was now part of our new life.

Colin has been very healthy thus far and we are so thankful for this. Colin has a bicuspid aortic valve which is a very common heart defect that we monitor but so far has not been an issue. We did recently find out that he will need hearing aids and since he is very verbal we were surprised by this.

Colin goes to occupational and physical therapy weekly and he is doing really well. At first I was overwhelmed by the appointments that seemed to consume the majority of our summer but then I remember that the reason for all of these appointments is to help Colin be the best that he can

be! We have been so lucky meeting all the wonderful people we have in the last few months.
We could not have asked for more wonderful doctors and therapists. It is comforting to feel you
have a village of people working for you to help your child strive.

I know that our journey
has only begun but I
am confident our story
will only get better
from here. Although it
has not been an easy
first year I wouldn't
change Colin for
anything. He is the
happiest, most loving
baby and has added
so much joy into our
family. He is adored

by his big sister, Makenna and virtually anyone else who meets him. I am thankful to have such
a great support system and know that although Colin having Down Syndrome is not the plan I
had dreamed and hoped for I thank God everyday for blessing our family with my beautiful boy.
I look into his beautiful brushfield spotted brown eyes and am instantly reminded he indeed was
"fearfully and wonderfully made".

~ Jessica , Colin's mom; 31; Iowa, United States

{A Missed Diagnosis}

A three hour car ride to Long Island, NY for my six months Well Woman Exam. Twice a year for me, sometimes three but today would be different. A new house, a new state, freshly engaged to be married but back to NY for the well planned, inevitable conversation with my long time Gynecologist. A baby, children or even the thought of having one, was not really in our future. My husband and I just did not have that drive or passion to be parents this day, or even our near future. Don't get me wrong, I like children, I really do. I have 3 great nephews, a few friends with cute kids here and there but was I meant to be a Mom, were my fiancé and I really ever meant to be parents? Not so much. It was never really was much of a thought to us. We use to say, " We like kids but we love them more when they go home at the end of the night". My visit to the Gynecologist went almost just as planned. I sat in the waiting room for the usual hour, patiently and dreadfully waiting for my turn. My stomach was a bit queasy and the wait time seemed to be never ending. I knew today, that this visit was going to have a meaning and it was time for me to finally "get off the fence" per say. I guess I should explain. In medical terms, I

had a 7 inch fibroid surrounded by a few more, living in the uterine-lining tissue outside and growing inside the uterus. It sounds painful I suppose, but more of an unnecessary burden. These obnoxious fibroids, one mainly, has led to many unfortunate health issues since it began to take up residence in my body. Let's just begin with two pulmonary embolisms, seconds away from multiple strokes, a

few hospital stays and not to mention ridiculous nonstop pain. Today, I will only have two sentences on my mind. "Just take it" and "Get it out, I'm done!" That was definitely the only words I was anticipating on saying but nature had a different plan on this day. You see, this day was supposed to be the day to end my 3 hour drives to the Gyno. This day was the day where we get the exact dimensions and location of that annoying monster of a fibroid. This day was supposed to be the day of the "conversation" where I explain to my doctor that I was ready to have them remove anything and everything, as long as it just took my pain away.   Again, like I said, not having children, well we were OK with "it". My spouse and I would be "alright" because children were just not in our future. We were happy enough after 10 years, just finally being together, in the same state, a new home, with our dogs and engaged! But again, nature did not have that same plan for us on this day. "Jennifer", my name was finally called. "Right this way. Gown opening to the front and have a seat up there, the doctor will be in shortly". "Up there", the dreadful table but thank goodness! Finally, it's time. Wait, hold one second.. I'm bleeding! How humiliating! It definitely was way too early for that "time of the month", so why am I bleeding I thought. Just great! A 3 hour drive for nothing! The doctor finally came in and I immediately apologized. I explained to her that "my friend" came a bit early this month and we would have to reschedule the exam. Instead we went to her office and spoke about my next step and began to pick out dates and potential surgeons to do my long waited surgery. We spoke about having a portion of my uterus removed and we spoke about not having children. My next step was to just have another dreadful internal ultrasound, which I would have done today but instead I will have to wait two weeks, post menstruation. We decided that we can basically do the next few steps in my own state, PA, which was great for having to save me time commuting. Over the next few weeks, I scheduled and had my internal ultrasound. The doctor confirmed the fibroid was at its largest and most painful peak. We chose a surgeon and scheduled my time off from work for the procedure and recovery.

February 26th 2012 - A random thought.

That "time of the month" incident that occurred at the doctor's office only lasted one day. I thought maybe stress, maybe it was the endometriosis, and maybe I'm pregnant. Pregnant, ha! That would be impossible or would it?   Ten years of intimacy and never once a scare. It had been Two years since my last pulmonary embolism, not being on Birth Control pills and not one scare. Pregnant?? Yea right! I remember this day like it was yesterday and the thoughts that went through my mind. How can I be pregnant right? I just had both a pelvic and internal sonogram of my uterus and my ovaries. I just gave another urine sample.. How can anyone not have noticed? Could it have just been missed because no one was looking? Well, 5 pregnancy tests later, the results were there..Black and White, Red line, Pink line, Plus signs, Digital, Yes! I was pregnant! Confirmation followed a few days later by my local Primary Care Physician, my surgery was canceled and my journey began.

March 23th, 2012 - My first visit to an OB.

The visit was pretty much routine. Height, beginning weight, prenatal vitamins, healthy eating tips and then the boot! I say the doctor "gave me the boot" and shipped me off to the Advanced Fetal Maternal Unit because if my age. 37 years old, with a medical rap sheet that is a mile long. Heart Surgery, PE's , Gastroperisis , Anemia, Vertigo, WPW etc.... oh and like they said "too old" .

March 28th 2012 - My first Ultrasound

Today I had my first sonogram followed up by my Sequential Screening, my non-invasive prenatal test blood draw and our first routine visit to the Genetic Counselor. I think back to that time now and I can't help but to wish that I would have maybe paid more attention, asked a few more questions or maybe just took home a few of those pamphlets hanging on the wall. You see, my whole life, childhood until present, I have always been misdiagnosed. It took years for the medical professionals to finally make the correct heart diagnosis, the correct gastrointestinal diagnosis and so on. On this day, 3/28/2012, our Diagnosis was "potential" Trisomy 21. "We just have to conduct some more routine testing to confirm" said the Genetic Counselor but let's go over your odds". Odds? 1 out of 5 chances that the baby that I am carrying , the baby that I did not plan for, the baby that slipped right in to my life, right before having a surgical procedure that would make it impossible to ever carry a child, may have Trisomy 21? Trisomy what? 21? "What is this Trisomy 21 nosense all about?" That is all that went through my mind. Is that a way to make more money off of my insurance company? Another co-pay? More time off of work to test for this Trisomy21 thing? Was it because I was "too old"? Because I definitely didn't feel old. I play some sports here and there, I work out, I hang out until all hours of the night , I love happy hour after work, I still get "I.D'ed" when buying a drink, I love going to music concerts. Old? I'm not "too old". This all must be routine right?

"Exactly what is too much fluid in the neck mean? *Nuchal fold scan?* Nuchal translucency screening test results? Chromosomal abnormalities?

So what was next", I asked. 16 Days of silence. 16 days of "What if's", 16 days of an unbearable weight on my shoulder, unspoken actions of confusion, two people that have been so much in love for 10 years, who plan to marry at the end of next month, who lay in bed as strangers, as cowards.

April 16, 2102 - My husband's Birthday and the day we finally received our results from the test.

A new, noninvasive test. A simple blood draw. Two vials of blood , 99.8 percent accuracy , results in 2 weeks you say? Why not?? Of course I will take those odds!

Give me that test!

The results were in. Our test shows no evidence of Trisomy 21, 13 and 18. NEGATIVE. If you have taken this test before and you have seen your results, you would know what I mean by the larger, bolded font in the upper right corner. NEGATIVE! That is right! Our child does not have Down syndrome! I knew they were wrong! Now let's get back in to wedding mode!! We're getting married in two short weeks!!

September 13, 2012 - The events of the next 48 hours, will forever change our lives .

Twelve Ultrasounds later, over 30 combined OB and Advance Fetal Maternal visits , tons of sono pics hanging on our refrigerator, cool tough name picked out, baby room almost done and a "Surprise" baby shower scheduled for today and a 50th Birthday party out in Long Island that weekend. Well, once again, nature changed its course. Although my due date was October 6th, our little boy was ready to make his appearance sooner than expected.

39 hours later, After being induced, pushing through low amniotic fluid, fighting his way through fetal distress, 2 epidurals, an emergency C-section and on
September 15, 2012 at 1:00 a.m., we welcomed our 5 pound bright blue eyed baby boy, Mason Lucas, in to our world and our journey began.

Mason was brought to nursery for body temperature regulation and I was brought to recovery with some minor medical issues. Mason stayed in the nursery until the next morning, where his temperature was slowly regulated. He was cleaned, changed , fed and swaddled by a few nurses. His Dad got to feed him and hold him while I stayed in bed recovering for the day. Pictures were taken, visitors came and went as did our doctors. Fast forward to what my husband calls the steady loud buzzing noise that occurs in your ears, after a bomb explodes. You know, that whistle noise that doesn't get any louder or less noisy. The one that you hear while you observe other people's mouths moving but you do not know exactly what they are saying. Yes, THAT noise. "We suspect that your child has Down Syndrome", queue in the 4 ft. 11inch doctor , with tons of make-up and cheap perfume. "Your child has some soft markers. He is kind of floppy, his eyes are almond shaped, and ears are a little low. He has what we call a sandal gap and a single crease in the palm of his hand".

"OK, So he has Asian eyes? Well so does my sister, my nephew and most of my mother's side of the family". Oh so he also has a single palm crease". "Look doctor so do I! Have you seen my Dad's ears?" Oh I can show you a picture of my other sister's huge sandal gap toe too, she can send me one, if you just give me a second. "YOUR SON HAS DOWN SYNDROME, we just ordered some tests to confirm but we already know just by his markers"

Exits the pediatric doctor on duty.

Enter the Cardiologist. "Great your here!!" as I greeted him. "Is my son's heart ok?" Throughout the pregnancy I was concerned about Mason's heart. I thought he may have inherited my heart defect but no issues were ever found "Did you do an EKG yet? Does he have Wolfe Parkinson's White like me?"

"Your son's PDA valve has not closed and he has a slight murmur but nothing to be alarmed about. It is very common with BABIES THAT HAVE DOWN SYNDROME." said so nonchalantly by our Cardiologist.

"Our baby does NOT have Down Syndrome . I have all of my medical records with me. Just give me a second I will show you my non-invasive prenatal test results. You know the new test. The one that our genetic counselor said had 99.8 percent accuracy, which is only a small difference from the Amniocentesis. Hold on, I will show you!" "I will show you my last 12 sono pictures too!

Doctor -"I have been a cardiologist for many years. I have seen many babies like your little boy. YOUR SON HAS DOWN SYNDROME".

Exits the Cardiologist.

24 hours later Mason was moved to the NICU. While they continued to say he had Down Syndrome, he began presenting signs of Breathing Apnea, slow heartbeat, low platelet count, temperature issues and jaundice.

Mason remained in the NICU for a week as I stayed in ICU for a collapsing lung and the potential to clot. Every day became more of a challenge to prove the doctor's wrong. I sat in my hospital bed day and night just researching every site I can find on the internet. My sad, confused husband was torn between waiting by my bed side or Mason's incubator in the NICU. More pictures were taken but these pictures were almost of a different baby. Pictures were taken of Mason's sandal gap , of his almond eyes , his palm of his hand and whatever else I can capture just to so I can hear someone say that the Doctors were wrong. The waiting period for the positive FISH test was followed by a longer, less hopeful wait time for the Chromosome Karyotype test results.

The comments and questions were the biggest heart breaker:

"Are they sure?"

"I don't see it."

"Can you get a second opinion?"

"Will you keep him?"

"I'm sorry."

Not only did they add more doubt to my thoughts but they gave me a feeling of failure. I was so worried about Mason's health during my pregnancy from the medication that I was on. I worried about his heart. I worried that my blood thinning medication may have caused delays. I worried because he never showed his face during our Ultrasound visits. I worried that I the coffee clerk may have slipped me caffeine rather than decaf once or twice. I worried that I may have had too much dairy. I worried about Autism but I hadn't thought about Down Syndrome after my test results came back as a "Negative." A week later, both Mason and I had finally received clearance to be discharged from the hospital. I was not really sure what that meant for us at that time. We did not have the best support from the hospital. Our doctor's now seemed to be our enemies and our baby was not who we expected. Sure, he was absolutely beautiful and he was getting stronger and he did not have all of the potential health issues that the internet said he would. He did not really have the face of the "googled image" children with Down syndrome. He smiled, ate well, he had a strong hand grip and he rolled over. Maybe our child can beat this thing, I thought. The doubt remained for a very long time. I cried for weeks for so many different reasons. I thought about how disappointed my husband may have been with me. I thought about how I "caused" Mason's Down syndrome. I thought about his future, our future. The feeling of never wanting children resurfaced. Should I leave them? Will my husband leave us? The emotions were a never ending roller coaster.

As each day passed, we grew stronger. I grew stronger. I began to see Mason as a beautiful angel that fought his way in to this world through so many obstacles. I thought about how close I was to not knowing he even existed, as mentioned in the beginning of the story. I thought about how he managed to skate under 12 sonogram radars and how he managed to cheat his way through a fetal DNA test. Weeks passed and more and more I began to finally realize that

Mason was meant to be here. I was meant to be his Mother and we were all meant to be a family. He may not be the baby that we expected or the child we ever wanted but he is more than what we have ever imagined and we are filled with so much love for him. I am going to end this Birth story here, on one note... Some people say that special children like Mason are gifts from the Angels above. I do believe that Mason is a gift. I believe he did chose us and I believe he has every right to walk on earth just like any other typical child. I know that there will be some obstacles ahead as we pass the ones that have occurred but we are prepared. We are ready and

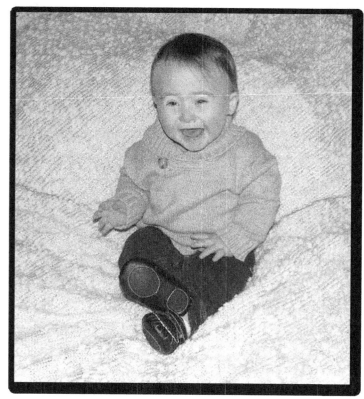

prepared to get through them as strong and as tough as Mason was when he was fighting to get in to our world. We can only hope to be as clever and strong as he was .After all the happiness he has brought us, we owe him that much. I love my little boy to the moon and back and although some days are rougher than others, I am so glad he found us.

~ Jenny, Mason's mom; 37; Pennsylvania, United States

{The Mixed-Up Test}

My parents always told me that our dreams signify either a fear or a desire. When I was pregnant with my second son, I had a vivid dream about a little girl. I knew she was mine, and she was beautiful. She had her hair in two pigtails and had glasses. She also had Down syndrome. My mother reassured me, "It's just fear honey, the baby is fine". At my 20 week ultrasound we found out we were having a boy, but the doctors found two markers for Down syndrome. Our little boy had a bright spot in his heart and one in his bowel. My heart sank. I knew he had it. Why would I have dreamt about this little girl with Down syndrome? An amnio confirmed Luke had typical chromosomes. Hesitantly, I confessed my dream to my husband. He couldn't believe it. He had the same dream as me. He dreamt of a little girl, his daughter. They were standing on the sidelines of a football game. She had Down syndrome.

When I became pregnant with our third and last child, my husband and I were nervous but thrilled. This was an unplanned surprise. We had already decided that two boys were the right amount of kids for us. They were 3 and 5, we were out of diapers! Our lives were getting more manageable as we both work full time. But this was happening and we embraced it. After the initial shock wore off we were beyond excited and grateful to welcome a new addition to our family.

My pregnancy was relatively uneventful except for my own personal issues, like gestational diabetes and thyroid problems. All ultrasounds of our surprise bundle were beautiful, then on my 34th birthday we found out what we were having, a baby girl. I was going to have a daughter. This was the best birthday present I could have asked for. My husband had tears in his eyes, he was convinced it was a third boy. I was so grateful and I couldn't believe it was really true. I spent the remainder of my pregnancy planning and daydreaming about this little girl.

At 12 weeks I had a quad screen done as well as a new test called maternit21. It is a new non-invasive blood test that can detect trisomies through the mother's blood. I was excited about this new test since it posed no risk to the baby. At my 16 week appointment my doctor gave me the news: baby is healthy, negative maternit21 test and quad screen is 1:450 for Down syndrome. I had better odds than someone else my age. I was so elated to hear our baby was healthy.

As she grew in my belly, her head was extended backward and touching her back. It was disturbing and no one could tell us what it meant. My doctor explained it could be nothing or could be a neurological or osteo issue. She was also in an oblique position. My friend at work immediately googled "hyper extended neck on baby" and the first thing she saw was a baby with Down syndrome. She asked me if the baby could have trisomy 21 and I immediately brushed it off, there's no way.

Then at 37 weeks I became sick with bronchitis. Our little girl was moving less and so I was sent in for non-stress tests and biophysical profiles. I had three in one week and I knew in my heart that she needed to come out. Something wasn't right. Then on January 3rd the ultrasound tech found that the chambers of her heart were different sizes. There was a pediatric cardiologist in the office that day and he took a look, confirming that her ductus has closed prematurely. They needed to get her out, and soon. We were scheduled for a c-section the following day.

January 4th, 2013 is the date of my daughter's birthday. This day will forever be burned in my memory as the most stressful, exciting, miraculous and life changing days of my life. My husband was by my side comforting me the whole way. As she was lifted from my body, I did not hear her cry. My husband barely got a glimpse of her when they whisked her away behind the heavy double doors. A few minutes later they called my husband back to see her. I was so scared. When he opened the door I heard music to my ears, a beautiful girlish cry was coming from the other room. My daughter. She was crying and is OK. I couldn't wait to hear all about her. I reminded my husband to take a picture. I couldn't wait to lay my eyes on her and to meet her. It felt like a lifetime waiting for this moment.

After he met her, he came back to my side. The look on his face said it all. He looked devastated. Through his tears he told me they suspected she had Down syndrome. I told him "there's no way, the test, I took the test, and it was negative! She doesn't have it!" I sobbed uncontrollably. I worried about my husband. I thought at that moment he was going to leave me with my three children. He was done having kids. This was my fault. He will never walk her down the aisle. What about my sons? This would change their lives too. It was all too much. My dream of having a daughter was shattered. It's amazing the amount of irrational thoughts you can have in such a short period of time. Then I said to him *"she's our girl, and we're going to love her"*. And he agreed.

That day my husband reminded me of our dream. It's like we were being prepared for this moment all along. This baby girl is meant to be ours. When I looked into her beautiful blue eyes with sparkles of white my fears melted away. When she looks at me it's like she's peering into my soul. She is more than I ever could have imagined. She is the light of our lives. Her brothers love her more than words can describe, and everyone who meets her is mesmerized by her. We named her Ellie, which means warrior, sun ray, and light. Little did we know four years ago that our dreams were not brought on by fear. They were in fact a desire. They predicted a happy ending we never could have dreamed of.

Ellie is a smiley 8 month old. She amazes us with how much she is growing and learning. She is now able to sit up on her own and is working on crawling. She loves all kinds of foods, but her favorite is applesauce and yogurt. She can't stand pureed peas! She knows how to give hugs and kisses now too, which melts our hearts every time. She is babbling up a storm and when she's upset she says "dadada" to her daddy's delight. Health-wise she has no issues and was cleared by the cardiologist at 2 months old. I thought our life was over when we received the diagnosis, I was 100% wrong. I am back at work full-time and am able to work from home on Fridays. Ellie loves to go boating and feel the wind on her face. She loves to giggle when her brothers tickle her. If you would have told me 8 months ago how "normal" our life would be I wouldn't have believed it. Except now our hearts are more open. We have joined a club that we didn't want to be a part of. I now see that we are the lucky ones. I'm proud to be a part of this club, I am proud she is my daughter. Our lives are better because of Ellie and I'm so grateful. I can't wait to see what Ellie can accomplish in her life. I know her future is bright. As my mother-in-law says, "having Ellie in my life is like winning the lottery" and I couldn't agree more.

Author's note: After some digging, I found that the Maternit21 test was never completed. My blood sample was never sent to the lab for testing, hence the negative result.

~ Tiffany, Ellie's mom; 34; Oregon, United States

Blogging @ www.our3lilbirds.blogspot.com

{Double Diagnosis}

I'm a Control Freak, a Perfectionist! I admit it! I've always needed things to be done my way. I had what I considered to be the perfect life. A nice house, a great career, an amazing husband and a beautiful, perfect daughter. And if things weren't perfect enough, the day before my 10 year wedding anniversary, I found out I was expecting Identical Twins. How PERFECT! How could I be so incredibly lucky?? How could I have been so blessed as to have been given TWO babies? Identical twins are so rare! I hit the jackpot! What an incredible gift!

The weeks following the initial ultrasound were pure bliss, that is, until an ultrasound at 12 weeks revealed that both babies could possibly have Down Syndrome. My heart sank. Surely this was a mistake. I wasn't even 35 yet! Down Syndrome didn't run in the family, I ate a very

healthy organic diet, and I was a good person, dammit!!! A very nice person!! What horrible thing did I do to deserve to be punished in this way? Why was this happening to ME?

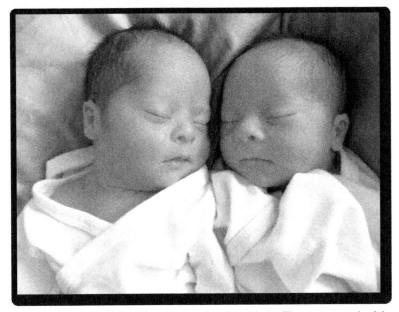

I knew what Down Syndrome was, and it wasn't good! Some of the grocery baggers at the supermarket had it. I would greet them with a strained

"Hello" feeling sorry for them. I've even seen some babies at the park with it. Those poor babies, I couldn't even look at them, smile at them like I did with other babies in strollers because I knew their mothers would think I was doing it out of pity. Poor mothers. Down Syndrome was not good, at all! It was the worst thing that could possibly happen.

My husband and I decided to confirm the diagnosis via a new, highly accurate, non-invasive blood test. We waited two grueling weeks for the results. They came back positive for Ds. We were devastated. I cried, a lot. I cursed the heavens above for this cruel joke. How could I have been given such a beautiful gift, then have it turned into something so abnormal? What would our family say? What would our friends think? What would our babies look like? What would their futures be like? I thought of all the times I looked away from the "poor babies" with Ds and felt tremendous pity for their mothers. Now I was one of them. My perfect life was now soiled and imperfect.

I was in pain. I was mourning the loss of the children I thought I would have. I had no control over this! Seeking some sort of solace, I reached out to several Ds Pregnancy support groups on the internet. I posted my introduction, reluctant and shameful, "Hi, I'm Venessa and my babies have Down Syndrome". I expected condolences, virtual hugs, some advice for not bursting into tears in front of my daugher. Instead, hundreds of people responded with "CONGRATULATIONS!". They all said nearly the same thing, that children with Ds are a blessing, they would change my life and the lives of the people around them in the most amazing and beautiful way. That they were perfection. "Perfection", really?

I looked over the flood of photos they shared with me of their adorable little babies, their toddlers, teenagers, adult children, their beloved aunts, uncles and cousins, all with Down Syndrome. They were photographed on vacation, at school, at parties. Just like us, they were living normal lives. It all seemed so positive, no doom and gloom. In my research I found out that Ds is a chromosomal abnormality. It can happen to anyone, at any age, of any race, regardless of their diet or whether or not they were "a good person".

Then I found a film on YouTube called Dakota's Pride. The film depicted so many wonderful adults with Ds that were excelling in all areas of life! They were athletes, business owners, public speakers, newlyweds! They were just like anyone else! There was no reason to pity them, no reason to look away!

At the next ultrasound I watched my babies, now confirmed to be boys, bounce around, playfully pushing each other. I could see their little arms, legs, hands and feet. Their beautiful profiles. Their hearts, beating. My boys. I loved them from the minute I found out I was expecting. They were my children and I was their mother.

In that moment I decided to let go. Let go of the grief. Let go of the guilt I felt for the weeks I spent crying. For letting the antiquated information I had about people with disabilities cloud my vision of "perfection". For letting the doctors fill my head with doubt and question whether or not my children were worthy of coming into this world because of their extra chromosome. Down Syndrome was not the worst thing in the world. They would have a future. My children would go to school, and parties and vacations! They would wake up on Christmas morning and open the gifts that Santa left. They would climb into our laps at bedtime to hear a story. They would chase each other in the back yard in the summer and fight over toys. They would ask for extra ice cream on the rare days that we ate it. They would live a life of limitless possibilities, a life full of LOVE!

I let go of the sadness and chose to be happy. I was about to embark on a great journey. I was going to have two children! And although the diagnosis of Down Syndrome wasn't anything I could control, my attitude and actions were. I had to be an advocate and the best mother I could be for them. So I began to celebrate them, Julian and Noel, two human beings that were coming into the world. I bought matching outfits, decorated their nursery and had a spectacular baby shower (which I planned, of course)! I did all the things any mother would do to welcome her new baby into the world.

I admit, I was scared, even terrified at times. Like a giant wave, the due date was fast approaching and my life was about to change forever, ready or not! Sometimes I would lie awake at night wondering how I would feel when they were finally here. Would I still be happy? When I looked at their faces and saw the almond shaped eyes, characteristic of Ds, would my heart break all over again? Would I cry out of grief and never stop?

On January 9th the wave finally came crashing in. My little boys made their debut, kicking and screaming! I frantically searched their face, looking for confirmation of Down Syndrome. They had my chin, my husband's lips, my daughters ears and beautiful almond shaped eyes--such

BEAUTIFUL eyes. I fell in love, a kind of love I had never known before. I cried...tears of joy! My boys were gorgeous. My boys were healthy and strong, not everyone is that fortunate. I WAS lucky, I WAS blessed! I held those two precious beings to my chest and thanked them for coming into our family, for choosing me to be their mother.

Soon after the delivery, a pediatrician cautiously approached my husband. He said he suspected the boys may have Down Syndrome. My husband, proudly holding his sons in his arms said, "Yes, we know. We've known for several months." The doctor smiled and said, "Well, it looks like they came to the right family then." Yes, yes they did. The perfect family.

~Venessa, Julian and Noel's mom; 34; New York, United States
Blogging @ www.organicsofrito.blogspot.com

Thank you for reading our stories. We believe that the connections to other families can make all the difference when receiving a new diagnosis. Whether you have a prenatal or birth diagnosis, we are here for you.

Please visit our websites and Facebook pages for additional resources and support:

{Unexpected} - http://www.missiont21.com/

Down Syndrome Diagnosis Network - http://www.dsdiagnosisnetwork.org/

CPSIA information can be obtained
at www.ICGtesting.com
Printed in the USA
FSOW03n1100030317
31499FS

9 781312 077119